Joseph L. Hyde, Editor

ARREST WARRANT AND INDICTMENT FORMS

2024
EDITION

The School of Government at the University of North Carolina at Chapel Hill works to improve the lives of North Carolinians by engaging in practical scholarship that helps public officials and citizens understand and improve state and local government. Established in 1931 as the Institute of Government, the School provides educational, advisory, and research services for state and local governments. The School of Government is also home to a nationally ranked Master of Public Administration program, the North Carolina Judicial College, and specialized centers focused on community and economic development, information technology, and environmental finance.

As the largest university-based local government training, advisory, and research organization in the United States, the School of Government offers up to 200 courses, webinars, and specialized conferences for more than 12,000 public officials each year. In addition, faculty members annually publish approximately 50 books, manuals, reports, articles, bulletins, and other print and online content related to state and local government. The School also produces the *Daily Bulletin Online* each day the General Assembly is in session, reporting on activities for members of the legislature and others who need to follow the course of legislation.

Operating support for the School of Government's programs and activities comes from many sources, including state appropriations, local government membership dues, private contributions, publication sales, course fees, and service contracts.

Visit sog.unc.edu or call 919.966.5381 for more information on the School's courses, publications, programs, and services.

Printed in the United States of America
28 27 26 25 24   1 2 3 4 5
ISBN 978-1-64238-099-6

If only a percentage of the knowledge of the
criminal law is in the books, where is the rest of it?

—Albert Coates
The Story of the Institute of Government

To L.D.

Contents

April 2024

Offenses Against the Habitation and Other Buildings

Offenses Against Property

Criminal Trespass

Offenses Against Public Morality and Decency

Offenses Against Public Justice

Chapter 20 (Motor Vehicles)

Chapter 49 (Bastardy)

Chapter 50B (Domestic Violence)

Chapter 58 (Insurance Fraud)

Chapter 75A (Boating and Water Safety)

Chapter 90 (Controlled Substances Act)

Preface to the 2024 Edition

Form books are not new. The most well-known is perhaps J.F. Archbold's treatise, *Pleading, Evidence and Practice in Criminal Cases,* which is cited in North Carolina appellate opinions from 1826 to 2003 and remains in print to this day. In 1965, the Institute of Government published a book called *A Guide to Drawing Warrants* (hereinafter *Guide*). As explained in a brief prefatory note, the forms that appeared therein were gathered from various sources by Judge Raymond B. Mallard and Horace L. Shaw, compiled to serve "only as a guide," and "not to be copied blindly."[1]

In 1968, in anticipation of a larger book, the Institute published a "temporarily abridged version" called *Arrest Warrant Forms,* which its editors called "a successor" to the *Guide* but carrying a different title "because it is a completely new work."[2] William Gerald Thornton, a research assistant with the Institute, was credited with revising the forms from the *Guide.* Like its predecessor, *Arrest Warrant Forms* included a disclaimer, cautioning the reader that "this booklet . . . is far from complete," and advising the user, when in doubt, to "turn to other materials."[3]

Various crime-specific supplements (and their updates) followed, including *Warrant Forms in Assault Cases, Warrant Forms in Drug Cases,* and *Warrant Forms in Burglary and Breaking and Entering Cases,* all produced in 1969, to name just a few. Another "temporarily abridged version" of the larger book was published in 1970, with gaps for material covered by the 1969 supplements.[4] In the years that followed, the Institute produced additional crime-specific supplements. The larger book, still titled *Arrest Warrant Forms,* appeared in 1980,[5] again followed by crime-specific supplements. The conception from the beginning seems to have been a practical manual compiled as a three-ring binder to which supplemental replacement material could be added as it became available.

A second edition of the larger book was released in 1981,[6] followed by crime-specific supplements. A third edition was published in 1984,[7] followed by general supplements in 1987 and 1991. The fourth edition, published in 1996 and followed by general supplements in 1997 and 2000, was the first to adopt the title, *Arrest Warrant and Indictment Forms.*[8] The fifth edition was published in 2005,[9] by which time the Institute had become the School of Government. The sixth edition was published in 2010,[10] followed by several updates available online.

Later editions would appear as single paperback volumes, the edition corresponding to the year of publication: 2019 Edition,[11] 2022 Edition,[12] 2023 Edition.[13] Jeff Welty asked me to prepare the 2024 Edition in November 2023.

---

1. Raymond B. Mallard & Horace L. Shaw, A Guide to Drawing Warrants i (UNC Inst. of Gov't 1965) (out of print).

2. William Gerald Thornton, Arrest Warrant Forms viii (UNC Inst. of Gov't 1968) (out of print).

3. *Id.* at ix.

4. William Gerald Thornton, Arrest Warrant Forms (UNC Inst. of Gov't 1970) (out of print).

5. Arrest Warrant Forms (Michael Crowell ed., UNC Inst. of Gov't 1980) (out of print).

6. Arrest Warrant Forms (2d ed., Joan G. Brannon & Robert L. Farb eds., UNC Inst. of Gov't 1981) (out of print).

7. Arrest Warrant Forms (3d ed., Robert L. Farb ed., UNC Inst. of Gov't 1984) (out of print).

8. Arrest Warrant and Indictment Forms (4th ed., Robert L. Farb ed., UNC Inst. of Gov't 1996) (out of print).

9. Arrest Warrant and Indictment Forms (5th ed., Robert L. Farb ed., UNC Sch. of Gov't 2005) (out of print).

10. Arrest Warrant and Indictment Forms (6th ed., Jeffrey B. Welty, UNC Sch. of Gov't 2010) (out of print).

11. Jeffrey B. Welty & Christopher Tyner, Arrest Warrant and Indictment Forms, 2019 Edition (UNC Sch. of Gov't) (out of print).

12. Jeffrey B. Welty, Christopher Tyner, & Jonathan Holbrook, Arrest Warrant and Indictment Forms, 2022 Edition (UNC Sch. of Gov't) (out of print).

13. Jeffrey B. Welty, Arrest Warrant and Indictment Forms, 2023 Edition (UNC Sch. of Gov't), available for purchase at www.sog.unc.edu/publications/books/arrest-warrant-and-indictment-forms-2023-edition.

This edition of *Arrest Warrant and Indictment Forms* contains eight completely new forms, fifteen significantly revised forms, and twenty-six forms to which new information has been added (additional notes or a change in the penalty) without substantially changing the charging language provided. One form, regarding the purchase, sale, or transfer of certain weapons without a permit, prohibited by Chapter 14, Section 402 of the North Carolina General Statutes (hereinafter G.S.), has been omitted to reflect the repeal of that statute. The remaining forms in this edition are carried forward from the previous edition unchanged. The introduction, providing an overview of the law concerning pleadings, has been entirely rewritten.

Some of the revisions are substantial and others are less so, but all are intended to ensure the issuance of legally sufficient pleadings. The revisions are based on legislative changes in the 2023 legislative session, as well as appellate cases issued through January 2024. A list of the new and revised forms is below.

New forms:

G.S. 14-32(d) .... Assault Upon Emergency Worker with Deadly Weapon Inflicting Serious Injury
G.S. 14-32(e) .... Assault upon Emergency Worker with Deadly Weapon with Intent to Kill
G.S. 14-32.5 .... Misdemeanor Crime of Domestic Violence
G.S. 14-33(c)(2a) .... Assault on a Pregnant Woman
G.S. 14-34.1A .... Discharging Firearm or Air Gun into Unoccupied Emergency Vehicle
G.S. 14-150.2 .... Injuring Energy Facility
G.S. 20-141.10 .... Street Takeover
G.S. 90-108(a)(12)–(12a) ... Equipment for Manufacturing a Controlled Substance or Counterfeit Controlled Substance

Revised Forms:

Common Law .... Going Armed to the Terror of the Public
G.S. 14-18.4 .... Death by Distribution of Controlled Substances
G.S. 14-34.2 .... Assault with a Firearm or Other Deadly Weapon on Government Officer or Employee or Company or Campus Police Officer
G.S. 14-34.6 .... Assault on a Firefighter or Specified Medical Personnel
G.S. 14-56 .... Breaking or Entering a Vehicle
G.S. 14-159.12 .... First-Degree Trespass
G.S. 14-159.13 .... Second-Degree Trespass
G.S. 14-190.1(a)(1) .... Disseminating Obscene Writing or Picture
G.S. 14-190.1(a)(4) .... Disseminating Obscene Movie, Video, etc.
G.S. 14-190.1(e) .... Possessing Obscenity with Intent to Disseminate
G.S. 14-190.9 .... Indecent Exposure
G.S. 14-288.2(c) .... Felony Riot
G.S. 14-288.2(d), (e) .... Inciting to Riot
G.S. 58-2-161 .... Insurance Fraud
G.S. 90-95.1 .... Continuing Criminal Enterprise

The preparation of this edition was a collaborative process, both inside and outside the School of Government. I appreciate the contributions of my colleagues to what, I hope, will be a useful reference.

—Joseph L. Hyde
UNC Chapel Hill, February 2024

There can be no trial, conviction or punishment without a formal and sufficient accusation. . . . [P]rosecuting officers should carefully read warrants and indictments before proceeding to trial.[1]

Introduction: Understanding Criminal Pleadings

Language matters. North Carolina has long adhered to the common law rule that a facial defect in an indictment deprives the trial court of jurisdiction.[2] Much of what makes this book vital is that so much depends on getting the language right. Challenges to an indictment may be raised at any time—despite a defendant's failure to object at trial and with no requirement to show prejudice—and a successful challenge justifies a court in vacating the judgment, despite years that may have passed since the conviction. Adherence to the forms prescribed preserves convictions.

Several recent North Carolina Supreme Court opinions seem to presage a coming change. In *In re J.U.*,[3] our Supreme Court criticized the common law rule that a defect in an indictment deprives the trial court of jurisdiction as "obsolete."[4] And in *State v. Lancaster*,[5] it cited with approval (apparently for the first time) the United States Supreme Court's decision in *United States v. Cotton*,[6] which abrogated the common law rule in the federal court system.[7]

Taken together, *J.U.* and *Lancaster* seem to be preparing the way for our Supreme Court to abolish the common law rule in state court as well. If using the proper language in an indictment is no longer necessary to confer jurisdiction, then strict adherence to prescribed forms is less important. To be sure, pleading defects might still qualify as errors of law, but it would be easier to fix them if timely raised, and they would be less likely to warrant relief years after a judgment is entered. The language would still matter—though somewhat less than it does now.

Arrest Warrant and Indictment Forms is about the language of criminal pleadings. Most of the manual consists of forms that may be used to draft pleadings that will withstand scrutiny. The forms are intended to be straightforward, but readers are more likely to use the forms correctly if they have a grasp of the applicable legal principles. Further, not every crime is included in the manual, so officers, prosecutors, and magistrates (and others) will sometimes need to draft criminal pleadings without a form to consult. This introduction is intended to cover the basics.

---

1. State v. Best, 265 N.C. 477, 481 (1965).
2. State v. Rankin, 371 N.C. 885, 897 (2018).
3. 384 N.C. 618 (2023).
4. *Id.* at 623 (quoting *Rankin*, 371 N.C. at 919 (Martin, C.J., dissenting)); *cf.* Chapter 4, Section 1 of the North Carolina General Statutes (hereinafter G.S.) (common law declared to be in force within this state except where, among other things, it has become obsolete).
5. 385 N.C. 459 (2023).
6. 535 U.S. 625 (2002).
7. *Lancaster*, 385 N.C. at 462.

I. Sources and Types of Criminal Pleadings

A. Constitutional Entitlement

The Fifth Amendment to the United States Constitution provides that no person shall be held to answer for a capital or otherwise infamous crime, unless on a presentment or indictment of a grand jury.[8] This provision reflects the founders' view that presentment or indictment represents a safeguard against abusive prosecution.[9] Unlike many provisions of the Bill of Rights, however, the Grand Jury Clause of the Fifth Amendment has never been incorporated against the states through the Due Process Clause of the Fourteenth Amendment.[10] There is therefore no federal constitutional guarantee of indictment for defendants charged in state court.[11]

The North Carolina Constitution provides that, except in misdemeanor cases initiated in the district court division, no person shall be put to answer any criminal charge but by indictment, presentment, or impeachment.[12] As used here, the term "indictment" signifies a written accusation of a crime drawn up by the prosecutor and submitted to the grand jury, and by them found and presented on oath or affirmation as a true bill.[13] The term "presentment" denotes an accusation made by a grand jury of an offense upon their own knowledge or observation, or upon information from others, without any bill of indictment having been submitted by the prosecutor.[14]

B. Statutory Recognition

By statute, the pleading in felony and misdemeanor cases initiated in the superior court division must be a bill of indictment, unless the defendant waives the right to indictment.[15] If the defendant waives indictment, the pleading must be a bill of information.[16] "A presentment by the grand jury may not serve as the pleading in a criminal case."[17] For a misdemeanor prosecuted in the district court, the pleading of the State may consist of the citation, criminal summons, warrant for arrest, magistrate's order, or a statement of charges.[18]

The following chart summarizes the role of each type of pleading.[19]

---

8. U.S. Const. amend. V.

9. *See* United States v. Calandra, 414 U.S. 338, 343 (1974) ("the protection of citizens against unfounded criminal prosecutions"); *cf.* John H. Langbein, Renee Lettow Lerner & Bruce P. Smith, History of the Common Law: The Development of Anglo-American Legal Institutions 216 (2019).

10. *See* State v. Hunt, 357 N.C. 257, 272 (2003); State v. Wallace, 351 N.C. 481, 508 (2000).

11. 1 Andrew D. Leipold, Federal Practice and Procedure: Criminal § 122 (5th ed. 2023). To be sure, the Sixth Amendment and the Due Process Clause require adequate notice of a criminal accusation, but such notice need not be endorsed by a grand jury.

12. N.C. Const. art. I, § 22. One who appeals from a misdemeanor conviction in district court may be tried in superior court on the original pleading, without an indictment. State v. Gay, 273 N.C. 125, 126 (1968).

13. State v. Thomas, 236 N.C. 454, 457 (1952).

14. *Id.* Impeachment initiates the process of disciplining an officeholder for malfeasance in office, and the punishment is limited to removal from office and disqualification from future office. *See* N.C. Const. art. IV, § 4.

15. G.S. 15A-923(a); *see also* G.S. 15A-642(c) (waiver of indictment must be (1) in writing, (2) signed by the defendant and his or her attorney, and (3) attached to or executed upon the bill of information).

16. G.S. 15A-923(a). Bills of information are generally subject to the same rules that govern indictments. *See* G.S. 15A-644(b).

17. G.S. 15A-923(a).

18. G.S. 15A-922(a). Except for the statement of charges, these instruments serve primarily as criminal process, requiring a person to come to court. *See* G.S. Ch. 15A, Art. 17 cmt.; *see also id.* Art. 19 cmt. (on misdemeanor pleadings).

19. Subject to the provisions of G.S. Chapter 15A, Article 49, each of these instruments may serve as pleadings of the State in criminal cases. G.S. 15A-921. But the pleading in felony cases initiated in the superior court must be a bill of indictment unless the right to indictment is waived. G.S. 15A-923(a); *cf.* G.S. 15A-642(a).

Name/Statute (G.S.)	Who May Issue	What Offenses May Be Charged	Notes
Citation 15A-302	Law enforcement officer	Misdemeanor or infraction	Directs a defendant to come to court on a specific day. A defendant may object to trial on a citation, and the prosecutor then must normally file a statement of charges. G.S. 15A-922(c).
Criminal Summons 15A-303	Justice, judge, magistrate, or clerk	Felony, misdemeanor, or infraction	Directs a defendant to come to court on a specific day.
Warrant for Arrest 15A-304	Justice, judge, magistrate, or clerk	Felony or misdemeanor	Orders that a defendant be arrested and held to answer a charge. Used when a judicial official determines "that the person named should be taken into custody." G.S. 15A-304(b)(1).
Magistrate's Order 15A-511(c)	Justice, judge, magistrate, or clerk	Felony or misdemeanor	Used when a defendant has been arrested without a warrant.
Statement of Charges 15A-922	Prosecutor	Misdemeanor or infraction	Used to supersede existing charges, not to initiate a new prosecution.
Information 15A-641, -644	Prosecutor	Felony and related misdemeanors	Requires consent of the defendant; information must contain or have attached a waiver of indictment signed by the defendant and his or her attorney.
Indictment 15A-641, -644	Grand jury	Felony and related misdemeanors	Requires concurrence of twelve or more grand jurors.

It bears repeating that a criminal defendant's right to indictment derives primarily from the state constitution—though that right is effectuated and supplemented by various statutes—and that the constitutional right to an indictment pertains to a grand jury's written accusation *of a crime*. Care must be taken to distinguish this right from a separate right to indictment created by statute.[20] Such purely statutory requirements do not implicate the state constitutional right to indictment.[21]

C. Related Instruments

Related instruments include presentments, juvenile petitions, and bills of particulars.

1. Presentments

As noted above, presentments are mentioned among the constitutionally permissible modes of prosecution in this state.[22] By statute, however, a presentment may not serve as a pleading.[23] In current practice, the prosecutor may solicit a presentment from the grand jury by submitting a draft

---

20. *See* G.S. 15A-924(a)(7); 15A-1340.16(a4) (nonstatutory aggravating factors must be alleged in indictment); *cf.* G.S. 15A-1340.16(a6) (requiring notice of all aggravating factors).

21. *See* State v. Roache, 358 N.C. 243, 267 (2004); *cf.* State v. Ross, 216 N.C. App. 337, 351 (2011) (failure to include aggravating factors in indictment was statutory, not constitutional, error).

22. N.C. Const. art. I, § 19. Historically, the terms "indictment" and "presentment" were used interchangeably, but by the eighteen century, the latter term was used to refer to an accusation presented by the grand jury upon its own motion. *See* Langbein, et al., *supra* note 9, at 215.

23. G.S. 15A-923(a).

presentment, followed by an indictment.[24] The benefit of doing so arises from the fact that, when a charge is initiated by presentment, the superior court has original jurisdiction to try a misdemeanor, allowing the State to bypass proceedings in the district court.[25]

2. Juvenile Petitions

In juvenile cases, the State's pleading is called a *petition*.[26] Because juvenile proceedings are civil rather than criminal, juvenile petitions are not criminal pleadings.[27] Still, petitions serve essentially the same function as indictments in providing notice to the accused, and juvenile petitions are generally held to the same standards as criminal indictments.[28]

3. Bills of Particulars

The function of a bill of particulars is to inform the defendant of the nature of the evidence which the State proposes to offer.[29] It is not part of the indictment, nor is it a substitute for or an amendment thereto.[30] Upon a defendant's motion, the trial court may order the State to file a bill of particulars containing "items of factual information . . . which pertain to the charge."[31] The trial court must order the State to file a bill of particulars if the information requested is necessary to enable the defendant adequately to prepare a defense.[32] Whether to order the State to file a bill of particulars is, however, within the sound discretion of the trial court.[33]

II. The Common Law and Statutes

A. English Antecedents

Although the state constitution is the source of a criminal defendant's right to indictment, most of the rules governing criminal pleadings may be found in statutes and caselaw. Determining the priority of these rules is not always easy.[34] Many of the rules advanced by the caselaw have their origin in the common law, that is, the law of England that the colonists were applying in this state at the time of the American Revolution.[35] Indeed, "[f]or many years, American courts demanded strict adherence to the technical niceties of common law pleading rules."[36]

---

24. *See* G.S. 15A-628(a)(4) (grand jury investigation may be initiated upon request of prosecutor); 15A-641 (prosecutor is obligated to investigate every presentment); *see also* State v. Baker, 263 N.C. App. 221, 228 (2018) (presentment and indictment submitted *simultaneously* were invalid absent intervening investigation).

25. G.S. 7A-271(a)(2).

26. G.S. 7B-1801.

27. State v. Adams, 345 N.C. 745, 748 (1997).

28. *In re* J.U., 384 N.C. 618, 622 (2023).

29. State v. Cameron, 283 N.C. 191, 194 (1973).

30. State v. Parker, 119 N.C. App. 328, 336 (1995); *cf.* G.S. 15A-925(e) (bill of particulars may not supply an omission or cure a defect in a criminal pleading).

31. G.S. 15A-925(b).

32. G.S. 15A-925(c).

33. State v. Garcia, 358 N.C. 382, 390 (2004).

34. It is not always apparent whether a statute is intended to codify preexisting law or to change it. *Compare* State v. McLymore, 380 N.C. 185, 190 (2022) (statute abolished common law right to perfect self-defense), *with* State v. Moorman, 320 N.C. 387, 392 (1987) (rape statutes codify common law of rape).

35. *See* G.S. 4-1 (common law declared to be in force within this state); State v. Vance, 328 N.C. 613, 617 (1991) ("the common law of England.").

36. 5 Wayne R. LaFave et al., Criminal Procedure § 19.1(a) (4th ed. 2015).

The technical pleading requirements of the common law could produce anomalous results. It is easy to ridicule decisions like *State v. Owen*,[37] which overturned a defendant's murder conviction based on the failure of the indictment to specify the length and depth of the mortal wounds.[38] On the other hand, the requirement for such an allegation was plainly stated in the available authorities,[39] and it does not seem entirely unreasonable to demand a degree of precision from the State in the formal accusation of a defendant who is on trial for his or her life.[40] In any event, the legislature responded to such decisions by eliminating the most egregious technicalities of the common law pertaining to indictments.[41]

B. Legislative Innovations

Another legislative attempt to alleviate burdensome common law pleading requirements came with the enactment of statutes authorizing "short-form" pleadings, statutes that prescribed simplified charging language.[42] The State was thus relieved of the obligation of alleging each element for specified offenses, as the common law had required.[43] Our statutes now recognize short-form pleadings for murder and manslaughter,[44] rape,[45] sex offense,[46] perjury,[47] and subornation of perjury.[48] In addition, the North Carolina Supreme Court has recognized a short-form pleading for attempted murder.[49] The short-form language has been consistently upheld against constitutional challenge.[50]

The General Assembly struck yet another blow at common law pleading requirements with the enactment of the Criminal Procedure Act of 1975.[51] Following adoption of the Act, the North Carolina

---

37. 5 N.C. (1 Mur.) 452 (1810).

38. *Id.* at 453; *see also* State v. Carter, 1 N.C. 406 (1801) (judgment arrested because indictment specified location of mortal wound as the left "brest," rather than breast); *cf.* Lawrence M. Friedman, A History of American Law 133–34 (1973) (discussing *Owen*). In their defense, the judges who formed the majority in *Owen* (the court split 3-2) frankly acknowledged their disapprobation of the rule but felt bound to apply the law as they found it and not as they wished it to be.

39. *E.g.*, 4 William Blackstone, Commentaries 302 ("in indictments for murder, the length and depth of the wound should in general be expressed").

40. Before the act of 1893 (now codified at G.S. 14-17) divided the offense into two degrees, there was but one offense of murder, and the penalty was death. State v. Gadberry, 117 N.C. 811, 813 (1895).

41. *See* G.S. 15-153 (pleading is sufficient "if it express the charge against the defendant in a plain, intelligible, and explicit manner; and the same shall not be quashed . . . by reason of any informality or refinement."); 15-155 (pleading not vitiated by omission of, among other things, any matter unnecessary to be proved, the words "with force and arms," the time of the offense when time is not of the essence, or for want of proper and perfect venue).

42. *See* 5 LaFave et al., *supra* note 36, § 19.1(c).

43. *See* State v. Jerrett, 309 N.C. 239, 259 (1983).

44. G.S. 15-144.

45. G.S. 15-144.1.

46. G.S. 15-144.2.

47. G.S. 15-145.

48. G.S. 15-146; *see also* G.S. 20-138.1(c) (prescribing short-form pleading for misdemeanor impaired driving).

49. State v. Jones, 359 N.C. 832, 838 (2005).

50. *See e.g.*, State v. Hunt, 357 N.C. 257, 274 (2003) (upholding short-form murder indictment); State v. Roberts, 310 N.C. 428, 434 (1984) (upholding short-form rape indictment).

51. State v. Mostafavi, 370 N.C. 681, 686 (2018) (Criminal Procedure Act of 1975 "sought to eliminate the technical pleading requirements previously recognized for criminal pleadings"); State v. Spivey, 368 N.C. 739, 742 (2016) (the 1975 Act was intended to simplify criminal proceedings).

Supreme Court overruled several well-established precedents that had perpetuated common law pleading requirements.[52] The full effect of the Act on common law rules is still being debated.[53]

C. Statutory Requirements

By statute (G.S. 15A-924), a criminal pleading must contain

1. the defendant's name or other form of identification,
2. a separate count for each offense charged,
3. the county in which each offense was committed,
4. the date on which each offense was committed,
5. a statement of facts supporting each element of the offense,
6. a citation to the applicable law alleged to have been violated, and
7. any nonstatutory aggravating sentencing factors.

1. The Defendant's Name

The complete omission of the defendant's name renders a pleading fatally defective.[54] This does not mean that the defendant must be identified by name in each count.[55] Further, under the doctrine of *idem sonans*, a slight misspelling in the defendant's name is not a fatal defect.[56] Many spelling errors can be corrected by amendment of the pleading.[57]

2. A Separate Count for Each Offense Charged

"Generally speaking, a bill of indictment which charges two offenses in the same count is bad for duplicity."[58] This rule is subject to exceptions, however. Acts constituting a single and continuous transaction may be charged together as a single offense; and where a single offense may be committed in different ways, it may be charged in a single count if the ways are not repugnant and are component parts of a single transaction.[59] Significantly, duplicity has not been treated as a jurisdictional defect: an objection based on duplicity is waived if not made in apt time, i.e., before plea, and is cured by

---

52. *See* State v. Oldroyd, 380 N.C. 613, 619 (2022) (indictment for armed robbery was not invalid for failure specifically to name the victim(s)); State v. Worsley, 336 N.C. 268, 280 (1994) (burglary indictment was not defective for failure to specify the felony that the defendant intended to commit within the victim's home); State v. Palmer, 293 N.C. 633, 640 (1977) (indictment for assault with a deadly weapon was sufficient even absent a detailed description of the weapon).

53. *Compare* State v. Lancaster, 385 N.C. 459, 462 (2023) ("the General Assembly's adoption of the Criminal Procedure Act represented a sharp departure from the demands of technical pleading."); *with* State v. Rankin, 371 N.C. 885, 898 (2018) ("The General Assembly acknowledged and approved of the common law remedy for invalid indictments with the enactment of the revised Criminal Procedure Act.").

54. State v. Simpson, 302 N.C. 613, 616 (1981) ("or a sufficient description if his name is unknown"); State v. Finch, 218 N.C. 511, 512 (1940) (when no name appears in the bill, judgment must be arrested).

55. G.S. 15A-924(a)(1) ("unless required for clarity"); *cf.* State v. Johnson, 77 N.C. App. 583, 584 (1985) (indictment that identified the defendant by name only in the caption was sufficient).

56. State v. Higgs, 270 N.C. 111, 113 (1967) (Buford Murril Higgs named in the indictment as Beauford Merrill Higgs); State v. Vincent, 222 N.C. 543, 544 (1943) ("'Vincent' and 'Vinson' sound almost alike"); *but see* State v. Overman, 257 N.C. 464, 468 (1962) (fatal variance when indictment identified the victim as Frank E. Nutley but evidence showed the victim was Frank E. Hatley).

57. *See* "Fixing Pleading Problems," *infra*.

58. State v. Dale, 218 N.C. 625 (1940); *cf.* 5 LaFave et al., *supra* note 36, § 19.3(d).

59. State v. O'Keefe, 263 N.C. 53, 56 (1964).

verdict.[60] And given timely objection, the prosecutor may elect to proceed with only one of the charges or may amend the pleading to separate the charges into separate counts.[61]

3. The County in Which Each Offense Was Committed

At common law, it was essential to name the county in which the offense was committed so that it might appear that the offense was within the jurisdiction of the court.[62] In North Carolina, venue likewise remains in the county where the crime was committed.[63] By statute, however, allegations of venue in a criminal pleading become conclusive absent timely objection.[64] Further, the place for returning an indictment is a matter of venue and not jurisdiction.[65] Accordingly, variances between the county alleged and the evidence at trial have been treated as immaterial.[66] And the prosecutor may amend a criminal pleading to reflect the proper county.[67]

4. The Date on Which Each Offense Was Committed

Except where time is of the essence of the offense, the date of offense set out in a pleading is immaterial and need not be proved, and a variance is not fatal, "the day being deemed merely a matter of form."[68] G.S. 15A-924(a)(4) did not change the law in this regard. The statute requires an allegation that the offense was committed on, or on or about, a designated date or during a designated period of time, but error as to a date or its omission is not grounds for dismissal of the charges or reversal of a conviction if time was not of the essence.[69] In cases involving sexual offenses against children, courts are particularly lenient with regard to the date of offense alleged.[70] Hence, the date alleged may generally be corrected by amendment.[71] Variance as to time becomes material when it deprives a defendant of the opportunity to prepare a defense. When a defendant relies on the date alleged to prepare his or her defense and the State's evidence substantially varies to the defendant's prejudice, a motion to dismiss will be granted.[72]

---

60. State v. Green, 266 N.C. 785, 789 (1966); State v. Beal, 199 N.C. 278, 294 (1930).

61. State v. Williamson, 250 N.C. 204, 209 (1959); *cf.* State v. Stephens, 188 N.C. App. 286, 293 (2008) (no error in allowing amendment of indictment); *cf.* G.S. 15A-924(b) (if a single count charges more than one offense, defendant may by motion require the State to elect a single offense).

62. State v. Flowers, 318 N.C. 208, 213 (1986).

63. G.S. Ch. 15A, Art. 3 cmt.

64. G.S. 15A-135.

65. G.S. 15A-631; *cf. Flowers*, 318 N.C. at 213 (noting legislature's power to extend grand jury's power beyond territorial limitation imposed by the common law).

66. *See* State v. Spencer, 187 N.C. App. 605, 611 (2007); State v. Brown, 85 N.C. App. 583, 588 (1987); *cf.* State v. Gardner, 84 N.C. App. 616, 618 (no error in denying motion to dismiss charge of receiving stolen goods because G.S. 14-71 permits indictment for receiving stolen goods in any county in which the thief may be tried), *aff'd per curiam*, 320 N.C. 789 (1987).

67. State v. Hyder, 100 N.C. App. 270, 273 (1990).

68. State v. Wise, 66 N.C. 120, 123 (1872); *accord* State v. Francis, 157 N.C. 612 (1911).

69. G.S. 15A-924(a)(4); *cf.* G.S. 15-155 (no judgment shall be stayed or reversed "for omitting to state the time at which the offense was committed in any case where time is not of the essence of the offense.")

70. State v. Everett, 328 N.C. 72, 75 (1991).

71. *E.g.*, State v. Price, 310 N.C. 596, 600 (1984).

72. State v. Stewart, 353 N.C. 516, 519 (2001).

5. A Statement of Facts Supporting Each Element of the Offense

The elements requirement is "clearly the most critical," and no pleading defect has resulted in more dismissals than failure to allege all the elements of the offense charged.[73] Assuming there is no authorized short-form pleading, a criminal pleading that omits an element will generally be deemed fatally defective.[74] Consistent with "traditional ideas," G.S. 15A-924(e) continues to require factual (but not evidentiary) allegations to support each element.[75] Thus, an indictment must allege lucidly and accurately all the essential elements of the offense charged.[76] While an indictment couched in the language of the statute is generally sufficient to charge a statutory offense,[77] if the words of the statute do not set forth all the elements, such elements must be alleged in the criminal pleading.[78] Still, the State is required to allege only the ultimate facts constituting each element of the crime; evidentiary matters need not be alleged.[79] There is conflicting authority on whether elements may be supplied by inference or implication, but the recent trend seems to be toward inferring elements from the facts alleged where possible.[80]

6. A Citation to the Applicable Law Alleged to Have Been Violated

By statute, a criminal pleading must contain, for each count, a citation of any applicable statute, rule, regulation, ordinance, or other provision of law alleged to have been violated.[81] But error in the citation or its omission is not grounds for dismissal of charges or reversal of a conviction.[82] On the other hand, citation to the proper statute will not cure a failure to allege each element of the offense charged.[83]

7. Any Nonstatutory Aggravating Sentencing Factors

Added in 2005, subdivision (a)(7) of G.S. 15A-924 requires the State to allege any nonstatutory aggravating sentencing factors it intends to use.[84] G.S. 15A-1340.16(d) prescribes aggravating factors that may be considered at sentencing in a felony case.[85] The last item in that subsection is a residual or catchall provision encompassing "[a]ny other aggravating factor reasonably related to the purposes of sentencing."[86] While the other factors need not be included in any indictment or other

---

73. 5 LaFave et al., *supra* note 36, § 19.3(b).

74. *E.g.*, State v. Murrell, 370 N.C. 187, 193 (2017); State v. Ellis, 368 N.C. 342, 344 (2015). As explained under "Legislative Innovations," *supra*, if the State uses an authorized short-form pleading, it need not allege all the elements of the offense charged. Similarly, a citation is sufficient that complies with G.S. 15A-302(c), albeit omitting elements, as explained under "Special Rules for Citations," *infra*.

75. G.S. 15A-924 cmt.

76. State v. Lofton, 372 N.C. 216, 221 (2019).

77. State v. Mostafavi, 370 N.C. 681, 685 (2018).

78. State v. Rankin, 371 N.C. 885, 887 (2018).

79. State v. Coker, 312 N.C. 432, 437 (1984) (driving while impaired (DWI) charge not required to specify impairing substance); State v. Palmer, 293 N.C. 633, 638 (1977) (charges for assault with a deadly weapon need not describe the weapon beyond identifying it as "a deadly weapon").

80. *Compare* State v. Lancaster, 385 N.C. 459, 469 (2023) (elements "clearly inferable"); *with* State v. Edwards, 190 N.C. 322, 324 (1925) (no element should be left to inference or implication). Elements cannot be supplied by reference to extrinsic evidence. State v. White, 372 N.C. 248, 254 (2019).

81. G.S. 15A-924(a)(6).

82. *Id.*; *see also* State v. Barnes, 333 N.C. 666, 677 (1993) ("mistake in the citation of the statute does not affect the validity of the trial"); State v. Collins, 221 N.C. App. 604, 613 (2012).

83. State v. McBane, 276 N.C. 60, 65 (1969); State v. Billinger, 213 N.C. App. 249, 257 (2011).

84. G.S. 15A-924(a)(7).

85. G.S. 15A-1340.16(d).

86. G.S. 15A-1340.16(d)(20).

charging instrument, an aggravating factor alleged under subdivision (d)(20) must be included in any indictment or other charging instrument.[87] Noncompliance with this provision results in the State being unable to use the aggravating factor at sentencing, and, if the aggravating factor is used, the defendant is entitled to resentencing.[88]

Other statutes contain additional requirements for particular pleadings.[89]

III. Additional Drafting Requirements

A. Formal Requirements

1. Extensive Detail Is Unnecessary

Federal indictments can reach a hundred pages in length and contain detailed accounts of the offense(s) charged.[90] By contrast, North Carolina pleadings are usually brief and do not contain much detail about the way the crime charged was committed.[91] As the North Carolina Supreme Court has said, "a very detailed account is not necessary for legally sufficient indictments[.]"[92] Indeed, it may be counterproductive to provide extensive detail, as some appellate decisions have held that the State is bound to prove even those allegations that need not have been included in the first place.[93]

2. Plead in the Conjunctive

"The use of the conjunctive form to express alternative theories of conviction is proper."[94] Since charging disjunctively or alternatively may render the allegations uncertain, the proper way to connect the various allegations in a pleading is with the word "and," not with the word "or."[95] This is true even when the statute defining the offense uses the word "or."[96] However, the rule against disjunctive pleading is not absolute.[97] In any event, the use of the conjunctive does not require the State to prove the alternative matters alleged.[98] Although the use of "and/or" has been criticized, its use is not per se fatal to an indictment.[99]

---

87. G.S. 15A-1340.16(a4).

88. *See* State v. Ortiz, 238 N.C. App. 508, 514 (2014).

89. *See* G.S. 15A-302 through -305 (misdemeanor pleadings); 15A-644 (indictment and information).

90. *See* James Jacobs & Tamara Crepet, *The Expanding Scope, Use, and Availability of Criminal Records*, 11 N.Y.U. J. Legis. & Pub. Pol'y 177, 183 n.36 (2008).

91. *Compare* Fed. R. Crim. P. 7(c)(1) ("a plain, concise, and definite written statement of the essential facts."), *with* G.S. 15A-924(a)(5) ("[a] plain and concise factual statement [that] asserts facts supporting every element").

92. State v. Rambert, 341 N.C. 173, 176 (1995).

93. *E.g.*, State v. Silas, 360 N.C. 377, 383 (2006) (burglary indictment need not specify the felony intended to be committed inside, but, if felony is named, State is bound by the allegation); State v. Williams, 303 N.C. 507, 510 (1981) (first-degree sexual offense indictment need not specify the sexual acts, etc.).

94. State v. Birdsong, 325 N.C. 418, 422 (1989).

95. *Id.*; *see also* State v. Lofton, 372 N.C. 216, 222 (2019) (manufacturing marijuana).

96. State v. Swaney, 277 N.C. 602, 612 (1971) (armed robbery indictment properly alleged "endangered and threatened," though G.S. 14-87 reads "endangered or threatened.").

97. State v. Rozier, 69 N.C. App. 38, 45 (1984).

98. State v. Lofton, 372 N.C. 216, 222 (2019); State v. Montgomery, 331 N.C. 559, 569 (1992); State v. Mitchell, 234 N.C. App. 423, 429 (2014).

99. State v. Haddock, 191 N.C. App. 474, 476 (2008).

3. Alleging Multiple Offenses in a Single Pleading

While an indictment must contain a separate count for each offense charged, a single pleading may charge multiple offenses. Two or more offenses may be joined in one pleading when the offenses are based on the same act or transaction or on a series of acts or transactions connected or constituting parts of a single scheme or plan.[100] In determining whether offenses have the requisite transactional connection, courts consider several factors: (1) the nature of the offenses charged, (2) any commonality of facts, (3) the lapse of time between the offenses, and (4) the unique circumstances of each case.[101]

There is no constitutional or statutory limit to the number of charges a single pleading may contain. However, there is an administrative limit of two charges per citation, and there are technical limits in various computer systems that limit to three the number of charges that may be contained in a single warrant, summons, or magistrate's order. Additional pleadings may be used when it is appropriate to charge a defendant with more crimes than will fit on a single pleading.[102]

B. Offense-Specific Requirements

1. For Statutory Offenses, Track the Language of the Statute

North Carolina recognizes both common law crimes and crimes created by statute.[103] For statutory offenses, an indictment couched in the language of the statute is generally sufficient.[104] Tracking the language of the statute does not, however, relieve the State of the burden of alleging each element of the offense.[105]

2. For Short-Form Eligible Offenses, Use the Form

As noted above, for several offenses the legislature has provided simplified charging language.[106] Most of these statutes appear in G.S. Chapter 15, the precursor to the more recent Chapter 15A (Criminal Procedure).[107] Slight deviation from the prescribed language may not be fatal so long as substantially equivalent words are used.[108]

---

100. G.S. 15A-926(a).

101. State v. Herring, 74 N.C. App. 269, 273 (1985), *aff'd per curiam*, 316 N.C. 188 (1986); *accord* State v. Perry, 142 N.C. App. 177, 181 (2001).

102. *See* Jeff Welty, *How Many Charges Can One Charging Document Contain?*, N.C. Crim. L.: A UNC Sch. Of Gov't Blog (Apr. 15, 2015), nccriminallaw.sog.unc.edu/how-many-charges-can-one-charging-document-contain/.

103. *See* G.S. 4-1 (common law declared to be in force within this state); *cf.* G.S. 14-51 ("two degrees in the crime of burglary as defined at the common law"); 14-58 ("two degrees of arson as defined at the common law").

104. State v. Mostafavi, 370 N.C. 681, 685 (2018); State v. Spivey, 368 N.C. 739, 742 (2016); State v. Williams, 368 N.C. 620, 626 (2016).

105. State v. Greer, 238 N.C. 325, 328 (1953) (general rule does not apply if the statute does not state all the elements of the offense); *accord* State v. Rankin, 371 N.C. 885, 887 (2018).

106. G.S. 15-144 (murder and manslaughter); 15-144.1 (rape); 15-144.2 (sex offense); 15-145 (perjury); 15-146 (subornation of perjury); *cf.* State v. Jones, 359 N.C. 832, 838 (2005) (attempted murder).

107. *See also* G.S. 14-76 (larceny of public records); 14-100 (false pretenses); 20-138.1(c) (impaired driving).

108. State v. Tart, 372 N.C. 73, 77 (2019) (upholding indictment for attempted murder that alleged that the defendant with malice did attempt to kill and *slay* the victim, as opposed to kill and *murder* the victim).

3. For Felonies, Include the Word "Feloniously"

The North Carolina Supreme Court has held that an indictment for a felony that fails to include the word "feloniously" is fatally defective.[109] This rule has been called into question by the North Carolina Court of Appeals, which has stated that the word "feloniously" is not required if the indictment references "the specific statute making the crime a felony."[110] Use of the word "feloniously" in a pleading charging a misdemeanor will be treated as surplusage.[111]

4. For Larceny, It Is Necessary to Identify the Victim

An indictment for larceny,[112] embezzlement,[113] injury to personal property,[114] and conversion by bailee[115] (but not armed robbery,[116] injury to real property,[117] or breaking and entering[118]) must allege an interest in the property by a natural person or a legal entity capable of owning property. A person named in the indictment may be either the person having a general interest in the property, i.e., the actual owner, or a person with a special interest in the property, i.e., the person who had possession and control of the property at the time it was stolen.[119] When alleging ownership in an entity, the indictment must specify that the owner is a corporation or otherwise capable of owning property, and the words "corporation," "incorporated," "limited," or "company," or their abbreviated forms, sufficiently identify a corporation.[120] Or the pleading may specifically identify the victim as "an entity capable of owning property."[121] For entities authorized by statute to own property, such as a church[122] or a university,[123] it is sufficient to name the entity or otherwise identify the entity as such.[124]

---

109. State v. Fowler, 266 N.C. 528, 530 (1966); State v. Price, 265 N.C. 703 (1965); State v. Whaley, 262 N.C. 536, 537 (1964).

110. State v. Blakney, 156 N.C. App. 671, 673 (2003). In *Blakney*, however, the North Carolina Court of Appeals found the indictment invalid as satisfying neither rule. *Id.* Since the result would be the same under the old rule (i.e., state supreme court precedent), the new rule (adopted by the court of appeals in *Blakney*) cannot be deemed authoritative.

111. State v. Mayes, 31 N.C. App. 694, 697 (1976).

112. State v. Campbell, 368 N.C. 83, 86 (2015).

113. State v. Linney, 138 N.C. App. 169, 173 (2000).

114. State v. Ellis, 368 N.C. 342, 345 (2015).

115. State v. Falana, 254 N.C. App. 329, 333 (2017).

116. State v. Thompson, 359 N.C. 77, 107 (2004).

117. State v. Spivey, 368 N.C. 739, 744 (2016).

118. State v. Norman, 149 N.C. App. 588, 592 (2002).

119. State v. Redmond, 281 N.C. App. 283, 287 (2022); *see also* State v. Linney, 138 N.C. App. 169, 173 (2000) (persons with a special interest include a bailee, custodian, or one who otherwise has possession and control of the property).

120. State v. Campbell, 368 N.C. 83, 86 (2015); *see also* State v. Speas, 265 N.C. App. 351, 353 (2019) ("Sears Roebuck and Company" was sufficient); State v. Cave, 174 N.C. App. 580, 583 (2005) ("N.C. FYE, Inc." was sufficient); *but see* State v. Garner, 252 N.C. App. 393, 396 (2017) ("Pinewood Country Club" was insufficient); State v. Brown, 184 N.C. App. 539, 542 (2007) ("Smoker Friendly Store" was insufficient); State v. Price, 170 N.C. App. 672, 674 (2005) ("City of Asheville Transit and Parking Services" was insufficient); State v. Phillips, 162 N.C. App. 719, 721 (2004) ("Parker's Marine" was insufficient); State v. Norman, 149 N.C. App. 588, 593 (2002) ("Quail Run Homes Ross Dotson" was insufficient); State v. Woody, 132 N.C. App. 788, 791 (1999) ("P&R unlimited" was insufficient).

121. State v. Brawley, 256 N.C. App. 78, 84 (2017) (Arrowood, J. dissenting) ("Belk's Department Stores, an entity capable of owning property"), *rev'd for reasons in dissent*, 370 N.C. 626 (2018).

122. *Campbell*, 368 N.C. at 87 ("Manna Baptist Church").

123. State v. Ellis, 368 N.C. 342, 345 (2015) ("North Carolina State University" was sufficient); State v. Edwards, 286 N.C. App. 306, 310 (2022) ("Graham County Schools" was sufficient).

124. State v. McNair, 253 N.C. App. 178, 193 (2017) ("Vision," identified in other counts as a place of religious worship, was sufficient).

Several other crimes have particular naming rules. Victims of sex crimes (rape and sex offense,[125] indecent liberties,[126] incest[127]) may be identified by initials, but identifying a person as "Victim #1" is insufficient.[128] For drug offenses, it is necessary to name the buyer, if known.[129]

5. Special Rules for Citations

The North Carolina Supreme Court has held that a citation is sufficient when it (1) identifies the crime charged, (2) contains the name and address of the person cited, (3) identifies the issuing officer, and (4) directs the person cited to appear in court at a certain date and time.[130] Whatever identifying the crime means, it is not necessary to allege each element of the offense.[131]

C. Alleging Prior Convictions

In general, an indictment may not be read to a petit jury.[132] Pleadings that contain allegations of prior convictions in particular are subject to additional restrictions, as stated herein. In determining which rules apply, prior convictions used *as an element of the offense charged* should be distinguished from those used *for purposes of sentencing*. Though the General Statutes allow indictment for habitual felon status,[133] habitual felon status is not a crime; it is a sentencing enhancement.[134] In alleging a prior conviction, it is generally sufficient to state that the defendant was at a certain time and place convicted of the prior offense, without otherwise fully alleging all the elements.[135]

1. As an Element of the Offense

For some crimes, it is necessary to prove prior convictions as an element of the offense.[136] When such crimes are charged by indictment or information, the prior conviction must be alleged in a separate indictment or information or as a separate count in the principal indictment.[137] If the name of the

---

125. State v. McKoy, 196 N.C. App. 650, 658 (2009).

126. State v. Sechrest, 277 N.C. App. 372, 377 (2021).

127. State v. Perkins, 286 N.C. App. 495, 503 (2022).

128. State v. Corey, 373 N.C. 225, 233 (2019); State v. White, 372 N.C. 248, 252 (2019); State v. Shuler, 263 N.C. App. 366, 369 (2018); *cf. In re* M.S., 199 N.C. App. 260, 266 (2009) (juvenile petition was invalid which alleged sexual offense with "a child.").

129. *See* State v. Bennett, 280 N.C. 167, 168 (1971) (under Uniform Narcotic Drug Act of 1935, where sale is prohibited it is necessary to allege the name of the person to whom the sale was made or that his or her name is unknown); State v. Ingram, 20 N.C. App. 464, 466 (1974) (applying *Bennett* to indictment under Controlled Substances Act of 1972); *accord* State v. Redd, 144 N.C. App. 248, 256 (2001).

130. State v. Jones, 371 N.C. 548, 555 (2018); *cf.* G.S. 15A-302(c).

131. *Jones*, 371 N.C. at 555 (citation for transporting an open container was sufficient even absent allegations that the defendant was driving, on a public road or highway, with a container in the passenger area of the vehicle); State v. Allen, 247 N.C. App. 179, 183 (2016) (citation for transporting an open container was sufficient even absent an allegation that the container was in the passenger area of defendant's vehicle).

132. G.S. 15A-1221(b). This statute applies only (1) during jury selection and the guilt phase of the trial and (2) to the indictment(s) for the case currently being tried. State v. Flowers, 347 N.C. 1, 35 (1997).

133. G.S. 14-7.3 (prosecutor may "charge" a person as an habitual felon; an indictment which charges a person with being an habitual felon must contain date of prior felonies, etc.).

134. State v. Patton, 342 N.C. 633, 635 (1996); State v. Roper, 328 N.C. 337, 363 (1991); State v. Allen, 292 N.C. 431, 435 (1977).

135. G.S. 15A-924(d).

136. *See e.g.*, G.S. 14-72(b)(6) (habitual larceny); 14-33.2 (habitual misdemeanor assault); 14-415.1 (possession of firearm by a felon); 20-138.5 (habitual impaired driving); 90-95(e) (certain drug offenses); State v. Howell, 370 N.C. 647, 655 (2018) (construing G.S. 90-95(e) to create greater offense not merely enhance punishment); *cf.* State v. Burch, 160 N.C. App. 394, 396 (2003) (regarding habitual offenses).

137. G.S. 15A-928(a) ("accompanied by a special indictment or information"), (b) (or "incorporated . . . as a separate count"); *cf.* G.S. 15A-645 (pleadings subject to G.S. 15A-928); 15A-924(c) (same).

offense refers to the prior conviction, the name may not be used in the indictment or information but should be altered to avoid reference to the prior conviction.[138] When a misdemeanor with such an element is tried de novo in superior court, the State must replace the pleading with a statement of charges that complies with these provisions.[139] But failure to comply with statutory separate-count provisions is not a jurisdictional defect.[140]

2. As an Aggravating Sentencing Factor

Even when a prior conviction is not an element of the offense charged, prior conviction(s) may justify a longer sentence. For the most part, prior convictions are factored into a determination of the defendant's prior record level or prior conviction level.[141] Under a few statutes, relevant prior convictions also constitute aggravating factors at sentencing, and the particular pleading requirements are set out in the pertinent statutes.[142]

3. As "Elements" of Habitual Felon Status

As noted above, being an habitual felon is not a crime.[143] "[T]he status of habitual felon merely enhances the punishment of another crime."[144] By statute, any person who has been previously convicted of three felony offenses may be charged as a status offender.[145] An habitual felon indictment must be separate from the indictment charging the principal felony.[146] Under G.S. 14-7.3, an habitual felon indictment must include (1) the date the prior felonies were committed, (2) the name of the state or sovereign against which the felonies were committed, (3) the dates the felony convictions were returned, and (4) the identity of the court where the convictions took place.[147] An habitual felon indictment is sufficient if it provides a defendant with notice of the prior felony convictions.[148] Hence, deviations from the requirements of G.S. 14-7.3 are not fatal so long as the defendant received adequate notice.[149]

---

138. G.S. 15A-928(a) ("improvised name or title must be used"). This manual contains forms that comply with G.S. 15A-928. It also contains simplified language that may be used in pleadings not subject to G.S. 15A-928.

139. G.S. 15A-928(d); *cf.* G.S. 15A-922(h).

140. State v. Newborn, 384 N.C. 656, 661 (2023) (construing G.S. 14-415.1(c), State v. Brice, 370 N.C. 244, 253 (2017) (construing G.S. 15A-928).

141. G.S. 15A-1340.14 (felony sentencing); 15A-1340.21 (misdemeanor sentencing).

142. *See* G.S. 15A-1340.16B(d) (Class B1 felony, victim under 13, and prior conviction of Class B1 felony); 20-179(a1)(1) (DWI appeal to superior court, defendant entitled to notice of aggravating factors).

143. *E.g.*, State v. Patton, 342 N.C. 633, 635 (1996). Yet cases persist in referring to prior convictions as "elements of the offense." *E.g.*, State v. Hefner, 289 N.C. App. 223, 232 (2023); State v. Griffin, 213 N.C. App. 625, 629 (2011).

144. State v. Roper, 328 N.C. 337, 363 (1991).

145. G.S. 14-7.1.

146. G.S. 14-7.3. An habitual felon indictment may be returned before or after the substantive felony indictment. State v. Blakney, 156 N.C. App. 671, 675 (2003). But an habitual felon indictment returned before the defendant has committed the principal offense will not support habitual felon status for that offense. *See* State v. Ross, 221 N.C. App. 185, 191 (2012).

147. G.S. 14-7.3.

148. State v. Briggs, 137 N.C. App. 125, 131 (2000); State v. Williams, 99 N.C. App. 333, 335 (1990) ("notice to a defendant that he is being tried as a recidivist"); *cf.* State v. Marshburn, 173 N.C. App. 749, 753 (2005) (notice is "the critical issue").

149. *See* State v. Griffin, 213 N.C. App. 625, 629 (2011) (misidentifying prior conviction); State v. Taylor, 203 N.C. App. 448, 455 (2010) (incorrect date); State v. Sinclair, 191 N.C. App. 485, 495 (2008) (failed to name state or sovereign); State v. Lewis, 162 N.C. App. 277, 285 (2004) (incorrect date and county); State v. Montford, 137 N.C. App. 495, 501 (2000) (state or sovereign); State v. Mason, 126 N.C. App. 318, 322 (1997) (same); State v. Hodge, 112 N.C. App. 462, 467 (1993) (same); State v. Smith, 112 N.C. App. 512, 516 (1993) (omitted date); *see also* Jeffrey B. Welty, *North Carolina's Habitual Felon, Violent Habitual Felon, and Habitual Breaking and Entering Laws*, Admin. of Just. Bull. No. 2013/07 (UNC School of Government, Aug. 2013).

IV. Fixing Pleading Problems

A prosecutor confronted with pleading errors has four main choices: (1) do nothing, an approach best suited for very minor problems; (2) move to amend the pleading, best suited for relatively minor problems; (3) supersede with a new pleading, used to address even serious problems; and (4) dismiss the case and recharge the defendant, similar in effect to superseding with a new pleading. Each of these approaches is discussed in greater detail below.

A. Doing Nothing

Minor problems that do not affect the validity of the pleading may be safely ignored. Examples of this type include slight misspellings in the name of the defendant[150] or the victim[151] or an error regarding the date or time of the offense when time is not of the essence.[152] Of course, a prosecutor is not obliged to ignore even minor issues, and these can be corrected by amendment.

B. Moving to Amend

In general, errors that may safely be ignored may also be corrected by amendment, whereas defects that render a pleading defective cannot be remedied by merely amending the pleading.[153] Obviously, this makes amendment a procedure of only limited utility. The text that follows summarizes the sorts of errors that might be addressed by amendment—the rules for indictments are ostensibly stricter than the rules for misdemeanor pleadings (see below)—and then considers the procedure a prosecutor should follow in amending a pleading.

By statute, a bill of indictment may not be amended.[154] The North Carolina Supreme Court has construed this to mean that a bill of indictment may not be amended in a manner that substantially

---

150. State v. Stroud, 259 N.C. App. 411, 417 (2018) (indictment listed the defendant's middle name as Rashawn, but his actual middle name was Rashaun; the defendant failed to show prejudice); State v. Spooner, 28 N.C. App. 203, 204 (1975) (indictment named the defendant as Mike Spooner, but the defendant said his name was Michael Charles Irwin Spooner; variance was "immaterial").

151. State v. Pender, 243 N.C. App. 142, 151 (2015) (indictment named the victim as Vera Alston, but the victim was Vera Pierson; no fatal variance); State v. Mason, 222 N.C. App. 223, 227 (2012) (indictment named the victim as You Xing Lin, but the victim's name was Lin You Xing; variance was immaterial); State v. Bailey, 97 N.C. App. 472, 475 (1990) (indictment named the victim as Pettress Cebron, but the victim's name was Cebron Pettress; no error in allowing amendment); State v. Isom, 65 N.C. App. 223, 226 (1983) (indictment named the victim as Eldred Allison, but the victim's name was Elton Alison; variance was "wholly immaterial"); *but see* State v. Abraham, 338 N.C. 315, 340 (1994) (trial court erred by allowing the prosecutor to amend the victim's name from Carlose Antoine Latter to Joice Hardin).

152. State v. Jones, 248 N.C. App. 418, 425 (2016) (indictment listed date of offense as 17 December 2009, but State's evidence showed that date of offense was 18 October 2009; defendant failed to show prejudice); State v. Avent, 222 N.C. App. 147, 151 (2012) (indictment listed date of offense as 28 December 2009, but evidence showed that date of offense was 27 December 2009; no error in allowing amendment); State v. Riggs, 100 N.C. App. 149, 153 (1990) (indictment listed date of offense as 17 May 1989, but State's evidence showed date of offense was 15 May 1989; defendant was not deprived of any defense).

153. *See* State v. Brinson, 337 N.C. 764, 767 (1994) (amendment was permissible to specify items were "deadly weapons" where original indictment was sufficient to identify the items as deadly weapons); State v. Madry, 140 N.C. App. 600, 603 (2000) (defective warrant could not be cured by amendment); *cf.* State v. White, 202 N.C. App. 524, 529 (2010) (surplusage could be amended).

154. G.S. 15A-923(e). This seems to have codified the common law rule. *See* State v. Jackson, 280 N.C. 563 (1972); 1 Leipold, *supra* note 11, § 128 ("the historic rule"); *cf.* G.S. 15A-923(d) (information may be amended only with consent of the defendant).

alters the charged offense.[155] Undoubtedly, a fatally defective indictment cannot be cured by amendment.[156]

In considering whether an amendment otherwise constitutes a substantial alteration, courts consider the purposes served by indictments, including enabling a defendant to prepare for trial.[157] Where time is not of the essence and the defendant has not been prejudiced, an amendment relating to the date of offense charged is permissible.[158] Likewise, an amendment that does not implicate the elements of the offense is less objectionable.[159] By contrast, an amendment that alters allegations relied on by the defendant in preparing a defense is prohibited.[160] Similarly, an amendment that results in a misdemeanor being elevated to a felony is a substantial alteration.[161] Whether changing a victim's name substantially alters the charge seems to depend on how drastically the name is changed.[162]

Misdemeanor pleadings may be amended at any time "when the amendment does not change the nature of the offense."[163] The substantial-alteration standard for indictments and the changed-nature standard for misdemeanor pleadings have been treated as essentially identical.[164] It should be noted, however, that by statute a warrant may be amended to correct allegations pertaining to the ownership of property.[165] This would seem to permit amendment of the victim's name in a larceny case to specify an entity capable of owning property, whereas such amendment may not be permissible for

---

155. State v. Farrar, 361 N.C. 675, 677 (2007).

156. State v. Maloney, 253 N.C. App. 563, 570 (2017); *see also* State v. De la Sancha Cobos, 211 N.C. App. 536, 541 (2011) (adding an element is substantially altering the indictment).

157. State v. Silas, 360 N.C. 377, 380 (2006).

158. State v. Price, 310 N.C. 596, 600 (1984) (murder); State v. Avent, 222 N.C. App. 147, 151 (2012) (murder); State v. Riffe, 191 N.C. App. 86, 94 (2008) (sexual exploitation of a minor); State v. Coltrane, 188 N.C. App. 498, 501 (2008) (possession of a firearm by a felon).

159. State v. Lawson, 285 N.C. App. 404, 411 (2022) (animal cruelty indictment properly amended to strike name of horse); State v. Stith, 246 N.C. App. 714, 717 (2016) (drug possession indictment amended to strike "Schedule II"), *aff'd per curiam*, 369 N.C. 516 (2017); State v. Tucker, 227 N.C. App. 627, 632 (2013) (embezzlement indictment amended to add "or agent"); State v. McCallum, 187 N.C. App. 628, 636 (2007) (robbery indictment amended to remove value of property); State v. Brady, 147 N.C. App. 755, 759 (2001) (indictment for obtaining controlled substance by fraud amended to change drug); State v. Parker, 146 N.C. App. 715, 719 (2001) (indictment for false pretenses amended to change items pawned); *but see* State v. Hill, 262 N.C. App. 113, 117 (2018) (kidnapping indictment impermissibly amended to add felony facilitated); State v. Simmons, 256 N.C. App. 347, 355 (2017) (drug trafficking indictment impermissibly amended from heroin to opiates); State v. Maloney, 253 N.C. App. 563, 570 (2017) (possession of precursor chemicals indictment impermissibly amended to add mens rea).

160. *Silas*, 360 N.C. at 383 (breaking and entering, changing the intended felony); State v. Frazier, 251 N.C. App. 840, 842 (2017) (negligent child abuse, changing the nature of the negligent conduct); State v. Morris, 185 N.C. App. 481, 484 (2007) (kidnapping, changing the alleged purpose of the confinement, restraint, or removal); State v. Moore, 162 N.C. App. 268, 274 (2004) (drug paraphernalia, changing "a can designed as a smoking device" to "a brown paper container").

161. State v. Winslow, 169 N.C. App. 137 (Hunter, J. dissenting in part), *rev'd based on dissent*, 360 N.C. 161, 623 S.E.2d 11 (2005); State v. Moses, 154 N.C. App. 332, 338 (2002).

162. State v. Abraham, 338 N.C. 315, 340 (1994) (impermissible amendment to change name from Carlose Antoine Latter to Joice Hardin); State v. Abbott, 217 N.C. App. 614, 618 (2011) (impermissible amendment struck "incorporated" from name of larceny victim); *but see* State v. McNair, 146 N.C. App. 674, 678 (2001) (no error in allowing amendment of victim's name from Donald Cook to Ronald Cook); State v. Hewson, 182 N.C. App. 196, 212 (2007) (Gail Hewson Tice to Gail Tice Hewson); State v. Holliman, 155 N.C. App. 120, 126 (2002) (Tamika to Tanika); *cf.* State v. Ingram, 160 N.C. App. 224, 226 (2003) (deleting one robbery victim's name), *aff'd per curiam*, 358 N.C. 147 (2004).

163. G.S. 15A-922(f) (statement of charges, criminal summons, warrant for arrest, citation, or magistrate's order).

164. State v. Reavis, 287 N.C. App. 322, 328 n.2 (2022) ("neither an indictment nor a statement of charges may be amended in a manner that changes the nature of the offense"); *but see* State v. Bohannon, 26 N.C. App. 486, 487 (1975) (distinguishing warrant defect cases from indictment defect cases).

165. G.S. 15-24.1 (abrogating State v. Cooke, 246 N.C. 518, 521 (1957)).

indictments.[166] As with indictments, misdemeanor charging documents may not be amended so as to charge the defendant with committing an entirely different offense.[167]

Assuming amendment is permissible, the amendment should be made in writing.[168] The usual practice is for the prosecutor to move to amend, for the court to rule on the motion, and for someone—the prosecutor, the clerk, or the judge—to mark the amendment on the court's copy of the pleading and to initial it. As for timing, North Carolina courts have permitted amendments to indictments as late as during trial.[169] By statute, misdemeanor pleadings may be amended at any time.[170]

C. Superseding with a New Pleading

Even fatal defects in an indictment or information can be remedied by obtaining a superseding indictment or information that correctly charges the offense.[171] It has long been the law in this state that prior indictment constitutes no legal impediment to putting the defendant on trial upon a later and more perfect bill.[172] By statute, if, before trial or plea, another indictment or information is filed in the same court charging the defendant with an offense charged or attempted to be charged in the first instrument, the first is superseded by the second "with respect to the offense."[173] But the first instrument is not superseded with respect to any count not charged in the second.[174] A superseding indictment may be used to eliminate unnecessary details in the original pleading upon which the defendant might rely to his or her prejudice.[175] A superseding indictment should not, however, be used to add unnecessary details to an otherwise valid pleading.[176]

In the district court, misdemeanor pleadings may be superseded by a statement of charges. By statute, when a statement of charges is filed, it supersedes all previous pleadings and constitutes the pleading of the State.[177] Because a statement of charges entirely supersedes the prior pleading (i.e., not only with respect to an offense previously charged[178]), a prosecutor must take care to include in the statement of charges any offenses he or she wishes to retain from a prior pleading. A statement of charges filed prior to arraignment in district court may charge the same offenses as a prior

---

166. *Compare* State v. Capps, 374 N.C. 621, 627 (2020) (no error in allowing amendment to victim's name in warrant for larceny from "Loves Truck Stop" to "Love's Truck Stops & Country Stores, Inc."); *with* State v. Cathey, 162 N.C. App. 350, 354 (2004) (larceny indictment could not be amended to add "Incorporated"), *overruled in part on other grounds by* State v. Campbell, 368 N.C. 83 (2015).

167. State v. Bryant, 267 N.C. App. 575, 578 (2019) (larceny to shoplifting); State v. Carlton, 232 N.C. App. 62, 66 (2014) (representative of an illegal lottery to possession of lottery tickets); *cf. In re* Davis, 114 N.C. App. 253, 256 (1994) (burning real property to burning personal property).

168. G.S. 15A-951 (in general, a motion must: (1) be in writing, (2) state the grounds, (3) set forth relief sought).

169. State v. Snyder, 343 N.C. 61, 64 (1996) (no error in allowing amendment at the close of the State's evidence); State v. Kamtsiklis, 94 N.C. App. 250, 255 (1989) (no error in allowing amendment on the morning of trial).

170. G.S. 15A-922(f) ("at any time prior to or after final judgment").

171. *See* State v. Camacho, 329 N.C. 589, 596 (1991) ("incomplete or defective"); State v. Bailey, 145 N.C. App. 13, 21 (2001) ("an error in the form"); State v. Allen, 144 N.C. App. 386, 391 n.5 (2001) (fatal defect).

172. State v. Carson, 320 N.C. 328, 333 (1987).

173. G.S. 15A-646; *cf.* State v. Stallings, 271 N.C. App. 148, 156 (2020) (rejecting the argument that the trial court lacked jurisdiction because a superseding information was not filed prior to the first day of trial).

174. G.S. 15A-646; State v. Bailey, 145 N.C. App. 13, 21 (2001) (charges not superseded).

175. State v. Silas, 360 N.C. 377, 381 (2006) (indictment for felony breaking and entering need not allege the felony that the defendant intended to commit inside the dwelling).

176. *See* State v. Fuller, 179 N.C. App. 61, 67 (2006) (aiding and abetting need not be alleged).

177. G.S. 15A-922(a) (statement of charges "supersedes all previous pleadings").

178. *Cf.* G.S. 15A-646.

misdemeanor pleading or charge additional or different offenses.[179] Unless the statement of charges makes no material change in the pleadings, a defendant, upon motion, is entitled to a continuance of three days after a statement of charges is filed or the defendant is first notified.[180]

D. Dismissing the Case and Re-Charging

When it is not practical or possible to amend or supersede an existing charging document, the prosecutor may choose to dismiss and recharge the defendant.[181] There is no double jeopardy problem with this procedure so long as the State dismisses the pleading before jeopardy attaches.[182] Even if trial has begun, there is no double jeopardy problem if the original pleading was fatally defective.[183] Later misdemeanor charges may, however, be barred by the statute of limitations.[184]

The new charge may be initiated in any way that is permissible for the offense in question. For a misdemeanor, an officer could issue a new citation or a judicial official could issue a new summons or warrant.[185] New felony charges could also be initiated by a new summons or warrant but would eventually require a new indictment or a waiver of indictment and information.[186] If the defendant posted bond on the original charge and appeared in court as required, the prosecutor should consider using a form of pleading that will not result in a new arrest.

---

179. G.S. 15A-922(d); *cf.* State v. Capps, 374 N.C. 621, 628 (2020) ("before arraignment a prosecutor may file a statement of charges that changes the nature of the offense, but after arraignment the prosecutor may only file a statement of charges that does not change the nature of the offense").

180. G.S. 15A-922(b)(2).

181. State v. Friend, 219 N.C. App. 338, 343 (2012) (no due process violation in refiling charges).

182. In superior court, jeopardy attaches when the jury is impaneled. State v. Schalow, 251 N.C. App. 334, 343 (2016). In district court, jeopardy attaches when the first witness begins to testify. State v. Ward, 127 N.C. App. 115, 121 (1997).

183. *See* State v. Brunson, 327 N.C. 244, 246 (1990).

184. G.S. 15-1 (establishing two-year statute of limitations for most misdemeanors but allowing one year from abandonment of defective charge); *cf.* G.S. 15A-931(b) (statute of limitations not tolled by voluntary dismissal).

185. G.S. 15A-922(a). Use of a statement of charges to initiate a prosecution is not authorized by statute. *Id.*

186. G.S. 15A-923(a); *cf.* State v. Fields, 374 N.C. 629, 636 (2020) (when judgment is arrested due to a fatally defective indictment, the State may seek a new indictment).

List of AOC Charging Forms

(Note: Check www.nccourts.org/Forms/FormSearch.asp for the current version of many of these forms.)

Form No.	Charging Instrument	Criminal Offense(s)
AOC-CR-100	Warrant for Arrest	Blank
AOC-CR-107	Warrant for Arrest	Misdemeanor Worthless Check
AOC-CR-113	Criminal Summons	Blank
AOC-CR-115	Criminal Summons	Misdemeanor Worthless Check
AOC-CR-116	Magistrate's Order	Blank
AOC-CR-120	Misdemeanor Statement of Charges	Blank
AOC-CR-122	Indictment	Blank
AOC-CR-123	Information	Blank
AOC-CR-124	Indictment	First- or Second-Degree Murder
AOC-CR-125	Indictment	First- or Second-Degree Forcible Rape (Female Victim)
AOC-CR-126	Indictment	First-Degree Burglary; Felonious Larceny; Felonious Possession of Stolen Goods
AOC-CR-127	Indictment	Voluntary or Involuntary Manslaughter
AOC-CR-128	Indictment	First- or Second-Degree Forcible Sexual Offense (Female or Male Victim)
AOC-CR-129	Indictment	Assault with Deadly Weapon with Intent to Kill Inflicting Serious Injury
AOC-CR-130	Indictment	Embezzlement
AOC-CR-131	Indictment	Felony Prison Escape by Failing to Return after Authorized Absence
AOC-CR-132	Indictment	Felony Prison Escape from Confines of State Prison Unit
AOC-CR-133	Indictment	Forgery; Uttering Forged Paper
AOC-CR-134	Indictment	Felonious Breaking and Entering; Felonious Larceny; Felonious Possession of Stolen Goods
AOC-CR-135	Indictment	Robbery with Dangerous Weapon
AOC-CR-136	Indictment	Common Law Robbery
AOC-CR-137	Indictment	Obtaining Property by False Pretenses
AOC-CR-138	Indictment	Felonious Larceny; Felonious Possession of Stolen Goods
AOC-CR-148	Indictment	First-Degree Statutory Rape (Female Child under 13)
AOC-CR-149	Indictment	First-Degree Statutory Sexual Offense (Female or Male Child under 13)
AOC-CR-150	Indictment	Indecent Liberties with Child
AOC-CR-151	Indictment	Possession with Intent to Manufacture, Sell, and Deliver; Sale and Delivery; Manufacture
AOC-CR-152	Indictment	Financial Transaction Card Theft; Financial Transaction Card Fraud
AOC-CR-154	Indictment	Habitual Impaired Driving

Form No.	Charging Instrument	Criminal Offense(s)
AOC-CR-156	Indictment	Related Misdemeanor
AOC-CR-909M	Magistrate's Order	Fugitive from Another State
AOC-CR-910M	Warrant for Arrest	Fugitive from Another State
AOC-CR-911M	Fugitive Affidavit	Fugitive from Another State
AOC-J-310	Juvenile Petition	Blank
AOC-J-311	Juvenile Petition	First- and Second-Degree Trespass
AOC-J-312	Juvenile Petition	Simple Assault; Assault Inflicting Serious Injury; Assault with a Deadly Weapon; Assault on a Person under 12; Assault by Pointing a Gun; Assault on Government Officer/Employee
AOC-J-313	Juvenile Petition	Felonious Breaking or Entering; Felonious Larceny
AOC-J-314	Juvenile Petition	Communicating Threats
AOC-J-315	Juvenile Petition	Concealment of Merchandise (Shoplifting)
AOC-J-316	Juvenile Petition	Weapon on School Campus/Property
AOC-J-317	Juvenile Petition	Indecent Liberties between Children
AOC-J-318	Juvenile Petition	Forgery; Uttering
AOC-J-319	Juvenile Petition	Felony/Misdemeanor Larceny; Felony/Misdemeanor Possession of Stolen Goods
AOC-J-320	Juvenile Petition	Unauthorized Use of Motor Vehicle
AOC-J-321	Juvenile Petition	Operate a Motor Vehicle without a License
AOC-J-322	Juvenile Petition	Injury to Real Property
AOC-J-323	Juvenile Petition	Injury to Personal Property
AOC-J-324	Juvenile Petition	Resist, Delay, and Obstruct an Officer
AOC-J-325	Juvenile Petition	Carrying a Concealed Weapon
AOC-J-326	Juvenile Petition	Disorderly Conduct at School
AOC-J-327	Juvenile Petition	Sale or Delivery of Controlled Substance
AOC-J-328	Juvenile Petition	Possession with Intent to Manufacture, Sell, or Deliver
AOC-J-329	Juvenile Petition	Possession of Schedule I Controlled Substance
AOC-J-330	Juvenile Petition	Possession of Schedule II, III, or IV Controlled Substance
AOC-J-331	Juvenile Petition	Felonious Possession of Schedule VI Controlled Substance; Aggravated Misdemeanor Possession; Simple Possession
AOC-J-332	Juvenile Petition	Possession of Drug Paraphernalia
AOC-J-333	Juvenile Petition	Simple Affray
AOC-J-334	Juvenile Petition	Possession of Stolen Property
AOC-J-335	Juvenile Petition	First-Degree Statutory Sexual Offense (Female or Male Child under 13)
AOC-J-336	Juvenile Petition	Second-Degree Sexual Offense
AOC-J-337	Juvenile Petition	First-Degree Forcible Sexual Offense

Common Law and G.S. 14-2.4
Conspiracy
April 2024
Page 1 of 2

Introductory Comment:
To charge a drug-trafficking conspiracy, use the drug-trafficking form, G.S. 90-95(h), (i). To charge conspiracy to commit bribery, see G.S. 14-217, which sets out an additional element, an overt act.

Charging Language:
. . . unlawfully, willfully, and feloniously did conspire with (*name the other conspirators and/or write* "persons unknown") to commit the (*choose one*: felony; misdemeanor) of (*name the crime and cite the statute*) against (*name the victim or otherwise generally describe the circumstances of the crime*).

Notes about Charging Language:
- If the conspiracy is a misdemeanor, allege "unlawfully and willfully" rather than "unlawfully, willfully, and feloniously."
- Indictments for conspiracy traditionally have included a number of other verbs such as "agree, plan, combine, conspire, and confederate, each with the other . . . ." However, the word "conspire" by itself is sufficient.
- In *State v. Gallimore*, 272 N.C. 528 (1968), the North Carolina Supreme Court ruled that a conspiracy indictment is valid if it simply says the defendant conspired "with others," though the preferred practice is to name the other conspirators if they are known.
- A conspiracy indictment is sufficient if it "allege[s] generally the object of the conspiracy." State v. Furr, 292 N.C. 711, #722 (1977). Although it may be enough to name the crime that was the object of the conspiracy, *cf.* State v. Nicholson, 78 N.C. App. 398 (1985), it is advisable to provide some additional detail.
- Regarding the crime that is the object of the conspiracy, this form prompts you to "name the crime and cite the statute." The statutory citation is requsted for clarity but probably is not legally required. Although G.S. 15A-924(a)(6) requires, "[f]or each count[,] a citation of any applicable statute . . . alleged therein to have been violated," in a conspiracy charge that requirement appears to be satisfied by the citation to the conspiracy statute, G.S. 14-2.4.

Sample Charge:
[Conspiracy to commit armed robbery]

. . . unlawfully, willfully, and feloniously did conspire with Allen T. Wilson, Fred R. Hastings, and other persons unknown to commit the felony of robbery with a dangerous weapon, G.S. 14-87, against Peter Gaithers.

AOC Forms for This Offense:
None.

Punishment:
G.S. 14-2.4 provides that unless a different classification is expressly stated—for example, drug trafficking conspiracies under G.S. 90-95(h), (i) and drug conspiracies under G.S. 90-98—a defendant who is convicted of a conspiracy to commit a felony is guilty of a felony that is one class lower than the felony the defendant conspired to commit, except that a conspiracy to commit a Class A or B1 felony is a Class B2 felony, a conspiracy to commit a Class B2 felony is a Class C felony, and a conspiracy to commit a Class I felony is a Class 1 misdemeanor. Unless a different classification is expressly stated, a defendant who is convicted of a conspiracy to commit a misdemeanor is guilty of a misdemeanor that is one class lower than the misdemeanor the defendant conspired to commit, except that a conspiracy to commit a Class 3 misdemeanor is a Class 3 misdemeanor.

Common Law and G.S. 14-2.5
Attempt
April 2024

Introductory Comment:
G.S. 15-170 provides that a defendant may be convicted of an attempt to commit a crime based on an indictment charging that crime. In effect, an attempt is a lesser-included offense of an indictment charging a crime. Thus, a prosecutor does not need to allege in an indictment that the defendant is charged with an attempt to commit the crime. Instead, the prosecutor may charge the completed crime and then announce that the State is prosecuting the defendant only for an attempt to commit that crime. See, for example, *State v. Arnold*, 285 N.C. 751 (1974), in which this procedure was upheld. If a prosecutor only wants to charge an attempt to commit a crime, the forms in this publication may be used with the addition of the words *attempt to* after the words "unlawfully, willfully, and feloniously did" and before the recitation of the elements of the offense.

Charging Language:

See above.

Notes about Charging Language:
None.

Sample Charge:
[Attempted second-degree forcible rape]

. . . unlawfully, willfully, and feloniously did attempt to ravish and carnally know Susan Jones by force and against her will.

AOC Forms for This Offense:
None.

Punishment:
Unless a different classification is expressly stated—as it is, for example, for attempts to commit armed robbery, discharging a firearm into occupied property, obtaining property by false pretenses, indecent liberties, and certain drug offenses—an attempt to commit a misdemeanor or a felony is punishable under the next lower classification as the offense the defendant attempted to commit. An attempt to commit a Class A or B1 felony is a Class B2 felony, an attempt to commit a Class B2 felony is a Class C felony, an attempt to commit a Class I felony is a Class 1 misdemeanor, and an attempt to commit a Class 3 misdemeanor is a Class 3 misdemeanor. *See generally* G.S. 14-2.5.

Common Law and G.S. 14-2.6
Solicitation to Commit a Crime
April 2024

Introductory Comment:
As to the circumstances under which solicitation to commit a misdemeanor is a crime, see Jessica Smith, *North Carolina Crimes: A Guidebook on the Elements of Crime* 52 (UNC School of Government, 7th ed. 2012).

Charging Language:

. . . unlawfully, willfully, and feloniously did solicit (*name the person solicited*) to commit the felony of (*name the crime to be committed, give the statutory citation, and name the intended victim or otherwise describe the circumstances of the crime, including the intended date if known*).

Notes about Charging Language:

- See the discussion under Punishment, below, to determine whether the solicitation is a felony or a misdemeanor.
- In *State v. Furr*, 292 N.C. 711, 722 (1977), the North Carolina Supreme Court ruled that an indictment charging solicitation need only "allege generally" the object of the solicitation. Because the limits of that ruling are not clear, it is advisable to include some detail beyond the name of the crime to be committed. If it is a misdemeanor, allege "unlawfully and willfully" rather than "unlawfully, willfully, and feloniously."

Sample Charge:
[Solicitation to commit first-degree murder]

. . . unlawfully, willfully, and feloniously did solicit Peter Smith to commit the felony of first-degree murder, G.S. 14-17, against Joan Coleman.

AOC Forms for This Offense:
None.

Punishment:
G.S. 14-2.6 provides that unless a different classification is expressly stated, a defendant who is convicted of a solicitation to commit a felony is guilty of a felony that is two classes lower than the felony the defendant solicited to commit, except that a solicitation to commit a Class A or B1 felony is a Class C felony, a solicitation to commit a Class B2 felony is a Class D felony, a solicitation to commit a Class H felony is a Class 1 misdemeanor, and a solicitation to commit a Class I felony is a Class 2 misdemeanor. Unless a different classification is expressly stated, a defendant who is convicted of a solicitation to commit a misdemeanor is guilty of a Class 3 misdemeanor.

Common Law and G.S. 14-3(b)

Increased Punishment for Infamous Misdemeanor, Misdemeanor Committed with Secrecy and Malice, or with Deceit and Intent to Defraud

April 2024

Introductory Comment:

G.S. 14-3(b) provides that if a misdemeanor for which no punishment is prescribed by statute—for example, common law forgery or common law obstruction of justice—is infamous, committed with secrecy and malice, or committed with deceit and intent to defraud (except when the offense is a conspiracy to commit a misdemeanor), the offense is a Class H felony. If the defendant is to be punished for the Class H felony, the State must allege and prove the factor that elevates the misdemeanor to the felony. Therefore, the language below must be added to the criminal pleading.

Charging Language:

This offense (*choose one or more*: is infamous; was committed with secrecy and malice; was committed with deceit and intent to defraud).

Notes about Charging Language:

- You may wish to include a short description of the secrecy, malice, deceit, etc., though that is probably not legally required.
- Because the elevated offense is a felony, the charging language should begin with the phrase "unlawfully, willfully, and feloniously" rather than just "unlawfully and willfully", as is typical for misdemeanor charges.

Sample Charge:

[Increased punishment for common law obstruction of justice]

. . . unlawfully, willfully, and feloniously did obstruct justice by pleading guilty to impaired driving in Guilford County District Court in 18 CR 14566, State v. Sam R. Jones, falsely representing to the court that he was Sam R. Jones, when in fact his name is Albert C. Pickens. This offense was committed with deceit and intent to defraud.

AOC Forms for This Offense:

None.

Punishment:

See Introductory Comment, above.

G.S. 14-3(c)
Increased Punishment for Misdemeanor Committed Because of Prejudice
April 2024

Introductory Comment:
G.S. 14-3(c) provides that if any Class 2 or Class 3 misdemeanor is committed because of the victim's race, color, religion, nationality, or country of origin, the defendant shall be guilty of a Class 1 misdemeanor. If any Class A1 or Class 1 misdemeanor is committed because of the victim's race, color, religion, nationality, or country of origin, the defendant shall be guilty of a Class H felony. If a defendant is to be convicted of the elevated offense, the prejudicial reason (race, nationality, etc.) for committing the underlying offense must be alleged in the criminal pleading and proven at trial. Therefore, the language below must be added to the criminal pleading.

Charging Language:

This offense was committed because of the victim's (*choose one or more*: race; color; religion; nationality; country of origin).

Notes about Charging Language:

- As indicated in the sample charges below, the word "feloniously" should be included if the elevated offense is a felony.
- You may wish to include a short description of the defendant's conduct that shows the defendant's prejudicial motivation, though that is probably not legally required.

Sample Charges:

I. Class A1 or Class 1 misdemeanor elevated to Class H felony

[Increased punishment for assault on a female]

. . . unlawfully, willfully, and feloniously did assault and strike Sally Jones, a female person, by punching her in the stomach. The defendant is a male person and was at least 18 years of age when the assault and striking occurred. This offense was committed because of the victim's race; the defendant called the victim a racial epithet just before assaulting her.

II. Class 2 or Class 3 misdemeanor elevated to Class 1 misdemeanor

[Increased punishment for simple assault]

. . . unlawfully and willfully did assault and strike Bill Smith by punching him in the stomach. This offense was committed because of the victim's race; the defendant called the victim a racial epithet just before assaulting him.

AOC Forms for This Offense:
None.

Punishment:
See Introductory Comment, above.

G.S. 14-4
Local Ordinance Violation
April 2024

Introductory Comment:
During the 2021 legislative session, the General Assembly passed a law that decriminalizes many local ordinance violations and adds a new defense to ordinance violations that remain criminal. That legislation is discussed in depth in Jeff Welty, *North Carolina's Decriminalization of Most Local Ordinance Violations*, N.C. Crim. L.: A UNC Sch. of Gov't Blog (Mar. 23, 2022), nccriminallaw.sog .unc.edu/north-carolinas-decriminalization-of-most-local-ordinance-violations/.

Charging Language:
. . . unlawfully and willfully did (*state the crime by following the language of the ordinance as closely as possible*), in violation of (*give citation and caption of the local ordinance*).

Notes about Charging Language:
- G.S. 160A-79 (for cities) and 153A-50 (for counties) require that both the section number and caption of the ordinance must be pleaded, unless the ordinance was not codified, in which case the caption must be pleaded. Although G.S. 160A-79 states that "it is not necessary to plead or allege the substance or effect of the ordinance unless the ordinance has no caption and has not been codified," this form asks for a statement of the crime that follows the language of the local ordinance. The benefit of this approach is clear from *State v. Hales*, 282 N.C. App. 178, 185 (2022), where the court ruled that a summons charging a local ordinance violation was valid despite citing the wrong subsection of the ordinance number because the charging language "indicat[ed] to Defendant the proper city ordinance subsection of which he was in violation."
- This form was previously listed under G.S. 153A-50 and 160A-79. It is now listed under G.S. 14-4 because *Hales* states that "[t]he summons listed N.C. Gen. Stat. § 14-4 as the statutory basis for the charge against Defendant, thus correctly identifying the crime with which Defendant was charged." 282 N.C. App. at 185.

Sample Charge:
. . . unlawfully and willfully did keep on his premises a dog that barks, howls, fights, and makes such other noises as to disturb the peace and quiet of the neighborhood and general public and to create a nuisance, after being warned by the police to stop the nuisance, in violation of Section 5-20, "Keeping of barking, howling, etc., dogs and dogs in unsanitary conditions prohibited," Lumley, N.C., Code of City Ordinances (2001).

AOC Forms for This Offense:
None.

Punishment:
Class 3 misdemeanor, with a maximum fine of $500, except that a fine may not exceed $50 unless the ordinance expressly states that the maximum fine is greater than $50. A violation of an ordinance regulating the operation or parking of vehicles is an infraction with a maximum penalty of $50.

Common Law
Aiding and Abetting
April 2024

Introductory Comment:
Because a person who aids and abets another in the commission of a crime is just as guilty of the crime as the person who actually commits it, the aider and abettor may simply be charged with the crime without any reference to his or her aiding and abetting. *See* State v. Ogleston, 177 N.C. 541 (1919); State v. Madry, 140 N.C. App. 600 (2000). Some prosecutors, however, may prefer to charge aiding and abetting specifically. If that is done, the charge for the offense, whatever it is, should be modified by starting with the language set forth below.

Charging Language:

. . . unlawfully, willfully, and feloniously did aid and abet [*name the person(s) who committed the crime and/or write* "persons unknown"] in unlawfully, willfully, and feloniously (*give charging language for the offense that was committed*).

Notes about Charging Language:

- *State v. Beach*, 283 N.C. 261 (1973), ruled that an indictment need not allege the way in which the defendant aided and abetted and that if the person who committed the crime is unknown, it is sufficient to state that the defendant aided and abetted "an unknown party."
- In *State v. Gunter*, 289 N.C. App. 45, 50 (2023), the North Carolina Court of Appeals found an indictment for aiding and abetting possession of a firearm by a felon sufficient that alleged that the defendant aided and abetted one Conner Wellmon by concealing two handguns for Conner Wellmon prior to a traffic stop knowing that Mr. Wellmon was convicted of obtaining property by false pretenses (including date of offense, date of conviction, sentence, county, and file number).

Sample Charge:
None.

AOC Forms for This Offense:
None.

Punishment:
A person who aids and abets the commission of a felony is guilty of that felony and is subject to punishment for committing that felony unless a statute specifically provides otherwise. A person who aids and abets the commission of a misdemeanor is guilty of that misdemeanor and is subject to punishment for committing that misdemeanor unless a statute specifically provides otherwise.

G.S. 14-5.2
Accessory Before the Fact to a Felony
April 2024

Introductory Comment:
G.S. 14-5.2 abolished all distinctions between accessories before the fact and principals to the commission of a felony. Therefore, a person who counsels, procures, commands, or aids the principal but is not present when the felony is committed should be charged with the substantive felony itself and not with being an accessory before the fact to that felony. *Cf.* State v. Gallagher, 313 N.C. 132 (1985). If, for some reason, a prosecutor wants to charge the theory of accessory before the fact specifically, the charge for the substantive offense may be modified using the language below.

Charging Language:
. . . unlawfully, willfully, and feloniously did be and become an accessory before the fact and thereby a principal under G.S. 14-5.2 to (*briefly describe crime*) by counseling, procuring, and commanding (*name person(s) who committed the crime*) to commit (*briefly describe crime*); and in confirmation of such counseling, procuring, and commanding by the defendant, (*name person(s) who committed the crime*) unlawfully, willfully, and feloniously did (*fully allege the crime*). The defendant was not present when the (*name offense*) was committed.

Notes about Charging Language:
- As with aiding and abetting, *see* State v. Lancaster, 37 N.C. App. 528 (1978), it is not necessary to allege the acts that constitute being an accessory. Some prosecutors, however, may prefer to specifically allege them.
- See *State v. Branch*, 288 N.C. 514 (1975), for a discussion of the sufficiency of an indictment charging accessory before the fact.

Sample Charge:
None.

AOC Forms for This Offense:
None.

Punishment:
A person who is an accessory before the fact to a felony is guilty of that felony and is punished for committing that felony. However, if a defendant is convicted of first-degree murder (which is a Class A felony) and the jury finds that the conviction was based solely on the uncorroborated testimony of one or more principals, co-conspirators, or accessories, the defendant is guilty of and punished for a Class B2 felony. *See* G.S. 14-5.2.

G.S. 14-7
Accessory After the Fact to a Felony
April 2024

Introductory Comment:
None.

Charging Language:
. . . unlawfully, willfully, and feloniously did become an accessory after the fact to the felony of (*name the crime committed and give the statutory citation*) that was committed by (*name the person who committed the crime*) against (*name the victim or otherwise give the circumstances of the crime*) on (*give the date of the crime*), in that the defendant, knowing that (*repeat the name of the person who committed the crime*) had committed that felony, did knowingly assist that person in attempting to escape and in escaping detection, arrest, and punishment by (*describe how the defendant aided the principal*).

Notes about Charging Language:
- See the discussion under Punishment, below, to determine whether the offense is a felony or a misdemeanor. If it is a misdemeanor, omit the word "feloniously."

Sample Charge:
. . . unlawfully, willfully, and feloniously did become an accessory after the fact to the felony of first-degree murder, G.S. 14-17, that was committed by Susan Langsford Blackwell against Harry Edwards on February 25, 2018, in that the defendant, knowing that Susan Langsford Blackwell had committed that felony, did knowingly assist that person in attempting to escape and in escaping detection, arrest, and punishment by hiding Susan Langsford Blackwell in his basement at 1826 Longleaf Drive, Charlotte, N.C., for three days and driving her in his car to Norfolk, Virginia.

AOC Forms for This Offense:
None.

Punishment:
Unless a different classification is expressly stated, the punishment is two classes lower than the felony the principal felon committed, except that being an accessory after the fact to a Class A or Class B1 felony is a Class C felony, being an accessory after the fact to a Class B2 felony is a Class D felony, being an accessory after the fact to a Class H felony is a Class 1 misdemeanor, and being an accessory after the fact to a Class I felony is a Class 2 misdemeanor. *See* G.S. 14-7.

G.S. 14-7.1
Habitual Felon
April 2024
Page 1 of 2

Introductory Comment:
This form is to be used in preparing an indictment that alleges that the defendant is a habitual felon. Do not use this form to charge a defendant with violent habitual felon status under G.S. 14-7.7 or with armed habitual felon status under G.S. 14-7.36. There are other indictment forms available to charge those statuses.

Charging Language:
The jurors for the State upon their oath present that (*name defendant*) is a habitual felon in that on or about (*give date the defendant committed felony*), (*name defendant*) did commit the felony of (*name felony and give statutory citation*), and that on or about (*give date the defendant was convicted of felony*), (*name defendant*) was convicted of the felony of (*name felony for which the defendant was convicted and the court and state in which the defendant was convicted*); and that on or about (*give date the defendant committed felony*), (*name defendant*) did commit the felony of (*name felony and give statutory citation*) and that on or about (*give date the defendant was convicted of felony*), (*name defendant*) was convicted of the felony of (*name felony for which the defendant was convicted and the court and state in which the defendant was convicted*); and that on or about (*give date the defendant committed felony*), (*name defendant*) did commit the felony of (*name felony and give statutory citation*), and that on or about (*give date the defendant was convicted of felony*), (*name defendant*) was convicted of the felony of (*name felony for which the defendant was convicted and the court and state in which the defendant was convicted*).

Notes about Charging Language:
- A charge that a defendant is a habitual felon should be brought by "[t]he district attorney," G.S. 14-7.3, not by, for example, a magistrate.
- A separate habitual felon indictment is not required for each principal felony indictment. One habitual felon indictment is sufficient. *See* State v. Patton, 342 N.C. 633 (1996).
- A habitual felon indictment need not allege the principal felony. *See* State v. Cheek, 339 N.C. 725 (1995).
- The State may allege more than three previous felonies. However, none of the felonies alleged in the indictment may be used to calculate the defendant's prior record level in the event of a conviction. *See* State v. Lee, 150 N.C. App. 701 (2003).
- For a longer discussion of charging issues in connection with habitual felon status, see Jeffrey B. Welty, *North Carolina's Habitual Felon, Violent Habitual Felon, and Habitual Breaking and Entering Laws*, Admin. of Just. Bull. No. 2013/07 (UNC School of Government, Aug. 2013), www.sog.unc.edu/sites/www.sog.unc.edu/files/reports/aojb1307.pdf.
- G.S. 14-7.3 provides that "[t]he indictment charging the defendant as an habitual felon shall be separate from the indictment charging him with the principal felony." However, the appellate courts have ruled that this requirement is satisfied so long as the habitual felon allegation is in a separate count from the substantive felony.

Sample Charge:
The jurors for the State upon their oath present that James Peter Kenly is a habitual felon in that on or about June 1, 2002, James Peter Kenly did commit the felony of armed robbery in violation of G.S. 14-87, and that on or about January 12, 2003, James Peter Kenly was convicted of the felony of armed robbery in the Superior Court of Wilson County, N.C.; and that on or about April 30, 2010, James Peter Kenly did commit the felony of felonious breaking and entering in violation of G.S. 14-54, and that on or about November 10, 2010, James Peter Kenly was convicted of felonious breaking and entering in the Superior Court of Cumberland County, N.C.; and that on or about August 30, 2015, James Peter Kenly did commit the felony of felonious larceny in violation of G.S. 14-72, and that on or about December 12, 2015, James Peter Kenly was convicted of the felony of felonious larceny in the Superior Court of Sampson County, N.C.

AOC Forms for This Offense:
None.

Punishment:
If the defendant is convicted of a principal felony and is then determined to be a habitual felon, he or she is sentenced as if the principal felony were four offense classes higher, but no higher than Class C. However, if the principal felony is a Class A, B1, or B2 offense, the defendant is sentenced according to the classification of the principal felony. When a defendant is convicted of multiple principal felonies to which a habitual felon indictment attaches, each is elevated according to the rules above, unless there is a reason to do otherwise, such as a plea agreement stipulating that one or more of the principal felonies will not be elevated.

G.S. 14-7.7
Violent Habitual Felon
April 2024
Page 1 of 2

Introductory Comment:
This form is to be used in preparing an indictment that alleges that the defendant is a violent habitual felon. Do not use this form to charge a defendant with habitual felon status under G.S. 14-7.1. There is another indictment form available to charge that status.

Charging Language:
The jurors for the State upon their oath present that (*name defendant*) is a violent habitual felon in that on or about (*give date the defendant committed felony*), (*name defendant*) did commit the violent felony of (*name felony and give statutory citation*), and that on or about (*give date the defendant was convicted of felony*), (*name defendant*) was convicted of the violent felony of (*name felony for which defendant was convicted and the court and state in which the defendant was convicted*); and that on or about (*give date the defendant committed felony*), (*name defendant*) did commit the violent felony of (*name felony and give statutory citation*), and that on or about (*give date the defendant was convicted of felony*), (*name defendant*) was convicted of the violent felony of (*name felony for which defendant was convicted and the court and state in which the defendant was convicted*).

Notes about Charging Language:
- A separate violent habitual felon indictment is not required for each substantive felony indictment. One violent habitual felon indictment is sufficient. *See* State v. Patton, 342 N.C. 633 (1996).
- A violent habitual felon indictment need not allege the predicate felony being tried. *See* State v. Cheek, 339 N.C. 725 (1995).
- The State may allege more than two previous felonies. However, none of the felonies alleged in the indictment may be used to calculate the defendant's prior record level in the event of a conviction. *See* State v. Lee, 150 N.C. App. 701 (2003).
- For a longer discussion of charging issues in connection with violent habitual felon status, see Jeffrey B. Welty, *North Carolina's Habitual Felon, Violent Habitual Felon, and Habitual Breaking and Entering Laws*, ADMIN. OF JUST. BULL. No. 2013/07 (UNC School of Government, Aug. 2013), www.sog.unc.edu/sites/www.sog.unc.edu/files/reports/aojb1307.pdf.
- G.S. 14-7.7 provides that "[t]he indictment charging the defendant as a violent habitual felon shall be separate from the indictment charging the defendant with the principal violent felony." As with charges of habitual felon, discussed above, it appears to be sufficient if the violent habitual felon allegation is in a separate count of the indictment.

Sample Charge:
The jurors for the State upon their oath present that David Louis Smith is a violent habitual felon in that on or about July 5, 2002, David Louis Smith did commit the violent felony of armed robbery in violation of G.S. 14-87, and that on or about January 12, 2003, David Louis Smith was convicted of the violent felony of armed robbery in the Superior Court of Wilson County, N.C.; and that on or about April 30, 2010, David Louis Smith did commit the violent felony of second-degree rape in violation of G.S. 14-27.3, and that on or about November 10, 2011, David Louis Smith was convicted of second-degree rape in the Superior Court of Cumberland County, N.C.

AOC Forms for This Offense:
None.

Punishment:
If the defendant is convicted of a violent felony and is then determined to be a violent habitual felon, the substantive felony is punished by imprisonment for life without parole. If there is more than one substantive felony conviction, each conviction is punished by imprisonment for life without parole. *Cf.* State v. Thomas, 82 N.C. App. 682 (1986).

Introductory Comment:
None.

Charging Language:
. . . is a habitual breaking and entering status offender under Article 2D of Chapter 14 of the North Carolina General Statutes in that, prior to committing (*choose one*: his; her) current felony offense of breaking and entering, (*choose one*: he; she) was previously convicted of the felony breaking and entering offense of (*name offense*). On or about (*enter date*), the defendant did commit the felony of (*name offense*)in violation of the laws of (*name the state or other jurisdiction*), and on or about (*enter date*), the defendant (*choose one*: did plead guilty to; was convicted of) the felony of (*name offense*) in (*name the court of conviction*), in case number (*insert file number*).

Notes about Charging Language:

- The principal breaking and entering felony must be committed after the defendant turns 18 years old.
- Under G.S. 14-7.25(1), "breaking and entering" means any of the following felony offenses: first-degree burglary (G.S. 14-51); second-degree burglary (G.S. 14-51); breaking out of dwelling house burglary (G.S. 14-53); breaking or entering buildings generally (G.S. 14-54(a)); breaking or entering with intent to terrorize or injure an occupant of the building (G.S. 14-54(a1)); breaking or entering a building that is a place of religious worship (G.S. 14-54.1); any repealed or superseded offense substantially equivalent to any of these listed offenses; any offense committed in another jurisdiction substantially similar to one of these listed offenses.
- Breaking or entering with intent to terrorize or injure an occupant of the building was added to the statute by S.L. 2017-176. The law states that it is "effective December 1, 2017, and applies to offenses committed on or after that date." Because it is not clear whether the phrase "offenses committed" refers only to principal breaking and entering charges or also to previous convictions, it is not clear whether a conviction for breaking or entering with intent to terrorize or injure an occupant of the building incurred prior to December 1, 2017, may be used as a previous conviction.
- G.S. 14-7.28(a) states that "The indictment charging the defendant as a status offender shall be separate from the indictment charging the person with the principal felony offense of breaking and entering."

Sample Charge:
. . . is a habitual breaking and entering status offender under Article 2D of Chapter 14 of the North Carolina General Statutes in that, prior to committing his current felony offense of breaking and entering, he was previously convicted of the felony breaking and entering offense of second-degree burglary. On or about April 26, 2011, the defendant did commit the felony of second-degree burglary in violation of the laws of North Carolina, and on or about November 10, 2011, the defendant did plead guilty to the felony of second-degree burglary in the Superior Court of Forsyth County, N.C., in case number 11 CRS 18401.

AOC Forms for This Offense:
None.

Punishment:
Upon conviction, the defendant's principal felony will be sentenced as a Class E felony.

G.S. 14-7.36
Armed Habitual Felon
April 2024
Page 1 of 2

Introductory Comment:
This offense may be charged only by the "district attorney, in the district attorney's discretion." G.S. 14-7.38(a). Therefore, it should not be charged by a magistrate or other judicial official. A detailed discussion of the armed habitual felon law can be found at Jeff Welty, *Armed Habitual Felon*, N.C. Crim. L.: A UNC Sch. of Gov't Blog (Feb. 25, 2014), nccriminallaw.sog.unc.edu /armed-habitual-felon/.

Charging Language:
The jurors for the State upon their oath present that (*name defendant*) is an armed habitual felon in that on or about (*give date*), (*name defendant*) did commit (*name previous firearm-related felony and give statutory citation*) against (*name the state or other sovereign against which the previous firearm-related felony was committed*), and that on or about (*give date of guilty plea or conviction of previous firearm-related felony*), in (*name court in which conviction took place*), (*name defendant*) was convicted of the firearm-related felony of (*name firearm-related felony for which defendant was convicted*).

Notes about Charging Language:
- A firearm-related felony is defined to mean a felony "in which the [defendant] used or displayed a firearm while committing the felony." G.S. 14-7.35(2). At least as to the defendant's previous conviction, G.S. 14-7.36 requires that evidence of the defendant's use or display of the gun "was needed to prove an element of the felony or was needed to establish the requirement for an enhanced or aggravated sentence."
- Because this statute is patterned on the habitual felon statute, it is likely that the principles that apply to charging habitual felon will be held to apply to armed habitual felon as well. For example, a separate armed habitual felon indictment likely is not required for each substantive armed felony. *Cf.* State v. Patton, 342 N.C. 633 (1996). An armed habitual felon indictment likely need not allege the substantive felony being tried, *cf.* State v. Cheek, 339 N.C. 725 (1995), and this form does not request that information. And, while the State may allege more than one previous armed felony, it is likely that none of the armed felonies alleged in the indictment may be used to calculate the defendant's prior record level in the event of a conviction. *Cf.* State v. Lee, 150 N.C. App. 701 (2003). For a longer discussion of charging issues in connection with habitual felon status, see Jeffrey B. Welty, *North Carolina's Habitual Felon, Violent Habitual Felon, and Habitual Breaking and Entering Laws*, Admin. of Just. Bull. No. 2013/07 (UNC School of Government, Aug. 2013), www.sog.unc.edu/sites/www.sog.unc.edu/files/reports/aojb1307.pdf.
- "The indictment charging the defendant [as an armed habitual felon] shall be separate from the indictment charging the person with the principal firearm-related felony." G.S. 14-7.38(a).

Sample Charge:
The jurors for the State upon their oath present that James Garman is an armed habitual felon in that on or about February 8, 2008, James Garman did commit assault with a deadly weapon with intent to kill inflicting serious injury, G.S. 14-32(b), against the State of North Carolina, and that on or about June 21, 2008, in Alleghany County Superior Court, James Garman was convicted of the firearm-related felony of assault with a deadly weapon with intent to kill inflicting serious injury.

AOC Forms for This Offense:
None.

Punishment:
If the defendant is convicted of a firearm-related felony and is then determined to be an armed habitual felon, the principal felony is punished as a Class C felony with a minimum active sentence of 120 months. The sentence may not be suspended and the defendant may not be placed on probation. G.S. 14-7.41.

G.S. 14-16.6
Assault on Court, Executive, or Legislative Officer
April 2024

Introductory Comment:
Amendments effective December 1, 2023, increased the penalty for assault inflicting serious bodily injury.

Charging Language:

I. Assault on court, executive, or legislative officer

. . . unlawfully, willfully, and feloniously did assault (*name victim*), (*name office*), by (*briefly describe the assault*).

II. Assault as retaliation for officer's exercise of duties

. . . unlawfully, willfully, and feloniously did assault (*name victim*) as retaliation against (*name officeholder and office*) because of the exercise of that officer's duties.

Notes about Charging Language:
- The statute covers the officials listed in G.S. 14-16.10, as well as people elected to one of the covered offices who have not yet taken the oath of office. G.S. 14-16.9.
- As to Offense II, it probably is not necessary to describe the specific duty performed by the officeholder that led to the retaliation. *Cf.* State v. Noel, 202 N.C. App. 715 (2010) (charge for assault on a public officer during the discharge of his or her duties under G.S. 14-33(c)(4) does not require the officer's duty to be specified).
- The statute also applies to a person who "makes a violent attack upon the residence, office, temporary accommodation or means of transportation" of a covered officer. G.S. 14-16.6(a). In an appropriate case, modify the charging language accordingly.
- When an assault is committed using a deadly weapon, it is a Class F felony. G.S. 14-16.6(b). In such a case, add an allegation that the defendant committed the assault using a deadly weapon, name or describe the weapon, and, if its deadly character is not obvious, allege that it is a deadly weapon.
- When an assault inflicts serious bodily injury to the official, it is a Class E felony. G.S. 14-16.6(c). In such a case, add an allegation that the assault inflicted a serious bodily injury. It is probably not necessary to detail the nature of the serious bodily injury, *see* State v. Gregory, 223 N.C. 415 (1943), though you may choose to include such information.

Sample Charge:

I. Assault on court, executive, or legislative officer
. . . unlawfully, willfully, and feloniously did assault Henry L. Raines, a superior court judge, by hitting the judge with his fist.

AOC Forms for This Offense:
None.

Punishment:
Offenses I and II are Class I felonies, except when enhanced to Class F or Class E felonies as described above.

G.S. 14-16.7
Threatening Court, Executive, or Legislative Officer
April 2024

Introductory Comment:
Pursuant to *State v. Taylor*, 379 N.C. 589, 605 (2021), the State must prove that the threat alleged under this statute was a "true threat," which is defined "as an objectively threatening statement communicated by a party which possesses the subjective intent to threaten a listener or identifiable group."

Charging Language:

I. Threatening court, executive, or legislative officer

. . . unlawfully, willfully, and feloniously did knowingly make a threat to (*choose one*: inflict serious bodily injury upon; kill) (*name victim*), (*name office*), by (*describe threat and manner in which it was made*).

II. Threatening as retaliation for officer's exercise of duties

. . . unlawfully, willfully, and feloniously did knowingly make a threat to (*choose one*: inflict serious bodily injury upon; kill) (*name victim*) as retaliation against (*name officeholder and office*) because of the exercise of that officer's duties, by (*describe threat and manner in which it was made*).

Notes about Charging Language:
- The statute covers the officials listed in G.S. 14-16.10, as well as people elected to one of the covered offices who have not yet taken the oath of office. *See* G.S. 14-16.9.
- As to Offense II, it probably is not necessary to describe the specific duty performed by the officeholder that led to the retaliation. *Cf.* State v. Noel, 202 N.C. App. 715 (2010) (ruling that a charge for assault on a public officer during the discharge of his or her duties under G.S. 14-33(c)(4) does not require the officer's duty to be specified, as the assault is the gist of the offense and the details of the duty are secondary).
- Subsection (b) of the statute makes it unlawful to put a letter or other document containing a threat to violate subsection (a) in the mail. In an appropriate case, modify the charging language accordingly.

Sample Charge:

I. Threatening court, executive, or legislative officer

. . . unlawfully, willfully, and feloniously did knowingly make a threat to kill Michael Sampson, the Governor of the State of North Carolina, by telephoning the governor's office on July 10, 2021, and telling Sarah Holmes, the governor's secretary, that he was in Raleigh with a .38-caliber pistol and would kill the governor before the week was over.

AOC Forms for This Offense:
None.

Punishment:
Class I felony.

G.S. 14-17
Murder
April 2024
Page 1 of 2

Introductory Comment:
Both first- and second-degree murder are typically charged using the short-form charging language provided in G.S. 15-144.

Charging Language:
. . . unlawfully, willfully, and feloniously did of malice aforethought kill and murder (*name victim*).

Notes about Charging Language:

- G.S. 15-144 provides that this charging language is sufficient to charge either first- or second- degree murder. The constitutionality of the short-form charging language was upheld in *State v. Hunt*, 357 N.C. 257 (2003), *State v. Garcia*, 358 N.C. 382 (2004), and other cases.
- Although G.S. 15-144 refers to the use of the averment "with force and arms," the absence of such language does not render an indictment defective. *See* G.S. 15-155.
- The effect of omitting the word "aforethought" is to charge second-degree murder only. *See* State v. McGee, 47 N.C. App. 280 (1980); *but see* State v. Davis, 305 N.C. 400, 425 (1982) (second-degree murder is an intentional and unlawful killing with malice aforethought); State v. Arnold, 107 N.C. 861, 862 (1890) (allegation of "malice aforethought" is necessary to murder indictment).
- The North Carolina Court of Appeals has held that this charging language is sufficient to charge Class B2 second-degree murder even where the provided check boxes on AOC-CR-124 indicating the legal theory upon which such an offense is based, an issue affecting punishment, are left blank. State v. Schmieder, 265 N.C. App. 95, 103 (2019) (so holding where the box labeled "second- degree" was checked but the box labeled "inherently dangerous without regard to human life" was not; reasoning that an indictment containing the statutory charging language is sufficient to inform the defendant that the State "will seek to prove second degree murder through any of the legal theories the law allows").
- 2017 legislation, S.L. 2017-94, amended G.S. 14-17 by adding a new subsection (a1), which provides that there is a rebuttable presumption that a murder is a "willful, deliberate, and premediated killing," and thus is first-degree murder, if the murder was perpetrated with malice, was committed against a person with whom the defendant had a specified domestic relationship, and was committed by a defendant with a previous criminal conviction for a specified type of offense—generally, a domestic violence offense—involving the same victim. It is not yet clear whether the charging language used in this form will be deemed sufficient to allege this type of first-degree murder. For a more complete discussion of the new subsection, see Jeff Welty, *Many Questions and a Few Answers about Britny's Law*, N.C. Crim. L.: A UNC Sch. of Gov't Blog (Aug. 28, 2017), www.sog.unc.edu/blogs/nc-criminal-law/many-questions-and-few-answers-about-britny%E2%80%99s-law.
- The North Carolina Supreme Court has held that a short-form murder indictment that used language intended for short-form manslaughter indictments by including the phrase "kill and slay" rather than "kill and murder" was not fatally defective where it also averred that the defendant acted with malice aforethought. State v. Tart, 372 N.C. 73 (2019). Nevertheless, the better practice is to use the charging language provided by the statute.

- 2023 legislation, S.L. 2023-14, amended G.S. 14-17 by adding a new subsection (c)(ii), which provides that it shall constitute murder where a child is born alive but dies as a result of an intentional, overt act performed after the child is born alive.

Sample Charge:
. . . unlawfully, willfully, and feloniously did of malice aforethought kill and murder John Franklin Jones.

AOC Forms for This Offense:
AOC-CR-124 (Indictment)

Punishment:
First-degree murder is a Class A felony punishable by death or by life imprisonment without parole, unless the defendant was under 18 at the time of the offense or is intellectually disabled. Second-degree murder is a Class B1 felony, except that second-degree murder is a Class B2 felony if the malice necessary to prove the crime is based on an inherently dangerous act or omission done in such a reckless and wanton manner as to manifest a mind utterly without regard for human life and social duty and deliberately bent on mischief.

Notes about punishment:
- 2023 legislation, S.L. 2023-123, amended G.S. 14-17(b) to omit as a second circumstance supporting punishment as a Class B2 felony that the murder is one that was proximately caused by the unlawful distribution of certain controlled substances and ingestion caused the death of the user. The same bill amended G.S. 14-18.4 (death by distribution).

G.S. 14-18
Manslaughter
April 2024

Introductory Comment:
Both voluntary and involuntary manslaughter are typically charged using the so-called short-form language provided in G.S. 15-144.

Charging Language:

. . . unlawfully, willfully, and feloniously did kill and slay (*name victim*).

Notes about Charging Language:

- G.S. 15-144 provides that this charging language is sufficient to charge either voluntary or involuntary manslaughter.
- Although G.S. 15-144 refers to the use of the averment "with force and arms," the absence of such language does not render an indictment defective. *See* G.S. 15-155.

Sample Charge:
. . . unlawfully, willfully, and feloniously did kill and slay Randolph Springer.

AOC Forms for This Offense:
AOC-CR-127 (Indictment)

Punishment:
Voluntary manslaughter is a Class D felony. Involuntary manslaughter is a Class F felony.

G.S. 14-18.4
Death by Distribution of Controlled Substances
April 2024
Page 1 of 2

Introductory Comment:
This offense was created by statute in 2019, effective for offenses committed on or after December 1, 2019. S.L. 2019-83. Amendments effective December 1, 2023, added delivery offenses (the statute had criminalized sale). The statute does not apply to deaths that result from professional prescribing and dispensing of controlled substances.

An indictment or an information for the recidivist offense defined in G.S. 14-18.4(c) and illustrated as Offense IV below must comply with G.S. 15A-928, which requires that the defendant's prior convictions be alleged either (1) in a separate count of the indictment or information than the substantive offense or (2) in a separate indictment or information. This requirement does not apply to arrest warrants or magistrates' orders, which explains why two sets of charging language for Offense IV appear below. G.S. 15A-928 also requires in indictments or informations that the name or title of an offense elevated by prior convictions must not make reference to such prior convictions. Therefore, a title such as "habitual death by distribution of controlled substances" probably would not be proper.

Charging Language:

I. Death by distribution through unlawful delivery of controlled substances G.S. 14-18.4(a1)

. . . unlawfully, willfully, and feloniously did deliver (*name controlled substance*), a "certain controlled substance" as defined in G.S. 14-18.4, to (*name purchaser*), and the ingestion of that controlled substance proximately caused the death of (*name user*), a user of that controlled substance.

II. Death by distribution through unlawful delivery with malice of controlled substances G.S. 14-18.4(a2)

. . . unlawfully, willfully, and feloniously did deliver (*name controlled substance*), acting with malice, a "certain controlled substance" as defined in G.S. 14-18.4, to (*name purchaser*), and the ingestion of that controlled substance proximately caused the death of (*name user*), a user of that controlled substance.

III. Death by distribution through unlawful sale of controlled substances G.S. 14-18.4(b)

. . . unlawfully, willfully, and feloniously did sell (*name controlled substance*), a "certain controlled substance" as defined in G.S. 14-18.4, to (*name purchaser*), and the ingestion of that controlled substance proximately caused the death of (*name user*), a user of that controlled substance.

IV. Aggravated death by distribution through unlawful sale of controlled substances G.S. 14-18.4(c)

A. Charging language for an arrest warrant or magistrate's order

. . . unlawfully, willfully, and feloniously did sell (*name controlled substance*), a "certain controlled substance" as defined in G.S. 14-18.4, to (*name purchaser*), and the ingestion of that controlled substance proximately caused the death of (*name user*), a user of that controlled substance. Within ten years of this offense as calculated under G.S. 14-18.4, on (*date of conviction*), the defendant was previously convicted of (*name offense*), in (*court and county or other jurisdiction*).

B. Charging language for an indictment or information

First count of indictment or information

. . . unlawfully, willfully, and feloniously did sell (*name controlled substance*), a controlled substance, to (*name purchaser*), and the ingestion of that controlled substance proximately caused the death of (*name user*), a user of that controlled substance.

Second count of indictment or information

Within ten years of the date of the offense charged above, as calculated under G.S. 14-18.4, on (*date of conviction*), the defendant was previously convicted of (*name offense*), in (*court and county or other jurisdiction*).

Notes about Charging Language:

- The statute defines a "certain controlled substance" as "includ[ing] any opium, opiate, or opioid; any synthetic or natural salt, compound, derivative, or preparation of opium, opiate, or opioid; cocaine or any other substance described in G.S. 90-90(1)(d); methamphetamine; a depressant described in G.S. 90-92(a)(1); or a mixture of one or more of these substances."
- Because the statute is new, it is not yet clear whether courts will require that the identity of the purchaser be alleged. Because that information must be included when otherwise alleging the sale of a controlled substance, this form includes that information.
- In the only reported case, the purchaser of the substance (fentanyl) and the user who died were not the same person. *See* State v. McCrorey, ___ N.C. App. ___, 896 S.E.2d 309 (2023). For Offense IV, a qualifying previous conviction includes a conviction "under this section, G.S. 90-95(a)(1), 90-95.1, 90-95.4, 90-95.6, or trafficking in violation of G.S. 90-95(h), or a prior conviction in any federal or state court in the United States that is substantially similar to an offense listed." The pleading should specify that the defendant's prior conviction is one of those listed or is a "substantially similar offense" to one of those listed.
- For Offense IV, the previous conviction must have been incurred "within ten years of the date of the offense," excluding "any period of time during which the person was incarcerated in a local, state, or federal detention center, jail, or prison."

Sample Charge:

I. Death by distribution of controlled substances G.S. 14-18.4(b)

. . . unlawfully, willfully, and feloniously did sell fentanyl, a "certain controlled substance" as defined in G.S. 14-18.4, to Edward Lee, and the ingestion of that controlled substance proximately caused the death of Edward Lee, a user of that controlled substance.

AOC Forms for This Offense:

None.

Punishment:

Offense I is a Class C felony. Offense II is a Class B2 felony. Offense III is a Class B2 felony. Offense IV is a Class B1 felony.

G.S. 14-23.2
Murder of an Unborn Child
April 2024
Page 1 of 2

Introductory Comment:
This statute does not create criminal liability for lawful abortions under G.S. 14-51.1. Nor may it be used to prosecute a pregnant woman who causes the miscarriage or stillbirth of her own unborn child. G.S. 14-23.3 through -23.6 create additional homicide and assault crimes related to unborn children.

Charging Language:

I. Murder of an unborn child with malice aforethought **G.S. 14-23.2(a)(1)**

. . . unlawfully, willfully, and feloniously did cause the death of (*name or describe child*), an unborn child, by willfully and maliciously committing an act, (*describe act committed*), with the intent to cause the death of the unborn child.

II. Murder of an unborn child in perpetration or attempted perpetration of a felony **G.S. 14-23.2(a)(2)**

. . . unlawfully, willfully, and feloniously did cause the death of (*name or describe child*), an unborn child, in the (*choose one or both*: perpetration; attempted perpetration) of [*choose one or more*: arson; rape; a sex offense; robbery; kidnapping; burglary; (*name felony*), a felony committed or attempted with a deadly weapon, (*describe weapon*)], by (*describe act committed*).

III. Murder of an unborn child while committing an inherently dangerous act **G.S. 14-23.2(a)(3)**

. . . unlawfully, willfully, and feloniously did cause the death of (*name or describe child*), an unborn child, by (*describe act*), an act that was inherently dangerous to human life and that was done so recklessly and wantonly that it reflected a disregard of life.

Notes about Charging Language:

- Offenses II and III do not require proof that (1) the offender knew or should have known that the victim was pregnant or (2) the offender intended to cause the death of, or bodily injury to, the unborn child.
- The statute defines "unborn child" as a human at any stage of development who is carried in the womb.

Sample Charge:

I. Murder of an unborn child with malice aforethought **G.S. 14-23.2(a)(1)**

. . . unlawfully, willfully, and feloniously did cause the death of a female child carried by Michelle Seegar, an unborn child, by willfully and maliciously committing an act, shooting Michelle Seegar in the abdomen, with the intent to cause the death of the unborn child.

AOC Forms for This Offense
None.

Punishment:
Offenses I and II are Class A felonies, punishable only by life in prison without parole. Offense III is "subject to the same sentence as if the person had been convicted of second degree murder pursuant to G.S. 14-17" and so is a Class B2 felony. G.S. 14-23.2(b)(2).

G.S. 14-27.21
First-Degree Forcible Rape
April 2024

Introductory Comment:
Prior to the 2015 legislative session, this offense was set forth in G.S. 14-27.2, and charging documents for offenses committed before December 1, 2015, should refer to that statute. Both first- and second-degree forcible rape are typically charged using the short-form charging language provided in G.S. 15-144.1.

Charging Language:
. . . unlawfully, willfully, and feloniously did ravish and carnally know (*name victim*), by force and against the victim's will.

Notes about Charging Language:
- G.S. 15-144.1 provides that this charging language is sufficient to charge either first- or second-degree rape. This statute was upheld in *State v. Lowe*, 295 N.C. 596 (1978), *State v. Hunter*, 299 N.C. 29 (1980), and other cases. It is not necessary to include information that elevates the rape to first degree, such as the infliction of serious injury, though such information may be included if desired.
- Although G.S. 15-144.1(a) refers to the use of the averment "with force and arms," the absence of such language does not render an indictment defective, *see* G.S. 15-155, and this form does not include it.
- Although both G.S. 15-144.1 and the charging language above indicate that the name of the victim should be supplied, the Court of Appeals of North Carolina has approved of the use of the victim's initials in at least one sexual assault case. State v. McKoy, 196 N.C. App. 650 (2009) (use of initials provided adequate notice to the defendant where the defendant admitted that he knew the victim and did not claim that the use of initials made it difficult to prepare his defense). By contrast, in another sexual assault case, the state supreme court disapproved of referring to the victim using the generic term "Victim #1." State v. White, 372 N.C. 248 (2019).

Sample Charge:
. . . unlawfully, willfully, and feloniously did ravish and carnally know Wilma C. Sutton, by force and against the victim's will.

AOC Forms for This Offense:
AOC-CR-125 (Indictment)

Punishment:
Class B1 felony.

G.S. 14-27.22
Second-Degree Forcible Rape
April 2024
Page 1 of 2

Introductory Comment:
Prior to the 2015 legislative session, this offense was set forth in G.S. 14-27.3, and charging documents for offenses committed before December 1, 2015, should refer to that statute. Both first- and second-degree rape are typically charged using the short-form charging language provided in G.S. 15-144.1.

Charging Language:

I. Forcible rape **G.S. 14-27.22(a)(1)**

. . . unlawfully, willfully, and feloniously did ravish and carnally know (*name victim*), by force and against the victim's will.

II. Victim who has a mental disability or who is mentally incapacitated or physically helpless **G.S. 14-27.22(a)(2)**

. . . unlawfully, willfully, and feloniously did carnally know and abuse (*name victim*), who at the time (*choose one or more:* had a mental disability; was mentally incapacitated; was physically helpless). The defendant (*choose one or both*: knew; should reasonably have known) that the victim (*choose one or more*: had a mental disability; was mentally incapacitated; was physically helpless).

Notes about Charging Language:

- G.S. 15-144.1 provides that this charging language is sufficient to charge either first- or second-degree rape. This statute has been upheld as providing "constitutionally sufficient" notice to the defendant. State v. Lowe, 295 N.C. 596 (1978). *See also* State v. Hunter, 299 N.C. 29 (1980).
- For Offense II, although G.S. 15-144.1 does not require the inclusion of an allegation regarding the defendant's knowledge of the victim's condition, this form includes such an allegation out of an abundance of caution and because the defendant's knowledge is an element of the offense. In *State v. Singleton*, 285 N.C. App. 630, *temp. stay granted*, ___ N.C. ___, 878 S.E.2d 286 (2022), the North Carolina Court of Appeals stated that the word "abuse" is a "means of describing" the essential element of the defendant's knowledge of the victim's condition. Thus, the inclusion of both "abuse" and an express allegation of the defendant's knowledge may be redundant. However, as of the preparation of the 2023 edition of this manual, *Singleton* was the subject of a stay by the state supreme court, so this form continues to include both out of an abundance of caution.
- Although G.S. 15-144.1 refers to the use of the averment "with force and arms," the absence of such language does not render an indictment defective, *see* G.S. 15-155, and this form does not include it.
- Although both G.S. 15-144.1 and the charging language above indicate that the name of the victim should be supplied, the North Carolina Court of Appeals has approved of the use of the victim's initials in sexual assault cases. *See* State v. McKoy, 196 N.C. App. 650 (2009) (use of initials provided adequate notice to the defendant where the defendant admitted that he knew the victim and did not claim that the use of initials made it difficult to prepare his defense); State v. Perkins, 286 N.C. App. 495 (2022) (approving use of initials and date of birth to identify victim). By contrast, in another sexual assault case, the state supreme court disapproved of referring to the victim using the generic term "Victim #1." State v. White, 372 N.C. 248 (2019).

Sample Charges:

I. Forcible rape **G.S. 14-27.22(a)(1)**

. . . unlawfully, willfully, and feloniously did ravish and carnally know Louisa G. Applemyer, by force and against the victim's will.

II. Victim who has a mental disability or who is mentally incapacitated or physically helpless **G.S. 14-27.22(a)(2)**

. . . unlawfully, willfully, and feloniously did carnally know and abuse Roberta G. Exeter, who was physically helpless. The defendant knew that the victim was physically helpless.

AOC Forms for This Offense:
AOC-CR-125 (Indictment)

Punishment:
Offenses I and II are Class C felonies.

G.S. 14-27.23
Statutory Rape of a Child by an Adult
April 2024

Introductory Comment:
Prior to the 2015 legislative session, this offense was set forth at G.S. 14-27.2A, and charging documents for offenses committed before December 1, 2015, should refer to that statute. According to G.S. 14-27.23(e), first-degree statutory rape under G.S. 14-27.24 is a lesser-included offense of this crime.

Charging Language:
. . . unlawfully, willfully, and feloniously did engage in vaginal intercourse with (*name victim*), a child who was under the age of 13 years, namely, (*state victim's age*) years old. At the time, the defendant was at least 18 years of age, namely, (*state defendant's age*) years old.

Notes about Charging Language:
- It is not clear that the specific ages of the victim and the defendant must be included when charging this offense. This form requests that information for clarity and out of an abundance of caution.
- Although both G.S. 15-144.1 and the charging language above indicate that the name of the victim should be supplied, the Court of Appeals of North Carolina has approved of the use of the victim's initials in at least one sexual assault case. State v. McKoy, 196 N.C. App. 650 (2009) (use of initials provided adequate notice to the defendant where the defendant admitted that he knew the victim and did not claim that the use of initials made it difficult to prepare his defense). By contrast, in another sexual assault case, the state supreme court disapproved of referring to the victim using the generic term "Victim #1." State v. White, 372 N.C. 248 (2019).

Sample Charge:
. . . unlawfully, willfully, and feloniously did engage in vaginal intercourse with Jennifer Smith, a child who was under the age of 13 years, namely, 11 years old. At the time, the defendant was at least 18 years of age, namely, 32 years old.

AOC Forms for This Offense:
None.

Punishment:
Class B1 felony, subject to a mandatory minimum sentence of 300 months and other special sentencing provisions.

G.S. 14-27.24
First-Degree Statutory Rape
April 2024

Introductory Comment:
Prior to the 2015 legislative session, this offense was included within G.S. 14-27.2, and charging documents for offenses committed before December 1, 2015, should refer to that statute. This offense is normally charged using the short-form charging language set forth in G.S. 15-144.1(b).

Charging Language:
. . . unlawfully, willfully, and feloniously did carnally know and abuse (*name victim*), a child under the age of 13 years.

Notes about Charging Language:
- G.S. 15-144.1(b) states that the language above may be used when the victim is "a female child under the age of 13 years." If the victim is a male child, it may be safer to draft charging language that tracks the language of G.S. 14-27.24 rather than using the short-form language.
- The short-form language above may be used in juvenile petitions as well as adult charging documents. *Cf. In re* J.F., 237 N.C. App. 218 (2014) (citing the statute regarding short-form indictments for sexual offenses, G.S. 15-144.1, in the context of a juvenile petition).
- Although both G.S. 15-144.1(b) and this form call for the name of the victim, the Court of Appeals of North Carolina has approved of the use of the victim's initials in sexual assault cases. *See* State v. Perkins, 286 N.C. App. 495, 503 (2022) (indictments included victim's date of birth and initials); State v. McKoy, 196 N.C. App. 650 (2009) (use of initials provided adequate notice to the defendant where the defendant admitted that he knew the victim and did not claim that the use of initials made it difficult to prepare his defense). By contrast, in another sexual assault case, the state supreme court disapproved of referring to the victim using the generic term "Victim #1." State v. White, 372 N.C. 248 (2019).

Sample Charge:
. . . unlawfully, willfully, and feloniously did carnally know and abuse Gina Alexander, a child under the age of 13 years.

AOC Forms for This Offense:
AOC-CR-148 (Indictment)

Punishment:
Class B1 felony.

G.S. 14-27.25
Statutory Rape of Person Who Is 15 Years Old or Younger
April 2024
Page 1 of 2

Introductory Comment:
Prior to the 2015 legislative session, this offense was set forth at G.S. 14-27.7A and applied only to victims aged 13, 14, or 15. Charging documents for offenses committed before December 1, 2015, should refer to that statute.

Charging Language:

I. Defendant who was at least six years older than victim G.S. 14-27.25(a)

. . . unlawfully, willfully, and feloniously did engage in vaginal intercourse with (*name victim*), a person of the age of (*give age, which must be 15 years or younger*) years. At the time of the offense, the defendant was at least 12 years old, at least six years older than the victim, and was not lawfully married to the victim.

II. Defendant who was more than four but less than six years older than victim G.S. 14-27.25(b)

. . . unlawfully, willfully, and feloniously did engage in vaginal intercourse with (*name victim*), a person of the age of (*give age, which must be 15 years or younger*) years. At the time of the offense, the defendant was at least 12 years old, was more than four but less than six years older than the victim, and was not lawfully married to the victim.

Notes about Charging Language:

- That the defendant was not married to the victim probably need not be alleged since it is an exception to the offense, but the allegation is included as a matter of caution. *Cf.* State v. Bishop, 119 N.C. App. 695 (1995) (ruling that an indictment for possession of a firearm by a convicted felon, G.S. 14-415.1, need not allege that the defendant did not possess the firearm in his home or place of business, which was at that time an exception to that offense).
- Although this form calls for the name of the victim, the Court of Appeals of North Carolina has approved of the use of the victim's initials in at least one sexual assault case. State v. McKoy, 196 N.C. App. 650 (2009) (use of initials provided adequate notice to the defendant where the defendant admitted that he knew the victim and did not claim that the use of initials made it difficult to prepare his defense). By contrast, in another sexual assault case, the state supreme court disapproved of referring to the victim using the generic term "Victim #1." State v. White, 372 N.C. 248 (2019).

Sample Charge:

I. Defendant who was at least six years older than victim G.S. 14-27.25(a)

. . . unlawfully, willfully, and feloniously did engage in vaginal intercourse with Susan Smith, a person of the age of 14 years. At the time of the offense, the defendant was at least 12 years old, at least six years older than the victim, and was not lawfully married to the victim.

AOC Forms for This Offense:
None.

Punishment:
Offense I is a Class B1 felony. Offense II is a Class C felony.

G.S. 14-27.26
First-Degree Forcible Sexual Offense
April 2024

Introductory Comment:
Prior to the 2015 legislative session, this offense was set forth in G.S. 14-27.4, and charging documents for offenses committed before December 1, 2015, should refer to that statute. Both first- and second-degree sexual offense are typically charged using the short-form charging language provided in G.S. 15-144.2.

Charging Language:
. . . unlawfully, willfully, and feloniously did engage in a sex offense with (*name victim*), by force and against the victim's will.

Notes about Charging Language:
- G.S. 15-144.2 sets out the requirements for an indictment for sexual offense. Under that statute, it is not necessary to allege the aggravating elements for first-degree sexual offense, such as use of a weapon or infliction of serious personal injury, although that information may be added if desired. This statute was upheld in *State v. Edwards*, 305 N.C. 378 (1982).
- It is not necessary to specify the sexual act the defendant committed, but if the State does specify the act, it may be bound by its pleadings. State v. Treadway, 208 N.C. App. 286 (2010) (noting that "the State was not required to specify in the indictment the sexual act alleged" but finding that "since the State specified digital penetration in the indictment, it was bound to provide substantial evidence at the trial that digital penetration occurred").
- Although G.S. 15-144.2(a) refers to the use of the averment "with force and arms," the absence of such language does not render an indictment defective, *see* G.S. 15-155, and this form does not include it.
- Although both G.S. 15-144.2 and this form call for the name of the victim, the Court of Appeals of North Carolina has approved of the use of the victim's initials in at least one sexual assault case. State v. McKoy, 196 N.C. App. 650 (2009) (use of initials provided adequate notice to the defendant where the defendant admitted that he knew the victim and did not claim that the use of initials made it difficult to prepare his defense). The North Carolina Supreme Court has held that the statutory requirement that the victim be named is not satisfied by referring to the victim using the generic term "Victim #1." State v. White, 372 N.C. 248 (2019).

Sample Charge:
. . . unlawfully, willfully, and feloniously did engage in a sex offense with Susan F. Underwood, by force and against the victim's will.

AOC Forms for This Offense:
AOC-CR-128 (Indictment)
AOC-J-337 (Juvenile Petition)

Punishment:
Class B1 felony.

G.S. 14-27.27
Second-Degree Forcible Sexual Offense

April 2024
Page 1 of 2

Introductory Comment:
Prior to the 2015 legislative session, this offense was set forth in G.S. 14-27.5, and charging documents for offenses committed before December 1, 2015, should refer to that statute. Both first- and second-degree sexual offense are typically charged using the short-form charging language provided in G.S. 15-144.2.

Charging Language:

I. Forcible sexual offense **G.S. 14-27.27(a)(1)**

. . . unlawfully, willfully, and feloniously did engage in a sex offense with (*name victim*), by force and against the victim's will.

II. Victim who has a mental disability or who is mentally incapacitated or physically helpless **G.S. 14-27.27(a)(2)**

. . . unlawfully, willfully, and feloniously did engage in a sex offense with (*name victim*), who at the time (*choose one or more*: had a mental disability; was mentally incapacitated; was physically helpless). The defendant (*choose one or both*: knew; should reasonably have known) that the victim (*choose one or more*: had a mental disability; was mentally incapacitated; was physically helpless).

Notes about Charging Language:

- G.S. 15-144.2 sets out the requirements for an indictment for sexual offense. This statute was upheld in *State v. Edwards*, 305 N.C. 378 (1982).
- It is not necessary to specify the sexual act the defendant committed, but if the State does specify the act, it may be bound by its pleadings. State v. Treadway, 208 N.C. App. 286 (2010) (noting that "the State was not required to specify in the indictment the sexual act alleged" but finding that "since the State specified digital penetration in the indictment, it was bound to provide substantial evidence at the trial that digital penetration occurred").
- For Offense II, although G.S. 15-144.2 does not require the inclusion of an allegation regarding the defendant's knowledge of the victim's condition, this form includes such an allegation out of an abundance of caution and because the defendant's knowledge is an element of the offense.
- Although G.S. 15-144.2(a) refers to the use of the averment "with force and arms," the absence of such language does not render an indictment defective, *see* G.S. 15-155, and this form does not include it.
- Although both G.S. 15-144.2 and this form call for the name of the victim, the Court of Appeals of North Carolina has approved of the use of the victim's initials in at least one sexual assault case. State v. McKoy, 196 N.C. App. 650 (2009) (use of initials provided adequate notice to the defendant where the defendant admitted that he knew the victim and did not claim that the use of initials made it difficult to prepare his defense). The North Carolina Supreme Court has held that the statutory requirement that the victim be named is not satisfied by rerring to the victim using the generic term "Victim #1." State v. White, 372 N.C. 248 (2019).

Sample Charge:

I. Forcible sexual offense **G.S. 14-27.27(a)(1)**

. . . unlawfully, willfully, and feloniously did engage in a sex offense with Wilbur S. Washington, by force and against the victim's will.

AOC Forms for This Offense:

AOC-CR-128 (Indictment)
AOC-J-336 (Juvenile Petition)

Punishment:

Offenses I and II are Class C felonies.

G.S. 14-27.28
Statutory Sexual Offense with a Child by an Adult
April 2024

Introductory Comment:
Prior to the 2015 legislative session, this offense was set forth at G.S. 14-27.4A, and charging documents for offenses committed before December 1, 2015, should refer to that statute. According to G.S 14-27.28(d), first-degree statutory sexual offense under G.S. 14-27.29 is a lesser-included offense of this crime.

Charging Language:
. . . unlawfully, willfully, and feloniously did engage in a sexual act with (*name victim*), a child who was under the age of 13 years, namely, (*state victim's age*) years old. At the time, the defendant was at least 18 years of age, namely, (*state defendant's age*) years old.

Notes about Charging Language:
- It is not clear that the specific ages of the victim and the defendant must be included when charging this offense. This form requests that information for clarity and out of an abundance of caution.
- It is not necessary to specify the sexual act the defendant committed, but if the State does specify the act, it may be bound by its pleadings. State v. Treadway, 208 N.C. App. 286, 297–98 (2010) (noting that "the State was not required to specify in the indictment the sexual act alleged" but finding that "since the State specified digital penetration in the indictment, it was bound to provide substantial evidence at the trial that digital penetration occurred").
- Although both G.S. 15-144.2 and this form call for the name of the victim, the Court of Appeals of North Carolina has approved of the use of the victim's initials in at least one sexual assault case. State v. McKoy, 196 N.C. App. 650 (2009) (use of initials provided adequate notice to the defendant where the defendant admitted that he knew the victim and did not claim that the use of initials made it difficult to prepare his defense). The North Carolina Supreme Court has held that the statutory requirement that the victim be named is not satisfied by referring to the victim using the generic term "Victim #1." State v. White, 372 N.C. 248 (2019).

Sample Charge:
. . . unlawfully, willfully, and feloniously did engage in a sexual act with Erik Erikson, a child who was under the age of 13 years, namely, 6 years old. At the time, the defendant was at least 18 years of age, namely, 24 years old.

AOC Forms for This Offense:
None.

Punishment:
Class B1 felony, subject to a mandatory minimum sentence of 300 months and other special sentencing provisions.

G.S. 14-27.29
First-Degree Statutory Sexual Offense
April 2024

Introductory Comment:
Prior to the 2015 legislative session, this offense was set forth in G.S. 14-27.4(a)(1), and charging documents for offenses committed before December 1, 2015, should refer to that statute.

Charging Language:
. . . unlawfully, willfully, and feloniously did engage in a sex offense with (*name victim*), a child under the age of 13 years.

Notes about Charging Language:
- This offense is typically charged using the short-form charging language set forth in G.S. 15-144.2. That language is used above. The statute was upheld in *State v. Edwards*, 305 N.C. 378 (1982).
- It is not necessary to specify the sexual act the defendant committed, but if the State does specify the act, it may be bound by its pleadings. State v. Treadway, 208 N.C. App. 286, 297–98 (2010) (noting that "the State was not required to specify in the indictment the sexual act alleged" but finding that "since the State specified digital penetration in the indictment, it was bound to provide substantial evidence at the trial that digital penetration occurred").
- Although both G.S. 15-144.2 and this form call for the name of the victim, the Court of Appeals of North Carolina has approved of the use of the victim's initials in sexual assault cases. *See* State v. Perkins, 286 N.C. App. 495, 503 (2022) (indictments included victim's date of birth and initials); State v. McKoy, 196 N.C. App. 650 (2009) (use of initials provided adequate notice to the defendant where the defendant admitted that he knew the victim and did not claim that the use of initials made it difficult to prepare his defense). The North Carolina Supreme Court has held that the statutory requirement that the victim be named is not satisfied by referring to the victim using the generic term "Victim #1." State v. White, 372 N.C. 248 (2019).

Sample Charge:
. . . unlawfully, willfully, and feloniously did engage in a sex offense with Walter R. Kincaid, a child under the age of 13 years.

AOC Forms for This Offense:
AOC-CR-149 (Indictment)
AOC-J-335 (Juvenile Petition)

Punishment:
Class B1 felony.

G.S. 14-27.30
Statutory Sexual Offense with a Person Who Is 15 Years Old or Younger
April 2024
Page 1 of 2

Introductory Comment:
Prior to the 2015 legislative session, this offense was set forth at G.S. 14-27.7A and applied only to victims aged 13, 14, or 15. Charging documents for offenses committed before December 1, 2015, should refer to that statute.

Charging Language:

I. Defendant who was at least six years older than victim G.S. 14-27.30(a)

. . . unlawfully, willfully, and feloniously did engage in a sexual act with (*name victim*), a person of the age of (*give age, which must be 15 years or younger*) years. At the time of the offense, the defendant was at least 12 years old, at least six years older than the victim, and was not lawfully married to the victim.

II. Defendant who was more than four but less than six years older than victim G.S. 14-27.30(b)

. . . unlawfully, willfully, and feloniously did engage in a sexual act with (*name victim*), a person of the age of (*give age, which must be 15 years or younger*) years. At the time of the offense, the defendant was at least 12 years old, was more than four but less than six years older than the victim, and was not lawfully married to the victim.

Notes about Charging Language:

- That the defendant was not married to the victim probably need not be alleged since it is an exception to the offense, but the allegation is included as a matter of caution. *Cf.* State v. Bishop, 119 N.C. App. 695 (1995) (ruling that an indictment for possession of a firearm by a convicted felon, G.S. 14-415.1, need not allege that the defendant did not possess the firearm in his home or place of business, which was at that time an exception to that offense).
- It is not necessary to specify the sexual act the defendant committed, but if the State does specify the act, it may be bound by its pleadings. State v. Treadway, 208 N.C. App. 286, 297–98 (2010) (noting that "the State was not required to specify in the indictment the sexual act alleged" but finding that "since the State specified digital penetration in the indictment, it was bound to provide substantial evidence at the trial that digital penetration occurred").
- Although this form calls for the name of the victim, the Court of Appeals of North Carolina has approved of the use of the victim's initials in at least one sexual assault case. State v. McKoy, 196 N.C. App. 650 (2009) (use of initials provided adequate notice to the defendant where the defendant admitted that he knew the victim and did not claim that the use of initials made it difficult to prepare his defense). The North Carolina Supreme Court has held that the statutory requirement that the victim be named is not satisfied by referring to the victim using the generic term "Victim #1." State v. White, 372 N.C. 248 (2019).

Sample Charge:

I. Defendant who was at least six years older than victim **G.S. 14-27.30(a)**

. . . unlawfully, willfully, and feloniously did engage in a sexual act with Susan Smith, a person of the age of 14 years. At the time of the offense, the defendant was at least 12 years old, at least six years older than the victim, and was not lawfully married to the victim.

AOC Forms for This Offense:
None.

Punishment:
Offense I is a Class B1 felony. Offense II is a Class C felony.

G.S. 14-27.31
Sexual Activity by a Substitute Parent or Custodian

April 2024
Page 1 of 2

Introductory Comment:

Prior to the 2015 legislative session, the offenses in this section were set forth at G.S. 14-27.7(a), and charging documents for offenses committed before December 1, 2015, should refer to that statute.

Charging Language:

I. Sexual activity by a substitute parent **G.S. 14-27.31(a)**

. . . unlawfully, willfully, and feloniously did, having assumed the position of a parent in the home in which (*name victim*), a minor child under the age of 18 years, was residing, engage in (*choose one or both*: vaginal intercourse; a sexual act) with (*name victim*).

II. Sexual activity by a custodian **G.S. 14-27.31(b)**

. . . unlawfully, willfully, and feloniously did engage in (*choose one or both*: vaginal intercourse; a sexual act) with (*name victim*) at a time when the victim was [*choose one*: in the custody of the defendant; in the custody of (*name person*) and the defendant was (*choose one or both*: an agent; an employee) of that person; in the custody of (*name institution*) and the defendant was (*choose one or both*: an agent; an employee) of that institution].

Notes about Charging Language:

- Consent is not a defense to the above offenses. G.S. 14-27.31(c).
- For Offense I, where it is alleged that the defendant had assumed the position of a parent in the home where the minor victim was residing, it is not necessary to allege that the defendant also resided in that home. State v. Scott, 278 N.C. App. 585 (2021).
- In a case involving a sexual act, it is not necessary to specify the sexual act the defendant committed, but if the State does specify the act, it may be bound by its pleadings. State v. Treadway, 208 N.C. App. 286, 297–98 (2010) (noting that "the State was not required to specify in the indictment the sexual act alleged" but finding that "since the State specified digital penetration in the indictment, it was bound to provide substantial evidence at the trial that digital penetration occurred").
- Although this form calls for the name of the victim, the Court of Appeals of North Carolina has approved of the use of the victim's initials in at least one sexual assault case. State v. McKoy, 196 N.C. App. 650 (2009) (use of initials provided adequate notice to the defendant where the defendant admitted that he knew the victim and did not claim that the use of initials made it difficult to prepare his defense). By contrast, in another sexual assault case, the state supreme court disapproved of referring to the victim using the generic term "Victim #1." State v. White, 372 N.C. 248 (2019).

Sample Charge:

II. Sexual activity by a custodian **G.S. 14-27.31(b)**

. . . unlawfully, willfully, and feloniously did engage in vaginal intercourse with Sally Wilson Montgomery at a time when the victim was in the custody of the Wake County Jail and the defendant was an employee of that institution.

AOC Forms for This Offense:
None.

Punishment:
Offenses I and II are both Class E felonies.

G.S. 14-27.32
Sexual Activity with Student by School Personnel
April 2024
Page 1 of 2

Introductory Comment:
Prior to the 2015 legislative session, the offenses defined in this section were set forth at G.S. 14-27.7(b), and charging documents for offenses committed before December 1, 2015, should refer to that statute. While the offenses defined in this section apply only when there has been vaginal intercourse or a sexual act, indecent liberties with a student, G.S. 14-202.4, may apply to additional conduct. Consent is not a defense to this charge. G.S. 14-27.32(d). Amendments effective December 1, 2023, redefined terminology and enhanced the penalty for a violation of this statute by school personnel who are less than four years older than the victim.

Charging Language:

I. Teacher, administrator, student teacher, safety officer, or coach **G.S. 14-27.32(a)**

. . . unlawfully, willfully, and feloniously did engage in (*choose one*: vaginal intercourse; a sexual act) with (*name student*). At the time of this offense, the defendant was a (*choose one*: teacher; student teacher; school administrator; school safety officer; coach) at (*name school*) and the victim was a student at this same school.

II. Other school personnel, at least four years older than victim **G.S. 14-27.32(a)**

. . . unlawfully, willfully, and feloniously did engage in (*choose one*: vaginal intercourse; a sexual act) with (*name student*). At the time of this offense, the defendant was school personnel, namely, (*describe position at school*), at (*name school*) and the victim was a student at this same school. At the time of this offense, the defendant was at least four years older than the victim.

III. Other school personnel, less than four years older than victim **G.S. 14-27.32(b)**

. . . unlawfully, willfully, and feloniously did engage in (*choose one*: vaginal intercourse; a sexual act) with (*name student*). At the time of this offense, the defendant was school personnel, namely, (*describe position at school*), at (*name school*) and the victim was a student at this same school. At the time of this offense, the defendant was less than four years older than the victim.

Notes about Charging Language:

- In a case involving a sexual act, it is not necessary to specify the sexual act the defendant committed, but if the State does specify the act, it may be bound by its pleadings. State v. Treadway, 208 N.C. App. 286, 297–98 (2010) (noting that "the State was not required to specify in the indictment the sexual act alleged" but finding that "since the State specified digital penetration in the indictment, it was bound to provide substantial evidence at the trial that digital penetration occurred").
- Offenses I and II also include sexual activity between one of the referenced school employees and a student after the employee and student are no longer present together at the same school, provided the student is still a student. (The term "student" is defined as a person enrolled in kindergarten or in grade 1 through 12 in any school within six months of a violation.) If that is the case, the charging language must be modified accordingly.

- For Offense III, it is not clear from the statute that the defendant and the victim need to have been present at the same school. However, because that requirement does exist for Offenses I and II and for the similar offenses under G.S. 14-202.4, and out of an abundance of caution, this form includes the same-school allegation.
- For Offenses I and II but not III, there is an exception in the statute if the defendant is married to the victim.
- Although this form calls for the name of the victim, the Court of Appeals of North Carolina has approved of the use of a minor victim's initials in sexual assault cases. *E.g.*, State v. McKoy, 196 N.C. App. 650 (2009) (use of initials provided adequate notice to the defendant where the defendant admitted that he knew the victim and did not claim that the use of initials made it difficult to prepare his defense). By contrast, in another sexual assault case, the state supreme court disapproved of referring to the victim using the generic term "Victim #1." State v. White, 372 N.C. 248 (2019).

Sample Charge:

I. Teacher, administrator, student teacher, safety officer, or coach G.S. 14-27.32(a)

. . . unlawfully, willfully, and feloniously did engage in vaginal intercourse with Phyllis Smith. At the time of this offense, the defendant was a teacher at South Park High School, Park Ridge, N.C., and the victim was a student at this same school.

AOC Forms for This Offense:

None.

Punishment:

Offenses I, II, and III are all Class G felonies.

G.S. 14-27.33
Sexual Battery
April 2024

Introductory Comment:
Prior to the 2015 legislative session, this offense was set forth in G.S. 14-27.5A, and charging documents for offenses committed before December 1, 2015, should refer to that statute.

Charging Language:
. . . unlawfully and willfully did for the purpose of (*choose one or more*: sexual arousal; sexual gratification; sexual abuse) engage in sexual contact, (*describe contact*), with another person, (*name person*),

(*choose one or both*)

- by force and against the will of the other person.
- who (*choose one or more*: had a mental disability; was mentally incapacitated; was physically helpless) and the defendant (*choose one or both*: knew; should reasonably have known) that the other person (*choose one or more*: had a mental disability; was mentally incapacitated; was physically helpless).

Notes about Charging Language:
- The term "sexual contact" is defined in G.S. 14-27.20(5).
- In *In re J.U.*, 384 N.C. 618, 626 (2023), the North Carolina Supreme Court found a juvenile petition alleging sexual battery was sufficient that alleged the juvenile engaged in sexual contact with the victim by touching her vaginal area against her will for the purpose of sexual gratification. The "element" of force, it said, was "clearly inferable" from these allegations. *Id.*

Sample Charge:
. . . unlawfully and willfully did for the purpose of sexual arousal and sexual gratification engage in sexual contact, placing his hands on the victim's breasts, with another person, Sallie Jones, by force and against the will of the other person.

AOC Forms for This Offense:
None.

Punishment:
Class A1 misdemeanor.

Introductory Comment:
Although there are three separate offenses set forth in G.S. 14-28, -29, and -30, they are sufficiently related that they are addressed together in this manual.

Charging Language:

I. Malicious castration or maiming of privy member **G.S. 14-28**

. . . unlawfully, willfully, and feloniously did with malice aforethought (*choose one or more*: castrate; cut off a privy member of; maim a privy member of; disfigure a privy member of) (*name the victim*), with the intent to (*choose one or more*: murder, maim; disfigure; disable; render impotent) that person, and as a result did permanently injure that privy member.

II. Castration or maiming without malice **G.S. 14-29**

. . . unlawfully, willfully, and feloniously did purposefully (*choose one or more*)

(1) (*choose one or more*: cut; slit; bite off; cut off) the nose;

(2) (*choose one or both*: bite off; cut off) the lip;

(3) (*choose one or both*: bite off; cut off) the ear;

(4) (disable) the (*name a limb or member*);

(5) (castrate);

(6) (*choose one or more*: cut off; maim; disfigure) a privy member

of (*name the victim*), with the intent to (*choose one or more*: kill; maim; disfigure; disable; render impotent) that person, and as a result did permanently injure that part of the victim's body.

III. Malicious maiming of tongue or eye **G.S. 14-30**

. . . unlawfully, willfully, and feloniously did with malice aforethought (*choose one or more*: cut out the tongue; disable the tongue; put out an eye) of (*name the victim*), with the intent to (*choose one or more*: murder; maim; disfigure) that person, and as a result did permanently injure the (*choose one or both*: tongue; eye) of that person.

Notes about Charging Language:

- "Privy member" appears to be an archaic term for the male genitals. It is likely a better practice to modify the above charging language to reflect the specific privy member(s) at issue. For example, an indictment could read, ". . . did with malice maim the privy member, to wit, the penis, of . . ."
- The language that the defendant "did permanently injure" the victim does not appear in the relevant statutes but may be required by *State v. Malpass*, 226 N.C. 403 (1945).

Sample Charge:

I. Malicious castration or maiming of privy member **G.S. 14-28**

. . . unlawfully, willfully, and feloniously did with malice aforethought cut off a privy member, to wit, the penis, of Randolph P. Jacobs, with the intent to maim, disfigure, disable, and render impotent that person, and as a result did permanently injure that privy member.

AOC Forms for This Offense:
None.

Punishment:
Offense I is a Class C felony. Offense II is a Class E felony. Offense III is a Class C felony.

G.S. 14-30.1
Malicious Throwing of Corrosive Acid or Alkali
April 2024

Introductory Comment:
None.

Charging Language:
. . . unlawfully, willfully, and feloniously did knowingly and with malice aforethought (*choose one*: throw; cause to be thrown) corrosive (*choose one*: acid; alkali) on (*name victim*), thereby inflicting serious injury on (*choose one*: him; her), to wit, (*describe injury*). This act was done with the intent to (*choose one or more*: murder; maim; disfigure) the victim.

Notes about Charging Language:
None.

Sample Charge:
. . . unlawfully, willfully, and feloniously did knowingly and with malice aforethought throw corrosive acid on Jamie Jones, thereby inflicting serious injury on him, to wit, severely scarring his face and blinding him in one eye. This act was done with the intent to maim and disfigure the victim.

AOC Forms for This Offense:
None.

Punishment:
Class E felony.

Note on Assault Terminology and Charging "Show of Violence" and Culpable Negligence Theories of Assault

April 2024

I. Assault Terminology

Under the common law, "assault" meant an attempted striking that did not actually result in contact, and a "battery" was the striking of another. Over the years the term "assault" has been used in North Carolina's statutes to cover both assaults and batteries. For example, G.S. 14-33 sets out the punishment for an "assault" inflicting serious injury; obviously, if serious injury was inflicted there must have been contact and thus a battery. These forms follow the statutory example and use the term "assault" to describe all assaults and batteries. The option of using the words "and strike" has been included for those situations where the assault actually did involve contact.

II. Charging "Show of Violence" Theory of Assault

North Carolina common law recognizes a theory of assault known as assault by show of violence. This form of assault occurs when (1) there is a show of violence by the defendant, (2) accompanied by the victim's reasonable apprehension of immediate bodily harm or injury, and (3) the show of violence caused the victim to engage in a course of conduct that he or she would not otherwise have followed. In *State v. Garcia*, 146 N.C. App. 745 (2001), the court ruled that the facts supporting this theory of assault must be alleged in the criminal pleading charging assault. The most common types of assault in which this theory would be alleged are simple assault or assault on a female, although the theory may apply to any other type of assault. The type of assault should be alleged the same as set out in this publication, and then the following statement should be included: "The defendant's show of violence (*describe how it occurred*) caused the victim's reasonable apprehension of immediate bodily harm and injury, and the show of violence caused the victim to engage in a course of conduct (*describe conduct*) that the victim would not otherwise have followed."

Sample Charge:

. . . unlawfully and willfully did assault Susan Riggins, a female person, by threatening to hit her with his fist if she continued to walk toward her house. The defendant is a male person and was at least 18 years of age when the assault occurred. The defendant's show of violence, his threat of hitting her, caused the victim's reasonable apprehension of immediate bodily harm and injury, and the show of violence caused the victim to engage in a course of conduct, deciding not to walk to her house, that the victim would not otherwise have followed.

III. Charging Culpable Negligence Theory of Assault

The State may establish the intent required to support an assault conviction by showing that the defendant acted with culpable negligence, sometimes also called criminal negligence. *See* State v. Jones, 353 N.C. 159, 164 (2000) (an assault conviction requires "either an actual intent to inflict injury or culpable or criminal negligence," meaning great recklessness or disregard of dangerous consequences). When the State seeks to rely on a culpable negligence theory, it must allege that theory in its pleading. *See, e.g.,* State v. Stevens, 228 N.C. App. 352, 358 (2013) (reversing a conviction where the judge's "instruction permitted the jury to convict Defendant on a criminal negligence theory of assault, a theory not alleged in the indictment"). A simple allegation that "The defendant acted with culpable negligence" should be sufficient.

G.S. 14-32(a)
Assault with Deadly Weapon with Intent to Kill Inflicting Serious Injury
April 2024

Introductory Comment:
None.

Charging Language:
. . . unlawfully, willfully, and feloniously did assault (*name victim*) with (*describe the deadly weapon*), a deadly weapon, with the intent to kill and inflicting serious injury.

Notes about Charging Language:
- The phrase "serious injury" means physical or bodily injury of real consequence; it means such physical injury as causes great pain and suffering. It may also include severe mental injury. State v. Everhardt, 326 N.C. 777 (1990).
- The nature of the serious injury need not be alleged. State v. Gregory, 223 N.C. 415 (1943); State v. Lanford, 225 N.C. App. 189, 199–200 (2013) ("Nothing requires the State to allege the body part to which serious injury was inflicted."); State v. Ebron, 173 N.C. App. 642 (2005) (unpublished) (indictment that alleged simply "serious injury" without further detail "allege[d] the necessary ultimate facts" and was sufficient).

Sample Charge:
. . . unlawfully, willfully, and feloniously did assault Randolph L. Mallott with a butcher knife with a twelve-inch blade, a deadly weapon, with the intent to kill and inflicting serious injury.

AOC Forms for This Offense:
AOC-CR-129 (Indictment)

Punishment:
Class C felony.

G.S. 14-32(b)
Assault with Deadly Weapon Inflicting Serious Injury
April 2024

Introductory Comment:
None.

Charging Language:
. . . unlawfully, willfully, and feloniously did assault (*name victim*) with (*describe the deadly weapon*), a deadly weapon, inflicting serious injury.

Notes about Charging Language:
- The phrase "serious injury" means physical or bodily injury of real consequence; it means such physical injury as causes great pain and suffering. It may also include severe mental injury. State v. Everhardt, 326 N.C. 777 (1990).
- The nature of the serious injury need not be alleged. State v. Gregory, 223 N.C. 415 (1943); State v. Lanford, 225 N.C. App. 189, 199–200 (2013) ("Nothing requires the State to allege the body part to which serious injury was inflicted."); State v. Ebron, 173 N.C. App. 642 (2005) (unpublished) (indictment that alleged simply "serious injury" without further detail "allege[d] the necessary ultimate facts" and was sufficient).

Sample Charge:
. . . unlawfully, willfully, and feloniously did assault Howard Smith with a butcher knife with a twelve-inch blade, a deadly weapon, inflicting serious injury.

AOC Forms for This Offense:
None.

Punishment:
Class E felony.

G.S. 14-32(c)
Assault with Deadly Weapon with Intent to Kill
April 2024

Introductory Comment:
None.

Charging Language:
. . . unlawfully, willfully, and feloniously did assault (*name victim*) with (*describe the deadly weapon*), a deadly weapon, with the intent to kill (*choose one*: him; her).

Notes about Charging Language:
None.

Sample Charge:
. . . unlawfully, willfully, and feloniously did assault Albert Davis with a .38-caliber pistol, a deadly weapon, with the intent to kill him.

AOC Forms for This Offense:
None.

Punishment:
Class E felony.

G.S. 14-32(d)
Assault Upon Emergency Worker with Deadly Weapon Inflicting Serious Injury
April 2024

Introductory Comment:
This offense was added to G.S. 14-32 by amendments effective December 1, 2023.

Charging Language:
. . . unlawfully, willfully, and feloniously did assault an emergency worker, (*name victim and describe employment*), with (*describe the deadly weapon*), a deadly weapon, inflicting serious injury.

Notes about Charging Language:
- For purposes of this section, an "emergency worker" is a law enforcement officer, firefighter, emergency medical technician, or medical responder. G.S. 14-32(f).
- For assault with a firearm, it is probably not necessary to describe the firearm. *See* State v. Lee, 218 N.C. App. 42, 48 (2012) (in an indictment for assault with a deadly weapon with intent to kill inflicting serious injury, it would have been sufficient to specify that the defendant used a "gun" to commit the offense).
- The phrase "serious injury" means physical or bodily injury of real consequence; it means such physical injury as causes great pain and suffering. It may also include severe mental injury. State v. Everhardt, 326 N.C. 777 (1990).
- The nature of the serious injury need not be alleged. State v. Gregory, 223 N.C. 415 (1943); State v. Lanford, 225 N.C. App. 189, 199–200 (2013) ("Nothing requires the State to allege the body part to which serious injury was inflicted."); State v. Ebron, 173 N.C. App. 642 (2005) (unpublished) (indictment that alleged simply "serious injury" without further detail "allege[d] the necessary ultimate facts" and was sufficient).

Sample Charge:
. . . unlawfully, willfully, and feloniously did assault an emergency worker, Howard Smith, an emergency medical technician with Buncombe County Emergency Medical Services, with a butcher knife with a twelve-inch blade, a deadly weapon, inflicting serious injury.

AOC Forms for This Offense:
None.

Punishment:
Class D felony.

G.S. 14-32(e)
Assault Upon Emergency Worker with Deadly Weapon with Intent to Kill
April 2024

Introductory Comment:
This offense was added to G.S. 14-32 by amendments effective December 1, 2023.

Charging Language:
. . . unlawfully, willfully, and feloniously did assault an emergency worker, (*name victim and describe employment*), with (*describe the deadly weapon*), a deadly weapon, with the intent to kill (*name victim*).

Notes about Charging Language:
- For purposes of this section, an "emergency worker" is a law enforcement officer, firefighter, emergency medical technician, or medical responder. G.S. 14-32(f).
- For assault with a firearm, it is probably not necessary to describe the firearm. *See* State v. Lee, 218 N.C. App. 42, 48 (2012) (in an indictment for assault with a deadly weapon with intent to kill inflicting serious injury, it would have been sufficient to specify that the defendant used a "gun" to commit the offense).

Sample Charge:
. . . unlawfully, willfully, and feloniously did assault an emergency worker, Albert Davis, an emergency medical technician with Buncombe County Emergency Medical Services, with a .38-caliber pistol, a deadly weapon, with the intent to kill Albert Davis.

AOC Forms for This Offense:
None.

Punishment:
Class D felony.

G.S. 14-32.1
Assaults on Individuals with a Disability
April 2024
Page 1 of 2

Introductory Comment:
G.S. 14-32.1 sets out two types of assault offenses against individuals with a disability: "simple" assaults and "aggravated" assaults. Both types of offenses are covered by this entry in this manual.

Charging Language:

I. Simple assault and battery **G.S. 14-32.1(f)**

. . . unlawfully and willfully did assault and strike (*name victim*), an individual with a disability, by (*describe the assault or the assault and battery*).

II. Aggravated assault **G.S. 14-32.1(e)**

. . . unlawfully, willfully, and feloniously did assault and strike (*name victim*), an individual with a disability, by (*describe the assault or the assault and battery*). In the course of the assault the defendant (*choose one or more*):

(1) used a deadly weapon, a (*describe deadly weapon*);
(2) inflicted serious injury on (*name victim*);
(3) intended to kill (*name victim*).

Notes about Charging Language:

- It is probably unnecessary to describe the assault. *Cf.* State v. Thorne, 238 N.C. 392 (1953) (upholding a simple assault charge that did not describe the manner in which the assault was committed); State v. Brooks, 190 N.C. App. 675 (2008) (unpublished) (holding that allegations regarding the specific manner in which the defendant committed an assault by strangulation were surplusage). However, this form requests that information for clarity.
- The phrase "individual with a disability" means a person who has a physical or mental disability or infirmity that substantially impairs the person's ability to defend himself or herself. G.S. 14-32.1(a). However, the specific nature of the victim's disability need not be described in the charging document. State v. Collins, 221 N.C. App. 604 (2012).
- The State must prove that the defendant knew that the victim had a disability in order to convict the defendant under G.S. 14-32.1. State v. Singletary, 163 N.C. App. 449 (2004). However, the defendant's knowledge is implicit in the term "willfully" and need not be separately alleged. State v. Collins, 221 N.C. App. 604 (2012).
- The phrase "serious injury" means physical or bodily injury of real consequence; physical injury that causes great pain and suffering. It also may include severe mental injury. State v. Everhardt, 326 N.C. 777 (1990). The nature of the serious injury need not be alleged in the charging document. State v. Gregory, 223 N.C. 415 (1943); State v. Lanford, 225 N.C. App. 189, 199–200 (2013) ("Nothing requires the State to allege the body part to which serious injury was inflicted."); State v. Ebron, 173 N.C. App. 642 (2005) (unpublished) (indictment that alleged simply "serious injury" without further detail "allege[d] the necessary ultimate facts" and was sufficient).

Sample Charge:

I. Simple assault and battery **G.S. 14-32.1(f)**

. . . unlawfully and willfully did assault and strike Douglas Herndon, an individual with a disability, by kicking him in the stomach with his foot.

AOC Forms for This Offense:
None.

Punishment:
Simple assault and battery on an individual with a disability is a Class A1 misdemeanor. Aggravated assault on an individual with a disability is a Class F felony.

G.S. 14-32.2
Patient Abuse and Neglect
April 2024
Page 1 of 2

Introductory Comment:
G.S. 14-32.2(g) previously provided that criminal process for this offense could be issued only upon the request of "a District Attorney;" therefore, a request by an assistant district attorney was not sufficient. The statute was amended in 2019 to read "a district attorney" without capitalization; it is unclear whether this change alters the prior rule.

Charging Language:
. . . unlawfully, willfully, and feloniously did physically abuse (*name patient or resident*), a (*choose one*: patient of a health care facility; resident of a residential care facility), (*name facility*).
(*choose one*)

(1) The physical abuse was the result of intentional conduct, (*describe conduct*), that proximately caused the death of (*name patient or resident*).
(2) The physical abuse was the result of a culpably negligent conduct, (*describe conduct*), that proximately caused the death of (*name patient or resident*).
(3) The physical abuse was the result of (*choose one or both*: willful; culpably negligent) conduct, (*describe conduct*), that proximately caused serious bodily injury to (*name patient or resident*).
(4) The physical abuse evinced a pattern of (*choose one or both*: willful; culpably negligent) conduct, (*describe conduct*), that proximately caused bodily injury to (*name patient or resident*).

Notes about Charging Language:

- When alleging abuse that causes bodily injury or serious bodily injury, the nature of the injury need not be alleged. State v. Gregory, 223 N.C. 415 (1943); State v. Lanford, 225 N.C. App. 189, 199–200 (2013) ("Nothing requires the State to allege the body part to which serious injury was inflicted."); State v. Ebron, 173 N.C. App. 642 (2005) (unpublished) (indictment that alleged simply "serious injury" without further detail "allege[d] the necessary ultimate facts" and was sufficient).

Sample Charge:
. . . unlawfully, willfully, and feloniously did physically abuse Sandra Withers, a patient of a residential care facility, Underwood's Health Care Home, in Morristown, N.C. The physical abuse was the result of willful and culpably negligent conduct, in that the defendant failed to attend to the patient's medical needs as a form of punishment for the patient's behavior, that proximately caused seriously bodily injury to Sandra Withers.

AOC Forms for This Offense:
None.

Punishment:

If intentional physical abuse proximately caused death [choice (1) in the charging language above], it is a Class C felony. If culpably negligent conduct proximately caused death [choice (2) in the charging language above], it is a Class E felony. If willful or culpably negligent conduct proximately caused serious bodily injury [choice (3) in the charging language above], it is a Class F felony. If a pattern of willful or culpably negligent conduct proximately caused bodily injury [choice (4) in the charging language above], it is a Class H felony.

G.S. 14-32.3
Domestic Abuse or Neglect of Disabled or Elder Adults
April 2024
Page 1 of 2

Introductory Comment:
This charge applies to abuse or neglect of a disabled or elder adult in a domestic setting. If a disabled or elder adult is abused or neglected while residing in a health care facility or a residential care facility, the proper charge is patient abuse or neglect under G.S. 14-32.2.

Charging Language:

I. Abuse of disabled or elder adult **G.S. 14-32.3(a)**

. . . unlawfully, willfully, and feloniously did knowingly and with malice aforethought, as a caretaker of a (*choose one or both*: disabled adult; elder adult), (*name disabled/elder adult*), who was residing in a domestic setting, (*choose one or more*)

(1) assault that adult;

(2) fail to provide (*choose one or both*: medical care; hygienic care) to that adult;

(3) confine and restrain that adult in a place and under a condition that was cruel and unsafe.

As a result of the defendant's (*choose one or both*: act; failure to act), the adult suffered (*choose one or both*: mental injury; physical injury). (*State if appropriate*: The injury was serious.)

II. Neglect of disabled or elder adult **G.S. 14-32.3(b)**

. . . unlawfully, willfully, and feloniously did (*choose one or more*: wantonly; recklessly, with gross carelessness), as a caretaker of a (*choose one or both*: disabled adult; elder adult), (*name disabled/elder adult*), who was residing in a domestic setting, (*choose one or both)*

(1) fail to provide (*choose one or both*: medical care; hygienic care) to that adult;

(2) confine and restrain that adult in a place and under a condition that was cruel and unsafe.

As a result of the defendant's (*choose one or both*: act; failure to act), the adult suffered (*choose one or both*: mental injury; physical injury). (*State if appropriate*: The injury was serious.)

Notes about Charging Language:

- As reflected in the charging language above, both abuse and neglect may be committed by improper confinement of an elder or disabled adult. The statute makes it illegal to "confine[] or restrain[] the disabled or elder adult in a place or under a condition that is cruel or unsafe." In some cases, it will be appropriate to charge only confinement or only restraint; or only cruelty or only lack of safety. In such a case, unnecessary language may be omitted.
- When alleging abuse that causes bodily injury or serious bodily injury, the nature of the injury need not be alleged. State v. Gregory, 223 N.C. 415 (1943); State v. Lanford, 225 N.C. App. 189, 199–200 (2013) ("Nothing requires the State to allege the body part to which serious injury was inflicted."); State v. Ebron, 173 N.C. App. 642 (2005) (unpublished) (indictment that alleged simply "serious injury" without further detail "allege[d] the necessary ultimate facts" and was sufficient).

Sample Charge:

I. Abuse of disabled or elder adult **G.S. 14-32.3(a)**

. . . unlawfully, willfully, and feloniously did knowingly and with malice aforethought, as a caretaker of an elder adult, Phyllis Smith, who was residing in a domestic setting, confine and restrain that adult in a place and under a condition that was cruel and unsafe. As a result of the defendant's act, the adult suffered mental injury and physical injury. The injury was serious.

AOC Forms for This Offense:
None.

Punishment:
Offense I is a Class F felony if the disabled or elder adult suffered "serious injury" and a Class H felony if the adult suffered "injury." Offense II is a Class G felony if the disabled or elder adult suffered "serious injury" and a Class I felony if the disabled or elder adult suffered "injury."

G.S. 14-32.4(a)
Assault Inflicting Serious Bodily Injury
April 2024

Introductory Comment:
None.

Charging Language:

. . . unlawfully, willfully, and feloniously did assault (*name victim*) and inflict serious bodily injury.

Notes about Charging Language:

- The nature of the serious bodily injury need not be alleged. State v. Gregory, 223 N.C. 415 (1943); State v. Lanford, 225 N.C. App. 189, 199–200 (2013) ("Nothing requires the State to allege the body part to which serious injury was inflicted."); State v. Ebron, 173 N.C. App. 642 (2005) (unpublished) (indictment that alleged simply "serious injury" without further detail "allege[d] the necessary ultimate facts" and was sufficient).

Sample Charge:
. . . unlawfully, willfully, and feloniously did assault Howard Smith and inflict serious bodily injury.

AOC Forms for This Offense:
None.

Punishment:
Class F felony.

G.S. 14-32.4(b)
Assault Inflicting Physical Injury by Strangulation
April 2024

Introductory Comment:
None.

Charging Language:
. . . unlawfully, willfully, and feloniously did assault (*name victim*) and inflict physical injury, by strangulation, (*describe method of strangulation*).

Notes about Charging Language:
- The nature of the physical injury need not be alleged. State v. Gregory, 223 N.C. 415 (1943); State v. Lanford, 225 N.C. App. 189, 199–200 (2013) ("Nothing requires the State to allege the body part to which serious injury was inflicted."); State v. Ebron, 173 N.C. App. 642 (2005) (unpublished) (indictment that alleged simply "serious injury" without further detail "allege[d] the necessary ultimate facts" and was sufficient).
- The specific method of strangulation is surplusage. State v. Williams, 201 N.C. App. 161 (2009). Thus, it need not be alleged. Nonetheless, this form requests that information.

Sample Charge:
. . . unlawfully, willfully, and feloniously did assault Susan Jones and inflict physical injury, by strangulation, using his hands to squeeze her throat.

AOC Forms for This Offense:
None.

Punishment:
Class H felony.

G.S. 14-32.5
Misdemeanor Crime of Domestic Violence
April 2024

Introductory Comment:
Created by statute effective December 1, 2023, this offense was apparently created in order to trigger federal firearm disqualification under 18 U.S.C. § 922(g)(9). *See* Brittany Bromell, *New Misdemeanor Crime of Domestic Violence*, N.C. CRIM. L.: A UNC SCH. OF GOV'T BLOG (June 6, 2023), nccriminallaw.sog.unc.edu/new-misdemeanor-crime-of-domestic-violence/.

Charging Language:
. . . unlawfully and willfully (*choose one or both:* used and attempted to use physical force/threatened the use of a deadly weapon) against another person, (*name victim*). The defendant is (*describe domestic relationship*).

Notes about Charging Language:
- To satisfy the domestic relationship requirement, the defendant must be one of the following:
  - a current or former spouse, parent, or guardian of the victim;
  - a person with whom the victim shares a child in common;
  - a person who is cohabitating with or has cohabitated with the victim as a spouse, parent, or guardian;
  - a person similarly situated to a spouse, parent, or guardian of the victim; or
  - a person who has a current or recent former dating relationship with the victim.
- For purposes of this section, the term "dating relationship" is as defined in 18 U.S.C. § 921. Under that statute, a "dating relationship" means a relationship between individuals who have or have recently had a continuing serious relationship of a romantic or intimate nature. 18 U.S.C. § 921(a)(37)(A). Whether a relationship constitutes a dating relationship is determined based on considerations of (1) the length of the relationship, (2) the nature of the relationship, and (3) the frequency and type of interaction between the individuals involved. 18 U.S.C. § 921(a)(37)(B). A casual acquaintanceship or ordinary fraternization in a business or social context does not constitute a dating relationship. 18 U.S.C. § 921(a)(37)(C).
- No caselaw has yet interpreted the phrase "threatens the use of a deadly weapon" for purposes of this offense. Comparable language in G.S. 14-27.21 (first-degree forcible rape) and 14-87 (armed robbery) has been interpreted as requiring the State to allege and prove the presence of a weapon. *See* State v. Murrell, 370 N.C. 187, 195 (2017) (for armed robbery, weapon must be alleged and proved); State v. Thompson, 290 N.C. 431, 444 (1976) (for rape, evidence is sufficient if victim knows, or reasonably believes, the weapon is "readily accessible").

Sample Charge:
. . . unlawfully and willfully used and attempted to use physical force against Mary Major. The defendant is the victim's spouse.

AOC Forms for This Offense:
None.

Punishment:
Class A1 misdemeanor

G.S. 14-33(a)
Simple Assault
April 2024

Introductory Comment:
None.

Charging Language:
. . . unlawfully and willfully did assault and strike (*name victim*) by (*describe the assault or assault and battery*).

Notes about Charging Language:
- If the defendant did not strike the victim, omit "and strike."

Sample Charge:
. . . unlawfully and willfully did assault and strike Douglas Smith by hitting him in the face with his fist and hand.

AOC Forms for This Offense:
AOC-J-312 (Juvenile Petition)

Punishment:
Class 2 misdemeanor.

G.S. 14-33(a)
Simple Affray
April 2024

Introductory Comment:
None.

Charging Language:
. . . unlawfully and willfully did make an affray to the terror and disturbance of other citizens at (*name public place where fight occurred*), a public place. At that public place the defendant and (*name other persons who were involved in the affray or write* "other persons whose names are not known") did assault and strike each other by (*describe the nature of the fight*).

Notes about Charging Language:
- One who provokes a fight by using abusive language against another can be guilty of affray without having a chance to strike a blow. If that situation occurs, leave out the words "and strike."

Sample Charge:
. . . unlawfully and willfully did make an affray to the terror and disturbance of other citizens at the parking lot of Silent Sam's Tavern in the Big Town Shopping Center in Random, N.C., a public place. At that public place the defendant and Sam Lupin did assault and strike each other by hitting each other with fists and tires and wooden crates.

AOC Forms for This Offense:
AOC-J-333 (Juvenile Petition)

Punishment:
Class 2 misdemeanor.

G.S. 14-33(c)(1)
Assault Inflicting Serious Injury
April 2024

Introductory Comment:
None.

Charging Language:
. . . unlawfully and willfully did assault and strike (*name victim*) by (*describe the assault*), thereby inflicting serious injury.

Notes about Charging Language:
- The phrase "serious injury" means physical or bodily injury of real consequence; it means such physical injury as causes great pain and suffering. It may also include severe mental injury. State v. Everhardt, 326 N.C. 777 (1990).
- The nature of the serious injury need not be alleged. State v. Gregory, 223 N.C. 415 (1943); State v. Lanford, 225 N.C. App. 189, 199–200 (2013) ("Nothing requires the State to allege the body part to which serious injury was inflicted."); State v. Ebron, 173 N.C. App. 642 (2005) (unpublished) (indictment that alleged simply "serious injury" without further detail "allege[d] the necessary ultimate facts" and was sufficient).

Sample Charge:
. . . unlawfully and willfully assault and strike Howard Smith by punching him in the mouth, thereby inflicting serious injury.

AOC Forms for This Offense:
AOC-J-312 (Juvenile Petition)

Punishment:
Class A1 misdemeanor.

G.S. 14-33(c)(1)
Assault with a Deadly Weapon
April 2024

Introductory Comment:
None.

Charging Language:
. . . unlawfully and willfully did assault (*name victim*) with (*describe the deadly weapon*), a deadly weapon, by (*briefly describe the assault and how the weapon was used*).

Notes about Charging Language:

- It is probably unnecessary to describe the assault and how the weapon was used. *Cf.* State v. Thorne, 238 N.C. 392 (1953) (upholding a simple assault charge that did not describe the manner in which the assault was committed); State v. Brooks, 190 N.C. App. 675 (2008) (unpublished) (holding that allegations regarding the specific manner in which the defendant committed an assault by strangulation were surplusage). However, out of an abundance of caution, this form requests that information.

Sample Charge:
. . . unlawfully and willfully did assault Charles Anderson with a knife with a six-inch blade, a deadly weapon, by thrusting the knife at Anderson many times.

AOC Forms for This Offense:
AOC-J-312 (Juvenile Petition)

Punishment:
Class A1 misdemeanor.

G.S. 14-33(c)(2)
Assault on a Female by a Male at Least 18
April 2024

Introductory Comment:
None.

Charging Language:
. . . unlawfully and willfully did assault and strike (*name victim*), a female person, by (*briefly describe the assault*). The defendant is a male person and was at least 18 years of age when the assault and striking occurred.

Notes about Charging Language:
- If the defendant did not strike the victim, omit "and strike" and "striking."
- It is probably unnecessary to describe the assault. *Cf.* State v. Thorne, 238 N.C. 392 (1953) (upholding a simple assault charge that did not describe the manner in which the assault was committed); State v. Brooks, 190 N.C. App. 675 (2008) (unpublished) (holding that allegations regarding the specific manner in which the defendant committed an assault by strangulation were surplusage). However, out of an abundance of caution, this form requests that information.

Sample Charge:
. . . unlawfully and willfully did assault and strike Susan Riggins, a female person, by throwing an empty whiskey bottle and hitting her on the left shoulder. The defendant is a male person and was at least 18 years of age when the assault and striking occurred.

AOC Forms for This Offense:
None.

Punishment:
Class A1 misdemeanor.

G.S. 14-33(c)(2a)
Assault on a Pregnant Woman
April 2024

Introductory Comment:
This subsection of G.S. 14-33 was added by statutory amendment effective December 1, 2023.

Charging Language:
. . . unlawfully and willfully did assault and strike (*name victim*), a pregnant woman, by (*briefly describe the assault*).

Notes about Charging Language:
- If the defendant did not strike the victim, omit "and strike."
- It is probably unnecessary to describe the assault. *Cf.* State v. Thorne, 238 N.C. 392 (1953) (upholding a simple assault charge that did not describe the manner in which the assault was committed); State v. Brooks, 190 N.C. App. 675 (2008) (unpublished) (holding that allegations regarding the specific manner in which the defendant committed an assault by strangulation were surplusage). However, out of an abundance of caution, this form requests that information.

Sample Charge:
. . . unlawfully and willfully did assault and strike Mary Major, a pregnant woman, by hitting her on the left leg with a golf club.

AOC Forms for This Offense:
None.

Punishment:
Class A1 misdemeanor.

G.S. 14-33(c)(3)
Assault on a Child under 12 Years of Age
April 2024

Introductory Comment:
None.

Charging Language:
. . . unlawfully and willfully did assault and strike (*name victim*), a child (*give age*) years of age and thus under 12 years of age, by (*briefly describe the assault*).

Notes about Charging Language:
- If the defendant did not strike the victim, omit "and strike."
- It is probably unnecessary to describe the assault. *Cf.* State v. Thorne, 238 N.C. 392 (1953) (upholding a simple assault charge that did not describe the manner in which the assault was committed); State v. Brooks, 190 N.C. App. 675 (2008) (unpublished) (holding that allegations regarding the specific manner in which the defendant committed an assault by strangulation were surplusage). However, out of an abundance of caution, this form requests that information.

Sample Charge:
. . . unlawfully and willfully did assault and strike Charles Fielding Lawson, a child 10 years of age and thus under 12 years of age, by hitting him on the left leg with a golf club.

AOC Forms for This Offense:
AOC-J-312 (Juvenile Petition, Assault on a Person under 12)

Punishment:
Class A1 misdemeanor.

G.S. 14-33(c)(4)
Assault on a Government Officer or Employee
April 2024

Introductory Comment:
None.

Charging Language:
. . . unlawfully and willfully did assault and strike (*name person assaulted*), an (*choose one*: officer; employee) of [*choose one*: the State; a political subdivision of the State, namely, (*name city or municipality*)], by (*describe assault*). At the time of the offense, the (*choose one*: officer; employee) was (*choose one or both*: discharging; attempting to discharge) a duty of (*choose one*: his; her) (*choose one*: employment; office).

Notes about Charging Language:
- If the defendant did not strike the victim, omit "and strike."
- The specific duty that the victim was discharging or attempting to discharge need not be alleged. State v. Noel, 202 N.C. App. 715 (2010); State v. Bethea, 71 N.C. App. 125 (1984); State v. Waller, 37 N.C. App. 133 (1978). However, the AOC forms for this offense request a description of the duty, and it is not improper to include such a description.
- It is probably unnecessary to describe the assault. *Cf.* State v. Thorne, 238 N.C. 392 (1953) (upholding a simple assault charge that did not describe the manner in which the assault was committed); State v. Brooks, 190 N.C. App. 675 (2008) (unpublished) (holding that allegations regarding the specific manner in which the defendant committed an assault by strangulation were surplusage). However, out of an abundance of caution, this form requests that information.

Sample Charge:
. . . unlawfully and willfully did assault and strike Bill Weathers, an officer of a political subdivision of the State, namely, the Town of Cary, by punching him in his chest. At the time of the offense, the officer was attempting to discharge a duty of his office.

AOC Forms for This Offense:
AOC-J-312 (Juvenile Petition)

Punishment:
Class A1 misdemeanor.

G.S. 14-33(c)(6)
Assault on School Personnel
April 2024

Introductory Comment:
None.

Charging Language:
. . . unlawfully and willfully did assault and strike (*name person assaulted*), a school (*choose one*: employee; volunteer) of the (*name school unit*), by (*describe assault*).
(choose one of the following)

(1) At the time of the offense, the victim was (*choose one or both*: discharging; attempting to discharge) (*choose one*: his; her) duties as a(n) (*choose one*: employee; volunteer).

(2) The victim was assaulted as a result of the (*choose one or both*: discharge; attempt to discharge) of (*choose one*: his; her) duties as a(n) (*choose one*: employee; volunteer).

Notes about Charging Language:
- If the defendant did not strike the victim, omit "and strike."
- The specific duty that the victim was discharging or attempting to discharge need not be alleged. *Cf.* State v. Bethea, 71 N.C. App. 125 (1984); State v. Waller, 37 N.C. App. 133 (1978). However, it is not improper to include such a description.
- It is probably unnecessary to describe the assault. *Cf.* State v. Thorne, 238 N.C. 392 (1953) (upholding a simple assault charge that did not describe the manner in which the assault was committed); State v. Brooks, 190 N.C. App. 675 (2008) (unpublished) (holding that allegations regarding the specific manner in which the defendant committed an assault by strangulation were surplusage). However, out of an abundance of caution, this form requests that information.

Sample Charge:
. . . unlawfully and willfully did assault and strike Bill Weathers, a school employee of the Durham Public Schools, by punching him in his chest. At the time of the offense, the victim was attempting to discharge his duties as an employee.

AOC Forms for This Offense:
None.

Punishment:
Class A1 misdemeanor.

G.S. 14-33(c)(7)
Assault on a Public Transit Operator
April 2024

Introductory Comment:
None.

Charging Language:
. . . unlawfully and willfully did assault and strike (*name person assaulted*), a public transit operator of the (*name government agency*), by (*describe assault*). At the time of the offense, the operator was (*choose one or both*: discharging; attempting to discharge) (*choose one*: his; her) duties as a public transit operator.

Notes about Charging Language:
- If the defendant did not strike the victim, omit "and strike."
- The specific duty that the victim was discharging or attempting to discharge need not be alleged. *Cf.* State v. Bethea, 71 N.C. App. 125 (1984); State v. Waller, 37 N.C. App. 133 (1978). However, it is not improper to include such a description.
- It is probably unnecessary to describe the assault. *Cf.* State v. Thorne, 238 N.C. 392 (1953) (upholding a simple assault charge that did not describe the manner in which the assault was committed); State v. Brooks, 190 N.C. App. 675 (2008) (unpublished) (holding that allegations regarding the specific manner in which the defendant committed an assault by strangulation were surplusage). However, out of an abundance of caution, this form requests that information.

Sample Charge:
. . . unlawfully and willfully did assault and strike Joan Butters, a public transit officer of the Triangle Transit Authority, by punching her in her chest. At the time of the offense, the operator was attempting to discharge her duties as a public transit operator.

AOC Forms for This Offense:
None.

Punishment:
Class A1 misdemeanor.

G.S. 14-33(d)
Assault in Presence of Minor
April 2024

Introductory Comment:
None.

Charging Language:
. . . unlawfully and willfully did, in the course of an (*choose one or more*: assault; assault and battery; affray), (*choose one or more*)

(1) inflict serious injury;

(2) use a deadly weapon, (*describe the weapon*),

on (*name victim*), a person with whom the defendant has a personal relationship, (*describe relationship*), and in the presence of a minor (*name minor and give age*).

Notes about Charging Language:

- It is probably unnecessary to describe the assault. *Cf.* State v. Thorne, 238 N.C. 392 (1953) (upholding a simple assault charge that did not describe the manner in which the assault was committed); State v. Brooks, 190 N.C. App. 675 (2008) (unpublished) (holding that allegations regarding the specific manner in which the defendant committed an assault by strangulation were surplusage). However, out of an abundance of caution, this form requests that information.
- The phrase "serious injury" means physical or bodily injury of real consequence; it means such physical injury as causes great pain and suffering. It may also include severe mental injury. State v. Everhardt, 326 N.C. 777 (1990).
- The nature of the serious injury need not be alleged. State v. Gregory, 223 N.C. 415 (1943); State v. Lanford, 225 N.C. App. 189, 199–200 (2013) ("Nothing requires the State to allege the body part to which serious injury was inflicted."); State v. Ebron, 173 N.C. App. 642 (2005) (unpublished) (indictment that alleged simply "serious injury" without further detail "allege[d] the necessary ultimate facts" and was sufficient).

Sample Charge:
. . . unlawfully and willfully did, in the course of an assault, inflict serious injury, a broken arm, on Stephanie Horne, a person with whom the defendant has a personal relationship, being her husband, and in the presence of a minor, Susan Horne, age 2.

AOC Forms for This Offense:
None.

Punishment:
Class A1 misdemeanor. If the defendant is sentenced to community punishment, the defendant must be placed on supervised probation in addition to any other punishment imposed by the court.

A defendant committing a second or subsequent offense must be sentenced to active punishment of no less than 30 days in addition to any other punishment imposed by the court. For this punishment to be imposed, the State must allege the prior conviction and prove it at trial.

G.S. 14-33.2
Habitual Misdemeanor Assault
April 2024
Page 1 of 2

Introductory Comment:
An indictment or an information for this offense must comply with G.S. 15A-928, which requires that the defendant's prior convictions be alleged either (1) in a separate count of the indictment or information than the substantive offense or (2) in a separate indictment or information. This requirement does not apply to arrest warrants or magistrates' orders, which explains why two sets of charging language appear below.

G.S. 15A-928 also requires that an "improvised name or title" be used so that the title of the indictment or information does not refer to the defendant's prior convictions. Therefore, an indictment or information charging habitual misdemeanor assault should be captioned "assault under G.S. 14-33.2" or something similar.

Charging Language:

I. Charging language for an arrest warrant or magistrate's order

. . . . . . unlawfully, willfully, and feloniously did (*insert proper charging language of a violation of G.S. 14-33 or -34*). This assault caused physical injury to the victim. The defendant has been previously convicted of two or more felony or misdemeanor assault offenses. The defendant has been previously convicted of the (*choose one*: misdemeanor; felony) assault of (*name offense*) on (*give date*), in (*name court*). The defendant has been previously convicted of the (*choose one*: misdemeanor; felony) assault of (*name offense*) on (*give date*), in (*name court*). The earlier of these convictions occurred no more than fifteen years prior to the date of the current violation.

II. Charging language for an indictment or information

First count of indictment or information

. . . unlawfully, willfully, and feloniously did (*insert proper charging language of a violation of G.S. 14-33 or G.S. 14-34*). This assault caused physical injury to the victim.

Second count of indictment or information

The defendant has been previously convicted of two or more felony or misdemeanor assault offenses. The defendant has been previously convicted of the (*choose one*: misdemeanor; felony) assault of (*name offense*) on (*give date*), in (*name court*). The defendant has been previously convicted of the (*choose one*: misdemeanor; felony) assault of (*name offense*) on (*give date*), in (*name court*). The earlier of these convictions occurred no more than fifteen years prior to the date of the current violation.

Notes about Charging Language:

- If the assault giving rise to this charge is assault by pointing a gun under G.S. 14-34, the allegation that the assault caused physical injury is unnecessary and may be deleted.
- More than two previous assault convictions may be alleged if desired.

- The nature of the physical injury need not be alleged. State v. Gregory, 223 N.C. 415 (1943); State v. Lanford, 225 N.C. App. 189, 199–200 (2013) ("Nothing requires the State to allege the body part to which serious injury was inflicted."); State v. Ebron, 173 N.C. App. 642 (2005) (unpublished) (indictment that alleged simply "serious injury" without further detail "allege[d] the necessary ultimate facts" and was sufficient).

Sample Charges:

I. Sample charge for an arrest warrant or magistrate's order

. . . unlawfully, willfully, and feloniously did assault and strike Susan Riggins, a female person, by throwing an empty whiskey bottle and hitting her with it on the left shoulder. The defendant is a male person and was at least 18 years of age when the assault and striking occurred. This assault caused physical injury to the victim. The defendant has been previously convicted of two or more felony or misdemeanor assault offenses. The defendant has been previously convicted of misdemeanor assault of assault on a female on October 14, 2010, in Wake County District Court. The defendant has been previously convicted of misdemeanor assault of assault on a female on December 13, 2016, in Wake County District Court. The earlier of these convictions occurred no more than fifteen years prior to the date of the current violation.

II. Sample charge for an indictment or information

First count of indictment or information
. . . unlawfully, willfully, and feloniously did assault and strike Susan Riggins, a female person, by throwing an empty whiskey bottle and hitting her on the left shoulder. The defendant is a male person and was at least 18 years of age when the assault and striking occurred. This assault caused physical injury to the victim.

Second count of indictment or information
The defendant has been previously convicted of two or more felony or misdemeanor assault offenses. The defendant has been previously convicted of misdemeanor assault of assault on a female on October 14, 2010, in Wake County District Court. The defendant has been previously convicted of misdemeanor assault of assault on a female on December 13, 2015, in Wake County District Court. The earlier of these convictions occurred no more than fifteen years prior to the date of the current violation.

AOC Forms for This Offense:
None.

Punishment:
Class H felony.

G.S. 14-34
Assault by Pointing a Gun
April 2024

Introductory Comment:
G.S. 14-34 provides that this offense is committed "whether such gun or pistol be loaded or not loaded" and whether the pointing is "either in fun or otherwise."

Charging Language:
. . . unlawfully and willfully did assault (*name victim*) by intentionally pointing a gun, (*describe gun*), at such person without legal justification.

Notes about Charging Language:
- The word "intentionally" is not used in the statute, but the cases stress the element.

Sample Charge:
. . . unlawfully and willfully did assault Richard Matthews by intentionally pointing a gun, a .22-caliber rifle, at such person without legal justification.

AOC Forms for This Offense:
AOC-J-312 (Juvenile Petition)

Punishment:
Class A1 misdemeanor.

G.S. 14-34.1
Discharging Firearm or Air Gun into Occupied Property
April 2024
Page 1 of 2

Introductory Comment:
G.S. 14-34.1 defines the basic offense of discharging a firearm into occupied property and the greater offense of discharging a firearm into an occupied dwelling or an occupied conveyance in operation. Either offense is elevated further if serious bodily injury results.

Charging Language:

I. Discharging into occupied property generally **G.S. 14-34.1(a)**

. . . unlawfully, willfully, and feloniously did discharge a (*describe the weapon used*), a firearm, into (*identify and describe the place or thing fired into*), a (*choose one*: building; structure; vehicle; aircraft; watercraft; conveyance; device; equipment; erection; enclosure) located at (*give the address*), while it was actually occupied by (*name any person who was in the particular place or thing at the time of the firing*). [*If appropriate, add*: This resulted in serious bodily injury to (*name victim*).]

II. Discharging into occupied dwelling or into occupied conveyance in operation **G.S. 14-34.1(b)**

. . . unlawfully, willfully, and feloniously did discharge a (*describe the weapon used*), a firearm, into (*identify and describe the place or thing fired into*), a (*choose one*: dwelling; vehicle; aircraft; watercraft; or conveyance) located at (*give the address*), while it was actually occupied by (*name any person who was in the particular place or thing at the time of the firing*) (*if the thing fired into was a conveyance, add*: and while it was in operation). [*If appropriate, add*: This resulted in serious bodily injury to (*name victim*).]

Notes about Charging Language:

- The statute also prohibits discharging or attempting to discharge a "barreled weapon capable of discharging shot, bullets, pellets, or other missiles at a muzzle velocity of at least 600 feet per second." If the weapon was not a firearm but qualifies under this definition, substitute the quoted phrase for "firearm."
- The statute also prohibits an attempt to discharge a firearm or qualifying air gun into occupied property. If there was only an attempt, substitute "attempt to discharge" for "discharge."
- If a very large number of persons were inside, name several and then put the phrase "and many other persons."
- The nature of the serious bodily injury need not be alleged. State v. Gregory, 223 N.C. 415 (1943); State v. Lanford, 225 N.C. App. 189, 199–200 (2013) ("Nothing requires the State to allege the body part to which serious injury was inflicted."); State v. Ebron, 173 N.C. App. 642 (2005) (unpublished) (indictment that alleged simply "serious injury" without further detail "allege[d] the necessary ultimate facts" and was sufficient).
- Each shot fired constitutes a separate offense, so long as each shot is a distinct volitional act. State v. Rambert, 341 N.C. 173 (1995).

Sample Charge:

I. Discharging into occupied property generally **G.S. 14-34.1(a)**

. . . unlawfully, willfully, and feloniously did discharge a shotgun, a firearm, into a McDonald's restaurant, a building located at 513 Caesar Lane, Greensboro, N.C., while it was actually occupied by Reginald Holiday, Marie Desimone, and many other persons.

AOC Forms for This Offense:

None.

Punishment:

Offense I is a Class E felony. Offense II is a Class D felony. Both offenses are Class C felonies if a serious bodily injury results.

G.S. 14-34.1A
Discharging Firearm or Air Gun into Unoccupied Emergency Vehicle
April 2024

Introductory Comment:
This offense was created by statute effective December 1, 2023, as part of the Protect Those Who Serve and Protect Act, which also amended G.S. 14-32 (assault with a deadly weapon), 14-34.2 (assault with a deadly weapon upon government officers), 14-34.5 (assault with a firearm on law enforcement officers), 14-34.7 (assaults on law enforcement officer), and 14-34.8 (use of laser device).

Charging Language:
. . . unlawfully, willfully, and feloniously did discharge a (*describe the weapon used*), a firearm, at or into a (*describe vehicle*), an unoccupied emergency vehicle.

Notes about Charging Language:
- For purposes of this section, the term "emergency vehicle" means any of the following:
  - A law enforcement vehicle
  - A fire department vehicle
  - A public or private ambulance
  - A rescue squad emergency service vehicle
  - A state or local emergency-management vehicle
  - A vehicle owned or operated by the North Carolina National Guard
  - A vehicle owned or operated by any branch of the Armed Forces of the United States
  - A vehicle owned or operated by the Department of Adult Correction
  - A vehicle owned or operated by the Division of Juvenile Justice of the Department of Public Safety
- It is probably not necessary to describe the firearm. *See* State v. Pickens, 346 N.C. 628, 646 (1997) (in indictment for discharging a firearm into occupied dwelling, language specifying type of firearm was "mere surplusage," and variance with evidence was immaterial).
- The statute also prohibits discharging or attempting to discharge a "barreled weapon capable of discharging shot, bullets, pellets, or other missiles at a muzzle velocity of at least 600 feet per second." If the weapon used was not a firearm but qualifies under this definition, substitute the quoted phrase for "firearm."
- The statute also prohibits an attempt to discharge a firearm or qualifying barreled weapon into an unoccupied emergency vehicle. If there was only an attempt, substitute "attempt to discharge" for "discharge." When in doubt, charge the completed offense. *See* G.S. 15-170 (indictment for completed offense will support conviction for attempt).
- For purposes of the offense created by G.S. 14-34.1 (discharging a firearm into occupied property), the North Carolina Supreme Court has held that each shot fired constitutes a separate offense, so long as each shot is a distinct volitional act. *See* State v. Rambert, 341 N.C. 173, 177 (1995).

Sample Charge:
. . . unlawfully, willfully, and feloniously did discharge a shotgun, a firearm, into a Buncombe County ambulance, an unoccupied emergency vehicle.

AOC Forms for This Offense:
None.

Punishment:
Class H felony.

G.S. 14-34.2
Assault with a Firearm or Other Deadly Weapon on Government Officer or Employee or Company or Campus Police Officer

April 2024

Introductory Comment:
If the defendant assaults a law enforcement officer with a firearm, it is usually preferable to charge assault with a firearm on a law enforcement officer in violation of G.S. 14-34.5, a Class D felony, instead of this offense. G.S. 14-34.2 was amended effective December 1, 2023, to remove the term "firearm" from the text (though it remains in the title) and to increase the penalty from a Class F to a Class E felony.

Charging Language:
. . . unlawfully, willfully, and feloniously did assault (*name officer or employee assaulted*), a (*choose one*: government officer; government employee; company police officer certified pursuant to the provisions of Chapter 74E of the General Statutes; campus police officer certified pursuant to the provisions of Chapter 74G, Chapter 17C, or Chapter 116 of the General Statutes) of (*name agency*), with a (*describe the deadly weapon used for the assault*), which is a deadly weapon, by (*briefly describe the assault*). At the time of the assault, the (*choose one*: officer; employee) was performing the following official duty of that office: (*describe the duty the officer or employee was performing*).

Notes about Charging Language:

- It is probably unnecessary to describe the assault. *Cf.* State v. Thorne, 238 N.C. 392 (1953) (upholding a simple assault charge that did not describe the manner in which the assault was committed); State v. Brooks, 190 N.C. App. 675 (2008) (unpublished) (holding that allegations regarding the specific manner in which the defendant committed an assault by strangulation were surplusage). However, out of an abundance of caution, this form requests that information.
- For assault with a firearm, it is probably not necessary to describe the firearm. *See* State v. Lee, 218 N.C. App. 42, 48 (2012) (in an indictment for assault with a deadly weapon with intent to kill inflicting serious injury, it would have been sufficient to specify that the defendant used a "gun" to commit the offense).

Sample Charge:
. . . unlawfully, willfully, and feloniously did assault John Allen Jones, a campus police officer certified pursuant to the provisions of Chapter 74G, Chapter 17C, or Chapter 116 of the General Statutes of the University of North Carolina Public Safety Department, with a knife, a deadly weapon, by stabbing Jones three times. At the time of the assault, the officer was performing the following official duty of that office: investigating a report of a break-in at the student union.

AOC Forms for This Offense:
None.

Punishment:
Class E felony.

Common Law
Going Armed to the Terror of the Public
April 2024

Introductory Comment:
The elements of the common law crime of going armed to the terror of the public are that the accused (1) went about armed with an unusual and dangerous weapon, (2) in a public place, (3) for the purpose of terrifying and alarming the peaceful people, and (4) in a manner which would naturally terrify and alarm the peaceful people. State v. Lancaster, 385 N.C. 459, 467 (2023).

Charging Language:
. . . unlawfully and willfully did arm (*choose one:* himself; herself) with (an) unusual and dangerous weapon(s), (*describe the weapon(s)*), for the unlawful purpose of terrifying and alarming the people of the county named above, and while thus armed the defendant went to (*describe location*), a public place, in a manner that would naturally terrify and alarm the people by (*describe manner in which defendant terrorized*).

Notes about Charging Language:
- Although the essential weapon is described as unusual *and* dangerous, it is probably sufficient if the weapon is unusual *or* dangerous. *See* State v. Huntly, 25 N.C. (3 Ired.) 418, 420 (1843) (quoting 4 William Blackstone, Commentaries 149). In any event, a firearm carried openly qualifies as an unusual and dangerous weapon. *See* State v. Lancaster, 385 N.C. 459, 469 (2023); State v. Dawson, 272 N.C. 535, 543 (1968).
- The crime of going armed to the terror of the public does not require that the offensive conduct occur about a public highway. *See* State v. Lancaster, 385 N.C. 459, 467–68 (2023) (overruling State v. Staten, 32 N.C. App. 495 (1977)).
- It is not necessary to enumerate the acts or threats of violence committed by the defendant while going thus armed. *See Dawson*, 272 N.C. at 549 ("such specific averments are not required").

Sample Charge:
. . . unlawfully and willfully did arm himself with unusual and dangerous weapons, a shotgun and a pistol, for the unlawful purpose of terrifying and alarming the people of the county named above, and while thus armed the defendant went about the public highways of that county, a public place, in a manner that would naturally terrify and alarm the people by driving down East Lee Street in Pickleborough, N.C., and firing the guns repeatedly from the windows of his truck and shouting obscenities and threats to the people living on that street.

AOC Forms for This Offense:
None.

Punishment:
Class 1 misdemeanor.

G.S. 14-34.5
Assault with a Firearm on a Law Enforcement Officer or a Related Professional
April 2024
Page 1 of 2

Introductory Comment:
None.

Charging Language:

I. Assault with a firearm on law enforcement officer, probation officer, or parole officer **G.S. 14-34.5(a)**

. . . unlawfully, willfully, and feloniously did assault (*name officer assaulted*), (*choose one*: a law enforcement officer of [*name law enforcement agency*]; a probation officer; a parole officer), with a firearm, (*describe firearm*), by (*describe assault*). At the time of this offense, the officer was performing a duty of (*choose one*: his; her) office, namely, (*describe duty*).

II. Assault with a firearm on member of North Carolina National Guard **G.S. 14-34.5(a1)**

. . . unlawfully, willfully, and feloniously did assault (*name victim*), a member of the North Carolina National Guard, with a firearm, (*describe firearm*), by (*describe assault*). At the time of this offense, the victim was performing (*choose one*: his; her) duties, namely, (*describe duty*).

III. Assault with a firearm on employee of state or local detention facility **G.S. 14-34.5(b)**

. . . unlawfully, willfully, and feloniously did assault (*name employee assaulted*), who was employed at a detention facility, (*describe detention facility*), operated under the jurisdiction of (*choose one*: the State of North Carolina; *name local government*), with a firearm, (*describe firearm*), by (*describe assault*). At the time of this offense, the employee was performing a duty of (*choose one*: his; her) employment, namely, (*describe duty*).

Notes about Charging Language:

- It is probably not legally necessary to describe the type of firearm used. *See* State v. Pickens, 346 N.C. 628 (1997) (ruling that, when alleging discharging a firearm into an occupied dwelling, it is sufficient to allege that the defendant employed "a firearm," and allegations regarding the specific type of firearm are surplusage). *But cf.* State v. Langley, 173 N.C. App. 194 (2005) (finding a fatal variance between an indictment charging the defendant with possession of a "handgun" and evidence that showed the defendant possessed a sawed-off shotgun; the court viewed the two types of weapons as belonging to different classes of firearms). However, this form requests that information for clarity.
- It is probably not legally necessary to describe how the defendant committed the assault. *Cf.* State v. Williams, 201 N.C. App. 161 (2009) (holding that the specific manner of strangulation was surplusage in a case in which the defendant was charged with assault by strangulation); State v. Muskelly, 6 N.C. App. 174, 176–77 (1969) (holding that the specific manner in which a firearm was used to injure the victim, i.e., whether the victim was shot or beaten with the gun, was surplusage and stating that "[t]he bill is complete without evidentiary matters descriptive of the manner and means by which the offense was committed"). However, this form requests that information for clarity.

- Although a description of the specific duty being performed is not required, State v. Waller, 37 N.C. App. 133 (1978), this form requests that information.

Sample Charge:

I. Assault with a firearm on law enforcement officer, probation officer, or parole officer **G.S. 14-34.5(a)**

. . . unlawfully, willfully, and feloniously did assault Susan Thomas, a law enforcement officer of the Smithville Police Department, with a firearm, a .22-caliber pistol, by shooting at her two times. At the time of this offense, the officer was performing a duty of her office, namely, investigating a breaking and entering of a house on 1212 Racine Street, Smithville, N.C.

AOC Forms for This Offense:
None.

Punishment:
For offenses committed on or after December 1, 2019, Offenses I and III are Class D felonies, while Offense II is a Class E felony. S.L. 2019-116. Prior to that date, Offenses I, II, and III were Class E felonies.

G.S. 14-34.6
Assault on a Firefighter or Specified Medical Personnel
April 2024
Page 1 of 2

Introductory Comment:
Amendments effective December 1, 2023, redefined the term "hospital personnel" and enhanced the penalties for assault inflicting serious bodily injury, assault with a deadly weapon, and assault with a firearm.

Charging Language:

I Assault causing physical injury **G.S. 14-34.6(a)**

. . . unlawfully, willfully, and feloniously did assault (*name person assaulted*), (*choose one*: an emergency medical technician; an emergency health care provider; a medical responder; a hospital employee; a medical practice employee; a licensed health care provider; an individual under contract to provide services at a hospital or medical practice; a firefighter; a hospital security personnel member) (*choose one*: with; working for [*name employer*]). The defendant (*describe assault*) and caused physical injury to the victim. At the time of this offense, the victim of the assault was (*choose one*: discharging; attempting to discharge) official duties (*describe duties*).

II. Assault inflicting serious bodily injury or using deadly weapon other than a firearm **G.S. 14-34.6(b)**

. . . unlawfully, willfully, and feloniously did assault (*name person assaulted*), (*choose one*: an emergency medical technician; an emergency health care provider; a medical responder; a hospital employee; a medical practice employee; a licensed health care provider; an individual under contract to provide services at a hospital or medical practice; a firefighter; a hospital security personnel member) (*choose one*: with; working for [*name employer*]). The defendant (*describe assault*) and (*choose one or both*: inflicted serious bodily injury to the victim; caused physical injury on the victim, and the assault was committed with a deadly weapon other than a firearm [*describe weapon*]). At the time of this offense, the victim of the assault was (*choose one*: discharging; attempting to discharge) official duties (*describe duties*).

III. Assault with a firearm **G.S. 14-34.6(c)**

. . . unlawfully, willfully, and feloniously did assault (*name person assaulted*), (*choose one*: an emergency medical technician; an emergency health care provider; a medical responder; a hospital employee; a medical practice employee; a licensed health care provider; an individual under contract to provide services at a hospital or medical practice; a firefighter; a hospital security personnel member) (*choose one*: with; working for [*name employer*]). The defendant (*describe assault*) and caused physical injury on the victim. The assault was committed with a firearm (*describe firearm*). At the time of this offense, the victim of the assault was (*choose one*: discharging; attempting to discharge) official duties (*describe duties*).

Notes about Charging Language:

- It is probably unnecessary to describe how the defendant committed the assault. *Cf.* State v. Williams, 201 N.C. App. 161 (2009) (holding that the specific manner of strangulation was surplusage in a case in which the defendant was charged with assault by strangulation); State v. Muskelly, 6 N.C. App. 174 (1969) (holding that the specific manner in which a firearm was used to injure the victim, i.e., whether the victim was shot or beaten with the gun, was surplusage). However, this form requests that information for clarity.
- The statute does not define "physical injury." However, G.S. 14-34.7 defines the term as cuts, scrapes, bruises, or other physical injury that is not a serious injury.
- It is not necessary to describe the nature of the injury inflicted. State v. Gregory, 223 N.C. 415 (1943); State v. Lanford, 225 N.C. App. 189, 199–200 (2013) ("Nothing requires the State to allege the body part to which serious injury was inflicted."); State v. Ebron, 173 N.C. App. 642 (2005) (unpublished) (indictment that alleged simply "serious injury" without further detail "allege[d] the necessary ultimate facts" and was sufficient).
- For assault with a firearm, it is probably not necessary to describe the firearm. *See* State v. Lee, 218 N.C. App. 42, 48 (2012) (in an indictment for assault with a deadly weapon with intent to kill inflicting serious injury, it would have been sufficient to specify that the defendant used a "gun" to commit the offense).
- Effective December 1, 2017, subdivision (a)(6) of the statute covers "[h]ospital security personnel." S.L. 2017-57, § 16B.3. Questions might arise regarding whether this term extends to security personnel assigned to work at a hospital but employed by a third-party security company.
- Offenses II and III apply "[u]nless [the] person's conduct is covered under some other provision of law providing greater punishment." G.S. 14-34.6(c).

Sample Charge:

I. Assault causing physical injury **G.S. 14-34.6(a)**

. . . unlawfully, willfully, and feloniously did assault Helen Smith, an emergency medical technician with McDowell County EMS. The defendant hit the victim on her arm and caused physical injury to the victim. At the time of this offense, the victim of the assault was discharging official duties in treating Howard Patton for a gunshot wound.

AOC Forms for This Offense:

None.

Punishment:

Offense I is a Class I felony. Offense II is a Class F felony. Offense III is a Class D felony.

G.S. 14-34.7
Assault on a Law Enforcement Officer or a Related Professional Inflicting Serious Bodily Injury or Physical Injury

April 2024
Page 1 of 3

Introductory Comment:
Prior to the 2015 legislative session, there was an inconsistency between the text of G.S. 14-34.7(a)–(b), which included the term "serious bodily injury," and the caption of the statute, which referred to "serious injury." Relying on the caption, the Court of Appeals of North Carolina ruled in *State v. Crawford*, 167 N.C. App. 777 (2005), that the legislature intended G.S. 14-34.7(a)–(b) to apply to assaults on covered persons resulting in "serious injury." However, in 2015, the General Assembly amended the caption, removing the reference to "serious injury." This appears to undermine *Crawford*, and this form now refers to "serious bodily injury" when addressing the offenses defined in G.S. 14-34.7(a)–(b) as well as the offense created in 2015 in G.S. 14-34.7(a1). Amendments effective December 1, 2023, increased the penalties provided herein.

Charging Language:

I. Assault inflicting serious bodily injury on law enforcement officer, probation officer, or parole officer **G.S. 14-34.7(a)**

. . . unlawfully, willfully, and feloniously did assault (*name officer assaulted*), (*choose one*: a law enforcement officer of [*name law enforcement agency*]; a probation officer; a parole officer), by (*describe the assault*), thereby inflicting serious bodily injury. At the time of this offense, the officer was (*choose one*: discharging; attempting to discharge) a duty of (*choose one*: his; her) office, namely, (*describe duty*).

II. Assault inflicting serious bodily injury on member of North Carolina National Guard **G.S. 14-34.7(a1)**

. . . unlawfully, willfully, and feloniously did assault (*name victim*), a member of the North Carolina National Guard, by (*describe the assault*), thereby inflicting serious bodily injury. At the time of this offense, the victim was (*choose one*: discharging; attempting to discharge) (*choose one*: his; her) official duties, namely, (*describe duty*).

III. Assault inflicting serious bodily injury on employee of state or local detention facility **G.S. 14-34.7(b)**

. . . unlawfully, willfully, and feloniously did assault (*name employee assaulted*), who was employed at a detention facility, (*describe detention facility*), operated under the jurisdiction of (*choose one*: the State of North Carolina; *name local government*), by (*describe the assault*), thereby inflicting serious bodily injury. At the time of this offense, the employee was performing a duty of (*choose one*: his; her) employment, namely, (*describe duty*).

IV. Assault inflicting physical injury on law enforcement officer, probation officer, or parole officer **G.S. 14-34.7(c)(1)**

. . . unlawfully, willfully, and feloniously did assault (*name officer assaulted*), (*choose one*: a law enforcement officer of [*name law enforcement agency*]; a probation officer; a parole officer), by (*describe *the assault*), thereby inflicting physical injury. At the time of this offense, the officer was (*choose one*: discharging; attempting to discharge) a duty of (*choose one*: his; her) office, namely, (*describe duty*).

V. Assault inflicting physical injury on employee of state or local detention facility **G.S. 14-34.7(c)(2)**

. . . unlawfully, willfully, and feloniously did assault (*name employee assaulted*), who was employed at a detention facility, (*describe detention facility*), operated under the jurisdiction of (*choose one*: the State of North Carolina; *name local government*), by (*describe the assault*), thereby inflicting physical injury. At the time of this offense, the employee was performing a duty of (*choose one*: his; her) employment, namely, (*describe duty*).

VI. Assault inflicting physical injury on member of North Carolina National Guard **G.S. 14-34.7(c)(3)**

. . . unlawfully, willfully, and feloniously did assault (*name victim*), a member of the North Carolina National Guard, by (*describe the assault*), thereby inflicting physical injury. At the time of this offense, the victim was (*choose one*: discharging; attempting to discharge) (*choose one*: his; her) official duties, namely, (*describe duty/duties*).

Notes about Charging Language:

- Although a description of the specific duty being performed is not required, State v. Waller, 37 N.C. App. 133 (1978), this form requests that information.
- It is probably unnecessary to describe how the defendant committed the assault *Cf.* State v. Williams, 201 N.C. App. 161 (2009) (holding that the specific manner of strangulation was surplusage in a case in which the defendant was charged with assault by strangulation); State v. Muskelly, 6 N.C. App. 174, 176–77 (1969) (holding that the specific manner in which a firearm was used to injure the victim, i.e., whether the victim was shot or beaten with the gun, was surplusage and stating that "[t]he bill is complete without evidentiary matters descriptive of the manner and means by which the offense was committed"). However, this form requests that information for clarity.
- It is not necessary to describe the nature of the injury inflicted. State v. Gregory, 223 N.C. 415 (1943); State v. Lanford, 225 N.C. App. 189, 199–200 (2013) ("Nothing requires the State to allege the body part to which serious injury was inflicted."); State v. Ebron, 173 N.C. App. 642 (2005) (unpublished) (indictment that alleged simply "serious injury" without further detail "allege[d] the necessary ultimate facts" and was sufficient).
- For Offenses I, II, and III, "serious bodily injury" is not defined in G.S. 14-34.7. A court likely would apply the definition in G.S. 14-32.4(a), which is "bodily injury that creates a substantial risk of death, or that causes serious permanent disfigurement, coma, a permanent or protracted condition that causes extreme pain, or permanent or protracted loss or impairment of the function of any bodily member or organ, or that results in prolonged hospitalization." *See generally* N.C.P.I.—Crim. 208.94 (incorporating this definition).

- For Offenses IV, V, and VI, "physical injury" is defined in G.S. 14-34.7 as "cuts, scrapes, bruises, or other physical injury which does not constitute serious injury."

Sample Charge:

I. Assault inflicting serious bodily injury on law enforcement officer, probation officer, or parole officer **G.S. 14-34.7(a)**

. . . unlawfully, willfully, and feloniously did assault Joe Fandango, a probation officer, by hitting him with a beer bottle, thereby inflicting serious bodily injury. At the time of this offense, the officer was discharging a duty of his office, namely, conducting a home visit at the defendant's residence.

AOC Forms for This Offense:
None.

Punishment:
Offenses I, II, and III are Class E felonies. Offenses IV, V, and VI are Class H felonies.

G.S. 14-34.10
Discharging a Firearm within an Enclosure to Incite Fear
April 2024

Introductory Comment:
None.

Charging Language:
. . . unlawfully, willfully, and feloniously did wantonly (*choose one*: discharge; attempt to discharge) a (*describe the firearm*), a firearm, within an occupied (*choose one and describe*: building; structure; motor vehicle; conveyance; erection; enclosure) with the intent to incite fear in another, (*name victim*).

Notes about Charging Language:

- It is probably not legally necessary to describe the firearm. State v. Pickens, 346 N.C. 628 (1997) (holding that language in an indictment for discharging a firearm into an occupied dwelling that specified the type of firearm was unnecessary "surplusage"). *Cf.* State v. Lee, 218 N.C. App. 42, 48 (2012) (stating that an indictment for assault with a deadly weapon with intent to kill inflicting serious injury would have been sufficient if it had simply alleged that the defendant used a "gun," as that "would have been sufficient to give notice to defendant of the allegation that he used some type of gun to commit the assault"). However, this form requests that information for clarity.
- In some instances the defendant may have intended to incite fear in a class of persons, such as all the patrons of a business within which the defendant discharged a firearm, rather than in a specific individual. In such a case, it may be appropriate to describe the victim or victims rather than to name them.

Sample Charge:
. . . unlawfully, willfully, and feloniously did wantonly discharge a Glock 9mm pistol, a firearm, within an occupied building, a house located at 224 Katie Lane, Farmville, N.C., with the intent to incite fear in another, Fatima Achour.

AOC Forms for This Offense:
None.

Punishment:
Class F felony.

G.S. 14-39
First-Degree Kidnapping
April 2024
Page 1 of 2

Introductory Comment:
None.

Charging Language:
. . . unlawfully, willfully, and feloniously did kidnap (*name victim*), a person (*choose one*: who had attained the age of 16 years; under the age of 16 years), by unlawfully [*choose one or more*: confining (*choose one*: him; her); restraining (*choose one*: him; her); removing (*choose one*: him; her) from one place to another], [*for victim 16 or over, state*: without (*choose one*: his; her) consent; *for victim under 16, state*: without the consent of (*choose one*: his; her) parent or legal guardian] and for the purpose of (*choose one or more*)

(1) holding (*choose one*: him; her) for ransom.
(2) holding (*choose one*: him; her) as a hostage.
(3) using (*choose one*: him; her) as a shield.
(4) facilitating the commission of a felony.
(5) facilitating the flight of (*name the defendant or other person fleeing*) following the commission of a felony.
(6) doing serious bodily harm to (*choose one*: him; her).
(7) terrorizing (*choose one*: him; her).
(8) holding (*choose one*: him; her) in involuntary servitude.
(9) trafficking (*choose one*: him; her) with the intent that (*choose one*: he; she) be held in involuntary servitude.
(10) trafficking (*choose one*: him; her) with the intent that (*choose one*: he; she) be held in sexual servitude.
(11) (*choose one or both*: subjecting; maintaining) (*choose one*: him; her) to/for sexual servitude.

(*Name victim*) (*choose one or more*: was not released by the defendant in a safe place; was seriously injured; was sexually assaulted).

Notes about Charging Language:

- With respect to purposes (4) and (5), the name of the felony is not required. If that information is included, the State may be bound by the felony (or felonies) named. State v. Yarborough, 198 N.C. App. 22 (2009).
- The statute states that the offense may be committed when the kidnapping is done for the purpose of doing serious bodily injury to or terrorizing someone other than the person kidnapped. If that is the case, strike the word "him" or "her" and substitute the name of the other person injured or terrorized.

- G.S. 14-43.10(a)(3) defines "involuntary servitude" as the performance of labor "[b]y deception, coercion, or intimidation using violence or the threat of violence or by any other means of coercion or intimidation."
- G.S. 14-43.10(a)(5) defines "sexual servitude" as, *inter alia*, sexual activity obtained by coercion or deception or from a person under 18 years of age.
- Alleging that the victim was "sexually assaulted" is sufficient; the indictment need not "allege or specify what crime constituted the underlying 'sexual assault.' " State v. Pabon, 273 N.C. App. 645, 668 (2020).
- By statute, felonious restraint is a lesser-included offense of kidnapping. G.S. 14-43.3. However, in order for felonious restraint to be submitted to the jury under a kidnapping indictment, the indictment must allege all the elements of felonious restraint, including transportation by motor vehicle or other conveyance. State v. Wilson, 128 N.C. App. 688 (1998). Appropriate language may be added if desired.

Sample Charge:
. . . unlawfully, willfully, and feloniously did kidnap Ronald Jacob Evans, Jr., a person under the age of 16 years, by unlawfully confining and restraining and removing him from one place to another, without the consent of his parent or legal guardian and for the purpose of holding him for ransom. Ronald Jacob Evans, Jr., was not released by the defendant in a safe place and was seriously injured.

AOC Forms for This Offense:
None.

Punishment:
Class C felony.

G.S. 14-39
Second-Degree Kidnapping
April 2024
Page 1 of 2

Introductory Comment:
None.

Charging Language:
. . . unlawfully, willfully, and feloniously did kidnap (*name victim*), a person (*choose one*: who had attained the age of 16 years; under the age of 16 years), by unlawfully [*choose one or more*: confining (*choose one*: him; her); restraining (*choose one*: him; her); removing (*choose one*: him; her) from one place to another], [*for victim 16 or over, state*: without (*choose one*: his; her) consent; for victim under 16, state: without the consent of (*choose one*: his; her) parent or legal guardian] and for the purpose of (*choose one or more*)

(1) holding (*choose one*: him; her) for ransom.
(2) holding (*choose one*: him; her) as a hostage.
(3) using (*choose one*: him; her) as a shield.
(4) facilitating the commission of a felony.
(5) facilitating the flight of (*name the defendant or other person fleeing*) following the commission of a felony.
(6) doing serious bodily harm to (*choose one*: him; her).
(7) terrorizing (*choose one*: him; her).
(8) holding (*choose one*: him; her) in involuntary servitude.
(9) trafficking (*choose one*: him; her) with the intent that (*choose one*: he; she) be held in involuntary servitude.
(10) trafficking (*choose one*: him; her) with the intent that (*choose one*: he; she) be held in sexual servitude.
(11) (*choose one or both*: subjecting; maintaining) (*choose one*: him; her) to/for sexual servitude.

Notes about Charging Language:

- With respect to purposes (4) and (5), the name of the felony is not required. If that information is included, the State may be bound by the felony (or felonies) named. State v. Yarborough, 198 N.C. App. 22 (2009).
- The statute states that the offense may be committed when the kidnapping is done for the purpose of doing serious bodily injury to or terrorizing someone other than the person kidnapped. If that is the case, strike the word "him" or "her" and substitute the name of the other person injured or terrorized.
- G.S. 14-43.10(a)(3) defines "involuntary servitude" as the performance of labor "[b]y deception, coercion, or intimidation using violence or the threat of violence or by any other means of coercion or intimidation."
- G.S. 14-43.10(a)(5) defines "sexual servitude" as, *inter alia*, sexual activity obtained by coercion or deception or from a person under 18 years of age.

- By statute, felonious restraint is a lesser-included offense of kidnapping. G.S. 14-43.3. However, in order for felonious restraint to be submitted to the jury under a kidnapping indictment, the indictment must allege all the elements of felonious restraint, including transportation by motor vehicle or other conveyance. State v. Wilson, 128 N.C. App. 688 (1998). Appropriate language may be added if desired.

Sample Charge:
. . . unlawfully, willfully, and feloniously did kidnap Ronald Jacob Evans, Jr., a person under the age of 16 years, by unlawfully confining and restraining and removing him from one place to another, without the consent of his parent or legal guardian and for the purpose of holding him for ransom.

AOC Forms for This Offense:
None.

Punishment:
Class E felony.

Common Law
False Imprisonment
April 2024

Introductory Comment:
False imprisonment is a lesser-included offense of kidnapping. The key difference is the purpose of the confinement or restraint of the victim. False imprisonment is typically charged when there is insufficient evidence of any of the purposes enumerated in the kidnapping statute.

Charging Language:
. . . unlawfully and willfully did restrain and detain (*name victim*), against (*choose one*: his; her) will, by (*describe how victim was restrained and detained*).

Notes about Charging Language:
- It is unnecessary to allege both "restrain" and "detain," but both are alleged here.
- If the victim is an unemancipated minor, then it is probably unnecessary to allege "against the victim's will" because the victim's consent would be irrelevant.

Sample Charge:
. . . unlawfully and willfully did restrain and detain Sally Jones, against her will, by forcing her into a storage closet at her home at 32 E. Main Street, Durham, N.C., and preventing her from getting out.

AOC Forms for This Offense:
None.

Punishment:
Class 1 misdemeanor.

G.S. 14-41
Abduction of Children
April 2024

Introductory Comment:
None.

Charging Language:
. . . unlawfully, willfully, and feloniously did without legal justification or defense abduct (*name child*), a minor who was at least four years younger than the defendant, from the (*choose one*: person; agency; institution), (*name person, agency, or institution*), lawfully entitled to the child's (*choose one or more*: custody; placement; care).

Notes about Charging Language:
- This statute also prohibits a person from inducing the child to leave a person, agency, or institution lawfully entitled to the child's custody, placement, or care. In such a case, modify the charging language accordingly.
- This statute provides that it does not apply to a public officer or employee who is performing his or her duties.

Sample Charge:
. . . unlawfully, willfully, and feloniously did without legal justification or defense abduct Susan Jones, a minor who was at least four years younger than the defendant, from the person, Samantha Jones, lawfully entitled to the child's custody.

AOC Forms for This Offense:
None.

Punishment:
Class F felony.

G.S. 14-43.3
Felonious Restraint
April 2024

Introductory Comment:
None.

Charging Language:
. . . unlawfully, willfully, and feloniously did restrain (*name victim*), a person (*choose one*: who had attained the age of 16 years; under the age of 16 years), and move (*choose one*: him; her) from the place of the initial restraint, (*describe place*), by transporting (*choose one*: him; her) in a (*choose one*: motor vehicle; conveyance), a (*describe motor vehicle or conveyance*). This act was done [*for victim 16 or over, state*: without (*choose one*: his; her) consent; *for victim under 16, state*: without the consent of (*choose one*: his; her) parent or legal guardian].

Notes about Charging Language:

- G.S. 14-43.3 provides that felonious restraint is a lesser-included offense of kidnapping. However, a trial judge may not submit felonious restraint as a lesser-included offense of first- or second-degree kidnapping unless the kidnapping indictment alleges the elements of felonious restraint—transporting the victim in a motor vehicle or other conveyance. State v. Wilson, 128 N.C. App. 688 (1998).

Sample Charge:
. . . unlawfully, willfully, and feloniously did restrain Sally Michaels, a person who had attained the age of 16 years, and move her from the place of the initial restraint, the Magnolia Grill restaurant in Durham, N.C., by transporting her in a motor vehicle, a 2004 Toyota Camry, N.C. license no. HME-111, owned by Charles Smith. This act was done without her consent.

AOC Forms for This Offense:
None.

Punishment:
Class F felony.

G.S. 14-49, -49.1
Malicious Injury or Damage by Explosives
April 2024
Page 1 of 2

Introductory Comment:
None.

Charging Language:

I. Injury to person **G.S. 14-49(a)**

. . . unlawfully, willfully, and feloniously did maliciously injure (*name the victim*) by the use of an explosive and incendiary device and material.

II. Damage to property **G.S. 14-49(b)**

. . . unlawfully, willfully, and feloniously did maliciously damage (*name or describe the property that was damaged*), the (*choose one or both*: real; personal) property of (*name the owner, occupier, or possessor of the property*), by the use of an explosive and incendiary device and material.

III. Damage to religious building **G.S. 14-49(b1)**

. . . unlawfully, willfully, and feloniously did maliciously damage a (*choose one*: church; synagogue; mosque; masjid; *name other building of worship*), the property of (*name the owner, occupier, or possessor of the property*), by the use of an explosive and incendiary device and material.

IV. Damage to government building **G.S. 14-49(b2)**

. . . unlawfully, willfully, and feloniously did maliciously damage [*choose one and give location*: the State Capitol; the Legislative Building; the Justice Building; a building owned or occupied by (*name state agency or unit of state or local government*)], by the use of an explosive and incendiary device and material.

V. Damage to occupied property **G.S. 14-49.1**

. . . unlawfully, willfully, and feloniously did maliciously damage (*name or describe the property that was damaged*), the (*choose one or both*: real; personal) property of (*name the owner, occupier, or possessor of the property*), while that property was occupied by (*name the person who was inside the property*), by the use of an explosive and incendiary device and material.

Notes about Charging Language:

- G.S. 14-50.1 defines "explosive or incendiary device or material" to include "nitroglycerine, dynamite, gunpowder, other high explosive incendiary bomb or grenade, other destructive incendiary device, or any other destructive incendiary or explosive device, compound, or formulation; any instrument or substance capable of being used for destructive explosive or incendiary purposes against persons or property, when the circumstances indicate some probability that such instrument or substance will be so used; or any explosive or incendiary part or ingredient in any instrument or substance included above, when the circumstances indicate some probability that such part or ingredient will be so used." If the kind of explosive or incendiary device or material is known, its name may be alleged in the criminal pleading.

Sample Charges:

I. Injury to person **G.S. 14-49(a)**

. . . unlawfully, willfully, and feloniously did maliciously injure Joan Davis by the use of an explosive and incendiary device and material.

IV. Damage to government building **G.S. 14-49(b2)**

. . . unlawfully, willfully, and feloniously did maliciously damage a building occupied by the Orange County Department of Social Services, located at 95 Elm Street, Hillsborough, N.C., by the use of an explosive and incendiary device and material.

AOC Forms for This Offense:

None.

Punishment:

Offense I is a Class D felony. Offense II is a Class G felony. Offenses III and IV are Class E felonies. Offense V is a Class D felony.

G.S. 14-51
First-Degree Burglary
April 2024

Introductory Comment:
None.

Charging Language:
. . . unlawfully, willfully, and feloniously did during the night-time break and enter the dwelling house of (*name the possessor of the house*), located at (*give address of dwelling house*). At the time of the breaking and entering, the dwelling house was actually occupied by (*name occupant*). The defendant broke and entered with the intent to commit a felony therein.

Notes about Charging Language:

- Although burglary must take place during the night-time, the specific hour of the offense need not be alleged. *See, e.g.*, State v. Wood, 286 N.C. 248 (1974).
- The offense may also be committed by breaking into a sleeping apartment. If that is the case, substitute the words "sleeping apartment" for "dwelling house" and describe the location of the sleeping apartment within the building.
- In *State v. Worsley*, 336 N.C. 268 (1994), the court ruled that an indictment need only allege that the defendant intended to commit a felony, without naming the felony. If the State elects to name a specific felony, it may be bound by that allegation. State v. Silas, 360 N.C. 377 (2006).
- The elements of burglary require that the defendant have the intent to commit a felony *or larceny*. Jessica Smith, North Carolina Crimes: A Guidebook on the Elements of Crime 293 (UNC School of Government, 7th ed. 2012). However, larceny committed pursuant to burglary is a felony under G.S. 14-72(b)(2). Therefore, *or larceny* is redundant, and this form omits it. It is not improper to include it if desired.

Sample Charge:
. . . unlawfully, willfully, and feloniously did during the night-time break and enter the dwelling house of Lloyd Rollins, located at 4455 Haggard Street, Wilmington, N.C. At the time of the breaking and entering, the dwelling house was actually occupied by Lloyd Rollins and Esther Rollins. The defendant broke and entered with the intent to commit a felony therein.

AOC Forms for This Offense:
AOC-CR-126 (Indictment)

Punishment:
Class D felony.

G.S. 14-51
Second-Degree Burglary
April 2024

Introductory Comment:
None.

Charging Language:
. . . unlawfully, willfully, and feloniously did during the night-time break and enter the dwelling house of (*name the possessor of the house*), located at (*give address of dwelling house*). The defendant broke and entered with the intent to commit a felony therein.

Notes about Charging Language:

- Although burglary must take place during the night-time, the specific hour of the offense need not be alleged. *See, e.g.*, State v. Wood, 286 N.C. 248 (1974).
- The offense may also be committed by breaking into a sleeping apartment, any other house within the curtilage of a dwelling house, or a building other than a dwelling house in which there is a sleeping apartment. If that is the case, strike the words "dwelling house" and substitute appropriate language.
- In *State v. Worsley*, 336 N.C. 268 (1994), the court ruled that an indictment need only allege that the defendant intended to commit a felony, without naming the felony. If the State elects to name a specific felony, it may be bound by that allegation. State v. Silas, 360 N.C. 377 (2006).
- The elements of burglary require that the defendant have the intent to commit a felony *or larceny*. Jessica Smith, North Carolina Crimes: A Guidebook on the Elements of Crime 293 (UNC School of Government, 7th ed. 2012). However, larceny committed pursuant to burglary is a felony under G.S. 14-72(b)(2). Therefore, *or larceny* is redundant, and this form omits it. It is not improper to include it if desired.

Sample Charge:
. . . unlawfully, willfully, and feloniously did during the night-time break and enter the dwelling house of Robert Lewis, located at 506 Windward Road, Creel, N.C. The defendant broke and entered with the intent to commit a felony therein.

AOC Forms for This Offense:
None.

Punishment:
Class G felony.

G.S. 14-54(a)–(a1)
Felonious Breaking or Entering
April 2024
Page 1 of 2

Introductory Comment:
None.

Charging Language:

I. Felony Breaking or Entering **G.S. 14-54(a)**

. . . unlawfully, willfully, and feloniously did break and enter a building, located at (*give address*), with the intent to commit a felony therein. The building was (*choose one*: owned by; occupied by) (*name owner or occupant*) (*if the building was in use, also state*: and was used as [*state use*]).

II. Breaking or Entering to Terrorize **G.S. 14-54(a1)**

. . . unlawfully, willfully, and feloniously did break and enter a building, located at (*give address*), with the intent to (*choose one or both*: terrorize; injure) an occupant of the building, (*name occupant*).

Notes about Charging Language:

- The statute makes it an offense to either break or enter; if there was only a breaking and no entry, you may strike the words "and enter." If there was an entry but no breaking, you may strike the words "break and."
- For Offense I, as long as the building is accurately identified by its address, it is not legally necessary to allege the ownership, occupancy, or use of the building. State v. Norman, 149 N.C. App. 588, 592 (2002) (ruling that "[a]s to the building itself, it was not necessary that the [breaking or entering] indictment allege ownership of the building," so long as the building was identified with reasonable particularity). However, this form requests that information for clarity and in case the address is unavailable or incorrect. State v. Shanklin, 16 N.C. App. 712 (1972) (upholding breaking or entering indictment that did not provide the address of the building but did identify the occupant of the building).
- In *State v. Worsley*, 336 N.C. 268 (1994), the court ruled that an indictment need only allege that the defendant intended to commit a felony in the building, without naming the felony. If the State elects to name a specific felony, it may be bound by that allegation. State v. Silas, 360 N.C. 377 (2006).
- The elements of felonious breaking or entering require that the defendant have the intent to commit a felony *or larceny*. G.S. 14-54(a). However, larceny committed pursuant to a breaking or entering is a felony under G.S. 14-72(b)(2). Therefore, *or larceny* is redundant, and this form omits it. It is not improper to include it if desired.
- For Offense II, in some instances the defendant may have intended to injure or terrorize a class of persons, such as all the residents of a house, rather than a specific individual. In such a case, it may be appropriate to describe the victim or victims rather than to name them.

Sample Charge:

I. Felony Breaking or Entering **G.S. 14-54(a)**

. . . unlawfully, willfully, and feloniously did break and enter a building, located at 5678 Maryville Drive, Commerce, N.C., with the intent to commit a felony therein. The building was occupied by Thomas Montgomery and was used as a residence.

AOC Forms for This Offense:
AOC-CR-134 (Indictment)
AOC-J-313 (Juvenile Petition, for Offense I only)

Punishment:
Offense I is a Class H felony. Offense II is a Class H felony.

G.S. 14-54(b)
Misdemeanor Breaking or Entering
April 2024

Introductory Comment:
None.

Charging Language:
. . . unlawfully and willfully did wrongfully break and enter a building located at (*give address*). The building was (*choose one*: owned by; occupied by) (*name owner or occupant*) (*if the building was in use, also state*: and was used as [*state use*]).

Notes about Charging Language:
- The statute makes it an offense to either break or enter; if there was only a breaking and no entry, you may strike the words "and enter." If there was an entry but no breaking, you may strike the words "break and."
- As long as the building is accurately identified by its address, it is not legally necessary to allege the ownership, occupancy, or use of the building. State v. Norman, 149 N.C. App. 588, 592 (2002) (ruling that "[a]s to the building itself, it was not necessary that the [breaking or entering] indictment allege ownership of the building," so long as the building was identified with reasonable particularity). However, this form requests that information for clarity and in case the address is unavailable or incorrect. State v. Shanklin, 16 N.C. App. 712 (1972) (upholding breaking or entering indictment that did not provide the address of the building but did identify the occupant of the building).

Sample Charge:
. . . unlawfully and willfully did wrongfully enter a building located at 1875 S. Williams Street, Beamville, N.C. The building was occupied by Granny's Clothing Attic, Inc., a corporation, and was used as a retail store.

AOC Forms for This Offense:
None.

Punishment:
Class 1 misdemeanor.

G.S. 14-54.1
Breaking or Entering a Place of Religious Worship
April 2024

Introductory Comment:
None.

Charging Language:
. . . unlawfully, willfully, and feloniously did wrongfully break and enter a building occupied by (*name the possessor of the building*) that is a place of religious worship, located at (*give the address*), with the intent to commit a felony therein.

Notes about Charging Language:
- The statute makes it an offense to either break or enter; if there was only a breaking and no entry, you may strike the words "and enter." If there was an entry but no breaking, you may strike the words "break and."
- G.S. 14-54.1(b) states that a place of religious worship includes "any church, chapel, meetinghouse, synagogue, temple, longhouse, or mosque, or other building that is regularly used, and clearly identifiable, as a place for religious worship."
- In *State v. Worsley*, 336 N.C. 268 (1994), the court ruled that an indictment need only allege that the defendant intended to commit a felony, without naming the felony. If the State elects to name a specific felony, it may be bound by that allegation. State v. Silas, 360 N.C. 377 (2006).
- The elements of this offense require that the defendant have the intent to commit a felony *or larceny*. G.S. 14-54.1. However, larceny committed pursuant to a breaking or entering is a felony under G.S. 14-72(b)(2). Therefore, *or larceny* is redundant, and this form omits it. It is not improper to include it if desired.

Sample Charge:
. . . unlawfully, willfully, and feloniously did break and enter a building occupied by the Fountain Assembly of God that is a place of religious worship, located at 404 Elm Drive, Cypress Creek, N.C., with the intent to commit a felony therein.

AOC Forms for This Offense:
None.

Punishment:
Class G felony.

G.S. 14-54.2
Breaking or Entering a Pharmacy
April 2024

Introductory Comment:
This offense was enacted by the General Assembly in the 2019 legislative session, S.L. 2019-40, effective for offenses committed on or after December 1, 2019.

Charging Language:

I. Breaking or entering a pharmacy **G.S. 14-52.2(b)**

. . . unlawfully, willfully, and feloniously did break and enter a pharmacy, (*name pharmacy and provide address*), with the intent to commit a larceny of a controlled substance.

II. Possession of controlled substance stolen from a pharmacy **G.S. 14-52.2(c)**

. . . unlawfully, willfully, and feloniously did (*choose one or both: receive; possess*) (*name substance*), a controlled substance, stolen in violation of G.S. 14-52.2(b). The defendant (*choose one or both: knew; had reasonable grounds to believe*) that the controlled substance was stolen

Notes about Charging Language:
- The statute makes it an offense to either break or enter. If there was a breaking but no entry, you may strike the words "and enter." If there was an entry but no breaking, you may strike the words "break and."
- Because the statute is new, it is not yet clear whether courts will require the inclusion of the address of the pharmacy. Because that information is normally included when charging breaking or entering, this form requests it.
- The statute defines a "pharmacy" as "[a] business that has a pharmacy permit under G.S. 90-85.21" and defines a "controlled substance . . . [a]s defined in G.S. 90-87(5)."
- Because the statute is new, it is not yet clear whether courts will require that the controlled substance in question be named. Because it may be impossible to know the substance that the defendant intended to take, this form does not request that information for Offense I, but because it normally will be possible to know what substance the defendant received or possessed, this form does request that information for Offense II.

Sample Charge:

I. Breaking or entering a pharmacy **G.S. 14-52.2(b)**

. . . unlawfully, willfully, and feloniously did break and enter a pharmacy, Family Pharmacy, 2105 Prince Street, Danville, N.C., with the intent to commit a larceny of a controlled substance.

AOC Forms for This Offense:
None.

Punishment:
Offense I is a Class E felony. Offense II is a Class F felony.

G.S. 14-55

Preparation to Commit Burglary/Possession of Burglar's Tools/etc.

April 2024

Page 1 of 2

Introductory Comment:

G.S. 14-55 creates three separate offenses. A criminal pleading must individually identify which offense is being charged. *See* State v. Searcy, 37 N.C. App. 68 (1978).

Charging Language:

I. Found armed with intent to break or enter

. . . unlawfully, willfully, and feloniously did have in the defendant's possession a (*name or describe the weapon*), a dangerous weapon, with the intent to break and enter the building of (*name the possessor of the building*), located at (*give the address of the building*). At the time the defendant had the dangerous weapon in his or her possession, the defendant had the intent to break and enter the building to commit a felony therein.

II. Possession of implements of housebreaking

. . . unlawfully, willfully, and feloniously did without lawful excuse have in the defendant's possession an implement of housebreaking, a (*name and describe the picklock, key, bit or other implement and, if necessary, state how it is used for housebreaking*).

III. Presence in building with intent to commit felony or larceny

. . . unlawfully, willfully, and feloniously did remain in the building of (*name the possessor of the building*), located at (*give the address of the building*). At the time the defendant was found in the building, he or she had the intent to commit a felony or larceny therein.

Notes about Charging Language:

- The statute also makes it an offense to have an "offensive weapon"; if the weapon is offensive but not dangerous, the word "offensive" may be substituted for "dangerous."
- The statute makes it an offense to have the intent to either break or enter; if there is an intent to break but not to enter, you may strike the words "and enter"; if there is an intent to enter but not to break, strike the words "break and."
- The statute makes it an offense to have the intent to break or enter "a dwelling, or other building whatsoever." If the building to be broken or entered was a dwelling house, the word "building" may be deleted and replaced with "dwelling."

Sample Charges:

I. Found armed with intent to break or enter

. . . unlawfully, willfully, and feloniously did have in his possession a .45-caliber pistol, a dangerous weapon, with the intent to break and enter the dwelling of Samuel Lenore Bodfred, located at 42 Willow Lane, Monroe, N.C. At the time he had the dangerous weapon in his possession, the defendant had the intent to break and enter the dwelling to commit a felony therein.

II. Possession of implements of housebreaking

. . . unlawfully, willfully, and feloniously did without lawful excuse have in his possession implements of housebreaking, a picklock, a crowbar, and a fourteen-inch screwdriver.

III. Presence in building with intent to commit felony or larceny

. . . unlawfully, willfully, and feloniously did remain in the building of Roman Wine Corner, Inc., a corporation, located at 1665 Admiral Dewey Way, Seaside, N.C. At the time the defendant was found in the building, he had the intent to commit a felony or larceny therein.

AOC Forms for This Offense:
None.

Punishment:
Class I felony.

G.S. 14-56
Breaking or Entering a Vehicle
April 2024
Page 1 of 2

Introductory Comment:
Amendments effective December 1, 2023, enhanced the punishment for violations of this statute depending on the aggregated value of any property taken.

Charging Language:
. . . unlawfully, willfully, and feloniously did break and enter a (*choose one*: motor vehicle; aircraft; boat; railroad car; trailer), a (*describe the vehicle or other thing broken into, including the name of the owner*), which contained things of value, with the intent to commit (*choose one*: larceny; a felony) therein. (*If applicable, add one of the following*:)

(1) The defendant took property (*describe the property taken*) having a value (*choose one*: exceeding $100,000; between $50,000 and $100,000; between $20,000 and $50,000) aggregated over a ninety-day period.

(2) The defendant took property (*describe the property taken*) having a value of between $1,500 and $20,000; the conveyance is owned or operated by (*choose one*: a law enforcement agency, (*identify*); the North Carolina National Guard; a branch of the Armed Forces of the United States, (*identify*)); and the defendant knew or reasonably should have known that the conveyance was so owned or operated.

Notes about Charging Language:

- The statute makes it an offense to either break *or* enter; if there was only a breaking and no entry, you may strike the words "and enter"; if there was an entry but no breaking, you may strike the words "break and."
- The statute also covers watercraft other than boats. If the vehicle broken into is a watercraft but not a boat, substitute "watercraft" for "boat."
- The statute also covers breaking out of a railroad car, motor vehicle, trailer, aircraft, or boat after having committed larceny or another felony therein. This form should be modified in such a case.
- Unlike larceny pursuant to a burglary or breaking or entering a building, larceny committed pursuant to this statute is not deemed a felony regardless of the value of the property taken. *See* G.S. 14-72(b)(2). Thus, if the defendant's intent was to steal items worth less than $1,000, it may be improper to allege that the defendant intended to commit a felony.
- The December 2023 amendments repealed subsection (a1) and enacted subsection (a2) of the statute, pinning a higher penalty to the correspondingly higher value of the property taken. (It is not entirely clear whether the legislature intended to add a taking element to the offense, which is otherwise lacking, but aggregating the value of any stolen property obviously requires that a taking occurred.)
- The December 2023 amendments also added subsection (c) to the statute, providing that violations occurring in more than one county and involving a taking may be aggregated into an alleged violation. Each county where a part of the charged offense occurred has concurrent venue per G.S. 15A-132.

- In the 2015 legislative session, the General Assembly enacted G.S. 14-56(b), which generally provides that it is not a violation of this statute to break or enter a vehicle in order to provide emergency medical assistance to a person therein. This appears to create an exception to the statute rather than to make the lack of such an emergency an element of the crime.

Sample Charge:
. . . unlawfully, willfully, and feloniously did break and enter a motor vehicle, a 2004 Oldsmobile belonging to Roger Leonard, which contained things of value, with the intent to commit larceny therein.

AOC Forms for This Offense:
None.

Punishment:
Class I felony. Offense 1 is Class C felony (property taken valued at > $100,000), Class F felony (property value of $50,000–$100,000), or Class G felony (property value of $20,000–$50,000). Offense 2 is a Class H felony.

G.S. 14-56.1
Breaking into a Coin- or Currency-Operated Machine
April 2024
Page 1 of 2

Introductory Comment:
An indictment or an information for the recidivist offense illustrated as Offense II below must comply with G.S. 15A-928, which requires that the defendant's prior convictions be alleged either (1) in a separate count of the indictment or information than the substantive offense or (2) in a separate indictment or information. This requirement does not apply to arrest warrants or magistrates' orders, which explains why two sets of charging language for Offense II appear below. G.S. 15A-928 also requires in indictments or informations that the name or title of an offense elevated by prior convictions must not make reference to such prior convictions.

Charging Language:

I. First offense

. . . unlawfully and willfully did [*choose one*: forcibly break into; use a key to open without authorization; use a (*name instrument*) to open without authorization] a (*choose one*: coin-operated; currency-operated) machine, a (*describe the machine*), which was the property of (*name the owner*), with the intent to steal any (*choose one or both*: money; property) therein.

II. Second or subsequent offense

A. Charging language for an arrest warrant or magistrate's order

. . . unlawfully, willfully, and feloniously did [*choose one*: forcibly break into; use a key to open without authorization; use a (*name instrument*) to open without authorization] a (*choose one*: coin-operated; currency-operated) machine, a (*describe the machine*), which was the property of (*name the owner*), with the intent to steal any (*choose one or both*: money; property) therein. The defendant was previously convicted of breaking into a (*choose one*: coin-operated; currency-operated) machine on the _____ day of ________________, ____, in the ______________ Court, ______________ County.

B. Charging language for an indictment or information

First count of indictment or information

. . . unlawfully, willfully, and feloniously did [*choose one*: forcibly break into; use a key to open without authorization; use a (*name instrument*) to open without authorization] a (*choose one*: coin-operated; currency-operated) machine, a (*describe the machine*), which was the property of (*name the owner*), with the intent to steal any (*choose one or both*: money; property) therein.

Second count of indictment or information

The defendant was previously convicted of breaking into a (*choose one*: coin-operated; currency-operated) machine on the _____ day of ________________, ____, in the ______________ Court, ______________ County.

Notes about Charging Language:

- The statute defines a coin- or currency-operated machine to include any coin- or currency-operated vending machine, pay telephone, telephone coin, or currency receptacle or other coin- or currency-activated machine.
- A charging document need not allege the owner of the coin- or currency-operated machine. State v. Price, 170 N.C. App. 672 (2005). However, because a charging document must identify the machine with reasonable particularity, this form asks for information about ownership.

Sample Charge:
. . . unlawfully and willfully did forcibly break into a coin-operated machine, a soft drink vending machine in the Durham County Courthouse, which was the property of Durham Concessions, Inc., with the intent to steal any money and property therein.

AOC Forms for This Offense:
None.

Punishment:
A first offense is a Class 1 misdemeanor. A second or subsequent offense is a Class I felony.

G.S. 14-56.2
Damaging a Coin- or Currency-Operated Machine
April 2024

Introductory Comment:
None.

Charging Language:
. . . unlawfully and willfully did maliciously (*choose one or both*: damage; destroy) a (*choose one*: coin-operated; currency-operated) machine, a (*describe the machine*), which was the property of (*name the owner*), by (*briefly describe how the machine was damaged or destroyed*).

Notes about Charging Language:
- The statute defines a coin- or currency-operated machine to include any coin- or currency-operated vending machine, pay telephone, telephone coin, or currency receptacle; or other coin or currency-activated machine.
- A charging document likely need not allege the owner of the coin- or currency-operated machine. *Cf.* State v. Price, 170 N.C. App. 672 (2005). However, because a charging document must identify the machine with reasonable particularity, this form asks for information about ownership.

Sample Charge:
. . . unlawfully and willfully did maliciously damage a coin-operated machine, a candy vending machine, located in the Knapp-Sanders Building on the UNC campus, Chapel Hill, N.C., which was the property of Triangle Caterers, Inc., by kicking the machine and hitting it with a bottle.

AOC Forms for This Offense:
None.

Punishment:
Class 1 misdemeanor.

G.S. 14-58
First-Degree Arson
April 2024

Introductory Comment:

The crime of arson may only be charged when a dwelling house is burned. If some other kind of building has been burned, choose the appropriate charge from the forms that follow in this publication. The dwelling must belong to someone other than the defendant, unless it is jointly occupied by the defendant and another person. If the defendant burns his or her own dwelling which is not jointly occupied, charge the offense in G.S. 14-65. First-degree arson should be charged when the dwelling house was occupied at the time of the burning; otherwise, second-degree arson is the proper charge.

Charging Language:

. . . unlawfully, willfully, and feloniously did maliciously burn the dwelling house inhabited by (*name owner or other possessor*) and located at (*give address of the dwelling house*). At the time of the burning, (*name person who was in the house at the time*) was in the dwelling house.

Notes about Charging Language:

- A burning requires some consumption of material, even though it may only constitute charring; a mere discoloration is insufficient.
- A "dwelling house" includes a mobile home. G.S. 14-58.2; State v. Hodge, 121 N.C. App. 209 (1995).

Sample Charge:

. . . unlawfully, willfully, and feloniously did maliciously burn the dwelling house inhabited by Albert R. Ramsey and Susan J. Ramsey and located at 4565 Cherry Lane, Pinetown, N.C. At the time of the burning, Susan J. Ramsey and Fred Ramsey were in the dwelling house.

AOC Forms for This Offense:

None.

Punishment:

Class D felony.

G.S. 14-58
Second-Degree Arson
April 2024

Introductory Comment:
The crime of arson may only be charged when a dwelling house is burned. If some other kind of building has been burned, choose the appropriate charge from the forms that follow in this publication. The dwelling must belong to someone other than the defendant, unless it is jointly occupied by the defendant and another person. If the defendant burns his or her own dwelling which is not jointly occupied, charge the offense in G.S. 14-65. First-degree arson should be charged when the dwelling house was occupied at the time of the burning; otherwise, second-degree arson is the proper charge.

Charging Language:
. . . unlawfully, willfully, and feloniously did maliciously burn the dwelling house inhabited by (*name owner or other possessor*) and located at (*give address of the dwelling house*).

Notes about Charging Language:
- A burning requires some consumption of material, even though it may only constitute charring; a mere discoloration is insufficient.
- A "dwelling house" includes a mobile home. State v. Hodge, 121 N.C. App. 209 (1995); *cf.* G.S. 14-58.2.

Sample Charge:
. . . unlawfully, willfully, and feloniously did maliciously burn the dwelling house inhabited by Albert R. Ramsey and Susan J. Ramsey and located at 4565 Cherry Lane, Pinetown, N.C.

AOC Forms for This Offense:
None.

Punishment:
Class E felony. (Class G felony for offenses committed prior to December 1, 2002. *See* S.L. 2022-8.)

G.S. 14-59
Burning of a Public Building
April 2024

Introductory Comment:
None.

Charging Language:
. . . unlawfully, willfully, and feloniously did wantonly (*choose one or more*: set fire to; burn; cause to be burned; aid the burning of; counsel the burning of; procure the burning of) a building owned by a governmental entity, (*name the governmental unit or agency owning or using the building*), and located at (*give the address of the building*).

Notes about Charging Language:

- The statute also covers the burning of buildings occupied by governmental agencies but not owned by them. If so, indicate the name of the actual owner and then add appropriate language such as "and occupied by a governmental entity, the Durham County Department of Social Services."
- The statute also covers the burning of buildings owned or occupied by "quasi-governmental entit[ies]," a term defined neither by statute nor case law. To charge the burning of such a building, modify the above language appropriately.
- Unlike arson, this offense may be committed when the building is set fire to, even though no burning takes place.

Sample Charge:
. . . unlawfully, willfully, and feloniously did wantonly burn a building owned by a governmental entity, Orange County, and located at 457 W. Franklin Street, Chapel Hill, N.C.

AOC Forms for This Offense:
None.

Punishment:
Class F felony.

G.S. 14-60
Burning of a Schoolhouse or Other Educational Building
April 2024

Introductory Comment:
This statute encompasses both public and private educational institutions.

Charging Language:
. . . unlawfully, willfully, and feloniously did wantonly (*choose one or more*: set fire to; burn; cause to be burned; aid the burning of; counsel the burning of; procure the burning of) a building owned by (*name the educational institution owning or using the building*), an educational institution, and located at (*give the address of the building*).

Notes about Charging Language:
- The statute also covers the burning of buildings leased or used by educational institutions but not owned by them. In a case involving such a building, give the name of the actual owner and then add appropriate language such as "and leased by the Durham Public Schools."
- Unlike arson, this offense may be committed when the building is set fire to, even though no burning takes place.

Sample Charge:
. . . unlawfully, willfully, and feloniously did wantonly set fire to a building owned by Burlington Properties, Inc., Burlington, N.C., and leased by the Alamance County Schools, an educational institution, and located at 600 Main Street, Burlington, N.C.

AOC Forms for This Offense:
None.

Punishment:
Class F felony.

G.S. 14-62
Burning of an Uninhabited House, Stable, etc.
April 2024

Introductory Comment:
This offense covers the burning of an uninhabited house, stable, coach house, or outhouse. Prior to December 1, 2022, it covered a wider range of structures, some of which are now covered by G.S. 14-62.3. *See* S.L. 2022-8. The same 2022 amendment made this offense applicable "[u]nless the conduct is covered under some other provision of law providing greater punishment." *Id.*

Charging Language:
. . . unlawfully, willfully, and feloniously did wantonly (*choose one or more*: set fire to; burn; cause to be burned; aid the burning of; counsel the burning of; procure the burning of) a(n) (*choose one:* uninhabited house; stable; coach house; outhouse), (*describe structure burned and its location*).

Notes about Charging Language:
- For this offense, the property burned need not be that "of another." A possessor who burns his or her own property violates the statute.
- Unlike arson, this offense may be committed when the building is set fire to, even though no burning takes place.

Sample Charge:
. . . unlawfully, willfully, and feloniously did wantonly set fire to an outhouse, a wooden structure located behind the log cabin at 414 Greenview Drive, Yanceyville, N.C.

AOC Forms for This Offense:
None.

Punishment:
Class F felony.

G.S. 14-62.1
Burning of a Building under Construction
April 2024

Introductory Comment:
As a result of S.L. 2022-8, as of December 1, 2022, this offense does not apply if "the conduct is covered under some other provision of law providing greater punishment."

Charging Language:
. . . unlawfully, willfully, and feloniously did wantonly (*choose one or more*: set fire to; burn; cause to be burned; aid the burning of; counsel the burning of; procure the burning of) a building in the process of construction (*choose one or both*: for use; for intended use) (*choose one*: as a dwelling house; in carrying on trade; in carrying on manufacture; *give other purpose*). The building is located at (*give address of building*).

Notes about Charging Language:
- The statute also covers the burning of "structures" under construction. If there is a question whether the object under construction is a building, the term "structure" might be substituted.
- The statute refers to buildings under construction "for use or intended to be used as a dwelling house or in carrying on any trade or manufacture, or otherwise. . . ." Because of that last phrase,
- the statute apparently covers all buildings under construction, no matter their intended use.
- For this offense, the property burned need not be that "of another." A possessor who burns his or her own property violates the statute.
- Unlike arson, this offense may be committed when the building is set fire to, even though no burning takes place.

Sample Charge:
. . . unlawfully, willfully, and feloniously did wantonly set fire to a building in the process of construction for use as a dwelling house. The building is located at 1109 Eastern Boulevard, Charlotte, N.C.

AOC Forms for This Offense:
None.

Punishment:
Class H felony.

G.S. 14-62.2
Burning of Churches or Certain Other Religious Buildings
April 2024

Introductory Comment:
This offense previously applied only to burnings of churches, chapels, and meetinghouses. Effective December 1, 2022, it was expanded to cover the additional types of premises set forth below. *See* S.L. 2022-8. The same bill added a provision stating that this offense does not apply if "the conduct is covered under some other provision of law providing greater punishment." *Id.*

Charging Language:
. . . unlawfully, willfully, and feloniously did wantonly (*choose one or more*: set fire to; burn; cause to be burned; aid the burning of; counsel the burning of; procure the burning of) a (*choose one and give description and location*: church; chapel; meetinghouse; synagogue; temple; longhouse; mosque; building that is regularly used, and clearly identifiable, as a place for religious worship).

Notes about Charging Language:
- No appellate case law clarifies the scope of the various types of premises set forth in the statute.
- Unlike arson, this offense may be committed when the building is set fire to, even though no burning takes place.

Sample Charge:
. . . unlawfully, willfully, and feloniously did wantonly burn a church, Siler Baptist Church, located at 2888 Old Canton Mill Road, Westville, N.C.

AOC Forms for This Offense:
None.

Punishment:
Class E felony.

G.S. 14-62.3
Burning of Commercial Structure
April 2024

Introductory Comment:
This offense was enacted by S.L. 2022-8 and is effective for offenses committed on or after December 1, 2022. For offenses committed prior to that date, consider whether the offense was covered by the version of G.S. 14-62 in effect at that time. This offense applies to conduct "[u]nless the conduct is covered under some other provision of law providing greater punishment." G.S. 14-62.3(b).

Charging Language:

I. Occupied structure

. . . unlawfully, willfully, and feloniously did wantonly (*choose one or more:* set fire to; burn; cause to be burned; aid the burning of; counsel the burning of; procure the burning of) (*choose one or both:* a commercial structure; the contents of a commercial structure), namely, (*describe structure, and if appropriate, contents*). The structure was occupied by (*name person*) at the time of the burning.

II. Unoccupied structure

. . . unlawfully, willfully, and feloniously did wantonly (*choose one or more:* set fire to; burn; cause to be burned; aid the burning of; counsel the burning of; procure the burning of) (*choose one or both*: a commercial structure; the contents of a commercial structure), namely, (*describe structure, and if appropriate, contents*). The structure was unoccupied at the time of the burning.

Notes about Charging Language:

- The statute provides that a "commercial structure" means "any building or structure that is designed principally for the manufacture, distribution, or exchange of goods or services, or for any other business or trade purpose."
- Unlike arson, this offense may be committed when the structure is set fire to, even if no burning takes place.
- The property burned need not be the property of another. A person who burns his or her own commercial structure may be charged with this offense.

Sample Charge:

I. Occupied structure

. . . unlawfully, willfully, and feloniously did wantonly set fire to a commercial structure, namely, Frank Hill's Locksmith Shop, located at 808 Elm Street, Fairview, N.C. The structure was occupied by Denise Hill at the time of the burning.

AOC Forms for This Offense:
None.

Punshment:
Offense I is a Class D felony. Offense II is a Class E felony.

G.S. 14-65
Occupant or Owner Burning Dwelling House
April 2024

Introductory Comment:
This offense is normally used when a person burns a dwelling that he or she alone occupies. Arson may be charged when a person burns a dwelling that he or she owns or occupies jointly with another person.

Charging Language:

I. Fire set for fraudulent purpose

. . . unlawfully, willfully, and feloniously did for a fraudulent purpose (*choose one or more*: set fire to; burn; cause to be burned; aid the burning of; counsel the burning of; procure the burning of) the dwelling house located at (*give the address of the dwelling house*). At the time of the offense, the defendant was the (*choose one*: owner; occupant) of the dwelling house, and the defendant did this act for the fraudulent purpose of (*indicate the fraudulent purpose for the burning*).

II. Fire set wantonly and willfully

. . . unlawfully, willfully, and feloniously did wantonly (*choose one or more*: set fire to; burn; cause to be burned; aid the burning of; counsel the burning of; procure the burning of) the dwelling house of which the defendant was at the time the (*choose one*: owner; occupant), and which was located at (*give the address of the dwelling house*).

Notes about Charging Language:
- The statute also covers the burning, by the building's owner, of a building designed or intended for use as a dwelling house. If the building was not at the time of the offense being used as a dwelling house but was designed or intended for that purpose, alter the charging language accordingly.
- Unlike arson, this offense may be committed when the building is set fire to, even though no burning takes place.
- Under some circumstances, it may be appropriate to charge insurance fraud in violation of G.S. 58-2-161 instead of, or in addition to, the fraudulent purpose offense set forth above.

Sample Charge:

I. Fire set for fraudulent purpose

. . . unlawfully, willfully, and feloniously did for a fraudulent purpose burn the dwelling house located at 910 Woodlawn Drive, Winston-Salem, N.C. At the time of the offense, the defendant was the owner of the dwelling house, and he did this act for the fraudulent purpose of collecting payments under a homeowner's insurance policy.

AOC Forms for This Offense:
None.

Punishment:
Class H felony.

G.S. 14-66
Burning of Personal Property
April 2024

Introductory Comment:
This statute covers the burning of goods, wares, merchandise, or other chattels or personal property of any kind with the intent to injure any person. The person injured may be, for example, the owner, an insurer of the property, a creditor, or some other person with an interest in the property. A person may be guilty of this offense for burning his or her own personal property if that burning would injure or prejudice another, such as a lien holder or insurer. Effective December 1, 2022, this offense was amended by S.L. 2022-8 so that it applies to burning property "any place other than a commercial structure as defined in G.S. 14-62.3." If the offense took place within a commercial structure, charge the offense in G.S. 14-62.3 instead.

Charging Language:
. . . unlawfully, willfully, and feloniously did wantonly (*choose one or more*: set fire to; burn; cause to be burned; aid the burning of; counsel the burning of; procure the burning of) the following personal property: (*describe the property burned*). This act was done with the intent to injure or prejudice (*name the person who suffered the harm and state his or her relationship to the property*). This act did not take place inside a commercial structure as defined in G.S. 14-62.3.

Notes about Charging Language:
- The allegation that the act did not take place within a commercial structure was added in case a court determines that is an element of the offense rather than an exception or an affirmative defense. *Cf.* State v. Rankin, 371 N.C. 885 (2018) (ruling that certain location-based provisions in the anti-littering statute were elements rather than exceptions).
- Unlike arson, this offense may be committed if the property is set fire to, even though no burning takes place.

Sample Charge:
. . . unlawfully, willfully, and feloniously did wantonly set fire to the following personal property: a 2004 Ford Mustang automobile, N.C. license no. FAB 747. This act was done with the intent to injure or prejudice Charles J. Lamb, the owner of the automobile. This act did not take place within a commercial structure.

AOC Forms for This Offense:
None.

Punishment:
Class H felony.

G.S. 14-69.1
Making a False Report Concerning a Destructive Device
April 2024
Page 1 of 2

Introductory Comment:
If a defendant is convicted of a violation of the public building offense set forth in G.S. 14-69.1(c), illustrated as Offense II below, within five years of an earlier conviction under G.S. 14-69.1(c), the later offense is elevated from a Class H to a Class G felony. An indictment or an information for the recidivist offense must comply with G.S. 15A-928, which requires that the defendant's prior convictions be alleged either (1) in a separate count of the indictment or information than the substantive offense or (2) in a separate indictment or information. In such a case, the separate count or separate indictment should set forth the date and court in which the prior conviction occurred. This requirement does not apply to arrest warrants or magistrates' orders, which still must allege the defendant's prior convictions but need not do so in a separate count or separate charging instrument. G.S. 15A-928 also requires in indictments or informations that the name or title of an offense elevated by prior convictions must not make reference to such prior convictions.

Charging Language:

I. False report concerning place other than public building **G.S. 14-69.1(a)**

. . . unlawfully, willfully, and feloniously did communicate a report, by (*describe means of communication*) to (*identify person, if known, who received communication*), (*choose one or both*: knowing; having reason to know) the report to be false, that there was located (*choose one*: in; in sufficient proximity to cause damage to) a (*choose one and describe*: building; house; structure; vehicle; aircraft; vessel; boat) a device designed to (*choose one or both*: destroy; damage) the (*choose one*: building; house; structure; vehicle; aircraft; vessel; boat) by (*choose one or more*: explosion; blasting; burning).

II. False report concerning public building **G.S. 14-69.1(c)**

. . . unlawfully, willfully, and feloniously did communicate a report, by (*describe means of communication*) to (*identify person, if known, who received communication*), (*choose one or both*: knowing; having reason to know) the report to be false, that there was located (*choose one*: in; in sufficient proximity to cause damage to) a public building, (*describe building*), a device designed to (*choose one or both*: destroy; damage) the public building by (*choose one or more*: explosion; blasting; burning).

Notes about Charging Language:

- The report may be made by any means of communication, including making the information available to another person by computer. G.S. 14-69.1(a), (e).
- The statute contains a definition of "public building." G.S. 14-69.1(c).

Sample Charge:

I. False report concerning place other than public building **G.S. 14-69.1(a)**

. . . unlawfully, willfully, and feloniously did communicate a report, by telephone to John Smith, knowing and having reason to know the report to be false, that there was located in a building, Food Lion Store, 23 Main Street, East End, N.C., a device designed to destroy and damage the building by explosion.

AOC Forms for This Offense:
None.

Punishment:
Class H felony. If a defendant is convicted of a violation of the public building offense set forth in G.S. 14-69.1(c) within five years of an earlier conviction under G.S. 14-69.1(c), the later offense is a Class G felony.

G.S. 14-71(a), -72(a)
Receiving Stolen Goods
April 2024
Page 1 of 2

Introductory Comment:
Two statutes address the receiving of stolen goods: G.S. 14-71(a) and -72(a). At best, the statutes are redundant. At worst, they are slightly inconsistent. For example, G.S. 14-71(a) allows any felonious taking to serve as the underlying theft, while G.S. 14-72(a) arguably applies only when the underlying theft is a larceny. And while G.S. 14-72(a) provides for both misdemeanor and felony possession offenses, G.S. 14-71(a) creates only a felony offense. Without carefully reconciling these statutes, courts generally have held that receiving stolen goods is a felony if (1) the goods are worth more than $1,000 or (2) the defendant knew or should have known that the goods were stolen under circumstances that amounted to felony larceny under G.S. 14-72(b). Otherwise, it is a misdemeanor. Receiving stolen goods is not an appropriate charge when the defendant stole the goods, but possession of stolen goods may be charged in that case.

Charging Language:
. . . unlawfully, willfully, and feloniously did receive (*describe the property*), the personal property of (*name the possessor*), valued at (*state value*), which property was stolen property, knowing and having reasonable grounds to believe the property to have been (*choose one*)

(1) feloniously stolen, taken, and carried away.
(2) feloniously stolen, taken, and carried away from the person of (*name person from whom taken*).
(3) feloniously stolen, taken, and carried away pursuant to a violation of Section (*insert* 14-51, 14-53, 14-54, 14-54.1, *or* 14-57, *as appropriate*) of the General Statutes.
(4) feloniously stolen, taken, and carried away in that it was a (*name or describe device*), an explosive or incendiary device or substance.
(5) feloniously stolen, taken, and carried away in that it was a (*name or describe firearm*), a firearm.
(6) feloniously stolen, taken, and carried away in that it was a (*choose one*: record; paper) in the custody of the North Carolina State Archives.
(7) if the charge is a misdemeanor, strike through "and feloniously," use option (1), and replace the word "feloniously" in option (1) with "unlawfully."

Notes about Charging Language:
- If the charge is a misdemeanor, strike through "and feloniously," use option (1), and replace the word "feloniously" in option (1) with "unlawfully."
- The statute covers a person receiving stolen goods either knowing or having reasonable grounds to believe they are stolen. If it is not clear that the defendant knew the goods were stolen, strike out the words "knowing and."
- It is not legally necessary to allege the possessor of the property. State v. Medlin, 86 N.C. App. 114 (1987). For clarity, however, this form requests that information.

Sample Charge:
. . . unlawfully and willfully did receive a blue nylon Sno-Tite two-man tent, the personal property of Willis Hagbarger, valued at $195, which property was stolen property, knowing and having reasonable grounds to believe the property to have been feloniously stolen, taken, and carried away.

AOC Forms for This Offense:
None.

Punishment:
Class 1 misdemeanor or Class H felony.

G.S. 14-71(b)
Receiving or Possessing Goods Represented as Stolen
April 2024

Introductory Comment:
None.

Charging Language:
. . . unlawfully, willfully, and feloniously did (*choose one both*: receive; possess) (*describe the property*), property in the custody of (*name agency*), a law enforcement agency, that was explicitly represented as stolen to the defendant by (*choose one*)

(1) (*name agent*), an agent of that law enforcement agency.

(2) (*name person*), a person authorized to act on behalf of that law enforcement agency.

Notes about Charging Language:
- It is not clear whether the indictment must name the person who made the representation to the defendant. It is safest to include it, so this form requests it.

Sample Charge:
. . . unlawfully, willfully, and feloniously did possess forty cans of Enfamil infant formula, property in the custody of the Hertford County Sheriff's Office, a law enforcement agency, that was explicitly represented as stolen to the defendant by Dawn Johnson, an agent of that law enforcement agency.

AOC Forms for This Offense:
None.

Punishment:
Class H felony.

Introductory Comment:

Two statutes address the possession of stolen goods: G.S. 14-71.1 and -72(a). At best, the statutes are redundant. At worst, they are slightly inconsistent. For example, G.S. 14-71.1 allows any felonious taking to serve as the underlying theft, while G.S. 14-72(a) arguably applies only when the underlying theft is a larceny. And while G.S. 14-72(a) provides for both misdemeanor and felony possession offenses, G.S. 14-71.1 creates only a felony offense. Without carefully reconciling these statutes, the courts generally have ruled that possessing stolen goods is a felony if (1) the goods are worth more than $1,000 or (2) the defendant knew or should have known that the goods were stolen under circumstances that amounted to felony larceny under G.S. 14-72(b). Otherwise, it is a misdemeanor. Unlike receiving stolen goods, possessing stolen goods may be an appropriate charge when the defendant stole the goods at issue.

Charging Language:

. . . unlawfully, willfully, and feloniously did possess (*describe the property*), the personal property of (*name the possessor*), valued at (*state value*), which property was stolen property, knowing and having reasonable grounds to believe the property to have been (*select one of the following*):

(1) feloniously stolen, taken, and carried away.
(2) feloniously stolen, taken, and carried away from the person of (*name person from whom taken*).
(3) feloniously stolen, taken, and carried away pursuant to a violation of Section (*insert* 14-51, 14-53, 14-54, 14-54.1, *or* 14-57, *as appropriate*) of the General Statutes.
(4) feloniously stolen, taken, and carried away in that it was a (*name or describe device*), an explosive or incendiary device or substance.
(5) feloniously stolen, taken, and carried away in that it was a (*name or describe firearm*), a firearm.
(6) feloniously stolen, taken, and carried away in that it was a (*choose one*: record, paper) in the custody of the North Carolina State Archives.
(7) feloniously taken and carried away in a manner amounting to (*name the felony*).

Notes about Charging Language:

- Strike through "and feloniously" after "willfully" if the charge is a misdemeanor, and strike through "feloniously" before "stolen, taken, and carried away." In such a case, it probably is not necessary to allege the value of the property. However, for clarity, this form requests that information.
- The statute covers a person possessing stolen goods with either (1) the knowledge that they are stolen or (2) reasonable grounds to believe that they are stolen. If it is not clear that the defendant knew the goods were stolen, strike out the words "knowing and."
- It is not legally necessary to allege the possessor of the property. State v. Medlin, 86 N.C. App. 114 (1987). For clarity, however, this form requests that information.

Sample Charge:
. . . unlawfully, willfully, and feloniously did possess a Sony radio, the personal property of Roger Watts, valued at $45, which property was stolen property, knowing and having reasonable grounds to believe the property to have been feloniously stolen, taken, and carried away pursuant to a violation of section 14-51 of the General Statutes.

AOC Forms for This Offense:
AOC-CR-126 (Indictment, with Burglary)
AOC-CR-134 (Indictment, with Felony Breaking/Entering and Felony Larceny)
AOC-CR-138 (Indictment, with Felony Larceny)
AOC-J-319 (Juvenile Petition, with Larceny)
AOC-J-334 (Juvenile Petition)

Punishment:
Class 1 misdemeanor or Class H felony.

G.S. 14-71.2
Possessing, Receiving, or Transferring Stolen Vehicle
April 2024

Introductory Comment:
None.

Charging Language:

I. Possessing stolen vehicle

. . . unlawfully, willfully, and feloniously did possess a vehicle, (*describe vehicle and owner*), which was stolen property and which the defendant knew and had reason to believe had been stolen and unlawfully taken.

II. Receiving stolen vehicle

. . . unlawfully, willfully, and feloniously did, with the intent to procure title to a vehicle, (*describe vehicle and owner*), which was stolen property and which the defendant knew and had reason to believe had been stolen and unlawfully taken, receive that vehicle from (*name person vehicle received from*).

III. Transferring stolen vehicle

. . . unlawfully, willfully, and feloniously did, with the intent to pass title to a vehicle, (*describe the vehicle and owner*), which was stolen property and which the defendant knew and had reason to believe had been stolen and unlawfully taken, transfer possession of that vehicle to (*name person vehicle transferred to*).

Notes about Charging Language:

- Although the charging language above says "knew and had reason to believe," the statute requires only that the defendant knew *or* had reason to believe; thus, you may omit one or the other of the allegations if appropriate.
- Although the charging language above says "had been stolen and unlawfully taken," the statute requires only that the vehicle be stolen *or* unlawfully taken; thus, you may omit one or the other of the allegations if appropriate.

Sample Charge:

I. Possessing stolen vehicle

. . . unlawfully, willfully, and feloniously did possess a vehicle, a 2004 Chevrolet, vehicle identification number TFN9912401, the property of Peter Graves, which was stolen property and which the defendant knew and had reason to believe had been stolen and unlawfully taken.

AOC Forms for This Offense:
None.

Punishment:
Class H felony.

Introductory Comment:
Use this form to charge misdemeanor larceny or larceny that is a felony because of the value of the goods taken (over $1,000). Other forms in this manual should be used to charge larceny that is a felony because it falls within one of the circumstances listed in G.S. 14-72(b), such as larceny of a firearm or larceny from the person.

Charging Language:
. . . unlawfully, willfully, and feloniously did steal, take, and carry away (*describe the property taken*), the personal property of (*name the possessor*), such property having a value of (*state value*).

Notes about Charging Language:

- Strike through "and feloniously" if the charge is a misdemeanor. Traditionally, the word "feloniously" was used even when the larceny is a misdemeanor. In *State v. Wesson*, 16 N.C. App. 683 (1972), the court of appeals ruled that this is not necessary.
- When a larceny is accomplished through misrepresentation, it is sometimes called "larceny by trick." A charging document need not "allege the manner in which the stolen property was taken and carried away, and the words 'by trick' need not be found in an indictment charging larceny." State v. Harris, 35 N.C. App. 401, 402 (1978). Of course, in many circumstances, a defendant who obtains property through misrepresentation may properly be charged with obtaining property by false pretenses.
- The possessor of the property is not necessarily the owner or the custodian of the property. The possessor is usually the one who has control over the property—thus the person who leases a piece of furniture is the possessor of it, not the company that owns the furniture. In some cases, however, a person will be in control of property only as part of his or her employment. In that case, the employer is the possessor, while the employee is only the custodian. If there is doubt about who the possessor is, list all of those who might be in possession and indicate their relationship to the property.
- The possessor of the property must be a person or an entity, such as a corporation, that is capable of owning property. If the possessor is an entity, indicate the nature of the entity in the manner shown in the first sample charge, below. At a bare minimum, allege the name of the entity and that the entity is capable of owning property. *See* State v. Brawley, 370 N.C. 626 (2018) (holding that "Belk's Department Stores, an entity capable of owning property," sufficiently identified the victim). If the possessor is a natural person, include the person's name.

Sample Charges:
. . . unlawfully and willfully did steal, take, and carry away a zircon ring, the personal property of Johnson's Jewelers, Inc., a corporation, such property having a value of $85.

. . . unlawfully, willfully, and feloniously did steal, take, and carry away an Apache 460 riding lawn mower, the personal property of L. G. Wilson, such property having a value of $1,075.

AOC Forms for This Offense:
AOC-CR-138 (Indictment, for felonies only)
AOC-J-319 (Juvenile Petition)

Punishment:
If the value of the property is $1,000 or less, the larceny is a Class 1 misdemeanor. If the value of the property is over $1,000, the larceny is a Class H felony.

G.S. 14-72(b)(1)
Larceny from the Person
April 2024

Introductory Comment:
None.

Charging Language:

. . . unlawfully, willfully, and feloniously did steal, take, and carry away (*describe the property taken*), the personal property of (*name the possessor*), from (*choose one*)

(1) (*choose one*: his; her) person.

(2) the person of (*name the person from whom the property was taken*).

Notes about Charging Language:

- The possessor of the property is not necessarily the owner or the custodian of the property. The possessor is usually the one who has control over the property—thus the person who leases a piece of furniture is the possessor of it, not the company that owns the furniture. In some cases, however, a person will be in control of property only as part of his or her employment. In that case, the employer is the possessor, while the employee is only the custodian. If there is doubt about who the possessor is, list all of those who might be in possession and indicate their relationship to the property.
- The possessor of the property must be a person or an entity, such as a corporation, that is capable of owning property. If the possessor is an entity, indicate the nature of the entity in the manner shown in the second sample charge, below. At a bare minimum, allege the name of the entity and that the entity is capable of owning property. *See* State v. Brawley, 370 N.C. 626 (2018) (holding that "Belk's Department Stores, an entity capable of owning property," sufficiently identified the victim).

Sample Charges:

. . . unlawfully, willfully, and feloniously did steal, take, and carry away a zircon ring consisting of a stone in a stainless steel setting, the personal property of Harlan Turner, from his person.

. . . unlawfully, willfully, and feloniously did steal, take, and carry away a zircon ring consisting of a stone in a stainless steel setting, the personal property of Johnson's Jewelers, Inc., a corporation, from the person of Harlan Turner.

AOC Forms for This Offense:
None.

Punishment:
Class H felony.

G.S. 14-72(b)(2)
Larceny Pursuant to Burglary or Breaking or Entering
April 2024
Page 1 of 2

Introductory Comment:
None.

Charging Language:
. . . unlawfully, willfully, and feloniously did steal, take, and carry away (*describe the property taken*), the personal property of (*name the possessor*), pursuant to a violation of Section (*choose* 14-51, 14-53, 14-54, 14-54.1, *or* 14-57) of the General Statutes of North Carolina.

Notes about Charging Language:

- The possessor of the property is not necessarily the owner or the custodian of the property. The possessor is usually the one who has control over the property—thus the person who leases a piece of furniture is the possessor of it, not the company that owns the furniture. In some cases, however, a person will be in control of property only as part of his or her employment. In that case, the employer is the possessor, while the employee is only the custodian. If there is doubt about who the possessor is, list all of those who might be in possession and indicate their relationship to the property.
- The possessor of the property must be a person or an entity, such as a corporation, that is capable of owning property. If the possessor is an entity, indicate the nature of the entity in the manner shown in the second sample charge, below. At a bare minimum, allege the name of the entity and that the entity is capable of owning property. *See* State v. Brawley, 370 N.C. 626 (2018) (holding that "Belk's Department Stores, an entity capable of owning property," sufficiently identified the victim).
- The offenses referenced in the charging language are as follows:
    - G.S. 14-51: First-Degree and Second-Degree Burglary
    - G.S. 14-53: Breaking Out of Dwelling
    - G.S. 14-54: Breaking or Entering Buildings
    - G.S. 14-54.1: Breaking or Entering Places of Worship
    - G.S. 14-57: Burglary with Explosives
- Note that larceny pursuant to breaking and entering a motor vehicle, boat, etc., under G.S. 14-56 is not automatically a felony. The goods taken must be valued at over $1,000 for that larceny to be a felony.

Sample Charges:
. . . unlawfully, willfully, and feloniously did steal, take, and carry away a Sony DVD player/recorder, serial no. 158234, the personal property of Frank Rugby, pursuant to a violation of Section 14-51 of the General Statutes of North Carolina.

. . . unlawfully, willfully, and feloniously did steal, take, and carry away a Stihl chain saw with a nineteen-inch blade, the personal property of Helverson's Hardware, Inc., a corporation, pursuant to a violation of Section 14-54 of the General Statutes of North Carolina.

AOC Forms for This Offense:
AOC-CR-126 (Indictment, with Burglary)
AOC-J-313 (Juvenile Petition, with Breaking or Entering)

Punishment:
Class H felony.

G.S. 14-72(b)(4)
Larceny of a Firearm
April 2024

Introductory Comment:
None.

Charging Language:
. . . unlawfully, willfully, and feloniously did steal, take, and carry away a (*name or describe the firearm*), a firearm, the personal property of (*name the possessor of the firearm*).

Notes about Charging Language:

- The statute defines a firearm as "any instrument used in the propulsion of a shot, shell or bullet by the action of gunpowder or any other explosive substance within it." The definition includes a firearm that is not capable of being fired at the time of the theft but that could be made to work. Air rifles and air pistols are specifically excluded from the definition.
- The possessor of the property is not necessarily the owner or the custodian of the property. The possessor is usually the one who has control over the property—thus the person who leases a piece of furniture is the possessor of it, not the company that owns the furniture. In some cases, however, a person will be in control of property only as part of his or her employment. In that case, the employer is the possessor, while the employee is only the custodian. If there is doubt about who the possessor is, list all of those who might be in possession and indicate their relationship to the property.
- The possessor of the property must be a person or an entity, such as a corporation, that is capable of owning property. If the possessor is an entity, indicate the nature of the entity in the manner shown in the first sample charge, below. At a bare minimum, allege the name of the entity and that the entity is capable of owning property. *See* State v. Brawley, 370 N.C. 626 (2018) (holding that "Belk's Department Stores, an entity capable of owning property," sufficiently identified the victim).

Sample Charges:
. . . unlawfully, willfully, and feloniously did steal, take, and carry away a 9mm Glock handgun, serial no. 42778462, the personal property of The Gunnery, Inc., a corporation.

. . . unlawfully, willfully, and feloniously did steal, take, and carry away a .38-caliber Smith and Wesson revolver, a firearm, the personal property of Joan Faulkner.

AOC Forms for This Offense:
None.

Punishment:
Class H felony.

G.S. 14-72(b)(6)
Habitual Misdemeanor Larceny
April 2024
Page 1 of 2

Introductory Comment:
An indictment or an information for this offense must comply with G.S. 15A-928, which requires that the defendant's prior convictions be alleged either in (1) a count of the indictment or information separate from the substantive offense or (2) a separate indictment or information. This requirement does not apply to arrest warrants or magistrates' orders, which explains why two sets of charging language appear below.

G.S. 15A-928 also requires that an "improvised name or title" be used so that the title of the indictment or information does not refer to the defendant's prior convictions. Therefore, an indictment or information charging habitual misdemeanor larceny should be captioned "larceny pursuant to G.S. 14-72(b)(6)" or something similar.

Charging Language:

I. Charging language for an arrest warrant or magistrate's order

. . . unlawfully, willfully, and feloniously did steal, take, and carry away (*describe the property taken*), the personal property of (*name the possessor*). This offense was committed after the defendant had been convicted of at least four previous larceny offenses. The defendant was convicted of the offense of (*name offense*) on (*give date of conviction*), in (*name court and, if desired, give case number*). The defendant was convicted of the offense of (*name offense*) on (*give date of conviction*), in (*name court and, if desired, give case number*). The defendant was convicted of the offense of (*name offense*) on (*give date of conviction*), in (*name court and, if desired, give case number*). The defendant was convicted of the offense of (*name offense*) on (*give date of conviction*), in (*name court and, if desired, give case number*).

II. Charging language for an indictment or information

First count of indictment or information

. . . unlawfully, willfully, and feloniously did steal, take, and carry away (*describe the property taken*), the personal property of (*name the possessor*).

Second count of indictment or information

The offense in count I, above, was committed after the defendant had been convicted of at least four previous larceny offenses. The defendant was convicted of the offense of (*name offense*) on (*give date of conviction*), in (*name court and, if desired, give case number*). The defendant was convicted of the offense of (*name offense*) on (*give date of conviction*), in (*name court and, if desired, give case number*). The defendant was convicted of the offense of (*name offense*) on (*give date of conviction*), in (*name court and, if desired, give case number*). The defendant was convicted of the offense of (*name offense*) on (*give date of conviction*), in (*name court and, if desired, give case number*).

Notes about Charging Language:

- When creating the portion of the charging document that alleges the current larceny, as opposed to the portion that alleges the defendant's prior convictions, it may be helpful to consult the notes contained in the form regarding misdemeanor larceny. Those notes are not reproduced here.
- More than four previous larceny convictions may be alleged if desired. However, previous convictions alleged in the charging document likely cannot be used when calculating the defendant's prior record level. *Cf.* State v. Cooper, 154 N.C. App. 521 (2002) (unpublished) (so holding, in the context of habitual misdemeanor assault); State v. Gentry, 135 N.C. App. 107 (1999) (so holding, in the context of habitual DWI).
- G.S. 14-72(b)(6) states that a conviction shall not count as a prior conviction for purposes of this offense unless the defendant was represented by counsel or waived counsel in connection with the prior conviction. The North Carolina Court of Appeals has held that this counsel requirement is not an essential element of the offense of habitual misdemeanor larceny and, thus, indictments for this offense need not allege that a defendant was represented by or waived counsel in connection with his or her prior convictions. State v. Edgerton, 266 N.C. App. 521 (2019).
- Attempted misdemeanor larceny does not qualify as an eligible prior conviction for purposes of charging this offense. State v. Irvins, 277 N.C. App. 101 (2021).

Sample Charges:

I. Charging language for an arrest warrant or magistrate's order

. . . unlawfully, willfully, and feloniously did steal, take, and carry away a Razor scooter, the personal property of Oliver Abrams. This offense was committed after the defendant had been convicted of at least four previous larceny offenses. The defendant was convicted of the offense of larceny on January 7, 2012, in Currituck County District Court. The defendant was convicted of the offense of larceny of a firearm on September 9, 2013, in Onslow County Superior Court. The defendant was convicted of the offense of larceny on July 17, 2018, in Horry County (South Carolina) Circuit Court. The defendant was convicted of the offense of larceny on August 3, 2020, in Onslow County District Court.

II. Charging language for an indictment or information

First count of indictment or information

. . . unlawfully, willfully, and feloniously did steal, take, and carry away a Razor scooter, the personal property of Oliver Abrams.

Second count of indictment or information

The offense in count I, above, was committed after the defendant had been convicted of at least four previous larceny offenses. The defendant was convicted of the offense of larceny on January 7, 2012, in Currituck County District Court. The defendant was convicted of the offense of larceny of a firearm on September 9, 2013, in Onslow County Superior Court. The defendant was convicted of the offense of larceny on July 17, 2018, in Horry County (South Carolina) Circuit Court. The defendant was convicted of the offense of larceny on August 3, 2020, in Onslow County District Court.

AOC Forms for This Offense:

None.

Punishment:

Class H felony.

G.S. 14-72.1
Shoplifting (Concealment of Merchandise)
April 2024
Page 1 of 3

Introductory Comment:
There are two ways in which the offense of shoplifting may be committed: (1) by concealing goods or merchandise while on the premises of a store and (2) by altering or replacing an item's price tag to reflect a lower price.

Under certain circumstances, repeat offenders face higher sentences, as described below. An indictment or an information for a recidivist offense must comply with G.S. 15A-928, which requires that the defendant's prior convictions be alleged either (1) in a separate count of the indictment or information than the substantive offense or (2) in a separate indictment or information. This requirement does not apply to arrest warrants or magistrates' orders, which still must allege the defendant's prior convictions but need not do so in a separate count or separate charging instrument. If charging the recidivist offense in an indictment or information, set forth the paragraph of the charging language relating to prior offenses in a separate count or in a separate indictment or information. Also note that in situations where a conviction for a recidivist offense is appealed from district to superior court for trial de novo, G.S. 15A-922(h) and -928(d) require the State to replace the pleading in the case with superseding statements of charges separately alleging the substantive offense and any prior convictions. G.S. 15A-928 also requires that the name or title of an offense elevated by prior convictions must not make reference to such prior convictions.

Charging Language:

I. Concealment of merchandise **G.S. 14-72.1(a)**

. . . unlawfully and willfully did without authority conceal (*describe the property*), the goods and merchandise of a store, (*name the store*), while still upon the premises of the store and not having theretofore purchased the goods and merchandise.

Fill in the paragraph below only if a prior offense (or offenses) is being charged.

The defendant was previously convicted of the crime of (*choose one*: willful concealment of a store's goods; willful transfer of price tag on merchandise presented for purchase; willful substitution of price tag on merchandise presented for purchase; willful marking merchandise at lower price and presenting it for purchase) on the _________ day of ___________________, _____, in the ______________ Court, ________________ County. And the defendant was previously convicted of the crime of (*choose one*: willful concealment of a store's goods; willful transfer of price tag on merchandise presented for purchase; willful substitution of false price tag on merchandise presented for purchase; willful marking merchandise at lower price and presenting it for purchase) on the _________ day of ___________________, _____, in the ______________ Court, ________________ County.

II. Substitution or transfer of price tag or marking goods at lower price **G.S. 14-72.1(d)**

. . . unlawfully and willfully did (*choose one*)

(1) transfer a price tag from merchandise to other merchandise, (*identify merchandise*), having a higher selling price, and present the merchandise for purchase at (*name the store*).

(2) substitute and superimpose a false price tag on merchandise, (*identify merchandise*), and present the merchandise for purchase at (*name the store*).

(3) mark merchandise, (*identify merchandise*), at a lower price and present the merchandise for purchase at (*name the store*).

Fill in the paragraph below only if a prior offense (or offenses) is being charged.

The defendant was previously convicted of the crime of (*choose one*: willful concealment of a store's goods; willful transfer of price tag on merchandise presented for purchase; willful substitution of price tag on merchandise presented for purchase; willful marking merchandise at lower price and presenting it for purchase) on the _________ day of ___________________, _____, in the ______________ Court, ________________ County. And the defendant was previously convicted of the crime of (*choose one*: willful concealment of a store's goods; willful transfer of price tag on merchandise presented for purchase; willful substitution of false price tag on merchandise presented for purchase; willful marking merchandise at lower price and presenting it for purchase) on the _________ day of ___________________, _____, in the ______________ Court, ________________ County.

Notes about Charging Language:

- Concealment of merchandise is a Class H felony if a person uses a lead-lined or aluminum-lined bag, a lead-lined or aluminum-lined article of clothing, or similar device to prevent the activation of any anti-shoplifting or inventory-control device. If that is the case, add the words "and feloniously" after "willfully" in the charging language above and add a sentence to the criminal pleading, such as "The defendant committed this offense by using a lead-lined bag to prevent the activation of an anti-shoplifting or inventory-control device."
- Allege one prior conviction only if it occurred within three years of the date of the current offense being charged. Allege two prior convictions only if they both occurred within five years of the date of the current offense being charged.

Sample Charge:

I. Concealment of merchandise **G.S. 14-72.1(a)**

. . . unlawfully and willfully did without authority conceal a set of 1/4-inch Black and Decker drill bits, the goods and merchandise of a store, Fred Fulcher d/b/a Fulcher-Mechilsen Hardware Store, while still upon the premises of the store and not having theretofore purchased the goods and merchandise.

The defendant was previously convicted of the crime of willful concealment of a store's goods on the 15th day of November, 2017, in the District Court, Durham County.

AOC Forms for This Offense:

AOC-J-315 (Juvenile Petition)

Punishment:
A first offense or a subsequent offense not covered by any of the provisions below is a Class 3 misdemeanor, with special requirements for sentencing as provided in G.S. 14-72.1(e)–(g).

A second offense committed within three years of a prior conviction of any offense under G.S. 14-72.1 is a Class 2 misdemeanor, with special requirements for sentencing as provided in G.S. 14-72.1(e)–(g).

A third offense committed within five years of two prior convictions of any offense under G.S. 14-72.1 is a Class 1 misdemeanor, with special requirements for sentencing as provided in G.S. 14-72.1(e)–(g).

It is a Class H felony to violate G.S. 14-72.1(a) by using a lead-lined or aluminum-lined bag, a lead-lined or aluminum-lined article of clothing, or similar device to prevent the activation of any antishoplifting or inventory-control device.

G.S. 14-72.2
Unauthorized Use of Motor-Propelled Conveyance
April 2024

Introductory Comment:
None.

Charging Language:

I. Motor-propelled conveyance other than aircraft

. . . unlawfully and willfully did, without the express or implied consent of the owner or person in lawful possession, take and operate (*describe motor vehicle, motorboat, or other conveyance taken*), a motor-propelled conveyance of another person, (*name owner or possessor of conveyance*).

II. Aircraft

. . . unlawfully, willfully, and feloniously did, without the express or implied consent of the owner or person in lawful possession, take and operate (*describe aircraft taken*), an aircraft of another person, (*name owner or possessor of aircraft*).

Notes about Charging Language:
None.

Sample Charges:

I. Motor-propelled conveyance other than aircraft

. . . unlawfully and willfully did, without the express or implied consent of the owner or person in lawful possession, take and operate a 2004 Lexus, a motor-propelled conveyance of another person, James Collier.

II. Aircraft

. . . unlawfully, willfully, and feloniously did, without the express or implied consent of the owner or person in lawful possession, take and operate a Piper Cub airplane, an aircraft of another person, James Collier.

AOC Forms for This Offense:
AOC-J-320 (Juvenile Petition)

Punishment:
Offense I is a Class 1 misdemeanor. Offense II is a Class H felony.

G.S. 14-72.5
Larceny of Motor Fuel
April 2024

Introductory Comment:
None.

Charging Language:
. . . unlawfully and willfully did take and carry away (*name motor fuel*), a motor fuel, valued at less than $1,000, namely, (*give value of motor fuel taken*), from (*name business and give location*), where the motor fuel was offered for retail sale, with the intent to steal the motor fuel.

Notes about Charging Language:
- "Motor fuel" is defined in G.S. 105-449.60(20).
- There are few appellate cases regarding this offense. It may therefore be advisable to follow the procedures that govern larceny charges more generally. For example, it may be advisable to make clear that the possessor of the motor fuel is an entity, such as a corporation, that is capable of owning property. The nature of the entity could be alleged in the charging document in the manner shown in the sample charge, below. At a bare minimum, allege the name of the entity and that the entity is capable of owning property. *See* State v. Brawley, 370 N.C. 626 (2018) (holding that "Belk's Department Stores, an entity capable of owning property," sufficiently identified the victim).

Sample Charge:
. . . unlawfully and willfully did take and carry away gasoline, a motor fuel, valued at less than $1,000, namely, $22.15, from Phil's Exxon, Inc., 125 Main Street, Marion, N.C., where the motor fuel was offered for retail sale, with the intent to steal the motor fuel.

AOC Forms for This Offense:
None.

Punishment:
Class 1 misdemeanor. The court must also report a final conviction to the Division of Motor Vehicles, which must revoke the defendant's driver's license for a second or subsequent conviction under this statute.

G.S. 14-72.6
Larceny from a Construction Site
April 2024

Introductory Comment:
None.

Charging Language:

I. Larceny from a permitted construction site **G.S. 14-72.6(a)(1)**

. . . unlawfully, willfully, and feloniously did steal, take, and carry away (*describe the property taken*), the personal property of (*name the possessor*), such property having a value of (*state value, which must be between $300 and $1,000*). The defendant took the property from a permitted construction site, (*describe site*).

II. Receiving or possessing goods stolen from a permitted construction site **G.S. 14-72.6(a)(2)**

. . . unlawfully, willfully, and feloniously did (*choose one both*: receive; possess) (*describe the property*), the personal property of (*name the rightful possessor*), such property having a value of (*state value, which must be between $300 and $1,000*). The defendant (*choose one or both*: knew; had reasonable grounds to believe) that the property was stolen from a permitted construction site, (*describe site*).

Notes about Charging Language:

- The possessor of the property is not necessarily the owner or the custodian of the property. The possessor is usually the one who has control over the property—thus the person who leases a tool is the possessor of it, not the company that owns the tool. In some cases, however, a person will be in control of property only as part of his or her employment. In that case, the employer is the possessor, while the employee is only the custodian. If there is doubt about who the possessor is, list all of those who might be in possession and indicate their relationship to the property.
- The possessor of the property must be a person or an entity, such as a corporation, that is capable of owning property. If the possessor is an entity, indicate the nature of the entity as shown in the sample charge, below. At a bare minimum, allege the name of the entity and that the entity is capable of owning property. *See* State v. Brawley, 370 N.C. 626 (2018) (holding that "Belk's Department Stores, an entity capable of owning property," sufficiently identified the victim).
- For Offense II, it likely is not legally necessary to allege the possessor of the property. *Cf.* State v. Medlin, 86 N.C. App. 114 (1987). For clarity, however, this form requests that information.

Sample Charge:

I. Larceny from a permitted construction site **G.S. 14-72.6(a)(1)**

. . . unlawfully, willfully, and feloniously did steal, take, and carry away two Stihl power saws, the personal property of Bloc Construction, Inc., such property having a value of $400. The defendant took the property from a permitted construction site, 14 Spencer Street, Durham, N.C.

AOC Forms for This Offense:
None.

Punishment:
Class I felony.

G.S. 14-72.8
Felony Larceny of Motor Vehicle Parts
April 2024

Introductory Comment:
This statute previously applied only to the theft of motor vehicle parts where the cost to repair the vehicle exceeded $1,000. Effective December 1, 2021, the General Assembly expanded the statute to apply to the theft of a catalytic converter, regardless of the cost to repair the vehicle. S.L. 2021-154.

Possession of a catalytic converter that has been removed from a motor vehicle is now also addressed by G.S. 14-164.1, which makes possession a Class I felony absent certain circumstances indicative of legitimate possession. That offense should be considered when evaluating this offense.

Charging Language:
. . . unlawfully, willfully, and feloniously did steal, take, and carry away (*describe part, including by stating "a catalytic converter" if applicable*), a motor vehicle part, the personal property of (*name the possessor of the part*). (*If applicable, add: The cost of repairing the motor vehicle is $1,000 or more.*)

Notes about Charging Language:
- This offense requires either that the part be a catalytic converter, that the cost of repairing the motor vehicle be $1,000 or more, or both. If neither circumstance is present, do not charge this offense. Consider other offenses such as misdemeanor larceny instead. If both circumstances are present, both may be alleged.
- In determining the cost of repairing a vehicle, include "the cost of any replacement part and any additional costs necessary to install the replacement part in the motor vehicle." G.S. 14-72.8(c).
- Although there is no appellate case on point under this specific statute, the law generally requires that when charging larceny, the possessor of the property must be a person or an entity, such as a corporation, that is capable of owning property. Thus, if the possessor is an entity, indicate the nature of the entity. At a bare minimum, allege the name of the entity and that the entity is capable of owning property. *See* State v. Brawley, 370 N.C. 626 (2018) (holding that "Belk's Department Stores, an entity capable of owning property," sufficiently identified the victim).

Sample Charge:
. . . unlawfully, willfully, and feloniously did steal, take, and carry away a catalytic converter from a 2019 Toyota Prius, a motor vehicle part, the personal property of Angela Towns.

AOC Forms for This Offense:
None.

Punishment:
Class I felony.

G.S. 14-72.9
Larceny of Law Enforcement Equipment from a Law Enforcement Vehicle
April 2024
Page 1 of 2

Introductory Comment:
This offense was created by S.L. 2021-167 and applies to offenses committed on or after December 1, 2021.

Charging Language:
. . . unlawfully, willfully, and feloniously did steal, take, and carry away (*describe the property taken*), law enforcement equipment valued at (*give value of property taken*), from (*describe the law enforcement vehicle from which property was taken*), a law enforcement vehicle (*choose one or both*: owned; operated) by (*name law enforcement agency*) and (*name agency's city or county*). The defendant (*choose one or both*: knew; reasonably should have known) that the vehicle was a law enforcement vehicle and that the property was law enforcement equipment.

Notes about Charging Language:
- "Law enforcement equipment" is defined in G.S. 14-72.9(a)(1) to mean "any equipment owned or operated by a law enforcement agency and used by law enforcement agencies to conduct law enforcement operations, including firearms and any other type of weapon, ammunition, radios, computers, handcuffs and other restraints, phones, cell site simulators, light bars, and sirens."
- "Law enforcement vehicle" is defined in G.S. 14-72.9(a)(2) to mean "any railroad car, motor vehicle, trailer, aircraft, boat, or other watercraft of any kind owned or operated by any law enforcement agency, the North Carolina National Guard, or any branch of the Armed Forces of the United States."
- There are no appellate cases regarding this new offense. It may therefore be advisable to follow the procedures that govern larceny charges more generally, which include alleging that legal entities are capable of owning property. The charging language accomplishes this by requiring that both the law enforcement agency and the agency's city or county be alleged. By statute, North Carolina cities and counties are capable of owning personal property, *see* G.S. 153A-158 (counties); G.S. 160A-240.1 (cities), and on this basis the North Carolina Court of Appeals has upheld a larceny indictment alleging that personal property was owned by a municipal corporation. *See* State v. Turner, 8 N.C. App. 73 (1970) (indictment sufficient where it alleged that a truck was owned by the "City of Hendersonville, North Carolina"). In cases involving a state or federal law enforcement agency, identify the state or the United States of America where the charging language asks for a city or county.
- It is not yet clear how specific the description of the equipment must be. Therefore, it is advisable to describe the property with as much specificity as reasonably possible, using identification numbers where applicable as modeled in the sample charge.

Sample Charge:
. . . unlawfully, willfully, and feloniously did steal, take, and carry away a Lenovo ThinkPad T15 laptop computer having the serial number 549012, law enforcement equipment valued at $2,189, from a Ford Police Interceptor Utility having the VIN number 295603821, a law enforcement vehicle owned and operated by the Greensboro Police Department and the City of Greensboro, North Carolina. The defendant knew and reasonably should have known that the vehicle was a law enforcement vehicle and that the property was law enforcement equipment.

AOC Forms for This Offense:
None.

Punishment:
Class H felony. Class G felony if the value of the law enforcement equipment exceeds one thousand dollars ($1,000).

G.S. 14-72.11
Larceny from a Merchant
April 2024
Page 1 of 3

Introductory Comment:
G.S. 14-72.11 describes five circumstances under which a person commits the offense of larceny from a merchant.

Charging Language:

I. Of property valued at more than $200, using certain exit doors **G.S. 14-72.11(1)**

. . . unlawfully, willfully, and feloniously did steal, take, and carry away (*describe property taken*), the personal property of (*name merchant and, if not a person, allege nature of legal entity capable of owning property, e.g., "a corporation"*), a merchant, without the merchant's consent and with the intent to permanently deprive the merchant of the property, such property having a value of more than $200, using to exit the premises an exit door erected and maintained to comply with the requirements of 29 C.F.R. §§ 1910.36 and 1910.37.

II. By tampering with an anti-shoplifting or inventory-control device **G.S. 14-72.11(2)**

. . . unlawfully, willfully, and feloniously did steal, take, and carry away (*describe property taken*), the personal property of (*name merchant and, if not a person, allege nature of legal entity capable of owning property, e.g., "a corporation"*), a merchant, without the merchant's consent and with the intent to permanently deprive the merchant of the property, by removing, destroying, and deactivating a component of an anti-shoplifting or inventory-control device to prevent the activation of any anti-shoplifting or inventory-control device.

III. By affixing a fraudulent product code **G.S. 14-72.11(3)**

. . . unlawfully, willfully, and feloniously did steal, take, and carry away (*describe property taken*), the personal property of (*name merchant and, if not a person, allege nature of legal entity capable of owning property, e.g., "a corporation"*), a merchant, without the merchant's consent and with the intent to permanently deprive the merchant of the property, by affixing a product code created for the purpose of fraudulently obtaining goods or merchandise from a merchant at less than its actual sale price.

IV. Of infant formula valued at more than $100 **G.S.14-72.11(4)**

. . . unlawfully, willfully, and feloniously did steal, take, and carry away (*describe property taken*), the personal property of (*name merchant and, if not a person, allege nature of legal entity capable of owning property e.g., "a corporation"*), a merchant, without the merchant's consent and with the intent to permanently deprive the merchant of the property, such property being infant formula and having a value of more than $100.

V. By exchanging stolen property **G.S. 14-72.11(5)**

. . . unlawfully, willfully, and feloniously did steal, take, and carry away (*choose one or more and describe*: cash; a gift card; a merchandise card; an item of value, [*describe item*]), the personal property of (*name merchant and, if not a person, allege nature of legal entity capable of owning property, e.g., "a corporation"*), a merchant, without the merchant's consent and with the intent to permanently deprive the merchant of the property, by exchanging (*describe property exchanged*) knowing and having reasonable grounds to believe that the exchanged property was stolen.

Notes about Charging Language:

- With respect to larceny offenses generally, it is not legally necessary to allege that the victim did not consent to the taking and that the defendant intended to deprive the victim of the property permanently. State v. Osborne, 149 N.C. App. 235, 245 (2002) (citing prior cases and ruling that a larceny indictment that did not contain those elements was sufficient as it met "the underlying purpose of an indictment" by putting the defendant on notice of the offense charged). This form includes those elements out of an abundance of caution in light of the statement in *State v. Justice*, 219 N.C. App. 642, 644 (2012), that "an indictment under section 14-72.11(2) must allege the four elements of larceny [including lack of consent and intent to deprive] and also removal of an antishoplifting or inventory control device."
- The possessor of the property must be a person or an entity, such as a corporation, that is capable of owning property. If the possessor is an entity, indicate the nature of the entity in the manner shown in the sample charge, below. At a bare minimum, allege the name of the entity and that the entity is capable of owning property. *See* State v. Brawley, 370 N.C. 626 (2018) (holding that "Belk's Department Stores, an entity capable of owning property," sufficiently identified the victim).
- For Offense I, the federal regulations referenced in the charging language set forth various requirements related to the design, construction, maintenance, etc., of exit routes.
- For Offenses I and IV, it probably is not necessary to allege the specific value of the stolen property. *Cf.* State v. Jones, 275 N.C. 432, 436 (1969) (stating that "an indictment for the [f]elony of larceny must charge . . . that the value of the stolen goods was more than two hundred dollars [under current law, $1,000]" and that the law "does not require that the jury fix the precise value of the stolen property"). However, that information may be added if desired.
- For Offense IV, the term "infant formula" has the same meaning as found in 21 U.S.C. § 321(z). G.S. 14-72.11(4). That federal statute provides as follows: "The term 'infant formula' means a food which purports to be or is represented for special dietary use solely as a food for infants by reason of its simulation of human milk or its suitability as a complete or partial substitute for human milk."
- For Offense V, if the property obtained by the defendant is cash, it is probably not legally necessary to state the amount of money obtained. *Cf.* State v. Mostafavi, 370 N.C. 681 (2018) (holding that "United States currency" adequately described the property that the defendant obtained by false pretenses). However, it is not erroneous to include the amount if known.

Sample Charge:

I. Of property valued at more than $200, using certain exit doors G.S. 14-72.11(1)

. . . unlawfully, willfully, and feloniously did steal, take, and carry away a Sony television, the personal property of Johnson's Electronics, Inc., a corporation, a merchant, without the merchant's consent and with the intent to permanently deprive the merchant of the property, such property having a value of more than $200, using to exit the premises an exit door erected and maintained to comply with the requirements of 29 C.F.R. §§ 1910.36 and 1910.37.

AOC Forms for This Offense:
None.

Punishment:
Offenses I through V are all Class H felonies.

G.S. 14-74
Larceny by Employee
April 2024

Introductory Comment:
Despite its name, larceny by employee is much more akin to embezzlement than to larceny. It requires that the employee receive a thing of value from the employer and then take it for his or her own purposes.

Charging Language:
. . . unlawfully, willfully, and feloniously did, being the employee of (*name employer*), go away with, embezzle, and convert to the defendant's own use (*describe money, goods, or chose in action taken by the defendant*), which had been delivered to be kept for (*choose one*: his; her) employer's use, with the intent to steal and to defraud the defendant's employer. This act was done without (*choose one*: his; her) employer's consent and contrary to the trust and confidence reposed in the defendant by (*choose one*: his; her) employer. [*Insert if appropriate*: The value of the items described above was (*give value, if $100,000 or more*).]

Notes about Charging Language:
- The statute is violated by going away with the property, embezzling the property, or converting the property to one's own use. If one of these does not apply, delete the inappropriate word(s).
- This offense does not apply to defendants who are "within the age of 16 years." However, the age of the defendant need not be alleged in the charging document. State v. Brown, 56 N.C. App. 228 (1982).
- In *State v. Booker*, 262 N.C. App. 290, 296 (2018), a case decided under G.S. 14-90 (embezzlement), the court made several rulings that may be pertinent to charges under G.S. 14-74: first, that an indictment alleging that the defendant "embezzle[d]" funds sufficiently alleged the defendant's fraudulent intent; and second, that the indictment was not "defective for failing to specify the acts constituting embezzlement."

Sample Charge:
. . . unlawfully, willfully, and feloniously did, being the employee of Bill James, go away with, embezzle, and convert to his own use $4,523 of United States currency, which had been delivered to be kept for his employer's use, with the intent to steal and to defraud the defendant's employer. This act was done without his employer's consent and contrary to the trust and confidence reposed in the defendant by his employer.

AOC Forms for This Offense:
None.

Punishment:
Class H felony. It is a Class C felony if the value of the items taken is $100,000 or more.

G.S. 14-75
Larceny of Chose in Action
April 2024

Introductory Comment:
This statute covers the larceny of checks and other financial instruments. It likely does not apply to the larceny of blank checks, the taking of which should normally be charged as misdemeanor larceny. *See* Jessica Smith, North Carolina Crimes: A Guidebook on the Elements of Crime 250 (UNC School of Government, 7th ed. 2012).

Charging Language:
. . . unlawfully, willfully, and feloniously did steal, take, and carry away another's chose in action, (*describe chose in action stolen*), of the value of (*state value*), from the possession of (*name possessor*).

Notes about Charging Language:
- A "chose in action" is defined in G.S. 14-75 as "any bank note, check or other order for the payment of money issued by or drawn on any bank or other society or corporation within this State or within any of the United States, or any treasury warrant, debenture, certificate of stock or other public security, or certificate of stock in any corporation, or any order, bill of exchange, bond, promissory note or other obligation, either for the payment of money or for the delivery of specific articles."
- The possessor of the property must be a person or an entity, such as a corporation, that is capable of owning property. Accordingly, if the possessor is an entity, indicate the nature of the entity by alleging, for example, that the item was taken from the possession of "Pepper's Restaurant, Inc., a corporation." At a bare minimum, allege the name of the entity and that the entity is capable of owning property. *See* State v. Brawley, 370 N.C. 626 (2018) (holding that "Belk's Department Stores, an entity capable of owning property," sufficiently identified the victim).
- See the discussion of possession in this manual under G.S. 14-72(a), misdemeanor larceny.

Sample Charge:
. . . unlawfully, willfully, and feloniously did steal, take, and carry away another's chose in action, a bank note in the amount of $300 issued by First National Bank, of the value of $300, from the possession of William Huffner.

AOC Forms for This Offense:
None.

Punishment:
Class H felony.

G.S. 14-81
Larceny of Dog or Livestock
April 2024

Introductory Comment:
None.

Charging Language:
. . . unlawfully, willfully, and feloniously did steal, take, and carry away a (*choose one*: dog; horse; mule; pig; hog; cow), (*describe the animal*), the property of (*identify the possessor*).

Notes about Charging Language:
- See the discussion of possession in this manual under G.S. 14-72(a), misdemeanor larceny.
- As with other larceny offenses, the possessor of the property—that is, the dog or livestock—may need to be a person or an entity, such as a corporation, that is capable of owning property. Accordingly, if the possessor is an entity, indicate the nature of the entity by alleging, for example, that the dog or livestock was the property of "Eastern Tarboro Family Farm, Inc., a corporation." At a bare minimum, allege the name of the entity and that the entity is capable of owning property. *See* State v. Brawley, 370 N.C. 626 (2018) (holding that "Belk's Department Stores, an entity capable of owning property," sufficiently identified the victim).

Sample Charge:
. . . unlawfully, willfully, and feloniously did steal, take, and carry away a horse, a female appaloosa, the property of James Edward Sanford.

AOC Forms for This Offense:
None.

Punishment:
Larceny of a horse, mule, pig, or cow is a Class H felony. Larceny of a dog is a Class I felony. This offense carries special sentencing requirements as described in G.S. 14-81(b).

G.S. 14-86.6
Organized Retail Theft
April 2024
Page 1 of 2

Introductory Comment:
This offense was substantially revised by S.L. 2022-30, effective December 1, 2022. The same legislation created a new offense for damaging property or committing an assault during organized retail theft. *See* G.S. 14-86.7. It also contains important provisions regarding the pretrial return of property to the victim of organized retail theft offenses.

Charging Language:

I. Organized retail theft by disposition of property **G.S. 14-86.6(a)(1)**

. . . unlawfully, willfully, and feloniously did conspire with another person, (*name person*), to commit theft of retail property, (*describe property*), from [a] retail establishment[s], (*name establishment[s]*), with the intent to sell that retail property for monetary and other gain, and (*choose one or both:* took that retail property to [*name retail property fence or other person*] in exchange for consideration; caused that retail property to be placed in the control of [*name retail property fence or other person*] in exchange for consideration). Aggregated over a ninety-day period, the retail property had a value exceeding (*choose one:* one thousand five hundred dollars ($1,500); twenty thousand dollars ($20,000); fifty thousand dollars ($50,000); one hundred thousand dollars ($100,000)).

II. Organized retail theft by receipt or possession of property **G.S. 14-86.6(a)(2)**

. . . unlawfully, willfully, and feloniously did (*choose one or both:* receive; possess) retail property, *(describe property),* that had been (*choose one or both:* taken; stolen) in violation of G.S. 14-86.6(a)(1) while knowing and having reasonable grounds to believe the property was stolen. Aggregated over a ninety-day period, the retail property had a value exceeding (*choose one:* one thousand five hundred dollars ($1,500); twenty thousand dollars ($20,000); fifty thousand dollars ($50,000); one hundred thousand dollars ($100,000)).

III. Organized retail theft by leadership **G.S. 14-86.6(a)(3)**

. . . unlawfully, willfully, and feloniously did conspire with two other people, (*name people*), as a(n) (*choose one or more:* organizer; supervisor; financier; leader; manager), to engage for profit in a (*choose one or both:* scheme; course of conduct) to effectuate the (*choose one or both:* transfer; sale) of property stolen from a merchant in violation of G.S. 14-86.6. Aggregated over a ninety-day period, the retail property had a value exceeding (*choose one:* one thousand five hundred dollars ($1,500); twenty thousand dollars ($20,000); fifty thousand dollars ($50,000); one hundred thousand dollars ($100,000)).

Notes about Charging Language:
- An allegation regarding the value of the retail property appears to be essential. If the value does not exceed $1,500, this offense does not apply.
- "Thefts of retail property occurring in more than one county may be aggregated into an alleged violation of this section." G.S. 14-86.6(c).

- For offense I, it is unclear whether the possessor of the property must be a person or an entity, such as a corporation, that is capable of owning property, as is the case for larceny offenses. A cautious prosecutor may wish to indicate the nature of the entity in the manner shown in the sample charge, below, or to allege the name of the entity and that the entity is capable of owning property. *See* State v. Brawley, 370 N.C. 626 (2018) (holding, in a larceny case, that "Belk's Department Stores, an entity capable of owning property," sufficiently identified the victim).

Sample Charge:

I. Organized retail theft by disposition of property **G.S. 14-86.6(a)(1)**

. . . unlawfully, willfully, and feloniously did conspire with another person, Patrick Stone, to commit theft of retail property, Sony PlayStation video game consoles, from retail establishments, Sam's Secondhand Electronics, Inc., in Taylorsville, N.C., and Linus's Like New Shop, Inc., in Dunn, N.C., with the intent to sell that retail property for monetary and other gain, and took that retail property to Brandon Gaines in exchange for consideration. Aggregated over a ninety-day period, the retail property had a value exceeding one thousand five hundred dollars ($1,500).

AOC Forms for This Offense:

None.

Punishment:

Offenses involving more than $1,500 are Class H felonies. Offenses involving more than $20,000 are Class G felonies. Offenses involving more than $50,000 are Class F felonies. Offenses involving more than $100,000 are Class C felonies. G.S. 14-86.6(a2). Any property "acquired or maintained in violation of this section" is subject to forfeiture. G.S. 14-86.6(b).

G.S. 14-87
Robbery with a Dangerous Weapon
April 2024
Page 1 of 2

Introductory Comment:
G.S. 14-87(a) addresses both robbery with a dangerous weapon and attempted robbery with a dangerous weapon. The statute provides that each crime is a Class D felony. Legislation effective December 1, 2017, amended G.S. 14-87 by adding new subsection (a1), which states that "[a]ttempted robbery with a dangerous weapon shall constitute a lesser-included offense of robbery with a dangerous weapon" and further provides that "evidence sufficient to prove robbery with a dangerous weapon shall be sufficient to support a conviction of attempted robbery with a dangerous weapon." S.L. 2017-31. This legislative change appears to clear up any confusion as to whether distinct crimes of robbery with a dangerous weapon and attempted robbery with a dangerous weapon exist, and whether evidence sufficient to prove the completed crime also is sufficient to prove the attempted crime.

Charging Language:
. . . unlawfully, willfully, and feloniously did steal, take, and carry away another's personal property, (*describe the property*), from (*choose one or both*)

(1) the person and presence of (*name the victim(s)*).

(2) (*identify the place from which taken*) when (*name the victim(s)*) was present.

The defendant committed this act having in (*choose one*: his; her) possession and with the use and threatened use of a (*choose one or more*: firearm; dangerous weapon, implement, or means), (*identify the firearm or dangerous weapon and, if not obvious, how used so as to be dangerous*), whereby the life of (*name the threatened victim(s)*) was threatened and endangered.

Notes about Charging Language:
- The statute makes clear that attempted armed robbery is punished as severely as armed robbery, that is, it is not a less-serious crime under the general rule for attempts set forth in G.S. 14-2.5. As noted above, attempted armed robbery is defined by statute as a lesser-included offense of armed robbery, and evidence sufficient to prove a completed armed robbery is sufficient to support a conviction for attempted armed robbery. *Cf.* G.S. 15-170 (stating the general rule that an indictment for a crime will support a conviction for an attempt to commit that crime).
- If a prosecutor only wants to charge attempted armed robbery, the charging language set out above may be used with the addition of the words "attempt to" after the words "unlawfully, willfully, and feloniously did" and before the recitation of the elements of the offense. For more information about charging attempt crimes, see the Attempt form in the General Offenses section of this manual.
- This form calls for the name of the victim or victims, but at least in some circumstances other identifiers may be adequate. *See* State v. Oldroyd, 380 N.C. 613 (2022) (holding that "employees of the Huddle House located at [a specific address]" adequately identified the victims).
- It is necessary to name or describe the weapon used by the defendant and either expressly allege that it was a dangerous weapon or allege facts that necessarily indicate its dangerous nature. *See* State v. Moorman, 370 N.C. 187 (2017).

Sample Charge:
. . . unlawfully, willfully, and feloniously did steal, take, and carry away another's personal property, a purse containing money and personal belongings, from the person and presence of Mary Sellers. The defendant committed this act having in his possession and with the use and threatened use of a dangerous weapon, implement, or means, a knife with a six-inch blade, whereby the life of Mary Sellers was threatened and endangered.

AOC Forms for This Offense:
AOC-CR-135 (Indictment)

Punishment:
Class D felony.

Common Law and G.S. 14-87.1
Common Law Robbery
April 2024

Introductory Comment:
None.

Charging Language:
. . . unlawfully, willfully, and feloniously did steal, take, and carry away another's personal property, (*describe the property taken*), from the person and presence of (*name the victim*) by means of (*choose one or both*)

(1) the forcible and violent taking of the property.

(2) putting (*choose one*: him; her) in fear of bodily harm by the threat of violence.

Notes about Charging Language:
This form calls for the name of the victim or victims, but at least in some circumstances other identifiers may be adequate. *See* State v. Oldroyd, 380 N.C. 613 (2022) (holding, in an armed robbery case, that "employees of the Huddle House located at [a specific address]" adequately identified the victims).

Sample Charge:
. . . unlawfully, willfully, and feloniously did steal, take, and carry away another's personal property, a wallet and watch, from the person and presence of Walter Kline by means of putting him in fear of bodily harm by the threat of violence.

AOC Forms for This Offense:
AOC-CR-136 (Indictment)

Punishment:
Class G felony.

G.S. 14-89.1
Safecracking
April 2024
Page 1 of 2

Introductory Comment:
This offense can be committed by opening a safe or vault or by removing a safe or vault from the premises.

Charging Language:

I. Opening safe **G.S. 14-89.1(a)**

. . . unlawfully, willfully, and feloniously did attempt to open and enter, and did open and enter, a (*choose one*: safe; vault) that was the property of (*name the owner*) and was located at (*state where the safe was located*), by means of (*choose one or more*)

(1) the use of explosives.
(2) the use of drills.
(3) the use of tools.
(4) the use of a stolen combination.
(5) the use of a stolen key.
(6) the use of a stolen electronic device.
(7) the use of a fraudulently acquired (*name or describe the implement or means used to open the safe or vault*).
(8) the use of a master key (*choose one*: made; obtained) in an unauthorized manner.
(9) the use of a duplicate key (*choose one*: made; obtained) in an unauthorized manner.
(10) the use of a (*name or describe the device*) (*choose one*: made; obtained) in an unauthorized manner.
(11) the use of a stethoscope.
(12) the use of a listening device, a *(describe the device).*
(13) the use of an electronic device, a *(describe the device).*
(14) the use of *(describe the other surreptitious means of entry).*
(15) the use of *(describe the other safecracking implement or means).*

II. Removing safe from premises **G.S. 14-89.1(b)**

. . . unlawfully, willfully, and feloniously did remove a (*choose one*: safe; vault) that was the property of (*name the owner of the safe or vault*), from the premises at (*describe the location of the safe or vault*), for the purpose of stealing, tampering with, and ascertaining its contents.

Notes about Charging Language:

- The statute makes it unlawful to either open or enter or attempt to open or enter a safe or vault. If one of those terms is not applicable to the case, it should be omitted.
- The statute makes it unlawful to remove the safe either to steal or tamper with it or to ascertain its contents. If the facts do not support one of those purposes, that purpose should be omitted.

Sample Charge:

I. Opening safe **G.S. 14-89.1(a)**

. . . unlawfully, willfully, and feloniously did attempt to open and enter, and did open and enter, a safe that was the property of Lucius T. Warren, Jr., and was located at Warren's Gulf Service Station, 785 Westway Avenue, Winston-Salem, N.C., by means of the use of drills and tools.

AOC Forms for This Offense:

None.

Punishment:

Class I felony.

G.S. 14-90
Embezzlement
April 2024
Page 1 of 2

Introductory Comment:
Amendments effective March 1, 2024, make this offense eligible for aggregation under the new G.S. 15A-1340.16F. See that statute for particulars of pleading, procedure, and punishment.

Charging Language:
. . . unlawfully, willfully, and feloniously did (*choose one or more of the following*)

(1) embezzle
(2) fraudulently misapply and convert to (*choose one*: his; her) own use
(3) knowingly misapply and convert to (*choose one*: his; her) own use
(4) with the intent to embezzle and fraudulently and knowingly misapply and convert to (*choose one*: his; her) own use, take and make away with
(5) with the intent to embezzle and fraudulently and knowingly misapply and convert to (*choose one*: his; her) own use, secrete

(*describe the money, goods, checks, or other property embezzled*) belonging to (*name person, corporation, or unincorporated organization to whom the property belonged*).

At the time the defendant was over 16 years of age and was the (*choose one or more*: agent; bailee; consignee; clerk; officer; servant; fiduciary) of (*repeat the name of the person, corporation, or unincorporated organization to whom the property belonged*) and in that capacity had been entrusted to receive the property described above, and in that capacity the defendant did receive and take into (*choose one*: his; her) care and possession that property.

[*Insert if appropriate*: The value of the items described above was (*give value, if $100,000 or more*).]

Notes about Charging Language:

- It is not clear whether age is an element of the offense or an affirmative defense; therefore, as a precaution, an allegation as to age is included in the above language. State v. Cook, 165 N.C. App. 630 (2004) (noting uncertainty and declining to resolve it); *cf.* State v. Brown, 56 N.C. App. 228 (1982) (age restriction in larceny by employee statute is an affirmative defense; age need not be alleged in charging document).
- In addition to agents, bailees, and the other categories listed above, the statute also specifically refers to guardians, administrators, executors, trustees, receivers, and persons holding public office or exercising a public trust. If one of those terms is appropriate, it may be substituted for the ones included above. In *State v. Booker*, 262 N.C. App. 290 (2018), the State used the term "employee" rather than one of the terms listed in the statute and the court of appeals did not comment negatively on it. However, it is safer to use one of the terms contained in the statute.
- The statute also specifically refers to "a settlement agent, as defined in G.S. 45A-3." In an appropriate case, the quoted phrase may be substituted for agent, bailee, etc., in the charging language. In such a case, you should also substitute "that were closing funds as defined in G.S. 45A-3" for "belonging to (*name person . . .*)."

- In *Booker*, 262 N.C. App. at 296, the court ruled that an indictment alleging that the defendant "embezzle[d]" funds sufficiently alleged the defendant's fraudulent intent. The court also rejected the defendant's argument that the indictment was "defective for failing to specify the acts constituting embezzlement."
- When a defendant commits a series of misapplications or conversions against a single victim, a prosecutor may choose whether to charge each separately or whether to aggregate them into a single count. *See* State v. Mullaney, 129 N.C. App. 506, 512 (1998) (note that the concurrence is the controlling law on this issue, and it affirms that "[t]he choice of how to proceed is with the district attorney"). Aggregating them may be attractive when the individual takings each involve less than $100,000 but the combination exceeds that amount.

Sample Charge:
. . . unlawfully, willfully, and feloniously did embezzle and fraudulently and knowingly misapply and convert to his own use, and with the intent to embezzle and fraudulently and knowingly misapply and convert to his own use, take and make away with and secrete $2,500 in U.S. currency and one IBM computer belonging to Harold R. Fleebucker. At the time, the defendant was over 16 years of age and was the agent and servant of Harold R. Fleebucker and in that capacity had been entrusted to receive the property described above, and in that capacity he did receive and take into his care and possession that property.

AOC Forms for This Offense:
AOC-CR-130 (Indictment)

Punishment:
Class H felony. It is a Class C felony if the value of the items embezzled is $100,000 or more.

G.S. 14-91
Embezzlement by State Officer or Employee
April 2024

Introductory Comment:
Amendments effective March 1, 2024, make this offense eligible for aggregation under the new G.S. 15A-1340.16F. See that statute for particulars of pleading, procedure, and punishment.

Charging Language:
. . . unlawfully, willfully, and feloniously did (*choose one or both*)

(1) embezzle

(2) knowingly misapply and convert to the defendant's own use

(*describe the property embezzled*), property belonging to the State of North Carolina. At the time, the defendant held the position of (*name defendant's office or title*) as an (*choose one*: officer; agent; employee) of the State of North Carolina and in that capacity had been entrusted with the property described above.

[*Insert if appropriate*: The value of the property described above was (*give value, if $100,000 or more*).]

Notes about Charging Language:

- Several of the notes regarding embezzlement under G.S. 14-90 may also apply to charging this offense.

Sample Charge:
. . . unlawfully, willfully, and feloniously did embezzle and knowingly misapply and convert to the defendant's own use $327 in U.S. currency, property belonging to the State of North Carolina. At the time, the defendant held the position of clerk in the Department of Transportation as an employee of the State of North Carolina and in that capacity had been entrusted with the property described above.

AOC Forms for This Offense:
None.

Punishment:
Class F felony. It is a Class C felony if the value of the property embezzled is $100,000 or more.

G.S. 14-92
Embezzlement by Local or Charitable Officer or Employee
April 2024
Page 1 of 2

Introductory Comment:
This statute creates two offenses. The first generally prohibits embezzlement by officers and employees of local governments and charities. The second specifically targets the embezzlement by local government officers of property held in trust. The second offense may overlap to some extent with the first. Amendments effective March 1, 2024, make this offense eligible for aggregation under the new G.S. 15A-1340.16F. See that statute for particulars of pleading, procedure, and punishment.

Charging Language:

I. Embezzlement of money or property of local government or charity

. . . unlawfully, willfully, and feloniously did embezzle and corruptly use and misapply (*describe money or property embezzled*), property belonging to (*name city, county, or charitable institution that property belonged to*). At the time, the defendant held the position of (*name or describe defendant's office or job*) as an (*choose one*: officer; agent; employee) of that (*choose one*: city; county; charitable institution) and in that capacity had been entrusted with the property described above.
[*Insert if appropriate*: The value of the property described above was (*give value, if $100,000 or more*).]

II. Embezzlement by local government officer of money or property held in trust for another

. . . unlawfully, willfully, and feloniously did (*choose one or more*)

(1) embezzle
(2) wrongfully convert to the defendant's own use
(3) corruptly use
(4) misapply
(5) fail to pay over and deliver to (*name person for whom the money or property was held*) when lawfully required to do so

(*describe money or property that was embezzled*), property that was held in trust for (*name person or corporation for whom/which the money or property was held*). At the time, the defendant was [*choose one*: Clerk of Superior Court of (*name county*); Sheriff of (*name county*); Treasurer of (*name city or county*); Register of Deeds of (*name county*); *or* (*name other public office held by defendant*)] and had received the property described above by virtue and color of that office.
[*Insert if appropriate*: The value of the property described above was (*give value, if $100,000 or more*).]

Notes about Charging Language:

- The first offense may be committed against any "unit or agency of local government," any "local board of education," or any "penal, charitable, religious, or educational institution." If the victim is not a city, county, or charitable institution but falls within the bounds of the statute, modify the above language accordingly.
- The second offense may be committed only by a "public officer of any . . . local government."
- Several of the notes regarding embezzlement under G.S. 14-90 may also apply to charging these offenses.

Sample Charges:

I. Embezzlement of money or property of local government or charity

. . . unlawfully, willfully, and feloniously did embezzle and corruptly use and misapply 150 feet of steel fence, 25 gallons of paint, 20 paint brushes, and 3 sledge hammers, property belonging to the Town of Smallville. At the time, the defendant held the position of public works manager as an employee of that town and in that capacity had been entrusted with the property described above.

II. Embezzlement by local government officer of money or property held in trust for another

. . . unlawfully, willfully, and feloniously did embezzle and wrongfully convert to his own use and corruptly use and misapply and fail to pay over and deliver to Henson G. Cunningham when lawfully required to do so $200 in U.S. currency, property that was held in trust for Henson G. Cunningham. At the time, the defendant was Clerk of Superior Court of Essex County and had received the property described above by virtue and color of that office.

AOC Forms for This Offense:
None.

Punishment:
Class F felony. It is a Class C felony if the value of the property embezzled is $100,000 or more.

G.S. 14-100
Obtaining Property by False Pretenses
April 2024
Page 1 of 2

Introductory Comment:
In the 2019 legislative session, the General Assembly amended G.S. 14-100 to add a provision that "[i]n any prosecution for violation of this section, the State is not required to establish that all of the acts constituting the crime occurred in this State or within a single city, county, or local jurisdiction of this State, and it is no defense that not all of the acts constituting the crime occurred in this State or within a single city, county, or local jurisdiction of this State." S.L. 2019-193. Amendments effective March 1, 2024, make this offense eligible for aggregation under the new G.S. 15A-1340.16F. See that statute for particulars of pleading, procedure, and punishment.

Charging Language:
. . . unlawfully, willfully, and feloniously did knowingly and designedly with the intent to cheat and defraud obtain (*describe the property*) from (*name person from whom defendant obtained or attempted to obtain the property*), a person within this state, by means of a false pretense which was calculated to deceive and did deceive.

The false pretense consisted of the following: (*briefly describe the false pretense*). [*Insert if appropriate*: The value of the items described above was (*give value, if $100,000 or more*).]

Notes about Charging Language:
- The statute also includes attempt to obtain property by false pretenses. Change language appropriately when an attempt is charged.
- The "person" from whom the property was obtained may be a natural person or an "association, consortium, corporation, body politic, partnership, or other group, entity, or organization."
- G.S. 14-100(a) addresses money, goods, or other things of value that are obtained or attempted to be obtained "from any person within this State." The appellate courts have not yet ruled on whether this reference to being within the state is an essential element of the offense; however, assuming *arguendo* that it is, evidence that the person or entity operated a place of business or maintained a presence within the state appears to be sufficient. *See* State v. Pierce, 279 N.C. App. 494 (2021). The phrase "a person within this state" is included in this form out of an abundance of caution.
- The false pretense may be of a past or subsisting fact or of a future fulfillment or event. Failure to fulfill a contractual obligation does not by itself establish false pretenses.
- The property obtained must be described with reasonable certainty. When the property is money, this can be challenging. Examples of descriptions deemed adequate by the courts include "United States currency," State v. Mostafavi, 370 N.C. 681 (2018), while examples of descriptions deemed insufficient include "money," State v. Reese, 83 N.C. 637 (1880), "credit," State v. Everette, 256 N.C. App. 244 (2017), and "services," State v. Jones, 367 N.C. 299 (2014). It is good practice to allege the amount of funds obtained, if known.

Sample Charge:
. . . unlawfully, willfully, and feloniously did knowingly and designedly with intent to cheat and defraud obtain $2,000 from Mary Smith, a person within this state, by means of a false pretense which was calculated to deceive and did deceive. The false pretense consisted of the following: the defendant told Mary Smith that if she would go to the bank, get out her life savings, and give it to the defendant to prove her good faith, the defendant would divide with Mary Smith a large sum of money which the defendant said he had found on the sidewalk, when in fact the defendant had not found any such money on the sidewalk and did not intend to divide any money with Mary Smith.

AOC Forms for This Offense:
AOC-CR-137 (Indictment)

Punishment:
Class H felony. It is a Class C felony if the value of the items is $100,000 or more.

G.S. 14-100.1
Possess Fraudulent Form of Identification
April 2024

Introductory Comment:
This statute creates two closely related offenses regarding false identification. However, the statute specifically exempts violations of G.S. 20-30 from its scope; that statute prohibits the use of false information to obtain a driver's license.

Charging Language:
I. Possession or manufacture of false or fraudulent form of identification — G.S. 14-100.1(a)

. . . unlawfully and willfully did knowingly (*choose one or both*: possess; manufacture) a (*choose one or both*: false; fraudulent) form of identification, (*describe identification*), for the purpose of (*choose one or more*: deception; fraud; *describe other criminal conduct*).

II. Obtaining a form of identification by the use of false or fraudulent information — G.S. 14-100.1(b)

. . . unlawfully and willfully did knowingly obtain a form of identification, (*describe identification*), by the use of (*choose one or more*: false; fictitious; fraudulent) information.

Notes about Charging Language:
- G.S. 14-100.1(d) provides that "form of identification" means any of the following or any replica thereof: (1) an identification card containing a picture, issued by any department, agency, or subdivision of the State of North Carolina, the federal government, or any other state; (2) a military identification card containing a picture; (3) a passport; or (4) an alien registration card containing a picture.

Sample Charge:
I. Possession or manufacture of false or fraudulent form of identification — G.S. 14-100.1(a)

. . . unlawfully and willfully did knowingly possess and manufacture a false and fraudulent form of identification, a military identification card containing a picture of the defendant, for the purpose of deception and fraud.

AOC Forms for This Offense:
None.

Punishment:
Class 1 misdemeanor.

G.S. 14-106
Obtaining Property by Worthless Check
April 2024

Introductory Comment:
Most, if not all, of the conduct covered by this statute is also covered by G.S. 14-107, which (1) arguably carries a lower burden of proof and (2) is subject to the special prima facie evidence provisions of G.S. 14-107.1. Thus, it is usually preferable to charge under G.S. 14-107.

Charging Language:
. . . unlawfully and willfully did, with intent to cheat and defraud (*name person or corporation*), obtain (*briefly describe property or other thing of value*) by means of a (*indicate one of the following*: check, draft, order) for (*give amount*) drawn by the defendant on (*name bank, person, or corporation*) payable to (*name payee*) and dated (*give date*). At the time in question, (*name bank, person, or corporation on which instrument was drawn*) was not indebted to the defendant, nor had the defendant made provision for payment or acceptance of the instrument. The instrument was not paid upon presentation.

Notes about Charging Language:
None.

Sample Charge:
. . . unlawfully and willfully did, with intent to cheat and defraud Franklin Jewelry Store, Inc., obtain one sterling silver knife, made by Reed and Barton, pattern Louis XIV, by means of a check for $155.75 drawn by the defendant on Republic State Bank payable to Franklin Jewelry Store and dated November 12, 2004. At the time in question, Republic State Bank was not indebted to the defendant, nor had the defendant made provision for payment or acceptance of the instrument. The instrument was not paid upon presentation.

AOC Forms for This Offense:
None.

Punishment:
Class 3 misdemeanor.

G.S. 14-107
Writing Worthless Checks
April 2024
Page 1 of 3

Introductory Comment:
This statute defines several offenses related to the writing of worthless checks. The offenses vary based on the value of the check, whether the account on which the check was drawn was closed or nonexistent, and the defendant's history of writing worthless checks.

Charging Language:

I. Felony worthless check (check in amount over $2,000)

. . . unlawfully, willfully, and feloniously did draw, make, utter, and issue and deliver to (*name person who received the check*) a check drawn upon (*name bank*) of (*name city*), (*name state*), for the payment of (*give amount*) in money. The check was payable to (*name payee*) and was dated (*give date*). The defendant knew at the time that the defendant (*choose one*: did not have sufficient funds on deposit in or credit with the bank with which to pay the check upon presentation; had previously presented the check for the payment of money or its equivalent).

II. Simple misdemeanor worthless check (check in amount of $2,000 or less)

. . . unlawfully and willfully did draw, make, utter, and issue and deliver to (*name person who received the check*) a check drawn upon (*name bank*) of (*name city*), (*name state*), for the payment of (*give amount*) in money. The check was payable to (*name payee*) and was dated (*give date*). The defendant knew at the time that the defendant (*choose one*: did not have sufficient funds on deposit in or credit with the bank with which to pay the check upon presentation; had previously presented the check for the payment of money or its equivalent).

III. Check written on nonexistent account

. . . unlawfully and willfully did draw, make, utter, and issue and deliver to (*name person who received the check*) a check drawn upon (*name bank*) of (*name city and state*), for the payment of (*give amount*) in money. The check was payable to (*name payee*) and was dated (*give date*). The check was drawn upon a nonexistent account, and the defendant knew at the time that the defendant did not have sufficient funds on deposit in or credit with the bank with which to pay the check upon presentation.

IV. Check written on closed account

. . . unlawfully and willfully did draw, make, utter, and issue and deliver to (*name person who received the check*) a check drawn upon (*name bank*) of (*name city*), (*name state*), for the payment of (*give amount*) in money. The check was payable to (*name payee*) and was dated (*give date*). The defendant knew at the time that the defendant (*choose one*: did not have sufficient funds on deposit in or credit with the bank with which to pay the check upon presentation; had previously presented the check for the payment of money or its equivalent). [*Choose one*: (1) The check was drawn upon an account that had been closed by the defendant before the time the check was drawn. (2) The check was drawn upon an account that the defendant knew to have been closed by the bank before the time the check was drawn.]

V. Simple misdemeanor worthless check: fourth or subsequent offense

. . . unlawfully and willfully did draw, make, utter, and issue and deliver to (*name person who received the check*) a check drawn upon (*name bank*) of (*name city*), (*name state*), for the payment of (*give amount*) in money. The check was payable to (*name payee*) and was dated (*give date*). The defendant knew at the time that the defendant (*choose one*: did not have sufficient funds on deposit in or credit with the bank with which to pay the check upon presentation; had previously presented the check for the payment of money or its equivalent). The defendant was convicted three times previously of the crime of writing a worthless check, on the ________ day of ______________, ____, in the ______________ Court, ______________ County; on the ________ day of ______________, ____, in the ______________ Court, ______________ County; and on the ________ day of ______________, ____, in the ______________ Court, ______________ County.

Notes about Charging Language:

- An indictment or an information for the recidivist offense illustrated above as Offense V must comply with G.S. 15A-928, which requires that the defendant's prior convictions be alleged either (1) in a separate count of the indictment or information than the substantive offense or (2) in a separate indictment or information. In such a case, the separate count or separate indictment should set forth the charging language provided above regarding the defendant's prior convictions. This requirement does not apply to arrest warrants or magistrates' orders, which still must allege the defendant's prior convictions, as is shown in the charging language above, but need not do so in a separate count or separate charging instrument. Also note that in situations where a conviction for a recidivist offense is appealed from district to superior court for trial de novo, G.S. 15A-922(h) and -928(d) require the State to replace the pleading in the case with superseding statements of charges separately alleging the substantive offense and any prior convictions. G.S. 15A-928 also requires that the name or title of an offense elevated by prior convictions must not make reference to such prior convictions.
- The statute applies to drafts also. If the instrument is a draft, substitute the word "draft" for the word "check" throughout.
- The date on the check should be the same as the date on which the check was drawn. There is no crime under this statute if the check was postdated. State v. Crawford, 198 N.C. 522 (1930).
- The aiding and abetting provisions of the statute apply to soliciting also. If appropriate, substitute the word "solicit" for the words "aid and abet."
- Under *State v. Edwards*, 190 N.C. 322 (1925), a charge under this section that refers only to the lack of "funds on deposit" and fails also to mention the lack of "credit with the bank" is fatally defective.

- Subsection (b) of the statute makes it a crime to aid and abet a worthless check offense. Generally, those who aid and abet worthless check offenses are punished the same as principal offenders. In an appropriate case, modify the charging language to allege aiding and abetting.

Sample Charge:

I. Felony worthless check (check in amount over $2,000)

. . . unlawfully, willfully, and feloniously did draw, make, utter, and issue and deliver to Peter Piper a check drawn upon Central Carolina Bank of Durham, N.C., for the payment of $2,112.95 in money. The check was payable to Peter Piper and was dated October 30, 2005. The defendant knew at the time that the defendant did not have sufficient funds on deposit in or credit with the bank with which to pay the check upon presentation.

AOC Forms for This Offense:

AOC-CR-107 (Arrest Warrant, for Offenses II and V only)

AOC-CR-115 (Criminal Summons, for Offenses II and V only)

Punishment:

Offense I is a Class I felony. Offense II is a Class 3 misdemeanor. Offenses III and IV are Class 1 misdemeanors. Offense V is a Class 1 misdemeanor, for which the defendant must be ordered, as a condition of probation, to refrain from maintaining a checking account or making or uttering a check for three years.

G.S. 14-110
Defrauding Innkeeper
April 2024

Introductory Comment:
Despite its name, this offense applies to those who defraud "a hotel, inn, boardinghouse, eating house [i.e., restaurant], or campground."

Charging Language:

. . . unlawfully and willfully did, with the intent to defraud, obtain (*choose one or more and describe*: food; lodging; other accommodations) at (*name victim and give location*) by (*describe conduct*).

Notes about Charging Language:
None.

Sample Charges:
. . . unlawfully and willfully did, with the intent to defraud, obtain food, breakfast costing $5.51, at Shoney's restaurant on U.S. Highway 64 in Setoma, N.C., by leaving the restaurant without paying for the food.

. . . unlawfully and willfully did, with the intent to defraud, obtain lodging costing $42.00, at the Holiday Inn located at 751 East Sherbourne Street, Raleigh, N.C., by leaving the Holiday Inn without paying for the lodging.

AOC Forms for This Offense:
None.

Punishment:
Class 2 misdemeanor.

G.S. 14-112.2
Exploitation of Older or Disabled Adult
April 2024
Page 1 of 2

Introductory Comment:
Amendments effective March 1, 2024, make this offense eligible for aggregation under the new G.S. 15A-1340.16F. See that statute for particulars of pleading, procedure, and punishment.

Charging Language:

I. Abuse of position of trust **G.S. 14-112.2(b)**

. . . unlawfully, willfully, and feloniously did knowingly, while (*choose one or both*: standing in a position of trust and confidence with; having a business relationship with) (*name older or disabled adult*), (*choose one*: an older adult; a disabled adult) within the meaning of G.S. 14-112.2(a), by (*choose one or both*: deception; intimidation), (*choose one or both*: obtain; use) the funds, assets, and property of (*name older or disabled adult*) with the intent to (*choose one or both*: deprive [*name older or disabled adult*] of the use, benefit, and possession of the funds, assets, and property; benefit someone other than [*name older or disabled adult*]). (*If the value of the funds, assets, and property was $20,000 or more, state*: The value of the funds, assets, and property was [*give value*]).

II. Exploitation of older or disabled adult **G.S. 14-112.2(c)**

. . . unlawfully, willfully, and feloniously did knowingly, by (*choose one or both*: deception; intimidation) (*choose one or both*: obtain; use) the funds, assets, and property of (*name older or disabled adult*), (*choose one*: an older adult; a disabled adult) within the meaning of G.S. 14-112.2(a), with the intent to (*choose one or both*: deprive [*name older or disabled adult*] of the use, benefit, and possession of the funds, assets, and property; benefit someone other than [*name older or disabled adult*]). (*If the value of the funds, assets, and property was $20,000 or more, state*: The value of the funds, assets, and property was [*give value*]).

Notes about Charging Language:

- Both offenses apply to the improper obtaining of funds, assets, or property. If any of those terms is inappropriate, you may delete it.
- Both offenses also apply to a defendant who "endeavor[s] to obtain or use" the victim's property. If the defendant tried to obtain the victim's property but failed, insert this language.
- Offense II also applies to a defendant who "conspire[s] with another" to obtain or use the victim's property. In an appropriate case, insert this language, naming the person with whom the defendant conspired, if possible, or stating that the identity of the co-conspirator is unknown.
- Offense II does not apply to "a person acting within the scope of that person's lawful authority as the agent for the older adult or disabled adult." G.S. 14-112.2(c).
- "Disabled adult" and "older adult" are defined in G.S. 14-112.2(a).

Sample Charge:

I. Abuse of position of trust **G.S. 14-112.2(b)**

. . . unlawfully, willfully, and feloniously did knowingly, while standing in a position of trust and confidence with Jean McCannon, an older adult within the meaning of G.S. 14-112.2(a), by deception obtain and use the assets of Jean McCannon with the intent to deprive Jean McCannon of the use, benefit, and possession of the assets. The value of the assets was $57,515.

AOC Forms for This Offense:
None.

Punishment:
Offense I is a Class F felony if the funds, assets, or property are valued at $100,000 or more; a Class G felony if $20,000 or more but less than $100,000; a Class H felony if less than $20,000. Offense II is a Class G felony if the funds, assets, or property are valued at $100,000 or more; a Class H felony if $20,000 or more but less than $100,000; a Class I felony if less than $20,000.

If the defendant is charged with a violation involving funds, assets, or property valued at more than $5,000, the district attorney may petition the court to freeze the defendant's funds, assets, or property in an amount up to 150 percent of the amount alleged in the offense for the purpose of ensuring restitution, as provided by G.S. 14-112.3.

G.S. 14-113.9(a)(1)
Financial Transaction Card Theft: Taking Card
April 2024

Introductory Comment:
This statute applies to those who steal others' financial transaction cards. G.S. 14-113.10 provides that "[w]hen a person has in his possession or under his control financial transaction cards issued in the names of two or more other persons other than members of his immediate family, such possession shall be prima facie evidence that such credit cards have been obtained in violation of subsection (a) of G.S. 14-113.9."

Charging Language:
. . . unlawfully, willfully, and feloniously did take, obtain, and withhold a financial transaction card, (*describe card, including issuer and person to whom issued*), from the person, possession, custody, and control of (*name person from whom card taken and, if that person is someone other than the cardholder, briefly describe reason why he or she is entitled to the card*). The taking, obtaining, and withholding was done without the consent of the cardholder, (*name cardholder*), and with the intent to use the financial transaction card.

Notes about Charging Language:
- Taking multiple cards from a single person supports multiple charges under this statute.

Sample Charge:
. . . unlawfully, willfully, and feloniously did take, obtain, and withhold a financial transaction card, a Kohl's credit card, no. 5543-8777-3233-2232, expiration date March 2021, issued by Kohl's Stores, Inc., to Samuel Winston Johnston, from the person, possession, custody, and control of Andrew Johnston, who is the son of the cardholder and who was given the card for his use by his father. This taking was done without the consent of the cardholder, Samuel Winston Johnston, and with the intent to use the financial transaction card.

AOC Forms for This Offense:
AOC-CR-152 (Indictment)

Punishment:
Class I felony.

G.S. 14-113.9(a)(1), (a)(2)
Financial Transaction Card Theft: Receiving Stolen or Lost Cards
April 2024

Introductory Comment:
None.

Charging Language:

I. Receiving stolen card **G.S. 14-113.9(a)(1)**

. . . unlawfully, willfully, and feloniously did receive a financial transaction card, (*describe card, including issuer and person to whom issued*), with the intent to (*choose one or more*: use it; sell it; transfer it to a person other than the issuer or the cardholder). At the time of receiving the financial transaction card, the defendant knew that a person had unlawfully, willfully, and feloniously taken, obtained, and withheld the financial transaction card from the person, possession, custody, and control of (*name person from whom card was taken*) without the consent of the cardholder, (*name cardholder*), and with the intent to use it.

II. Receiving lost or misdelivered card **G.S. 14-113.9(a)(2)**

. . . unlawfully, willfully, and feloniously did receive a financial transaction card, (*describe card, including issuer and person to whom issued*), that the defendant knew had been lost, mislaid, and mistakenly delivered, and did retain possession of the financial transaction card with the intent to (*choose one or more*: use it; sell it; transfer it to a person other than the issuer or the cardholder).

Notes about Charging Language:
None.

Sample Charge:

I. Receiving stolen card **G.S. 14-113.9(a)(1)**

. . . unlawfully, willfully, and feloniously did receive a financial transaction card, a Smithtown Bank Visa credit card, no. 2222-2287-9093-1234, expiration date December 2015, issued to Howard Jones, with the intent to use it. At the time of receiving the financial transaction card, the defendant knew that a person had unlawfully, willfully, and feloniously taken, obtained, and withheld the financial transaction card from the person, possession, custody, and control of Howard Jones without the consent of the cardholder, Howard Jones, and with the intent to use it.

AOC Forms for This Offense:
None.

Punishment:
Class I felony.

G.S. 14-113.9(a)(3)
Financial Transaction Card Theft: Selling or Buying Card
April 2024

Introductory Comment:
None.

Charging Language:

I. Selling card

. . . unlawfully, willfully, and feloniously did sell to (*name buyer*) a financial transaction card, (*describe card, including issuer and person to whom issued*). The defendant was not the issuer of the financial transaction card sold.

II. Buying card

. . . unlawfully, willfully, and feloniously did buy from (*name seller*) a financial transaction card, (*describe card, including issuer and person to whom issued*). Neither the defendant nor (*name seller*) was the issuer or an agent of the issuer of the financial transaction card purchased.

Notes about Charging Language:
None.

Sample Charge:

II. Buying card

. . . unlawfully, willfully, and feloniously did buy from Peter Heard a financial transaction card, an Exxon Oil Company credit card, no. 5553-2398-0512-2384, expiration date June 2011, issued by Exxon Oil Company to Amy Brooks. Neither the defendant nor Peter Heard was the issuer or an agent of the issuer of the financial transaction card purchased.

AOC Forms for This Offense:
None.

Punishment:
Class I felony.

G.S. 14-113.9(a)(5)
Financial Transaction Card Theft: Using Scanning Device
April 2024

Introductory Comment:
None.

Charging Language:
. . . unlawfully, willfully, and feloniously did, with the intent to defraud (*name person or entity defrauded*),
(*choose one or both*)

(1) use a scanning device to (*choose one or more*: access; read; obtain; memorize; store) (*choose one or both*: temporarily; permanently) information encoded on another person's financial transaction card, (*describe card and name person to whom it belonged*).

(2) receive encoded information from another person's financial transaction card, (*describe card and name person to whom it belonged*).

Notes about Charging Language:
- G.S. 14-113.8(10) defines "scanning device" to include a scanner, reader, or any other device that is used to access, read, scan, obtain, memorize, or store, temporarily or permanently, information encoded on a financial transaction card.

Sample Charge:
. . . unlawfully, willfully, and feloniously did, with the intent to defraud Sallie Jones, use a scanning device to access, read, and obtain permanently information encoded on another person's financial transaction card, a Master Card, no. 5431-7154-6639-7592, expiration date January 2016, issued by Suntrust Bank to Sallie Jones.

AOC Forms for This Offense:
None.

Punishment:
Class I felony.

G.S. 14-113.9(a)(6)

Financial Transaction Card Theft: Possessing, Selling, or Delivering a Skimming Device

April 2024

Introductory Comment:

This offense was created by S.L. 2021-68 and applies to offenses committed on or after December 1, 2021.

Charging Language:

. . . unlawfully, willfully, and feloniously did knowingly (*choose one or more*: possess; sell; deliver) a skimming device as defined by G.S. 14-113.8, (*describe the skimming device*).

Notes about Charging Language:

- G.S. 14-113.8(11) defines a "skimming device" as a "self-contained device that (i) is designed to read and store in the device's internal memory information encoded on the computer chip, magnetic strip or stripe, or other storage mechanism of a financial transaction card or from another device that directly reads the information from a financial transaction card and (ii) is incapable of processing the financial transaction card information for the purpose of obtaining, purchasing, or receiving goods, services, money, or anything else of value from a merchant."
- G.S. 14-113.9(a)(6) states that this offense does not apply to an employee, officer, or agent of any of the following while acting within the scope of the person's official duties: a law enforcement agency; a State or federal court; an agency or department of the State, local, or federal government; a financial or retail security investigator employed by a merchant.

Sample Charge:

. . . unlawfully, willfully, and feloniously did knowingly possess a skimming device as defined by G.S. 14-113.8, having a yellow plastic body and internal electronics.

AOC Forms for This Offense:

None.

Punishment:

Class I felony.

G.S. 14-113.11
Financial Transaction Card Forgery
April 2024
Page 1 of 2

Introductory Comment:
This statute criminalizes a variety of conduct that falls under the general umbrella of forgery, including making bogus cards, adding information to cards to make them appear valid, electronically altering cards, or signing cards without authorization. G.S. 14-113.12 provides that the possession of two or more forged cards, under certain circumstances, makes out a prima facie case of a crime.

Charging Language:
. . . unlawfully, willfully, and feloniously did, with the intent to defraud (*name intended victim*), (*choose one or more of the alternatives listed below*)

(1) falsely make a purported financial transaction card by (*describe process of making the card*). This card purported to be issued by (*name purported issuer*) to (*name purported cardholder*) and was made without authorization by the purported issuer.

(2) falsely make a purported financial transaction card by altering a validly issued financial transaction card, (*describe card*), by (*describe how it was altered*).

(3) falsely emboss a purported financial transaction card by completing a financial transaction card issued by (*name issuer and identify card*). The matter added included information required by the issuer to appear on its cards before use by cardholders, (*describe matter added, other than signature, which is covered in alternative (8), below*).

(4) utter a falsely made and embossed purported financial transaction card by (*describe the uttering*). The purported financial transaction card was falsely made and embossed by [*adapt wording from alternatives (1), (2), or (3) above*].

(5) falsely encode information on a financial transaction card by (*describe the false encoding*), without authorization of the purported issuer of that card.

(6) falsely alter encoded information on a financial transaction card by (*describe alteration*), without the authorization of the purported issuer of that card.

(7) utter a falsely encoded purported financial transaction card by (*describe the uttering*). The purported financial transaction card was falsely encoded by [*adapt wording from alternatives (5) or (6) above*].

(8) sign a financial transaction card issued by (*name issuer*) to (*name person to whom card issued and give card number and other pertinent information*), when the defendant was neither the cardholder nor authorized by the cardholder to sign the card.

Notes about Charging Language:

- The statute describes the victim intended to be defrauded as including "a purported issuer, a person or organization providing money, goods, services, or anything else of value, or any other person."
- G.S. 14-113.8 provides a detailed definition of "financial transaction card." In addition to credit cards, the term includes cards used in withdrawing and transferring funds—in other words, debit cards—and cards used in connection with overdraft privilege accounts. This offense, though, does not cover misuse of certain telephone-related numbers, which are covered by G.S. 14-113.1 through -113.7A.

Sample Charges:

. . . unlawfully, willfully, and feloniously did, with the intent to defraud Bank Americard, Inc., and Stevens Hardware Store, Inc., 515 Market Street, Rayville, N.C., utter a falsely made and embossed purported financial transaction card by giving the financial transaction card to Stevens Hardware Store for the purpose of charging against the financial transaction card $25.50 worth of goods: one $20.00 rake and one $5.50 pair of scissors. The purported financial transaction card was falsely made and embossed by altering a valid Visa card issued by Smithtown Bank, N.C., to Randolph E. Taylor, a Bank Americard, no. 5411-6502-3623-1045, with an expiration date of September 2022, by means of altering the card number to read 5471-6502-3633-7045, without being authorized to do so by its issuer.

. . . unlawfully, willfully, and feloniously did, with the intent to defraud Central Carolina Bank, North Carolina, sign a financial transaction card issued by Central Carolina Bank, North Carolina, to Jennifer F. Jones, a Master Card, no. 5431-8652-4713-0456, with an expiration date of January 2025, when she was neither the cardholder nor authorized by the cardholder to sign the card.

AOC Forms for This Offense:

None.

Punishment:

Class I felony.

Introductory Comment:
G.S. 14-113.13 defines several crimes that fall under the general rubric of financial transaction card fraud. The crimes break down into two major categories. The first, obtaining property fraudulently, is committed when a customer misuses a card. The second, furnishing property fraudulently, is committed when a merchant engages in fraudulent activity, as when a merchant knowingly allows a customer to misuse a card.

Charging Language:

I. Obtaining property fraudulently **G.S. 14-113.13(a)**
. . . unlawfully, willfully, and feloniously did, with the intent to defraud (*name victim*), (*choose one of the alternatives listed below*)

(1) use for the purpose of obtaining (*describe thing of value sought to be obtained*) a financial transaction card, (*describe card*), obtained and retained by (*choose one*: financial transaction card theft under G.S. 14-113.9; financial transaction card forgery under G.S. 14-113.11).
(2) use a financial transaction card, (*describe card*), for the purpose of obtaining (*describe thing of value sought to be obtained*) after having received that card with knowledge that it was obtained and retained by (*choose one*: financial transaction card theft under G.S. 14-113.9; financial transaction card forgery under G.S. 14-113.11).
(3) use a financial transaction card, (*describe card*), for the purpose of obtaining (*describe thing of value sought to be obtained*) when the defendant knew that card was (*choose one or more*: forged; altered; expired; revoked; obtained by fraudulent application).
(4) obtain (*describe thing of value obtained*) by representing, without consent of the cardholder, (*name cardholder*), that the defendant was the holder of a financial transaction card, (*describe card*).
(5) obtain (*describe thing of value obtained*) by presenting a financial transaction card, (*describe card*), without the authorization or permission of the cardholder, (*name cardholder*).
(6) obtain (*describe thing of value obtained*) by representing that the defendant was the holder of a financial transaction card, (*describe card*), when such card had not in fact been issued.
(7) obtain (*describe thing of value obtained*) by using a financial transaction card, (*describe card*), to knowingly and willfully exceed (*choose one*: the actual balance of a demand deposit account; the actual balance of a time deposit account; an authorized credit line by [*give amount by which credit line exceeded*]), which exceeds the authorized credit line by (*choose whichever is greater as applied to the line of credit in question*: fifty percent (50%) of the authorized credit line; $500).

(8) obtain control over a financial transaction card, (*describe card*), as a security for a debt.

(9) deposit a (*choose one or more*: false; fictitious; forged; altered; counterfeit) (*choose one*: check; draft; money order; [*name other kind of document*]), (*describe the check, etc.*), into an account, (*indicate whose account*), by means of an automatic banking device.

(10) receive (*describe thing of value received*) as a result of a (*choose one or more*: check; draft; money order; [*name other kind of document*]), (*describe the check, etc.*), having been deposited into an account, (*indicate whose account*), knowing at the time of receiving the above items that the deposited document described above was (*choose one or more, consistent with the choice made above*: false; fictitious; forged; altered; counterfeit; not the defendant's lawful property).

(*Add the following paragraph if charging a felony offense*)

The (*choose one or more*: money; goods; services; other things of value) described above were obtained and furnished within a period of six months, (*give dates*), and had a value in excess of $500.

II. Furnishing property fraudulently **G.S. 14-113.13(b)**

. . . unlawfully, willfully, and feloniously did, with the intent to defraud (*name issuer of card or cardholder*), commit the offense of financial transaction card fraud. The defendant was authorized by (*name issuer*), the issuer of the financial transaction card in question, to furnish goods, money, services, and things of value upon presentation of a financial transaction card from such issuer by an authorized cardholder. The financial transaction card fraud was committed by (*choose one of the alternatives listed below*)

(1) furnishing (*describe thing of value furnished*) upon presentation of a financial transaction card, (*describe card*), obtained and retained by financial transaction card theft under G.S. 14-113.9.

(2) furnishing (*describe thing of value furnished*) upon presentation of a financial transaction card, (*describe card*), that the defendant knew was (*choose one or more*: forged; expired; revoked).

(3) failing to furnish (*describe thing of value*), which the defendant represented in writing to the issuer as having been furnished.

(*Add the following paragraph if charging a felony offense*)

The (*choose one or more*: money; goods; services; other things of value) described above were obtained and furnished within a period of six months, (*give dates*), and had a value in excess of $500.

Notes about Charging Language:

- Strike through the words "and feloniously" if a misdemeanor is being charged. Both obtaining property fraudulently and furnishing property fraudulently are misdemeanors if the value of all money, goods, and other things of value furnished in violation of law does not exceed $500 in any six-month period. G.S. 14-113.13(b).
- The statute describes the victims intended to be defrauded as including "the issuer, a person or organization providing money, goods, services or anything else of value, or any other person."
- G.S. 14-113.8 provides a detailed definition of "financial transaction card." In addition to credit cards, the term includes cards used in withdrawing and transferring funds—in other words, debit cards—and cards used in connection with overdraft privilege accounts.

Sample Charges:

I. Obtaining property fraudulently **G.S. 14-113.13(a)**

. . . unlawfully and willfully did, with the intent to defraud BP Oil Corp. and Sam's BP Service Station, Sanford, N.C., use for the purpose of obtaining fifteen gallons of gasoline and five quarts of oil a financial transaction card, a BP Oil credit card, no. 5413-7277-3343-9092, expiration date June 2023, issued to Bernard Sampson, obtained and retained by financial transaction card theft under G.S 14-113.9.

II. Furnishing property fraudulently **G.S. 14-113.13(b)**

. . . unlawfully, willfully, and feloniously did, with the intent to defraud NationsBank, Inc., commit the offense of financial transaction card fraud. The defendant was authorized by NationsBank, Inc., the issuer of the financial transaction card in question, to furnish goods, money, services, and things of value upon presentation of a financial transaction card from such issuer by an authorized cardholder. The financial transaction card fraud was committed by furnishing one white faux fur cape; one blue wool dress, style no. 5438; and one blue and green flowered long chiffon dress, style no. 6531, upon presentation of a financial transaction card, a Visa card, no. 5143-7265-4313-4928, expiration date December 2025, issued to Mary Tyler Jones, that the defendant knew was expired and revoked. The goods described above were furnished within a period of six months, from January 1 to February 15, 2019, and had a value in excess of $500.

AOC Forms for This Offense:

AOC-CR-152 (Indictment, for obtaining property fraudulently, option (1) only)

Punishment:

Class 2 misdemeanor, unless the value of all money, goods, and other things of value furnished in violation of law exceeds $500 in any six-month period, in which case, Class I felony.

G.S. 14-113.13(c), (d)
Financial Transaction Card Fraud: False Statements
April 2024
Page 1 of 2

Introductory Comment:
G.S. 14-113.13 criminalizes two types of false statements by cardholders or applicants for cards. Subsection (c) criminalizes certain false statements made on card applications, while subsection (d) criminalizes certain false statements made about the theft, loss, or disappearance of a card.

Charging Language:

I. False statement in application **G.S. 14-113.13(c)**

. . . unlawfully and willfully did, in an application to (*name issuer of card*) for a financial transaction card, (*name or describe kind of card*), for the purpose of influencing the issuer to issue such a card, (*choose one or more of the following*)

(1) make and cause to be made a false statement and report relative to the defendant's (*choose one or more*: name; occupation; financial condition; assets; liabilities) in that the defendant stated (*describe false statement and tell why it is false*).

(2) substantially overvalue the defendant's assets in that the defendant stated (*describe what he or she stated and tell how it differed from the truth*).

(3) omit a statement of indebtedness to (*describe indebtedness that was omitted from application*).

(4) substantially undervalue the defendant's indebtedness by stating (*describe what he or she stated and tell how it differed from the true state of his or her indebtedness*).

II. False report concerning card **G.S. 14-113.13(d)**

. . . unlawfully and willfully did, with the intent to defraud (*name victim*), submit to (*name person or company to whom false report was submitted*) a false notice and report of the (*choose one or more*: theft; loss; disappearance; non-receipt) of a financial transaction card in that the defendant stated (*describe false report and tell why it was false*).

Notes about Charging Language:

- The statute says that the victim intended to be defrauded may be "the issuer, a person or organization providing money, goods, services, or anything else of value, or any other person."
- G.S. 14-113.8 provides a detailed definition of "financial transaction card." In addition to credit cards, the term includes cards used in withdrawing and transferring funds—in other words, debit cards—and cards used in connection with overdraft privilege accounts.

Sample Charge:

I. False statement in application **G.S. 14-113.13(c)**

. . . unlawfully and willfully did, in an application to Suntrust Bank for a financial transaction card, a Master Card, for the purpose of influencing the issuer to issue such a card, make and cause to be made a false statement and report relative to the defendant's occupation and financial condition, in that the defendant stated that the defendant was a physician and had an income of $145,000 annually, when in fact the defendant was unemployed and had no regular income.

AOC Forms for This Offense:
None.

Punishment:
Class 2 misdemeanor.

G.S. 14-113.13(c1)
Financial Transaction Card Fraud: Payment for Non-Sale
April 2024

Introductory Comment:
None.

Charging Language:
. . . unlawfully and willfully did, being a person authorized by an acquirer, (*name acquirer*), to furnish money, goods, services, and anything else of value on presentation of a financial transaction card or account number by a cardholder, with intent to defraud the issuer, acquirer, and cardholder, remit to the (*choose one and describe*: acquirer; issuer) for payment a financial transaction card record of a sale, (*describe purported sale*), which sale was not made by the defendant, the defendant's agent, or the defendant's employee.

Notes about Charging Language:
- The statute also imposes criminal liability on an agent or employee of an authorized person. If that occurs, substitute the words "an agent of a person" or "an employee of a person" for "a person."
- G.S. 14-113.8 defines an "acquirer" as a business organization, financial institution, or an agent of a business organization or financial institution that authorizes a merchant to accept payment by financial transaction card for money, goods, services, or anything else of value. It defines "issuer" as the business organization or financial institution or its duly authorized agent that issues a financial transaction card.
- G.S. 14-113.8 provides a detailed definition of "financial transaction card." In addition to credit cards, the term includes cards used in withdrawing and transferring funds—in other words, debit cards—and cards used in connection with overdraft privilege accounts.

Sample Charge:
. . . unlawfully and willfully did, being a person authorized by an acquirer, NationsBank, to furnish money, goods, services, and anything of value on presentation of a financial transaction card or account number by a cardholder, with intent to defraud the issuer, acquirer, and cardholder, remit to the acquirer, NationsBank, for payment a financial transaction card record of a sale, $79.99 worth of jewelry to Sally Jones on a NationsBank Visa credit card, which sale was not made by the defendant, the defendant's agent, or the defendant's employee.

AOC Forms for This Offense:
None.

Punishment:
Class 2 misdemeanor.

Introductory Comment:
None.

Charging Language:

I. Possession of more than one incomplete card **G.S. 14-113.14(a)(1)**

. . . unlawfully, willfully, and feloniously did possess (*give number, which must be more than one*) incomplete financial transaction cards with intent to complete them without the consent of the issuer. The cards were incomplete with respect to the information required by their issuer to appear on the cards, in that (*describe issuer and condition of each card, indicating the matter other than the signature of the cardholder that the issuer required to appear on each card before use*). That information had not yet been stamped, embossed, imprinted, or written upon the cards.

II. Possession of machinery to make cards **G.S. 14-113.14(a)(2)**

. . . unlawfully, willfully, and feloniously did possess, with knowledge of its character, (*choose one or more*: machinery; plates; a contrivance), a (*describe the machinery, plate, or other contrivance*) designed to reproduce instruments purporting to be financial transaction cards of (*identify purported issuer*), who had not consented to the preparation of such financial transaction cards.

Notes about Charging Language:

- G.S. 14-113.8 provides a detailed definition of "financial transaction card." In addition to credit cards, the term includes cards used in withdrawing and transferring funds—in other words, debit cards—and cards used in connection with overdraft privilege accounts.

Sample Charges:

I. Possession of more than one incomplete card **G.S. 14-113.14(a)(1)**

. . . unlawfully, willfully, and feloniously did possess two incomplete financial transaction cards with intent to complete them without the consent of the issuers. The cards were incomplete with respect to the information required by their issuer to appear on the cards, in that card number 1 was a Belk credit card issued by Belk Co., Durham, N.C., which had the card number 5565-7821-9843-7732 imprinted on it, and card number 2 was a Belk credit card issued by Belk Co., Durham, N.C., which had the card number 5565-7821-9843-7731 imprinted on it. Before a card may be used, Belk Co. requires the name and address of the cardholder and the expiration date of the card to be imprinted on the card. That information had not yet been stamped, embossed, imprinted, or written upon the cards.

II. Possession of machinery to make cards **G.S. 14-113.14(a)(2)**

. . . unlawfully, willfully, and feloniously did possess, with knowledge of its character, machinery and plates, an AB Dick embossing machine and a plate for a Mobil Oil Credit card, designed to reproduce instruments purporting to be financial transaction cards of Mobile Oil Company, who had not consented to the preparation of such financial transaction cards.

AOC Forms for This Offense:
None.

Punishment:
Class I felony.

G.S. 14-113.15
Receiving Goods or Services Obtained by Financial Transaction Card Fraud
April 2024

Introductory Comment:
This offense is akin to possessing or receiving stolen goods, but it applies when the goods in question were obtained through financial transaction card fraud. The offense can be a misdemeanor or a felony, depending on the value of the goods.

Charging Language:
I. Goods worth $500 or less

. . . unlawfully and willfully did receive (*choose one or more*: money; goods; services; a thing of value), (*describe what was received*), which had been obtained by financial transaction card fraud in violation of G.S. 14-113.13(a) and which, at the time of such receiving, the defendant knew and believed to have been so obtained.

II. Goods worth more than $500

. . . unlawfully, willfully, and feloniously did receive (*choose one or more*: money; goods; services; a thing of value), (*describe what was received*), which had been obtained by financial transaction card fraud in violation of G.S. 14-113.13(a) and which, at the time of such receiving, the defendant knew and believed to have been so obtained. The things and services described above were received within a period of six months, (*give dates*), and had a value in excess of $500.

Notes about Charging Language:
- G.S. 14-113.16 provides: "A person who obtains at a discount price a ticket issued by an airline, railroad, steamship or other transportation company from other than an authorized agent of such company which was acquired in violation of G.S. 14-113.13(a) without reasonable inquiry to ascertain that the person from whom it was obtained had a legal right to possess it shall be presumed to know that such ticket was acquired under circumstances constituting a violation of G.S. 14-113.13(a)."

Sample Charge:
II. Goods worth more than $500

. . . unlawfully, willfully, and feloniously did receive one Sony 37-inch LCD TV, model no. 54358963, which had been obtained by financial transaction card fraud in violation of G.S. 14-113.13(a). At the time of such receiving, the defendant knew that such goods had been fraudulently obtained. The things and services described above were received within a period of six months, on or about March 17, 2019, to on or about September 17, 2019, and had a value in excess of $500.

AOC Forms for This Offense:
None.

Punishment:
Offense I is a Class 2 misdemeanor. Offense II is a Class I felony.

G.S. 14-113.15A
Criminal Factoring of Financial Transaction Card Records
April 2024

Introductory Comment:
None.

Charging Language:
. . . unlawfully, willfully, and feloniously did, without the express authorization of an acquirer, (*name acquirer*), solicit an authorized merchant, (*name merchant*), to remit to an (*choose one and identify*: acquirer; issuer) for payment a financial transaction card record of a sale, (*describe purported sale*), which sale was not made by the merchant, the merchant's agent, or the merchant's employee.

Notes about Charging Language:
- G.S. 14-113.8 defines an "acquirer" as a business organization, financial institution, or an agent of a business organization or financial institution that authorizes a merchant to accept payment by a financial transaction card for money, goods, services, or anything else of value. It defines "issuer" as the business organization or financial institution, or its duly authorized agent, that issues a financial transaction card.
- The statute also applies to a defendant who "employs" a merchant. If that occurs, substitute "employ" for "solicit" or use both terms if appropriate.
- The statute also applies to the soliciting of an agent or employee of the merchant. If that occurs, substitute the appropriate language.

Sample Charge:
. . . unlawfully, willfully, and feloniously did, without the express authorization of an acquirer, Wachovia National Bank, solicit an authorized merchant, Robert Smith of Smith's Jewelry Store, Inc., to remit to an acquirer, Wachovia National Bank, for payment a financial transaction card record of a sale, $1,200 for a diamond ring, to Howard Wilkins, on a Wachovia Visa credit card, which sale was not made by the merchant, his agent, or his employee.

AOC Forms for This Offense:
None.

Punishment:
Class I felony.

G.S. 14-113.20
Identity Theft
April 2024

Introductory Comment:
None.

Charging Language:
. . . unlawfully, willfully, and feloniously did knowingly (*choose one or more*: obtain; possess; use) identifying information, (*describe identifying information*), of another person, (*name person, living or dead*), with the intent to fraudulently represent that the defendant was the other person for the purpose of (*choose one or more and describe*: avoiding legal consequences; making financial transactions in the other person's name; making credit transactions in the other person's name; obtaining anything of value, benefit, or advantage).

Notes about Charging Language:
- G.S. 14-113.20(b) defines "identifying information" as Social Security or tax identification numbers; driver's license or state identification card numbers; passport numbers; checking account numbers; savings account numbers; credit card numbers; debit card numbers; PIN codes as defined in G.S. 14-113.8(6); electronic identification numbers; email addresses and certain other Internet-related information; digital signatures; any other numbers or information that can be used to access a person's financial resources; biometric data; fingerprints; passwords; and parents' legal surnames before marriage. In *State v. Miles*, 267 N.C. App. 78, 91 (2019), the court of appeals ruled that "a person's name, date of birth, and address constitutes identifying information under the statute."
- In *State v. Faucette*, 285 N.C. App. 501 (2022), the court of appeals ruled that the identifying information must belong to an "actual person." Thus, a defendant who gave a false name and date of birth did not commit this offense where, although the State located a person with the same name the defendant provided, the person's date of birth did not match and there was no indication "that anyone could have used the information given by Defendant to identify any real person."
- This offense is aggravated if (1) the victim is arrested, detained, or convicted as a proximate result of this offense or (2) the defendant possesses identifying information pertaining to three or more separate people. G.S. 14-113.22. If either of these is the case, the appropriate facts must be alleged. For example: "The victim was arrested as a proximate result of this offense" or "The defendant possessed the identifying information pertaining to three or more separate people, (*name people*)."

Sample Charge:
. . . unlawfully, willfully, and feloniously did knowingly obtain, possess, and use identifying information, a Social Security number, of another person, Peter Jones, with the intent to fraudulently represent that the defendant was the other person for the purpose of making financial transactions in the other person's name, by fraudulently opening a checking account in the name of Peter Jones.

AOC Forms for This Offense:
None.

Punishment:
Class G felony, unless aggravated as described above, in which case, Class F felony.

G.S. 14-113.20A
Trafficking in Stolen Identities
April 2024

Introductory Comment:
None.

Charging Language:
. . . unlawfully, willfully, and feloniously did (*choose one or more*: sell to; transfer to; purchase from [*name person to whom sold or transferred, or from whom purchased, if known, or state* "an unknown person"]) the identifying information, (*describe information*), of another person, (*name person*), (*choose one or both*: with the intent to commit identity theft; to assist another person, [*name person*], in committing identity theft) as set forth in G.S. 14-113.20.

Notes about Charging Language:
- G.S. 14-113.20(b) defines "identifying information" as Social Security or tax identification numbers; driver's license or state identification card numbers; passport numbers; checking account numbers; savings account numbers; credit card numbers; debit card numbers; PIN codes as defined in G.S. 14-113.8(6); electronic identification numbers; email addresses and certain other Internet-related information; digital signatures; any other numbers or information that can be used to access a person's financial resources; biometric data; fingerprints; passwords; and a parent's legal surname before marriage. In *State v. Miles*, 267 N.C. App. 78, 91 (2019), the court of appeals ruled that "a person's name, date of birth, and address constitutes identifying information under the statute."
- At least when charging this offense based on the sale or transfer of identifying information, it is necessary to allege "the name of the recipient or that the recipient's name is unknown." State v. Jones, 367 N.C. 299, 309 (2014).

Sample Charge:
. . . unlawfully, willfully, and feloniously did sell to James Bell the identifying information, the Social Security number, of another person, Phyllis Brown, to assist another person, James Bell, in committing identity theft as set forth in G.S. 14-113.20.

AOC Forms for This Offense:
None.

Punishment:
Class E felony.

G.S. 14-114
Disposing of Secured (Mortgaged) Personal Property
April 2024

Introductory Comment:
This offense applies when a person improperly sells, destroys, or otherwise disposes of property that is subject to a security agreement, that is, in which a creditor has a security interest. Proof that the maker possessed the property embraced in the security agreement after signing the agreement, and proof that the sheriff or other officer acting under an order to seize the property cannot after due diligence find the property, creates a presumption that the maker intended to violate the statute. However, this presumption may be rebutted by evidence that the property has—through no fault of the defendant—been stolen, lost, damaged beyond repair, or otherwise disposed of by the defendant without the intent to defeat the rights of the secured party.

Charging Language:
. . . unlawfully and willfully did, after executing a security agreement for a lawful purpose to (*name secured party*), dispose of the following personal property embraced in the security agreement: (*list property disposed of*), with the intent to defeat the rights of (*name secured party*).

Notes about Charging Language:
- This offense is also committed by any person who buys property subject to a security agreement with the intent to defeat the creditor's rights. In that case, modify the charging language appropriately.
- A person's refusal to turn over secured property to a secured party who is attempting to repossess the property without a judgment or order for possession is not, by itself, a violation of this statute.

Sample Charge:
. . . unlawfully and willfully did, after executing a security agreement for a lawful purpose to Raleigh Rent to Own Furniture Company, dispose of the following personal property embraced in the security agreement: one RCA 42-inch plasma TV and one Queen Anne couch with green and white striped upholstery, with the intent to defeat the rights of Raleigh Rent to Own Furniture Company.

AOC Forms for This Offense:
None.

Punishment:
Class 2 misdemeanor.

G.S. 14-115
Secreting Personal Property to Hinder Enforcement of Security Interest
April 2024

Introductory Comment:
None.

Charging Language:
. . . unlawfully and willfully did (*choose one or more*: remove; exchange; secrete; refuse to surrender to a law enforcement officer) personal property, (*name property*), on which a security interest to (*name secured party*) existed, with the intent to prevent and hinder the enforcement of the security interest after (*choose one*: a judgment; an order) had been issued for possession of that personal property.

Notes about Charging Language:
- The statute also protects a lien on personal property. Substitute "lien" for "security interest" if appropriate.

Sample Charge:
. . . unlawfully and willfully did refuse to surrender to a law enforcement officer personal property, a 21–cubic foot Hotpoint refrigerator, model CV105, on which a security interest to Grogan's Appliance, Inc., existed, with the intent to prevent and hinder the enforcement of the security interest after an order had been issued for possession of that personal property.

AOC Forms for This Offense:
None.

Punishment:
Class 2 misdemeanor.

G.S. 14-118.4
Extortion
April 2024

Introductory Comment:
None.

Charging Language:
. . . unlawfully, willfully, and feloniously did threaten and communicate a threat to (*name victim*) with the intent wrongfully to obtain (*name thing of value, acquittance, advantage, or immunity sought*) by (*describe threat*).

Notes about Charging Language:
The North Carolina Court of Appeals has held that the specific identity of the victim is not an element of this offense. *See In re* J.A.D., 283 N.C. App. 8 (2022) (upholding the validity of a juvenile petition alleging only that the juvenile made a threat to "another"). However, this form requests that information for clarity and out of an abundance of caution.

Sample Charge:
. . . unlawfully, willfully, and feloniously did threaten and communicate a threat to Lawrence Jones with the intent wrongfully to obtain $1,500 by threatening to kidnap the daughter of Lawrence Jones if he did not pay the defendant $1,500.

AOC Forms for This Offense:
None.

Punishment:
Class F felony.

G.S. 14-118.5
Theft of Cable Television Service
April 2024

Introductory Comment:
This offense criminalizes the theft of cable television service. It does not apply to the theft of satellite television service. *See* G.S. 14-118.5(f).

The statute provides that proof that cable television equipment has been tampered with is prima facie evidence that the tampering was done by the customer or by the person regularly receiving benefits as a result of the tampering. Note that while G.S. 14-118.5(b) criminalizes the sale or distribution of descramblers and similar devices that can facilitate the theft of cable television service, that offense is charged infrequently, and this manual therefore does not contain charging language for it.

Charging Language:

. . . did unlawfully, willfully, and knowingly

(choose one or both)

(1) (*choose one or both*: attach; maintain) a(n) (*choose one or more*: electronic connection; mechanical connection; *name other type of connection*) to

(2) (*choose one or more*: remove; tamper with; modify; alter)

a (*choose one or more*: cable; wire; decoder; converter; device; *name other piece of equipment*) of a cable television system, (*name system*), for the purpose of (*choose one or both*: intercepting; receiving) unauthorized (*choose one or both*: programming; service) of that system.

Notes about Charging Language:
None.

Sample Charge:
. . . did unlawfully, willfully, and knowingly tamper with and modify a wire of a cable television system, Spectrum Cable of Raleigh, N.C., for the purpose of receiving unauthorized programming and service of that system.

AOC Forms for This Offense:
None.

Punishment:
Class 3 misdemeanor, "which may include a fine not exceeding five hundred dollars." G.S. 14-118.5(a).

Forging and Counterfeiting of Currency, Notes, Checks, and Securities

Introductory Comment:
None.

Charging Language:
. . . unlawfully, willfully, and feloniously did forge and counterfeit an instrument, (*select one of the following*)

(1) (*choose one*: a bill; a note; a warrant; a check; an order; *name similar instrument*) drawn on a (*choose one*: mutual fund; money market fund; credit union; savings and loan association; bank; *name similar institution*; governmental unit), (*name financial institution or governmental unit*),

(2) a security purporting to be issued by a (*choose one*: mutual fund; money market fund; credit union; savings and loan association; bank; governmental unit; corporation), (*name financial institution, governmental unit, or corporation*),

(3) currency of the (*name governmental unit, such as* United States),

which is described as follows: (*describe instrument*). The forgery and counterfeiting consisted of the following: (*describe how the instrument was forged and counterfeited*). The defendant acted without authority and with the intent to injure and defraud.

Notes about Charging Language:

- The statute only requires proof of forgery or counterfeiting. You may delete one of the words if appropriate. "Counterfeit" is defined in G.S. 14-119(b)(1) to mean "manufacture, copy, reproduce, or forge an instrument that purports to be genuine, but is not, because it has been falsely copied, reproduced, forged, manufactured, embossed, encoded, duplicated or altered."
- A "governmental unit" includes the United States, any United States territory, any state of the United States, any political subdivision of any state, and any foreign jurisdiction. G.S. 14-119(c)(3).
- The court of appeals has held that a charging document need not describe the manner in which the instrument was forged. State v. King, 178 N.C. App. 122 (2006). This form nonetheless requests that information.
- It is not necessary to name the particular person or entity intended to be defrauded. *See* G.S. 15-151; *cf.* State v. McAllister, 287 N.C. 178, 190 (1975) (uttering forged checks).

Sample Charge:
. . . unlawfully, willfully, and feloniously did forge and counterfeit an instrument, a check drawn on a bank, Smithtown Bank, Charlotte, N.C., which is described as follows:

> Check number 2576, in the amount of $156.15, dated July 17, 2019, drawn on the account of Samuel Smith and payable to Nancy Tilden.

The forgery and counterfeiting consisted of the following: the defendant filled out the check and signed it without the authorization of Samuel Smith. The defendant acted without authority and with the intent to injure and defraud.

AOC Forms for This Offense:
AOC-CR-133 (Indictment)
AOC-J-318 (Juvenile Petition)

Punishment:
Class I felony.

G.S. 14-119(a), (b)
Possessing or Transporting Counterfeit Instruments
April 2024
Page 1 of 2

Introductory Comment:
None.

Charging Language:

I. Possess counterfeit instrument **G.S. 14-119(a)**

. . . unlawfully, willfully, and feloniously did possess a counterfeit instrument, (*select one of the following*)

(1) (*choose one*: a bill; a note; a warrant; a check; an order; *name similar instrument*) drawn on a (*choose one*: mutual fund; money market fund; credit union; savings and loan association; bank; *name similar institution*; governmental unit), (*name financial institution or governmental unit*),

(2) a security purporting to be issued by a (*choose one*: mutual fund; money market fund; credit union; savings and loan association; bank; governmental unit; corporation), (*name financial institution, governmental unit, or corporation*),

(3) currency of the (*name governmental unit, such as* United States),

which is described as follows: (*describe instrument*). The counterfeiting consisted of the following: (*describe how the instrument was counterfeited*). The defendant acted without authority and with the intent to injure and defraud.

II. Possess or transport five or more counterfeit instruments **G.S. 14-119(b)**

. . . unlawfully, willfully, and feloniously did (*choose one or both*: possess; transport) five or more, namely, (*insert actual number*), counterfeit instruments without authority and with the intent to injure or defraud.

For each of the instruments, describe as follows: The counterfeit instrument was

(1) (*choose one*: a bill; a note; a warrant; a check; an order; *name similar instrument*) drawn on a (*choose one*: mutual fund; money market fund; credit union; savings and loan association; bank; *name similar institution*; governmental unit), (*name financial institution or governmental unit*),

(2) a security purporting to be issued by a (*choose one*: mutual fund; money market fund; credit union; savings and loan association; bank; governmental unit; corporation), (*name financial institution, governmental unit, or corporation*),

(3) currency of the (*name governmental unit, such as* United States),

which is described as follows: (*describe instrument*). The counterfeiting consisted of the following: (*describe how the instrument was counterfeited*).

Notes about Charging Language:

- "Counterfeit" is defined in G.S. 14-119(b)(1) to mean "manufacture, copy, reproduce, or forge an instrument that purports to be genuine, but is not, because it has been falsely copied, reproduced, forged, manufactured, embossed, encoded, duplicated or altered."
- A "governmental unit" includes the United States, any United States territory, any state of the United States, any political subdivision of any state, and any foreign jurisdiction. G.S. 14-119(c)(3).
- The court of appeals has held that a charging document need not describe the manner in which the instrument was forged. State v. King, 178 N.C. App. 122 (2006). This form nonetheless requests that information.
- It is not necessary to name the particular person or entity intended to be defrauded. *See* G.S. 15-151; *cf.* State v. McAllister, 287 N.C. 178, 190 (1975) (uttering forged checks).

Sample Charge:

I. Possess counterfeit instrument **G.S. 14-119(a)**

. . . unlawfully, willfully, and feloniously did possess a counterfeit instrument, a check drawn on a bank, Smithtown Bank, Charlotte, N.C., which is described as follows:

> Check number 2576, in the amount of $156.15, dated July 17, 2019, drawn on the account of Samuel Smith and payable to Nancy Tilden.

The counterfeiting consisted of the following: the check was filled out and signed without the authorization of Samuel Smith. The defendant acted without authority and with the intent to injure and defraud.

AOC Forms for This Offense:
None.

Punishment:
Offense I is a Class I felony. Offense II is a Class G felony.

Common Law
Common Law Forgery
April 2024

Introductory Comment:
When a forgery involves an "instrument" as defined in G.S. 14-119, that statutory offense is usually charged rather than common law forgery.

Charging Language:
. . . unlawfully, willfully, and feloniously did forge and falsely make (*describe forged paper*), which was apparently capable of effecting a fraud, by (*describe what defendant did*). The defendant acted without authority and with deceit and the intent to injure and defraud.

Notes about Charging Language:
- Common law forgery is a felony if done with deceit as well as with the intent to injure and defraud. *See generally* G.S. 14-3(b). Because deceit will usually be present, the charging language above includes "feloniously" and the allegation "with deceit." If deceit is not present and only a misdemeanor is to be charged, strike through "feloniously" and "with deceit."
- In the context of the statutory forgery offense in G.S. 14-119, the court of appeals has held that a charging document need not describe the manner in which a document was forged. State v. King, 178 N.C. App. 122 (2006). Although that case may have some application to common law forgery, this form nonetheless requests a description of the general manner in which the defendant forged the document in question.

Sample Charge:
. . . unlawfully, willfully, and feloniously did forge and falsely make an admission ticket to the UNC-Chapel Hill vs. N.C. State football game played in Raleigh, N.C., on October 15, 2019, which was apparently capable of effecting a fraud, by making an admission ticket that looked similar to a valid ticket and by which the defendant gained admission to the game. The defendant acted without authority and with deceit and the intent to injure and defraud.

AOC Forms for This Offense:
None.

Punishment:
Class H felony, *see* G.S. 14-3(b), unless done without deceit, in which case, Class 1 misdemeanor.

Common Law
Common Law Uttering of Forged Paper
April 2024

Introductory Comment:
When an uttering involves an "instrument" as defined in G.S. 14-119, the statutory uttering offense set forth in G.S. 14-120 is usually charged rather than common law uttering.

Charging Language:
. . . unlawfully, willfully, and feloniously did utter as true to (*identify one who received forged paper*) a falsely made and forged (*describe forged paper*), which was apparently capable of effecting a fraud because (*describe why the paper was capable of effecting a fraud*). The defendant acted without authority and with deceit and the intent to injure and defraud.

Notes about Charging Language:
- Common law uttering is a felony if done with deceit as well as with the intent to injure and defraud. *See generally* G.S. 14-3(b). Because deceit will usually be present, the charging language above includes "feloniously" and the allegation "with deceit." If deceit is not present and only a misdemeanor is to be charged, strike through "feloniously" and "with deceit."

Sample Charge:
. . . unlawfully, willfully, and feloniously did utter as true to Samuel Jones a falsely made and forged admission ticket to the UNC vs. N.C. State football game played in Raleigh, N.C., on October 13, 2019, which was apparently capable of effecting a fraud because the falsely made and forged admission ticket looked similar to a valid ticket and was used to gain admission to the game. The defendant acted without authority and with deceit and the intent to injure and defraud.

AOC Forms for This Offense:
None.

Punishment:
Class H felony, *see* G.S. 14-3(b), unless done without deceit, in which case, Class 1 misdemeanor.

G.S. 14-120
Uttering Forged Paper
April 2024

Introductory Comment:
None.

Charging Language:
. . . unlawfully, willfully, and feloniously did utter, publish, pass, and deliver as true to (*identify one who received forged paper*) a falsely made and forged (*choose one*: bill; note; order; warrant; check; security; *and describe in the same manner as in the charge for G.S. 14-119*). The defendant acted for the sake of gain and with the intent to injure and defraud and with knowledge that the instrument was falsely made and forged.

Notes about Charging Language:
None.

Sample Charge:
. . . unlawfully, willfully, and feloniously did utter, publish, pass, and deliver as true to Jones State Bank a falsely made and forged check drawn on Acme State Bank, an incorporated bank of the State of North Carolina, payable to John Doe and dated January 1, 2019. The defendant acted for the sake of gain and with the intent to injure and defraud and with knowledge that the instrument was falsely made and forged.

AOC Forms for This Offense:
AOC-CR-133 (Indictment)
AOC-J-318 (Juvenile Petition)

Punishment:
Class I felony.

G.S. 14-120
Forging Endorsement
April 2024

Introductory Comment:
None.

Charging Language:
. . . unlawfully, willfully, and feloniously did falsely make and forge an endorsement of (*name person whose endorsement was forged*) on a (*choose one*: bill; note; warrant; check; order; security; *and describe in the same manner as in the charge for G.S. 14-119*). The defendant acted for the sake of gain and with the intent to injure and defraud.

Notes about Charging Language:
None.

Sample Charge:
. . . unlawfully, willfully, and feloniously did falsely make and forge an endorsement of Sally Victim on a check drawn on Acme State Bank, an incorporated bank of the State of North Carolina, payable to John Defendant and dated January 1, 2019. The defendant acted for the sake of gain and with the intent to injure and defraud.

AOC Forms for This Offense:
None.

Punishment:
Class I felony.

G.S. 14-120
Uttering Paper with Forged Endorsement
April 2024

Introductory Comment:
None.

Charging Language:
. . . unlawfully, willfully, and feloniously did utter, publish, pass, and deliver as true to (*identify recipient*) a (*choose one*: bill; warrant; note; order; check; security; *and describe in the same manner as in the charge for G.S. 14-119*), which contained a forged and falsely made endorsement of (*name person whose endorsement was forged*). The defendant knew at the time that the endorsement was falsely made and forged and acted for the sake of gain and with the intent to injure and defraud.

Notes about Charging Language:
None.

Sample Charge:
. . . unlawfully, willfully, and feloniously did utter, publish, pass, and deliver as true to Acme State Bank a check of Jones National Bank, an incorporated bank of North Carolina, payable to John Defendant and dated January 1, 2019, which contained a forged and falsely made endorsement of Sally Victim. The defendant knew at the time that the endorsement was falsely made and forged and acted for the sake of gain and with the intent to injure and defraud.

AOC Forms for This Offense:
None.

Punishment:
Class I felony.

G.S. 14-127
Injury to Real Property
April 2024

Introductory Comment:
None.

Charging Language:
. . . unlawfully and willfully did wantonly damage, injure, and destroy real property, (*describe and provide address of real property*), the property of (*describe the person or entity that owns the property*).

Notes about Charging Language:
- "Ideally, an indictment for injury to real property should include the street address or other clear designation . . . of the real property alleged to have been injured." State v. Spivey, 368 N.C. 739, 743 (2016).
- It is not a legal requirement that the ownership of the property must be alleged, much less that the owner is legally capable of owning property. *See Spivey*, 368 N.C. at 740 ("The indictment needs to identify the real property itself, not the owner or ownership interest."). However, this form requests information about ownership because it may be helpful in identifying the property in question.

Sample Charge:
. . . unlawfully and willfully did wantonly damage, injure, and destroy real property, two windows of a house at 49 Main Street, Apex, N.C., the property of Howard and Betty Jones.

AOC Forms for This Offense:
AOC-J-322 (Juvenile Petition)

Punishment:
Class 1 misdemeanor.

Common Law
Forcible Trespass
April 2024

Introductory Comment:
This offense is distinct from the statutory first- and second-degree trespass offenses that are more commonly charged. It occurs only when the defendant uses force or intimidation against the occupant during a trespass.

Charging Language:
. . . unlawfully and willfully did enter with a strong hand upon the lands located at (*give location of land*) by using force against and intimidating the occupant of the lands, (*name occupant*), who was present at the time of entry and was in peaceful possession of the lands. The defendant (*describe force or intimidation used*).

Notes about Charging Language:
- If the defendant entered the property legally but remained after being asked to leave, include the following at the end of the charging language above: The entry and presence by the defendant was unlawful in that the defendant remained after being asked to leave by (*name person who asked defendant to leave*).
- This offense may also be committed when the occupant is not present at the time of entry if the occupant appears while the trespasser is still present. For a discussion of the elements of this offense, see Jessica Smith, *North Carolina Crimes: A Guidebook on the Elements of Crime* 394–95 (UNC School of Government, 7th ed. 2012).

Sample Charge:
. . . unlawfully and willfully did enter with a strong hand upon the lands located at 245 Mossdale Avenue, Livingston, N.C., the home of Robert Smith, by using force against and intimidating the occupant of the lands, Robert Smith, who was present at the time of entry and was in peaceful possession of the lands. The defendant entered the lands with a stick, threatening to beat Robert Smith and telling him that nobody was going to stop him.

AOC Forms for This Offense:
None.

Punishment:
Class 1 misdemeanor.

G.S. 14-132(a)(1)
Disorderly Conduct in Public Building or Facility
April 2024

Introductory Comment:
Although G.S. 14-132 defines several crimes, such as defacing a public building, G.S. 14-132(a)(2), and committing a nuisance in a public building, G.S. 14-132(a)(3), this manual provides sample charging language only for the most commonly-charged offense defined in the statute, namely, disorderly conduct in a public building, G.S. 14-132(a)(1).

Charging Language:
. . . unlawfully and willfully did commit disorderly conduct (*describe disorderly conduct*) (*choose one or both*: in; near) a public building and facility, (*describe building or facility and give its location*).

Notes about Charging Language:
- Disorderly conduct is not defined in this statute. Courts would likely apply the definition of disorderly conduct in G.S. 14-288.4.
- A "public building or facility" is defined in G.S. 14-132(c) to include a building or facility (1) to which the public or a portion of the public has access and which is owned or controlled by the state, any subdivision of the state, any other public agency, or any private institution or agency of a charitable, educational, or eleemosynary nature; (2) dedicated to the use of the general public primarily for public recreation, cultural activities, and other public events; or (3) designated as public by the Director of the State Bureau of Investigation pursuant to G.S. 143B-987. The definition also includes the surrounding grounds and premises of a building or facility used in the connection with the operation or functioning of the building or facility.

Sample Charge:
. . . unlawfully and willfully did commit disorderly conduct by fighting with three other people, Sam Jones, Peter Fink, and Sally Jones, in a public building and facility, the Division of Motor Vehicles license office at 12 Trent Street, Middletown, N.C.

AOC Forms for This Offense:
None.

Punishment:
Class 2 misdemeanor.

G.S. 14-134.3
Domestic Criminal Trespass
April 2024
Page 1 of 2

Introductory Comment:
None.

Charging Language:

I. Misdemeanor domestic criminal trespass **G.S. 14-134.3(a)**

. . . unlawfully and willfully did, at (*give full address of premises, including apartment number, if any*), (*choose one or both*: enter the premises after being forbidden to do so; remain in the premises after being ordered to leave) by (*name occupant*), the lawful occupant, the premises then being occupied by (*choose one of the following*)

(1) the present spouse of the defendant,
(2) the former spouse of the defendant,
(3) a person with whom the defendant has lived as if married,

who was living separate and apart from the defendant at the time of the entry and refusal to leave.

II. Felony domestic criminal trespass **G.S. 14-134.3(b)**

. . . unlawfully, willfully, and feloniously did, at (*name place and give location*), operated as a safe house and haven for victims of domestic violence, (*choose one or both*: enter the premises after being forbidden to do so; remain in the premises after being ordered to leave) by (*name occupant*), the lawful occupant, the premises then being occupied by
(*choose one of the following*)

(1) the present spouse of the defendant,
(2) the former spouse of the defendant,
(3) a person with whom the defendant has lived as if married,

who was living separate and apart from the defendant at the time of the entry and refusal to leave. At the time of this offense, the defendant was armed with a deadly weapon, (*name deadly weapon*).

Notes about Charging Language:
None.

Sample Charge:

I. Misdemeanor domestic criminal trespass

. . . unlawfully and willfully did at 453 Randall Lane, Charlotte, N.C., enter the premises after being forbidden to do so and remain in the premises after being ordered to leave by Teresa Weldon Simpson, the lawful occupant, the premises then being occupied by the former spouse of the defendant, who was living separate and apart from the defendant at the time of the entry and refusal to leave.

AOC Forms for This Offense:
None.

Punishment:
Offense I is a Class 1 misdemeanor. Offense II is a Class G felony.

G.S. 14-148, -149
Desecrating Grave Site
April 2024
Page 1 of 2

Introductory Comment:
G.S. 14-148 and -149 define several offenses related to the desecration of grave sites. Charging language for the most common of these offenses appears below.

Charging Language:

I. Desecrating human remains **G.S. 14-149(a1)**

. . . unlawfully, willfully, and feloniously did knowingly, without the authorization of law or the consent of the (*choose one*: surviving spouse; next of kin), (*name person if known or state* "name unknown"), (*choose one or more*: disturb; destroy; remove; vandalize; desecrate) the human remains of (*name person if known or state* "a person unknown"), which were interred in a cemetery, (*name cemetery and give location*).

II. Desecrating caskets **G.S. 14-149(a)(1)**

. . . unlawfully, willfully, and feloniously did knowingly, without the authorization of law or the consent of the (*choose one*: surviving spouse; next of kin), (*name person if known or state* "name unknown"), (*choose one or more*: open; disturb; destroy; remove; vandalize; desecrate) a [*choose one or more*: casket; repository of human remains, a (*describe repository*),] by (*briefly describe the method of desecration*).

III. Desecrating grave markers **G.S. 14-149(a)(2)**

. . . unlawfully, willfully, and feloniously did knowingly, without the authorization of law or the consent of the (*choose one*: surviving spouse; next of kin), (*name person if known or state* "name unknown"), (*choose one or more*: take away; disturb; vandalize; destroy; tamper with; deface) a [*choose one or more*: tombstone; headstone; monument; grave marker; grave ornamentation; grave artifact (*describe item if a marker, ornament, or other artifact*)] that was erected or placed within a cemetery, (*name cemetery and give location*), to designate the place where the human remains of (*name person if known or state* "a person unknown") were interred and to preserve and perpetuate the memory and the name of that person, by (*briefly describe the method of desecration*).

IV. Tampering with plants designating a grave **G.S. 14-148(a)(3)**

. . . unlawfully and willfully did, without the authorization of law or the consent of the (*choose one*: surviving spouse; next of kin), (*name person if known or state* "name unknown"), (*choose one or more*: take away; disturb; vandalize; destroy; tamper with) [*choose one or more*: shrubbery; flowers; plants; an article (*describe article*)] that was/were planted or placed within a cemetery, (*name cemetery and give location*), to designate the place where the human remains of (*name person if known or state* "a person unknown") were interred and to preserve and perpetuate the memory and the name of that person, by (*briefly describe the method of desecration*).

Notes about Charging Language:

- Offense IV is a felony if the damage caused by the violation is $1,000 or more. In that case, substitute "unlawfully, willfully, and feloniously" for "unlawfully and willfully," and add the following at the end of the charging language above: "The damage caused by the defendant was $1,000 or more."

Sample Charge:

III. Desecrating grave markers **G.S. 14-149(a)(2)**

. . . unlawfully, willfully, and feloniously did knowingly, without the authorization of law or the consent of the surviving spouse, Janet Smith, vandalize a tombstone that was erected or placed within a cemetery, Peaceful Rest Cemetery, 2538 Pine Road, Cliffsburg, N.C., to designate the place where the human remains of Lance Smith were interred and to preserve and perpetuate the memory and the name of that person, by spray painting the image of a pentagram on the tombstone.

AOC Forms for This Offense:

None.

Punishment:

Offense I is a Class H felony. Offenses II and III are Class I felonies. Offense IV is a Class 1 misdemeanor unless the damage is $1,000 or more, in which case it is a Class I felony.

G.S. 14-150.2
Injuring Energy Facility
April 2024
Page 1 of 2

Introductory Comment:
Enacted in response to attacks on power substations in Moore County and Randolph County in December 2022 and January 2023, G.S. 14-150.2 (effective December 1, 2023) makes it a felony to damage an energy facility or obstruct its services. The bill that created this offense also amended G.S. 14-154 (injuring wires or other fixtures) and 14-159.12 (first-degree trespass).

Charging Language:

I. Damaging an energy facility

. . . unlawfully, willfully, and feloniously did destroy, injure, and damage an energy facility, (*identify the facility*), by (*describe the conduct*). (*If applicable add:* This conduct resulted in the death of another person, (*name the victim*).)

II. Obstructing the services of an energy facility

. . . unlawfully, willfully, and feloniously did obstruct, impede, and impair the services or transmissions of an energy facility, (*identify the facility*), by (*describe the conduct*), resulting in (*describe how services were impeded*). (*If applicable add*: This conduct resulted in the death of another person, (*name the victim*).)

Notes about Charging Language:

- For purposes of this section, "energy facility" means any facility involved in (1) the production, storage, transmission, or distribution of electricity, fuel, or another form or source of energy or (2) research, development, or demonstration related to the production, storage, transmission, or distribution of electricity, fuel, or another form or source of energy.
- The term "energy facility" includes any (1) facility in operation, under construction, or otherwise not functioning; (2) line, wire, pipe, or other property or equipment used as part of the normal operation of the facility; and (3) hardware, software, or other digital infrastructure necessary for the operations of a facility.
- The statute also prohibits an attempt to damage or obstruct the services of an energy facility. If there was only an attempt, include the phrase "attempt to." When in doubt, charge the completed offense. *See* G.S. 15-170 (indictment for completed offense will support conviction for attempt).
- Each violation constitutes a separate offense and shall not merge with any other offense. As the statute enumerates two forms, (i) or (ii), they are similarly enumerated above. Each instance of damage or obstruction might constitute a separate count. *See* State v. Applewhite, 281 N.C. App. 66, 77 (2021) (interpreting comparable provisions of G.S. 14-43.11, human trafficking), *discretionary review allowed*, ___ N.C. ___, 871 S.E.2d 511 (2022).
- This statute does not apply to demolition work and other activity that is performed by the owner or operator of an energy facility or an agent thereof authorized to perform such work.

Sample Charge:
. . . unlawfully, willfully, and feloniously did destroy, injure, and damage an energy facility, a Duke Energy substation located in the city of Thomasville, N.C., by breaching the gates and firing a gun at the facility, striking a transformer.

AOC Forms for This Offense:
None.

Punishment:
Class C felony. A violation that results in a death is a Class B2 felony. Fine of $250,000.

G.S. 14-151
Interfering with Utility Meters
April 2024

Introductory Comment:
This offense is a felony for repeat offenders. In such a case, insert "unlawfully, willfully, and feloniously" in place of "unlawfully and willfully" and add an allegation regarding the defendant's previous conviction. An indictment or an information for the recidivist offense must comply with G.S. 15A-928, which requires that the defendant's prior convictions be alleged either (1) in a separate count of the indictment or information than the substantive offense or (2) in a separate indictment or information. This requirement does not apply to arrest warrants or magistrates' orders, which still must allege the defendant's prior convictions but need not do so in a separate count or separate charging instrument. G.S. 15A-928 also requires in indictments or informations that the name or title of an offense elevated by prior convictions must not make reference to such prior convictions.

Charging Language:
. . . unlawfully and willfully did, with intent to (*choose one or both*: injure; defraud), (*choose one or more*: obstruct; alter; bypass; tamper with; injure; prevent the action of) a (*choose one*: meter; instrument) used to measure the quantity of (*choose one*: illuminating fuel; natural gas; water; electricity) passing through such meter. At the time of the offense, the defendant was not an employee of (*name company*), the company (*choose one or both*: owning; supplying) the (*choose one*: gas; water; electric) meter.

Notes about Charging Language:
- Previously, some utility-theft cases were charged under G.S. 14-151.1. However, in 2013 the General Assembly repealed that section and expanded this one.
- The charging language above is for a violation of subdivision (a)(2) of G.S. 14-151. The subdivision is confusingly drafted, and other interpretations are possible.
- There are several other subdivisions in the statute dealing with different means of utility theft, such as re-connecting a utility that was lawfully shut off, subdivision (a)(9).
- This offense is a felony if the crime results in significant property damage or public endangerment. In such a case, insert "unlawfully, willfully, and feloniously" in place of "unlawfully and willfully" and add an allegation regarding the damage or endangerment.
- This offense is a felony if the crime results in death. In such a case, insert "unlawfully, willfully, and feloniously" in place of "unlawfully and willfully" and add an allegation regarding the death.

Sample Charge:
. . . unlawfully and willfully did, with intent to defraud, tamper with a meter used to measure the quantity of natural gas passing through such meter. At the time of the offense, the defendant was not an employee of Blue Ridge Energy, the company owning and supplying the gas meter.

AOC Forms for This Offense:
None.

Punishment:
Class 1 misdemeanor. This offense is a Class H felony for a second or subsequent offense, a Class F felony if it results in significant property damage or public endangerment, and a Class D felony if it results in death.

G.S. 14-159.12
First-Degree Trespass
April 2024

Introductory Comment:
Enacted in 1987, G.S. 14-159.12 makes it a Class 2 misdemeanor to enter or remain, without authorization, in a building or enclosed premises of another. As of 2018, first-degree trespassing also includes entering upon the lands of the Eastern Band of the Cherokee Indians after banishment. Amendments effective December 1, 2023, increased the penalty for trespassing on facilities used for electric power, natural gas, public water, or agricultural activities.

Charging Language:
. . . unlawfully and willfully did, without authorization, enter and remain (*choose one*)

(1) in the building of (*name the owner or possessor of the building*), located at (*give location*).

(2) on the premises of (*name the owner or possessor of the premises*), located at (*give location*), so enclosed and secured as to demonstrate clearly an intent to keep out intruders.

(3) on the lands of the Eastern Band of Cherokee Indians after the person has been excluded by a resolution passed by the Eastern Band of Cherokee Indian Tribal Council, (*give date*).

Notes about Charging Language:
- G.S. 14-159.11 defines "building" as a "structure or part of a structure, other than a conveyance, enclosed so as to permit reasonable entry only through a door and roofed to protect it from the elements."
- G.S. 14-159.14 provides that first- and second-degree trespass are lesser-included offenses of the breaking or entering offenses in G.S. 14-54 (felonious and misdemeanor breaking or entering of a building) and 14-56 (felonious breaking or entering of motor vehicle, boat, etc.).
- There are aggravated versions of this offense involving trespass on certain energy facilities, utility facilities, public water facilities, or agricultural facilities. The aggravated offenses are felonies. Because these are rarely charged, this form does not include charging language for them. *Cf.* G.S. 14-150.2 (injuring energy facility).

Sample Charge:
. . . unlawfully and willfully did, without authorization, enter and remain in the building of Samuel Jones, located at 123 East Main Street, Patterson, N.C.

AOC Forms for This Offense:
AOC-J-311 (Juvenile Petition)

Punishment:
Class 2 misdemeanor.

G.S. 14-159.13
Second-Degree Trespass
April 2024

Introductory Comment:
Enacted in 1987, G.S. 14-159.13 recreated the older statutory offense of entering upon the lands of another after being forbidden to do so (G.S. 14-134), but it prescribed two forms for notice: direct communication by an authorized person or the posting of signs on the property. The statute was amended effective December 1, 2023, to add a third form of second-degree trespassing: being on the curtilage of another between midnight and 6:00 a.m.

Charging Language:
. . . unlawfully and willfully did, without authorization, enter and remain on the premises of (*name owner or possessor*), located at (*give location*), (*choose one*)

(1) after the defendant had been notified not to enter and remain there by (*name person*), (*choose one or more*: the owner of the premises; the person in charge of the premises; the lawful occupant of the premises; an authorized person).

(2) which was posted, in a manner reasonably likely to come to the attention of intruders, with notice not to enter the premises.

(3) on the curtilage of (his/her) dwelling between the hours of midnight and 6:00 a.m.

Notes about Charging Language:
- A sign prohibiting entry need not take the form of a "No Trespassing" sign. *See In re* S.M.S., 196 N.C. App. 170, 173 (2009) (sign marked "Girl's Locker Room" was reasonably likely to give respondent notice that he was not authorized to enter).
- G.S. 14-159.14 provides that first- and second-degree trespass are lesser-included offenses of the breaking or entering offenses in G.S. 14-54 (felonious and misdemeanor breaking or entering of a building) and 14-56 (felonious breaking or entering of motor vehicle, boat, etc.).

Sample Charge:
. . . unlawfully and willfully did, without authorization, enter and remain on the premises of Susan Kelly, located at 214 South Valley Road, Englishtown, N.C., after the defendant had been notified not to enter and remain there by Susan Kelly, the owner of the premises and the person in charge of the premises.

AOC Forms for This Offense:
AOC-J-311 (Juvenile Petition)

Punishment:
Offenses (1) and (2) above are Class 3 misdemeanors. Offense (3) is a Class 2 misdemeanor.

G.S. 14-160
Injury to Personal Property
April 2024

Introductory Comment:
None.

Charging Language:
. . . unlawfully and willfully did wantonly injure personal property, (*describe property*), the property of (*name owner or person in possession of the property*). (*Add if appropriate*: The damage caused was in excess of $200.)

Notes about Charging Language:
- The owner or possessor of the property must be a person or an entity, such as a corporation, that is capable of owning property. State v. Price, 170 N.C. App. 672 (2005). If the possessor is an entity, indicate the nature of the entity in the manner that you would when charging larceny.
- It is sufficient to allege as the victim a person or entity with a "special interest" in the property—that is, a person or entity in possession and control of the property—even if that person is not the actual owner. *See* State v. Redmond, 281 N.C. App. 283 (2022) (finding no fatal variance where a magistrate's order alleged that a damaged painting was "the property of Jonas Gerard," while the evidence at trial showed that the painting actually belonged to Jonas Gerard Fine Arts, Inc.; the evidence revealed that Mr. Gerard controlled his paintings during creation and even revisited them afterwards, giving him a "special interest" in them). *Cf.* G.S. 15-148 (describing permitted manner of alleging joint ownership).

Sample Charge:
. . . unlawfully and willfully did wantonly injure personal property, two lawn chairs, the property of Sally Jones.

AOC Forms for This Offense:
AOC-J-323 (Juvenile Petition)

Punishment:
Class 2 misdemeanor, unless the damage exceeded $200; then, Class 1 misdemeanor.

G.S. 14-160.1
Altering or Removing Permanent Identification Marks
April 2024
Page 1 of 2

Introductory Comment:
This offense applies to altering or removing identification marks, such as serial numbers, from personal property generally. If the property is a firearm, the felony offense set forth in G.S. 14-160.2 may be more appropriate.

Charging Language:

I. Altering, removing, or destroying identification **G.S. 14-160.1(a)**

. . . unlawfully, willfully, and feloniously did alter, deface, destroy, and remove the [choose one: permanent serial number; manufacturer's identification plate; permanent distinguishing number; permanent identification mark (*if necessary for clarity, describe the identification mark*)] from an item of personal property, a (*describe the property*) (*give value of property*), which was the property of (*name the owner or possessor*), with the intent to conceal and misrepresent the identity of the property.

II. Selling, buying, or possessing property with identification removed **G.S. 14-160.1(b)**

. . . unlawfully, willfully, and feloniously did knowingly (choose one or more)

(1) sell to (name the person to whom the property was sold)

(2) buy from (name the person from whom the property was bought)

(3) have and possess

an item of personal property, a (describe the property) (give value of property), which was the property of (name the owner or possessor), and on which the [choose one: permanent serial number; manufacturer's identification plate; permanent distinguishing number; permanent identification mark (if necessary for clarity, describe the identification mark)] had been altered, defaced, destroyed, and removed for the purpose of concealing and misrepresenting the identity of that property.

Notes about Charging Language:

- This offense is a Class H felony if the value of the property at the time of the offense exceeds one thousand dollars ($1,000). If charging a misdemeanor offense, change the phrase "unlawfully, willfully, and feloniously" in the charging language to "unlawfully and willfully."
- The statute includes altering, defacing, destroying, or removing the identification number. If one of those terms is not appropriate, it should be omitted.
- As to Offense II, the statute is applicable if the purpose was to either conceal or misrepresent the true identity of the property. If one of those terms is not appropriate, it should be omitted.
- It may be necessary to allege that the owner or possessor of the property is a person or an entity, such as a corporation, that is capable of owning property. *Cf.* State v. Price, 170 N.C. App. 672 (2005) (so holding, as to the offense of injury to personal property). If the possessor is an entity, indicate the nature of the entity in the manner that you would when charging larceny.

Sample Charge:

I. Altering, removing, or destroying identification **G.S. 14-160.1(a)**

. . . unlawfully, willfully, and feloniously did destroy and remove the permanent serial number from an item of personal property, a 55-inch Sony LCD television set having a value of $1,200, which was the property of Floyd T. Randolph, with the intent to conceal and misrepresent the identity of the property.

AOC Forms for This Offense:
None.

Punishment:
Class H felony. Class 1 misdemeanor if the value of the property at the time of the offense does not exceed one thousand dollars ($1,000).

G.S. 14-160.2

Alteration, Destruction, or Removal of Serial Number from Firearm; Possession of Firearm with Serial Number Removed

April 2024

Introductory Comment:

None.

Charging Language:

I. Altering or removing serial number **G.S. 14-160.2(a)**

. . . unlawfully, willfully, and feloniously did (*choose all that apply*: alter; deface; destroy; remove) the (*choose one or both*: permanent serial number; manufacturer's identification plate) from a firearm, (*describe firearm*), with the intent thereby to conceal and misrepresent the identity of the firearm.

II. Possessing firearm with serial number removed **G.S. 14-160.2(b)**

. . . unlawfully, willfully, and feloniously did knowingly (*choose all that apply*: sell; buy; possess) a firearm, (*describe firearm*), on which the (*choose one or both*: permanent serial number; manufacturer's identification plate) has been (*choose all that apply*: altered; defaced; destroyed; removed) for the purpose of concealing and misrepresenting the identity of the firearm.

Notes about Charging Language:

- Offenses I and II may also be committed when any "other permanent distinguishing number or identification mark" is removed from a firearm. In such a case, replace "permanent serial number" or "manufacturer's identification plate" with a description of the number or mark removed and a statement that it is a "permanent distinguishing number" or a "permanent identification mark," as the case may be.

Sample Charge:

I. Altering or removing serial number **G.S. 14-160.2(a)**

. . . unlawfully, willfully, and feloniously did alter, deface, destroy, and remove the permanent serial number from a firearm, a Glock 17 9mm pistol, with the intent thereby to conceal and misrepresent the identity of the firearm.

AOC Forms for This Offense:

None.

Punishment:

Offenses I and II are both Class H felonies.

G.S. 14-164.1
Possession of Catalytic Converter Removed from a Motor Vehicle
April 2024

Introductory Comment:
This offense was enacted by S.L. 2022-68, effective December 1, 2022. It applies unless another provision of law provides greater punishment. When considering whether to charge this offense, a prosecutor may also wish to consider whether to charge a violation of G.S. 14-72.8, felony larceny of motor vehicle parts.

Charging Language:
. . . unlawfully, willfully, and feloniously did knowingly possess a catalytic converter that was removed from a motor vehicle. The defendant was not a person authorized to possess a catalytic converter under G.S. 14-164.1(1)–(3).

Notes about Charging Language:
- The charging language above does not call for a description of the catalytic converter itself or of the vehicle from which the catalytic converter was removed, as such detail does not appear to be necessary to establish the elements of the offense. Such information could be included if desired.
- It is unclear whether the absence of any of the conditions justifying possession of a catalytic converter in G.S. 14-164.1(1)–(3) is an element of the offense or whether the presence of one those conditions is an affirmative defense. *Cf.* State v. Rankin, 371 N.C. 885 (2018) (ruling that certain aspects of the anti-littering statute were elements rather than defenses or exceptions). Out of an abundance of caution, this form affirmatively alleges the absence of any of those conditions.

Sample Charge:
. . . unlawfully, willfully, and feloniously did knowingly possess a catalytic converter that was removed from a motor vehicle. The defendant was not a person authorized to possess a catalytic converter under G.S. 14-164.1(1)–(3).

AOC Forms for This Offense:
None.

Punishment:
Class I felony.

G.S. 14-167
Failure to Return Rental Property
April 2024

Introductory Comment:
This offense should not be charged when the property is the subject of a *written* rent-to-own contract. In that case, charge the offense defined in G.S. 14-168.4. When there is intent to defraud involved in failing to return a rental motor vehicle, particularly one below the $4,000 threshold for felony status under this offense, consider charging G.S. 20-106.1 (rental vehicle fraud), which is a felony violation.

Charging Language:

I. Misdemeanor failure to return

. . . unlawfully and willfully did fail to return property, (*describe property*), to the possession of (*name person, firm, corporation, or owner*), from whom the defendant rented it, at the expiration of the time for which it was rented.

II. Felony failure to return

. . . unlawfully, willfully, and feloniously did fail to return a (*choose one*: truck; automobile; motor vehicle), (*describe vehicle*), to the possession of (*name person, firm, corporation, or owner*), from whom the defendant rented it, at the expiration of the time for which it was rented. The (*choose one*: truck; automobile; motor vehicle) was worth more than $4,000 at the time of the rental.

Notes about Charging Language:
None.

Sample Charge:

II. Felony failure to return

. . . unlawfully, willfully, and feloniously did fail to return a motor vehicle, a 2013 Honda Civic sedan, VIN number 317KADKJ37AWKFSJ8, to the possession of Rent-a-Wreck of Smithfield, Inc., from whom the defendant rented it, at the expiration of the time for which it was rented. The motor vehicle was worth more than $4,000 at the time of the rental.

AOC Forms for This Offense:
None.

Punishment:
Class 3 misdemeanor, unless the property is a motor vehicle worth more than $4,000, in which case it is a Class H felony.

G.S. 14-168.1
Conversion of Property by Bailee, Lessee, etc.
April 2024

Introductory Comment:
This offense is related to embezzlement. It is a felony if the value of the property converted is more than $400. This form assumes that the offense is a felony, but a later note explains how to modify the form to charge a misdemeanor.

Charging Language:
. . . unlawfully, willfully, and feloniously did, being entrusted with property, (*describe property*), owned by (*name owner*), as a (*choose one or more*: bailee; lessee; tenant; lodger; person with a power of attorney to sell or transfer the property), fraudulently

(*choose one or more*)

(1) convert the property to the defendant's own use.

(2) convert the proceeds of the property to the defendant's own use.

(3) secrete the property with the fraudulent intent to convert it to the defendant's own use.

The value of the property was in excess of $400.00.

Notes about Charging Language:
- If a misdemeanor is charged, strike the words "and feloniously." Also strike the allegation of value.

Sample Charge:
. . . unlawfully, willfully, and feloniously did, being entrusted with property, a 2005 Buick LeSabre car, N.C. license HME 856, owned by Smithville Buick Motors, Inc., as a bailee, fraudulently convert the property to the defendant's own use. The value of the property was in excess of $400.

AOC Forms for This Offense:
None.

Punishment:
Class 3 misdemeanor, unless the property converted is worth more than $400, in which case it is a Class H felony.

G.S. 14-168.4
Failure to Return Rental Property with Written Purchase Option
April 2024

Introductory Comment:
This offense should be charged only when the property is the subject of a *written* rent-to-own contract. Otherwise, failure to return rental property should be charged under G.S. 14-167.

Charging Language:
. . . unlawfully and willfully did fail to return property, (*describe rental property*), that was rented pursuant to a written agreement in which there was an option to purchase the property, when an event, (*describe event*), occurred that terminated the agreement, with the intent to defeat the rights of the owner, (*name owner*).

Notes about Charging Language:
- The event that terminated the rental agreement can be the passage of the termination date of the rental contract or an event that prematurely terminates the contract, such as the defendant's failure to pay rent according to the agreement's terms.

Sample Charge:
. . . unlawfully and willfully did fail to return property, a 42-inch Sony LCD television set, that was rented pursuant to a written agreement in which there was an option to purchase the property, when an event, the defendant's failure to pay rent on time, occurred that terminated the agreement, with the intent to defeat the rights of the owner, Easy-To-Rent Company, Apex, N.C.

AOC Forms for This Offense:
None.

Punishment:
Class 3 misdemeanor.

G.S. 14-177
Crime Against Nature
April 2024

Introductory Comment:
Enacted in 1837, the first North Carolina statute on this offense merely prescribed a punishment (death) for the common law offense of sodomy (referred to only obliquely using Blackstone's euphemism, "the abominable and detestable crime against nature"), which included anal intercourse and bestiality but not oral penetration. The statute was construed by the North Carolina Supreme Court in *State v. Fenner*, 166 N.C. 247 (1914), to include oral penetration. It now encompasses anal intercourse, fellatio, cunnilingus, analingus, and object penetration. The scope of G.S. 14-177 has been narrowed by the United States Supreme Court's decision in *Lawrence v. Texas*, 539 U.S. 558 (2003) (declaring unconstitutional a Texas statute that criminalized private homosexual conduct between consenting adults).

Charging Language:
. . . unlawfully, willfully, and feloniously did commit the abominable and detestable crime against nature with (*name the victim or describe the beast*).

Notes about Charging Language:
- It is not necessary to describe how the offense was committed, i.e., the details of the sexual contact. *See In re* J.F., 237 N.C. App. 218 (2014).

Sample Charge:
. . . unlawfully, willfully, and feloniously did commit the abominable and detestable crime against nature with Fred W. Wilson, Jr.

AOC Forms for This Offense:
None.

Punishment:
Class I felony.

G.S. 14-178
Incest
April 2024
Page 1 of 2

Introductory Comment:
Incest was not a common law crime. For a thorough legislative history of the statutory offense of incest in North Carolina, see *State v. Palacio*, 287 N.C. App. 667, 675–81 (2023).

Charging Language:

I. Incest **G.S. 14-178(b)(3)**

. . . unlawfully, willfully, and feloniously did have carnal intercourse with (*name the person with whom the defendant had vaginal intercourse*), who is the defendant's (*choose one*: child; stepchild; legally adopted child; brother; sister; grandchild; parent; grandparent; nephew; niece; aunt; uncle). The defendant knew that he or she was related to the victim as described above.

II. Incest with a person who is under 13 when the defendant is at least four years older than the person **G.S. 14-178(b)(1)(a)**

. . . unlawfully, willfully, and feloniously did have carnal intercourse with (*name the person with whom the defendant had vaginal intercourse*), who is the defendant's (*choose one*: child; stepchild; legally adopted child; brother; sister; grandchild; parent; grandparent; nephew; niece; aunt; uncle), at a time when (*name person*) was under the age of 13 and the defendant was at least 12 years old and was at least four years older than the child. The defendant knew that he or she was related to the victim as described above.

III. Incest with a person who is 13, 14, or 15 when the defendant is at least six years older than the person **G.S. 14-178(b)(1)(b)**

. . . unlawfully, willfully, and feloniously did have carnal intercourse with (*name the person with whom the defendant had vaginal intercourse*), who is the defendant's (*choose one*: child; stepchild; legally adopted child; brother; sister; grandchild; parent; grandparent; nephew; niece; aunt; uncle), at a time when (*name person*) was (*choose one*: 13 years old; 14 years old; *or* 15 years old) and the defendant was at least six years older than the child. The defendant knew that he or she was related to the victim as described above.

IV. Incest with a person who is 13, 14, or 15 when the defendant is more than four but less than six years older than the person **G.S. 14-178(b)(2)**

. . . unlawfully, willfully, and feloniously did have carnal intercourse with (*name the person with whom the defendant had vaginal intercourse*), who is the defendant's (*choose one*: child; stepchild; legally adopted child; brother; sister; grandchild; parent; grandparent; nephew; niece; aunt; uncle), at a time when (*name person*) was (*choose one*: 13 years old; 14 years old; *or* 15 years old) and the defendant was more than four but less than six years older than the child. The defendant knew that he or she was related to the victim as described above.

Notes about Charging Language:

- "Carnal intercourse" means vaginal intercourse. State v. Collins, 44 N.C. App. 27 (1979).
- A "brother" or "sister" may be a sibling of "the half or whole blood." G.S. 14-178. The term "niece" does not, however, include a niece-in-law. State v. Palacio, 287 N.C. App. 667, 681 (2023).
- Where the victim was under 13 years of age, the North Carolina Court of Appeals found an indictment sufficient that identified the victim only by her initials and date of birth. *See* State v. Perkins, 286 N.C. App. 495, 503 (2022).

Sample Charge:

II. Incest with a person who is under 13 when the defendant is at least four years older than the person **G.S. 14-178(b)(1)(a)**

. . . unlawfully, willfully, and feloniously did have carnal intercourse with Barbara Smith, who is the defendant's niece, at a time when Barbara Smith was under the age of 13 and the defendant was at least 12 years old and was at least four years older than the child. The defendant knew that he was related to the victim as described above.

AOC Forms for This Offense:

None.

Punishment:

Offense I is a Class F felony. Offenses II and III are Class B1 felonies. Offense IV is a Class C felony.

G.S. 14-190.1(a)(1)
Disseminating Obscene Writing or Picture
April 2024

Introductory Comment:
Enacted in 1971, G.S. 14-190.1 made it unlawful for any person, firm, or corporation to disseminate obscenity in any public place. The "public place" language was deleted by amendments in 1985 that also rewrote the definition of "sexual conduct." Amendments effective December 1, 2023, made this section applicable to persons "18 years of age or older" (as well as to firms and corporations) and enhanced the penalty for a violation "in the presence of a minor under 18 years of age."

Charging Language:
. . . unlawfully, willfully, and feloniously did intentionally disseminate obscenity by (*choose one or more*: selling; delivering; providing; offering to sell; offering to deliver; offering to provide) to (*name person*) (*describe where sale, delivery, etc., took place*) an obscene (*choose one or more*: writing; picture; record; representation and embodiment of the obscene), (*describe obscene item).* The defendant was (*give age*) and thus was 18 years of age or older at the time of this offense. (*If applicable add*: This conduct was committed knowingly in the presence of a minor, (*name the minor*), who was (*give age*) and thus was under 18 years of age.)

Notes about Charging Language:
- The statute applies to any person 18 years of age or older and to any firm or corporation. If the defendant is a firm or corporation, the language regarding the defendant being over 18 years old should be omitted.
- The statute also prohibits agreeing to sell, agreeing to deliver, and agreeing to provide obscene material.
- The term "record" as used above applies to a visual record; sound recordings are covered by G.S. 14-190.1(a)(4).
- The term "obscene material" is defined in G.S. 14-190.1(b). Generally, it requires a patently offensive depiction of certain types of sexual conduct that appeals to the "prurient interest in sex" and that lacks literary, artistic, political, or scientific value.
- G.S. 14-190.20 provides that a search warrant or criminal process (arrest warrant, criminal summons, citation, order for arrest) may be issued for this offense only upon the request of a prosecutor.

Sample Charge:
. . . unlawfully, willfully, and feloniously did intentionally disseminate obscenity by selling to Jonathan Edwards at the Triple X Bookstore, Bergen, N.C., obscene writings and pictures, a magazine entitled *Something Completely Different: Hot, Raunchy Sex with Transvestites, Gourmet Edition, The Insatiables #36.* The defendant was 40 years old and thus was 18 years of age or older at the time of this offense.

AOC Forms for This Offense:
None.

Punishment:
Except as otherwise provided, violation is a Class I felony. A violation committed knowingly in the presence of a minor under 18 years of age is a Class H felony.

G.S. 14-190.1(a)(4)
Disseminating Obscene Movie, Video, etc.
April 2024

Introductory Comment:
Enacted in 1971, G.S. 14-190.1 made it unlawful for any person, firm, or corporation to disseminate obscenity in any public place. The "public place" language was deleted by amendments in 1985 that also rewrote the definition of "sexual conduct." Amendments effective December 1, 2023, made this section applicable to persons "18 years of age or older" (as well as to firms and corporations) and enhanced the penalty for a violation "in the presence of a minor under 18 years of age."

Charging Language:
. . . unlawfully, willfully, and feloniously did intentionally disseminate obscenity by (*choose one or more*: exhibiting; renting; selling; providing; offering to exhibit; offering to rent) to (*name person*) (*describe where exhibiting, renting, selling, etc., took place*) an obscene (*choose one or more*: motion picture; film; filmstrip; projection slide; material which is a representation, embodiment, performance, and publication of the obscene), (*describe obscene item*). The defendant was (*give age*) and thus was 18 years of age or older at the time of this offense. (*If applicable add*: This conduct was committed knowingly in the presence of a minor, (*name the minor*), who was (*give age*) and thus was under 18 years of age.)

Notes about Charging Language:
- The statute applies to any person 18 years of age or older and to any firm or corporation. If the defendant is a firm or corporation, the language regarding the defendant being over 18 years old should be omitted.
- The statute also prohibits presenting; offering to present or provide; or agreeing to exhibit, present, rent, or provide obscene material.
- The statute also covers a sound recording, sound tape, or soundtrack.
- The term "obscene material" is defined in G.S. 14-190.1(b). Generally, it requires a patently offensive depiction of certain types of sexual conduct that appeals to the "prurient interest in sex" and that lacks literary, artistic, political, or scientific value.
- G.S. 14-190.20 provides that a search warrant or criminal process (arrest warrant, criminal summons, citation, order for arrest) may be issued for this offense only upon the request of a prosecutor.

Sample Charge:
. . . unlawfully, willfully, and feloniously did intentionally disseminate obscenity by selling to Sandra Billman at Triple X Bookstore, Bergen, N.C., obscene material which is a representation, embodiment, performance, and publication of the obscene, a DVD entitled "Deviations." The defendant was 40 years old and thus was 18 years of age or older at the time of this offense.

AOC Forms for This Offense:
None.

Punishment:
Except as otherwise provided, violation is a Class I felony. A violation committed knowingly in the presence of a minor under 18 years of age is a Class H felony.

G.S. 14-190.1(e)
Possessing Obscenity with Intent to Disseminate
April 2024

Introductory Comment:
Enacted in 1971, G.S. 14-190.1 made it unlawful for any person, firm, or corporation to disseminate obscenity in any public place. The "public place" language was deleted by amendments in 1985 that also rewrote the definition of "sexual conduct." Amendments effective December 1, 2023, made this section applicable to persons "18 years of age or older" (as well as to firms and corporations) and enhanced the penalty for a violation "in the presence of a minor under 18 years of age."

Charging Language:
. . . unlawfully, willfully, and feloniously did knowingly and intentionally (*choose one or more*: possess; buy; create; procure) obscene material, (*describe material*), with the purpose and intent of disseminating it unlawfully. The defendant was (*give age*) and thus was 18 years of age or older at the time of this offense. (*If applicable add*: This conduct was committed knowingly in the presence of a minor, (*name the minor*), who was (*give age*) and thus was under 18 years of age.)

Notes about Charging Language:
- The statute applies to any person 18 years of age or older and to any firm or corporation. If the defendant is a firm or corporation, the language regarding the defendant being over 18 years old should be omitted.
- Obscene material is defined in G.S. 14-190.1(b). Generally, it requires a patently offensive depiction of certain types of sexual conduct that appeals to the "prurient interest in sex" and that lacks literary, artistic, political, or scientific value.
- G.S. 14-190.20 provides that a search warrant or criminal process (arrest warrant, criminal summons, citation, order for arrest) may be issued for this offense only upon the request of a prosecutor.

Sample Charge:
. . . unlawfully, willfully, and feloniously did knowingly and intentionally possess obscene material, twenty-five copies of a magazine entitled *Something Completely Different: Hot, Raunchy Sex with Transvestites, Gourmet Edition, The Insatiables #36*, with the purpose and intent of disseminating it unlawfully. The defendant was 40 years old and thus was 18 years of age or older at the time of this offense.

AOC Forms for This Offense:
None.

Punishment:
Except as otherwise provided, violation is a Class I felony. A violation committed knowingly in the presence of a minor under 18 years of age is a Class H felony.

G.S. 14-190.5
Preparing Obscene Photograph
April 2024

Introductory Comment:
G.S. 14-190.20 provides that a search warrant or criminal process (arrest warrant, criminal summons, citation, and order for arrest) may be issued for this offense only on request of a prosecutor.

Charging Language:
. . . unlawfully and willfully did knowingly (*choose one*)

(1) photograph (*name person, which can include the defendant*) for the purpose of preparing an obscene (*choose one or more and describe*: film; photograph; negative; slide; motion picture) for the purpose of dissemination.

(2) (*choose one or more*: model in; pose in; act in; assist in the preparation of) an obscene (*choose one or more and describe*: film; photograph; negative; slide; motion picture) for the purpose of dissemination.

Notes about Charging Language:
- Obscene material is defined in G.S. 14-190.1(b). Generally, it requires a patently offensive depiction of certain types of sexual conduct that appeals to the "prurient interest in sex" and that lacks literary, artistic, political, or scientific value.

Sample Charge:
. . . unlawfully and willfully did knowingly photograph himself for the purpose of preparing an obscene photograph, a picture of himself masturbating, for the purpose of dissemination.

AOC Forms for This Offense:
None.

Punishment:
Class 1 misdemeanor.

G.S. 14-190.5A
Disclosure of Private Images
April 2024
Page 1 of 2

Introductory Comment:
This offense was enacted in the 2015 legislative session and is commonly called the "revenge porn" statute. The statute contains certain exceptions, including for the disclosure of images in the course of law enforcement activities and medical proceedings. G.S. 14-190.5A(d). The statute was amended and the offense expanded somewhat effective December 1, 2017. S.L. 2017-93.

If the defendant is under 18, a second or subsequent offense is a felony. An indictment or an information for the recidivist offense must comply with G.S. 15A-928, which requires that the defendant's prior convictions be alleged either (1) in a separate count of the indictment or information than the substantive offense or (2) in a separate indictment or information. In such a case, the separate count or separate indictment should set forth the date and court in which the prior conviction occurred. This requirement does not apply to arrest warrants or magistrates' orders, which still must allege the defendant's prior convictions but need not do so in a separate count or separate charging instrument. G.S. 15A-928 also requires in indictments or informations that the name or title of an offense elevated by prior convictions must not make reference to such prior convictions.

Charging Language:
. . . unlawfully, willfully, and feloniously did knowingly disclose an image of (*name victim*) with the intent to

(*choose one or both*)

(1) (*choose one or more*: coerce; harass; intimidate; demean; humiliate; cause financial loss to)

(2) cause others to (*choose one or more*: coerce; harass; intimidate; demean; humiliate; cause financial loss to)

(*name victim*). (*Name victim*) was identifiable from the disclosed image itself and information offered in connection with the image. (*Choose one or both*: The victim's intimate parts were exposed in the disclosed image; The victim was engaged in sexual conduct in the disclosed image). The defendant disclosed the image without the affirmative consent of the victim. The defendant (*choose one or both*: obtained the image without the consent of the victim; obtained the image under circumstances such that the defendant knew and should have known that the victim expected the image to remain private.) (*If applicable, state*: The defendant was 18 years of age or older at the time of the offense.)

Notes about Charging Language:

- The statute defines terms, including "disclose," "image," "intimate parts," and "sexual conduct." Of note, "image" includes still and video recordings as well as "live transmission[s]."
- If the defendant is under 18, a first offense is a misdemeanor. In such a case, strike "feloniously" from the charging language set out above.
- Although the general rule is that the name of the victim should be included when charging a crime, the Court of Appeals of North Carolina has approved of the use of the victim's initials in at least one sexual assault case. State v. McKoy, 196 N.C. App. 650 (2009) (use of initials provided adequate notice to the defendant where the defendant admitted that he knew the victim and did not claim that the use of initials made it difficult to prepare his defense). It is possible that a court

would follow *McKoy* in connection with this offense. By contrast, in another sexual assault case, the state supreme court disapproved of referring to the victim using the generic term "Victim #1." State v. White, 372 N.C. 248 (2019).
- If the victim is identifiable only from the disclosed image and not from any information offered in connection with the image, it would not be erroneous to strike "any information offered in connection with the image" from the charging document. It also likely would not be erroneous to leave that phrase in the charging document as surplusage.

Sample Charge:
. . . unlawfully, willfully, and feloniously did knowingly disclose an image of Samantha Scott with the intent to harass, intimidate, demean, and humiliate Samantha Scott. Samantha Scott was identifiable from the disclosed image itself and information offered in connection with the image. The victim was engaged in sexual conduct in the disclosed image. The defendant disclosed the image without the affirmative consent of the victim. The defendant obtained the image under circumstances such that the defendant knew and should have known that the victim expected the image to remain private. The defendant was 18 years of age or older at the time of the offense.

AOC Forms for This Offense:
None.

Punishment:
If the defendant is 18 or older, Class H felony. If the defendant is under 18, Class 1 misdemeanor, unless it is the defendant's second or subsequent offense, in which case, Class H felony. The court may also order the destruction of any image "made in violation of this section."

G.S. 14-190.6
Using Minor to Assist in Obscenity Offense
April 2024

Introductory Comment:
This offense was created by statute in 1971 as part of the same bill that created the offense of disseminating obscenity. See Note to G.S. 14-190.1. Amendments effective December 1, 2023, enhanced the penalty for this offense.

Charging Language:
. . . unlawfully, willfully, and feloniously did intentionally (*choose one or more*: hire; employ; use; permit) (*name minor*), a minor (*give age*) and thus under the age of 16 years, (*choose one or both and describe*: to do an act; to assist in doing an act) constituting an offense under Article 26 of General Statutes Chapter 14, (*name offense*), and involving (*choose one or more and describe*: material; an act; a thing) that the defendant knew and reasonably should have known to be obscene within the meaning of G.S. 14-190.1. The defendant was (*give age*), and thus 18 years of age or older at the time of the offense.

Notes about Charging Language:
- Obscene material is defined in G.S. 14-190.1(b). Generally, it requires a patently offensive depiction of certain types of sexual conduct that appeals to the "prurient interest in sex" and that lacks literary, artistic, political, or scientific value.

Sample Charge:
. . . unlawfully, willfully, and feloniously did intentionally use Susan Thomas, a minor of 14 years of age and thus under the age of 16 years, to do an act, being photographed masturbating while completely nude, constituting an offense under Article 26 of General Statutes Chapter 14, second-degree sexual exploitation of a minor under G.S. 14-190.17, and involving material, an obscene photograph of a minor, that the defendant knew and reasonably should have known to be obscene within the meaning of G.S. 14-190.1. The defendant was 30 years old, and thus 18 years of age or older at the time of the offense.

AOC Forms for This Offense:
None.

Punishment:
Class H felony.

G.S. 14-190.7
Disseminate Obscenity to Minor under 16
April 2024

Introductory Comment:
This offense was created by statute in 1971 as part of the same bill that created the offense of disseminating obscenity. See Note to G.S. 14-190.1. Amendments effective December 1, 2023, enhanced the penalty for this offense.

Charging Language:
. . . unlawfully, willfully, and feloniously did knowingly disseminate to (*name person*), a minor (*give age*) and thus under the age of 16 years, material, (*describe material*), which the defendant knew and reasonably should have known to be obscene within the meaning of G.S. 14-190.1. The defendant was (*give age*) and thus was 18 years of age or older at the time of this offense.

Notes about Charging Language:
- Obscene material is defined in G.S. 14-190.1(b). Generally, it requires a patently offensive depiction of certain types of sexual conduct that appeals to the "prurient interest in sex" and that lacks literary, artistic, political, or scientific value.

Sample Charge:
. . . unlawfully, willfully, and feloniously did knowingly disseminate to Peter Jones, a minor of the age of 13 years and thus under the age of 16 years, material, a photograph of a 13-year-old girl masturbating while completely nude, which the defendant knew and reasonably should have known to be obscene within the meaning of G.S. 14-190.1. The defendant was 40 years old and thus was 18 years of age or older at the time of this offense.

AOC Forms for This Offense:
None.

Punishment:
Class H felony.

G.S. 14-190.8
Disseminate Obscenity to Minor under 13
April 2024

Introductory Comment:
This offense was created by statute in 1971 as part of the same bill that created the offense of disseminating obscenity. See Note to G.S. 14-190.1. Amendments effective December 1, 2023, enhanced the penalty for this offense.

Charging Language:

. . . unlawfully, willfully, and feloniously did knowingly disseminate to (*name person*), a minor (*give age*) and thus under the age of 13 years, material, (*describe material*), which the defendant knew and reasonably should have known to be obscene within the meaning of G.S. 14-190.1. The defendant was (*give age*) and thus was 18 years of age or older at the time of this offense.

Notes about Charging Language:

- Obscene material is defined in G.S. 14-190.1(b). Generally, it requires a patently offensive depiction of certain types of sexual conduct that appeals to the "prurient interest in sex" and that lacks literary, artistic, political, or scientific value.

Sample Charge:
. . . unlawfully, willfully, and feloniously did knowingly disseminate to Peter Jones, a minor of the age of 10 years and thus under the age of 13 years, material, a photograph of a 13-year-old girl masturbating while completely nude, which the defendant knew and reasonably should have known to be obscene within the meaning of G.S. 14-190.1. The defendant was 40 years old and thus was 18 years of age or older at the time of this offense.

AOC Forms for This Offense:
None.

Punishment:
Class G felony.

G.S. 14-190.9
Indecent Exposure
April 2024
Page 1 of 2

Introductory Comment:
Indecent exposure was a misdemeanor at common law and by statute in North Carolina since at least 1907. G.S. 14-190.9 dates from 1971. Subsections (a2), (a4), and (a5) of this statute (pertaining to indecent exposure on private property) were added in 2015; this form does not provide charging language for those offenses because they seem unlikely to be charged frequently. Amendments effective December 1, 2023, to subsections (a1) and (a4) changed the description of the victim from "any other person less than 16 years of age" to "a minor as defined in G.S. 14-190.13."

Charging Language:

I. Misdemeanor indecent exposure **G.S. 14-190.9(a)**

. . . unlawfully and willfully did expose (*choose one*: his; her) private parts, (*describe parts*), in a public place, (*describe place*), in the presence of (*choose one*: another person; other persons), (*name person or persons*).

II. Felony indecent exposure **G.S. 14-190.9(a1)**

. . . unlawfully, willfully, and feloniously did expose (*choose one*: his; her) private parts, (*describe parts*), in a public place, (*describe place*), in the presence of another person, (*name person*), who was a minor as defined in G.S. 14-190.13, for the purpose of arousing and gratifying the defendant's sexual desire. At the time of this offense, the defendant was at least 18 years old, namely, (*give age*).

Notes about Charging Language:
- Appellate court rulings on the meaning of "private parts" and "public place" are summarized in Jessica Smith, *North Carolina Crimes: A Guidebook on the Elements of Crime* 290 (UNC School of Government, 7th ed. 2012). This charge cannot be based on the exposure of a woman's breast during breastfeeding. G.S. 14-190.9(b).
- For Offense I, the statute exempts exposure in places designated for a public purpose where same-sex exposure is incidental to a permitted activity.
- Offense I also covers a person who as owner, manager, lessee, director, promoter, or agent who knowingly hires, leases, or permits the land, building, or premises of which he or she is owner, lessee, or tenant, or over which he or she has control, to be used for the commission of this offense. Of course, the charging language above would need to be altered in such a situation.
- Offense II is not a lesser-included offense of G.S. 14-202.1 (taking indecent liberties with children).

Sample Charge:

II. Felony indecent exposure **G.S. 14-190.9(a1)**

. . . unlawfully, willfully, and feloniously did expose his private parts, his penis, in a public place, on Main Street, Billingham, N.C., in the presence of another person, Peter Jones, who was a minor as defined in G.S. 14-190.13, for the purpose of arousing and gratifying the defendant's sexual desire. At the time of this offense, the defendant was at least 18 years old, namely, 43 years old.

AOC Forms for This Offense:
None.

Punishment:
Offense I is a Class 2 misdemeanor. Offense II is a Class H felony.

G.S. 14-190.16
First-Degree Sexual Exploitation of a Minor
April 2024
Page 1 of 2

Introductory Comment:
Very generally, this offense concerns the production of child pornography. The statute contains several subsections. Charging language for the most-common subsections is set forth below, but the statute also prohibits permitting a minor under one's custody to be involved in the production of child pornography, G.S. 14-190.16(a)(2), and transporting a minor for the purpose of producing child pornography, G.S. 14-190.16(a)(3).

Charging Language:

I. Using minor in live performance or material **G.S. 14-190.16(a)(1)**

. . . unlawfully, willfully, and feloniously did (*choose one or more*: use; employ; induce; coerce; encourage; facilitate) a minor, (*name minor and give age; if name and age are unknown, state that and give approximate age*), to (*choose one or both*: engage in; assist others to engage in) sexual activity, (*describe the sexual activity*), for (*choose one or both*: a live performance; the purpose of producing material containing a visual representation depicting this activity), (*describe the performance or material*), the defendant knowing the character and content of the (*choose one or both*: performance; material).

II. Commercial recording or duplication of material **G.S. 14-190.16(a)(4)**

. . . unlawfully, willfully, and feloniously did (*choose one or more*: record; photograph; film; develop; duplicate) for (*choose one or both*: sale; pecuniary gain) material, (*describe material*), containing a visual representation depicting a minor, (*name minor and give age; if name and age are unknown, state that and give approximate age*), engaged in sexual activity, (*describe the sexual activity*), the defendant knowing the material's character and content.

Notes about Charging Language:

- G.S. 14-190.13(3) defines "minor" as one who is less than 18 years old and is not married or judicially emancipated. G.S. 14-190.16(c) provides that mistake of age is no defense to a prosecution of this offense.
- G.S. 14-190.13(5) defines "sexual activity" to include, among other acts, masturbation; vaginal, anal, or oral intercourse; insertion of an object into a person's anus or vagina; the lascivious exhibition of a person's genitals or pubic area; and touching—in apparent sexual stimulation or sexual abuse—of the genitals, pubic area, or buttocks. See the statute for the complete list of prohibited acts.
- G.S. 14-190.13(2) defines "material" as pictures, drawings, video recordings, films, or other visual depictions or representations, but not material consisting entirely of written words.
- Violations of the statute that are committed in close succession may nonetheless be charged separately. *Cf.* State v. Howell, 169 N.C. App. 58 (2005).

Sample Charge:

I. Using minor in live performance or material **G.S. 14-190.16(a)(1)**

. . . unlawfully, willfully, and feloniously did use, employ, induce, and coerce a minor, James Edwards, 10 years old, to engage in sexual activity, in that the defendant fondled the penis of this minor for the apparent purpose of sexual stimulation, for the purpose of producing material containing a visual representation depicting this activity, a video recording, the defendant knowing the character and content of the material.

AOC Forms for This Offense:
None.

Punishment:
Offenses I and II are both Class C felonies.

G.S. 14-190.17
Second-Degree Sexual Exploitation of a Minor
April 2024
Page 1 of 2

Introductory Comment:
Very generally, this offense concerns the distribution or noncommercial recording or duplication of child pornography. Commercial recording or duplication is covered by first-degree sexual exploitation of a minor, G.S. 14-190.16.

Charging Language:

I. Noncommercial recording or duplication of material **G.S. 14-190.17(a)(1)**

. . . unlawfully, willfully, and feloniously did (*choose one or more*: record; photograph; film; develop; duplicate) material, (*describe material*), containing a visual representation of a minor, (*name minor and give age; if name and age are unknown, state that and give approximate age*), engaged in sexual activity, (*describe the sexual activity*), the defendant knowing the material's character and content.

II. Distribution of material **G.S. 14-190.17(a)(2)**

. . . unlawfully, willfully, and feloniously did (*choose one or more*: distribute; transport; exhibit; receive; sell; purchase; exchange; solicit) (*if known, name person to whom material was distributed, exhibited, sold, etc.*) material, (*describe material*), containing a visual representation of a minor, (*name minor and give age; if name and age are unknown, state that and give approximate age*), engaged in sexual activity, (*describe the sexual activity*), the defendant knowing the material's character and content.

Notes about Charging Language:

- G.S. 14-190.13(3) defines "minor" as one who is less than 18 years old and is not married or judicially emancipated. G.S. 14-190.17(c) provides that mistake of age is no defense to a prosecution of this offense.
- G.S. 14-190.13(5) defines "sexual activity" to include, among other acts, masturbation; vaginal, anal, or oral intercourse; insertion of an object into a person's anus or vagina; the lascivious exhibition of a person's genitals or pubic area; and touching—in apparent sexual stimulation or sexual abuse—of the genitals, pubic area, or buttocks. See the statute for the complete list of prohibited acts.
- G.S. 14-190.13(2) defines "material" as pictures, drawings, video recordings, films, or other visual depictions or representations, but not material consisting entirely of written words.
- Violations of the statute that are committed in close succession may nonetheless be charged separately. *Cf.* State v. Howell, 169 N.C. App. 58 (2005).

Sample Charge:

II. Distribution of material **G.S. 14-190.17(a)(2)**

. . . unlawfully, willfully, and feloniously did distribute to Billy Jones material, a digital photograph, containing a visual representation of a minor, a male minor child, name unknown, approximately 6 years old, engaged in sexual activity, oral intercourse with an adult male, the defendant knowing the material's character and content.

AOC Forms for This Offense:
None.

Punishment:
Offenses I and II are both Class E felonies.

G.S. 14-190.17A
Third-Degree Sexual Exploitation of a Minor
April 2024

Introductory Comment:
Very generally, this offense concerns the possession of child pornography.

Charging Language:
. . . unlawfully, willfully, and feloniously did possess material, (*describe material*), containing a visual representation of a minor, (*name minor and give age; if name and age are unknown, state that and give approximate age*), engaging in sexual activity, (*describe the sexual activity*), the defendant knowing the material's character and content.

Notes about Charging Language:
- G.S. 14-190.13(3) defines "minor" as one who is less than 18 years old and is not married or judicially emancipated. G.S. 14-190.17A(c) provides that mistake of age is no defense to a prosecution of this offense.
- G.S. 14-190.13(5) defines "sexual activity" to include, among other acts, masturbation; vaginal, anal, or oral intercourse; insertion of an object into a person's anus or vagina; the lascivious exhibition of a person's genitals or pubic area; and touching—in apparent sexual stimulation or sexual abuse—of the genitals, pubic area, or buttocks. See the statute for the complete list of prohibited acts.
- G.S. 14-190.13(2) defines "material" as pictures, drawings, video recordings, films, or other visual depictions or representations, but not material consisting entirely of written words.
- Violations of the statute that are committed in close succession may nonetheless be charged separately. *Cf.* State v. Howell, 169 N.C. App. 58 (2005).

Sample Charge:
. . . unlawfully, willfully, and feloniously did possess material, a digital photograph, containing a visual representation of a minor, a male minor child, name unknown, approximately 6 years old, engaging in sexual activity, oral intercourse with an adult male, the defendant knowing the material's character and content.

AOC Forms for This Offense:
None.

Punishment:
Class H felony.

Introductory Comment:
G.S. 14-196(a)(1) (profane and indecent language on the telephone) has been declared unconstitutional by a federal court whose jurisdiction includes the state of North Carolina. Radford v. Webb, 446 F. Supp. 608 (W.D.N.C.), *aff'd per curiam*, 596 F.2d 1205 (4th Cir. 1979). Therefore, no charging language for this offense has been provided.

Charging Language:

I. Threatening language **G.S. 14-196(a)(2)**

. . . unlawfully and willfully did use words and language in a telephone communication with (*name other party to conversation*) threatening to inflict [*choose one or both*: bodily harm on (*name person threatened*); physical injury to the property of (*name person whose property was threatened*)].

II. Harassing calls **G.S. 14-196(a)(3)**

. . . unlawfully and willfully did telephone (*name person telephoned*) repeatedly for the purpose of (*choose one or more*: annoying; threatening; terrifying; harassing; embarrassing) (*name person at the called number*) at the called number.

III. Disrupt service of another **G.S. 14-196(a)(4)**

. . . unlawfully and willfully did make a telephone call to (*name person telephoned*) and fail to hang up and disengage the connection with the intent to disrupt the service of (*name person whose service was interrupted*).

IV. False statement about death, injury **G.S. 14-196(a)(5)**

. . . unlawfully and willfully did telephone (*name person with whom the defendant talked*) and knowingly make a false statement about the (*choose one or more*: death; injury; illness; disfigurement; indecent conduct; criminal conduct) of [*choose one*: (*name person with whom the defendant talked*); (*name person about whom the defendant spoke*), a member of (*name person with whom the defendant talked*)'s family] with the intent to (*choose one*: abuse; annoy; threaten; terrify; harass; embarrass).

Notes about Charging Language:

- This statute also applies to communications made or received by a telephone answering machine or recorder, telefacsimile machine, or computer modem. Make appropriate changes to the charging language in such cases.
- This statute also applies to any person who knowingly permits a telephone under his or her control to be used to commit any of the above offenses. G.S. 14-196(a)(6).

Sample Charges:

I. Threatening language **G.S. 14-196(a)(2)**

. . . unlawfully and willfully did use words and language in a telephone communication with Maureen Smith threatening to inflict bodily harm on Maureen Smith.

II. Harassing calls **G.S. 14-196(a)(3)**

. . . unlawfully and willfully did telephone Samuel Jones repeatedly for the purpose of annoying and harassing Samuel Jones at the called number.

AOC Forms for This Offense:
None.

Punishment:
Class 2 misdemeanor.

G.S. 14-196.3
Cyberstalking
April 2024
Page 1 of 2

Introductory Comment:
None.

Charging Language:

I. Threatening language **G.S. 14-196.3(b)(1)**

. . . unlawfully and willfully did use words and language in an (*choose one or both*: electronic communication; electronic mail) to (*name person with whom communicated*) threatening to inflict (*choose one or more*: bodily harm on [*name person threatened*]; physical injury to the property of [*name person whose property was threatened*]).

II. Extorting language **G.S. 14-196.3(b)(1)**

. . . unlawfully and willfully did use words and language in an (*choose one or both*: electronic communication; electronic mail) to (*name person with whom communicated*) for the purpose of extorting money or other things of value from (*name person who was the object of the extortion*).

III. Harassing communications **G.S. 14-196.3(b)(2)**

. . . unlawfully and willfully did (*choose one or both*: electronically communicate with; electronically mail [*name person to whom the defendant communicated*]) repeatedly for the purpose of (*choose one or more*: abusing; annoying; threatening; terrifying; harassing; embarrassing [*name person the defendant intended to abuse, annoy, threaten, etc.*]).

IV. False statement about death, injury **G.S. 14-196.3(b)(3)**

. . . unlawfully and willfully did in an (*choose one or both*: electronic communication; electronic mail) to (*name person to whom the defendant communicated*) knowingly make a false statement about the (*choose one or more*: death; injury; illness; disfigurement; indecent conduct; criminal conduct) of (*choose one*: [*name person with whom communicated*]; [*name person about whom communicated*]), a member of (*name person with whom communicated*)'s (*choose one or both*: family; household) with the intent to (*choose one*: abuse; annoy; threaten; terrify; harass; embarrass).

V. Use of electronic tracking device without consent **G.S. 14-196.3(b)(5)**

. . . unlawfully and willfully did knowingly (*choose one or more*: install; place; use; cause to be installed; cause to be placed; cause to be used) an electronic tracking device to track the location of (*name victim*) without the consent of (*name victim*).

Notes about Charging Language:

- "Electronic communication" is defined in G.S. 14-196.3(a)(1).
- "Electronic mail" is defined in G.S. 14-196.3(a)(2).
- "Electronic tracking device" is defined in G.S. 14-196.3(a)(3).
- This statute also applies to any person who knowingly permits an electronic communication device under his or her control to be used to commit any of the above offenses. G.S. 14-196.3(b)(4).
- For Offense I, the statute covers "words or language threatening to inflict bodily harm to **any person** or to that person's child, sibling, spouse, or dependent." G.S. 14-196.3(b)(1) (emphasis added). Given the use of the broad term "any person", it does not seem that the reference to "that person's child, sibling, spouse, or dependent" places any limitation on the scope of this offense. Perhaps one could argue that the statute was intended to require that the recipient of the communication be either the person threatened or the parent, sibling, etc., of the person threatened. To avoid any possible issue in this regard, you may wish to specify the relationship between the person receiving the communication and the person threatened if it is one of the relationships listed in the statute.
- The statute contains several exceptions to Offense V, allowing tracking devices to be used for certain business purposes, certain law enforcement purposes, and for certain investigations conducted by licensed private investigators. *See* G.S. 14-196.3(b)(5). These appear to be exceptions to the offense rather than elements, and so the lack of applicability of the exceptions is not included in the charging language above.

Sample Charge:

III. Harassing communications **G.S. 14-196.3(b)(2)**

. . . unlawfully and willfully did electronically communicate with Samuel Jones repeatedly for the purpose of annoying and harassing Samuel Jones.

AOC Forms for This Offense:
None.

Punishment:
Class 2 misdemeanor.

G.S. 14-202
Secret Peeping
April 2024
Page 1 of 3

Introductory Comment:
G.S. 14-202(i) provides for increased punishments for certain second or subsequent convictions under this statute. An indictment or an information for a recidivist offense must comply with G.S. 15A-928, which requires that the defendant's prior convictions be alleged either (1) in a separate count of the indictment or information than the substantive offense or (2) in a separate indictment or information. In such a case, the separate count or separate indictment should set forth the date and court in which the prior conviction occurred. This requirement does not apply to arrest warrants or magistrates' orders, which still must allege the defendant's prior convictions but need not do so in a separate count or separate charging instrument. Also note that in situations where a conviction for a recidivist offense is appealed from district to superior court for trial de novo, G.S. 15A-922(h) and -928(d) require the State to replace the pleading in the case with superseding statements of charges separately alleging the substantive offense and any prior convictions. G.S. 15A-928 also requires that the name or title of an offense elevated by prior convictions must not make reference to such prior convictions.

Charging Language:

I. Peeping into room **G.S. 14-202(a)**

. . . unlawfully and willfully did peep secretly into a room, (*name room, such as a bedroom, and give address of building in which room is located*), occupied by another person, (*name person, if known*).

II. Peeping under clothing with device **G.S. 14-202(a1)**

. . . unlawfully and willfully did secretly and surreptitiously peep (*choose one or both*: underneath; through) clothing being worn by another person, (*name person, if known*), through the use of a (*choose one or both*: mirror; *name other device*), for the purpose of viewing (*choose one or both*: the body of; the undergarments worn by) that other person, without (*choose one*: his; her) consent.

III. Peeping into room while possessing photo device **G.S. 14-202(c)**

. . . unlawfully and willfully did, while in possession of a device, (*name device*), which may be used to create a photographic image, peep secretly into a room, (*name room, such as a bedroom, and give address of building in which room is located*).

IV. Peeping into room and creating photo **G.S. 14-202(d)**

. . . unlawfully, willfully, and feloniously did, while secretly peeping into a room, (*name room, such as a bedroom, and give address of building in which room is located*), use a device, (*name device*), to create a photographic image of another person, (*name person, if known*), in that room for the purpose of arousing and gratifying the sexual desire of a person, (*name person, if known*).

V. Using device to create photo underneath or through clothing **G.S. 14-202(e)**

. . . unlawfully, willfully, and feloniously did secretly and surreptitiously use a device, (*name device*), to create a photographic image of another person, (*name person, if known*), (*choose one or both*: underneath; through) the clothing being worn by that other person, for the purpose of viewing the (*choose one or both*: body of; undergarments worn by) that other person, without that person's consent.

VI. Installing photo device in room **G.S. 14-202(f)**

. . . unlawfully, willfully, and feloniously did, for the purpose of arousing and gratifying the sexual desire of a person, (*name person, if known*), secretly and surreptitiously (*choose one or both*: use; install) in a room, (*name room, such as a bedroom, and give address of building in which room is located*), a device, (*name device*), that can be used to create a photographic image, with the intent to capture the image of another person, (*name person, if known*), without that person's consent.

VII. Possessing photo obtained by peeping violation **G.S. 14-202(g)**

. . . unlawfully, willfully, and feloniously did knowingly possess a photographic image, (*describe image*), that the defendant (*choose one or both*: knew; had reason to believe) was obtained in violation of G.S. 14-202, (*describe violation*).

VIII. Disseminating photo obtained by peeping violation **G.S. 14-202(h)**

. . . unlawfully, willfully, and feloniously did (*choose one or both*: disseminate; allow to be disseminated) to (*name person to whom disseminated, if known)* images, (*describe images*), that the defendant (*choose one or both*: knew; should have known) were obtained as a result of a violation of G.S. 14-202, (*describe violation*), and the dissemination was without the consent of the person, (*name person, if known*), in the photographic image.

Notes about Charging Language:

- If an offense is elevated from a misdemeanor to a felony by virtue of the increased punishment for recidivist offenses described in the introductory comment, be sure to include "and feloniously" in the charging language.
- The definition of "room" in G.S. 14-202(b)(2) includes, but is not limited to, a bedroom, a rest room, a bathroom, a shower, and a dressing room.
- G.S. 14-202(b)(1) defines "photographic image" to mean any photograph or photographic reproduction, still or moving, or any videotape, motion picture, or live television transmission, or any digital image of any individual.

Sample Charges:

I. Peeping into room **G.S. 14-202(a)**

. . . unlawfully and willfully did peep secretly into a room, the bedroom at the home of Wendy Smith at 3504 Main Street, Charlotte, N.C., occupied by another person, Wendy Smith.

II. Peeping under clothing with device **G.S. 14-202(a1)**

. . . unlawfully and willfully did secretly and surreptitiously peep underneath clothing being worn by another person, Susan Jones, through the use of a mirror, for the purpose of viewing the undergarments worn by that other person, without her consent.

III. Peeping into room while possessing photo device — G.S. 14-202(c)

. . . unlawfully and willfully did, while in possession of a device, a cell phone camera, which may be used to create a photographic image, peep secretly into a room, a bathroom at the YMCA, 12 James Street, Livingston, N.C.

AOC Forms for This Offense:
None.

Punishment:
Offenses I and II are Class 1 misdemeanors. Offense III is a Class A1 misdemeanor. Offenses IV, V, VI, and VII are Class I felonies. Offense VIII is a Class H felony. As noted above, G.S. 14-202(i) provides for increased penalties for certain recidivists.

G.S. 14-202.1
Taking Indecent Liberties with Children
April 2024

Introductory Comment:
None.

Charging Language:

I. Immoral, improper, and indecent liberties **G.S. 14-202.1(a)(1)**

. . . unlawfully, willfully, and feloniously did take and attempt to take immoral, improper, and indecent liberties with (*name child*), who was under the age of 16 years at the time, for the purpose of arousing and gratifying sexual desire. At the time, the defendant was over 16 years of age and at least five years older than that child.

II. Lewd and lascivious act **G.S. 14-202.1(a)(2)**

. . . unlawfully, willfully, and feloniously did commit and attempt to commit a lewd and lascivious act upon the body of (*name child*), who was under the age of 16 years at the time. At the time, the defendant was over 16 years of age and at least five years older than that child.

Notes about Charging Language:

- It is not necessary to describe the act that constitutes the indecent liberty. State v. Youngs, 141 N.C. App. 220 (2000).

Sample Charge:

I. Immoral, improper, and indecent liberties **G.S. 14-202.1(a)(1)**

. . . unlawfully, willfully, and feloniously did take and attempt to take immoral, improper, and indecent liberties with Sally Jones, who was under the age of 16 years at the time, for the purpose of arousing and gratifying sexual desire. At the time, the defendant was over 16 years of age and at least five years older than that child.

AOC Forms for This Offense:
AOC-CR-150 (Indictment)

Punishment:
Offenses I and II are Class F felonies.

G.S. 14-202.3
Solicit Child by Computer to Commit Sex Act
April 2024

Introductory Comment:
None.

Charging Language:
. . . unlawfully, willfully, and feloniously did knowingly, with the intent to commit an unlawful sex act, (*name sex act*), (*choose one or more*: entice; advise; coerce; order; command), by means of a computer, (*describe how defendant contacted child*), (*name child and give age*), a child less than 16 years of age and at least five years younger than the defendant, to meet with (*choose one or both*: the defendant; *if appropriate, name other person*) for the purpose of committing the unlawful sex act. The defendant was (*give age of defendant*) and thus 16 years of age or older at the time of the commission of this offense.

Notes about Charging Language:

- This offense also occurs when a defendant solicits "a person the defendant believes to be" under 16 and at least five years younger than the defendant. G.S. 14-202.3(a). If that is the case, modify the charging language accordingly.
- This offense is not limited to computers but can also be committed by any "device capable of electronic data storage or transmission." If that is the case, modify the charging language accordingly.
- Consent is not a defense to this offense. G.S. 14-202.3(a).
- This offense is a Class G felony, rather than a Class H felony, if either the defendant or any other person with whom the defendant was arranging to meet actually appears at the meeting location. If that is the case, add the following to the charge: "(*Choose one or both*: The defendant; *name other person*) actually appeared at the meeting location, (*briefly describe location*)."

Sample Charge:
. . . unlawfully, willfully, and feloniously did knowingly, with the intent to commit an unlawful sex act, crime against nature, entice by means of a computer, by contacting the victim through an Internet chat room, Susan Miller, 12 years of age, a child less than 16 years of age and at least five years younger than the defendant, to meet with the defendant for the purpose of committing the unlawful sex act. The defendant was 44 years old and thus 16 years of age or older at the time of the commission of this offense.

AOC Forms for This Offense:
None.

Punishment:
Class H felony. As noted above, it is a Class G felony if either the defendant or any other person with whom the defendant was arranging to meet actually appears at the meeting location.

G.S. 14-202.4
Taking Indecent Liberties with Student by School Personnel
April 2024
Page 1 of 2

Introductory Comment:
This offense applies to a variety of sexual activity between school personnel and students. If the conduct includes intercourse or a "sexual act," the offense set forth in G.S. 14-27.32 may apply. Amendments effective December 1, 2023, redefined terminology and enhanced the penalty for a violation of this statute by school personnel who are less than four years older than the victim

Charging Language:
I. Teacher, administrator, student teacher, safety officer, or coach **G.S. 14-202.4(a)**

. . . unlawfully, willfully, and feloniously did take indecent liberties with (*name student*). At the time of this offense, the defendant was a (*choose one*: teacher; school administrator; student teacher; school safety officer; coach) at (*name school*), and the victim was a student at this same school.

II. Other school personnel, at least four years older than victim **G.S. 14-202.4(a)**

. . . unlawfully, willfully, and feloniously did take indecent liberties with (*name student*). At the time of this offense, the defendant was school personnel, namely, (*describe position at school*), at (*name school*), and the victim was a student at this same school. At the time of this offense, the defendant was at least four years older than the victim.

III. Other school personnel, less than four years older than victim **G.S. 14-202.4(b)**

. . . unlawfully, willfully, and feloniously did take indecent liberties with (*name student*). At the time of this offense, the defendant was school personnel, namely, (*describe position at school*), at (*name school*), and the victim was a student at this same school. At the time of this offense, the defendant was less than four years older than the victim.

Notes about Charging Language:
- "Indecent liberties" is defined in G.S. 14-202.4(d)(1). It does not include vaginal intercourse or a sexual act—see G.S. 14-27.32 for an offense that includes these sex acts.
- It is not necessary to describe the act that constitutes the indecent liberty. *Cf.* State v. Youngs, 141 N.C. App. 220 (2000) (construing G.S. 14-202.1 (indecent liberties with a child)).
- "School personnel" is defined in G.S. 14-202.4(d)(3).
- "School safety officer" is defined in G.S. 14-202.4(d)(3a).
- "Student" is defined in G.S. 14-202.4(d)(4) (a person enrolled in K–12 plus six months).
- "School" is defined in G.S. 14-202.4(d)(2), and "same school" is defined in G.S. 14-202.4(d)(1a).
- At least Offenses I and II also include the taking of indecent liberties by school personnel with a student after the employee and student are no longer present together at the same school, provided the student is still enrolled in a K–12 school system (plus six months; see statutory definition of "student"). If that is the case, the charging language must be modified accordingly.
- G.S. 14-202.4(c) provides that consent is not a defense to this offense.
- G.S. 14-202.4(a) states in part that, "[a] person is not guilty of taking indecent liberties with a student if the person is lawfully married to the student." Whether this limitation applies to Offense III, which is defined in G.S. 14-202.4(b), is not clear.

Sample Charge:

I. Teacher, administrator, student teacher, safety officer, or coach **G.S. 14-202.4(a)**

. . . unlawfully, willfully, and feloniously did take indecent liberties with Phyllis Smith. At the time of this offense, the defendant was a teacher at South Park High School, Park Ridge, N.C., and the victim was a student at this same school.

AOC Forms for This Offense:

None.

Punishment:

Offenses I, II, and III are all Class G felonies.

G.S. 14-204
Prostitution
April 2024

Introductory Comment:
Minors are immune from prosecution under G.S. 14-204(c) and should instead be "taken into temporary protective custody as . . . undisciplined juvenile(s)."

Charging Language:
. . . unlawfully and willfully did (*choose one or more*: perform; offer to perform; agree to perform) (*choose one or more*: vaginal intercourse; [*describe sexual act*], a sexual act as defined in G.S. 14-27.20; [*describe sexual contact*], sexual contact as defined in G.S. 14-27.20), for the purpose of sexual arousal and gratification and for (*choose one or more*: money; consideration, [*describe consideration*]).

Notes about Charging Language:
None.

Sample Charge:
. . . unlawfully and willfully did offer to perform and agree to perform fellatio, a sexual act as defined in G.S. 14-27.20, for the purpose of sexual arousal and gratification and for money.

AOC Forms for This Offense:
None.

Punishment:
Class 1 misdemeanor. First offenders may be eligible for conditional discharge after probation, as described in G.S. 14-204(b).

Introductory Comment:
A minor suspected of soliciting as a prostitute is immune from prosecution under this section and instead shall be taken into custody as an undisciplined juvenile. G.S. 14-205.1(b).

Offense I is a felony if it is the defendant's second or subsequent offense. In such a case, substitute "unlawfully, willfully, and feloniously" for "unlawfully and willfully." An indictment or an information for a recidivist offense must comply with G.S. 15A-928, which requires that the defendant's prior convictions be alleged either (1) in a separate count of the indictment or information than the substantive offense or (2) in a separate indictment or information. In such a case, the separate count or separate indictment should set forth the date and court in which the prior conviction occurred. This requirement does not apply to arrest warrants or magistrates' orders, which still must allege the defendant's prior convictions but need not do so in a separate count or separate charging instrument. G.S. 15A-928 also requires in indictments or informations that the name or title of an offense elevated by prior convictions must not make reference to such prior convictions.

Charging Language:

I. Solicitation of prostitution

. . . unlawfully and willfully did solicit another, (*name person solicited, if known*), for the purpose of prostitution.

II. Solicitation of minor for prostitution

. . . unlawfully, willfully, and feloniously did solicit a minor, (*name person solicited, if known*), for the purpose of prostitution. The defendant was 18 years of age or older at the time of the solicitation.

III. Solicitation of person with a mental disability for prostitution

. . . unlawfully, willfully, and feloniously did solicit a person who had a (*choose one or both*: severe; profound) mental disability, (*name person solicited, if known*), for the purpose of prostitution.

Notes about Charging Language:

- For Offense II, this form calls for the name of the minor who was solicited. The Court of Appeals of North Carolina has approved of the use of the victim's initials in at least one sexual assault case. State v. McKoy, 196 N.C. App. 650 (2009) (use of initials provided adequate notice to the defendant where the defendant admitted that he knew the victim and did not claim that the use of initials made it difficult to prepare his defense). By contrast, in another sexual assault case, the state supreme court disapproved of referring to the victim using the generic term "Victim #1." State v. White, 372 N.C. 248 (2019). It is unclear whether it would be permissible to use initials to identify the minor in Offense II.
- For Offense III, it is probably not necessary to describe the nature of the mental disability. *Cf.* State v. Collins, 221 N.C. App. 604 (2012) (holding, in the context of assault on a handicapped person, that it is not necessary to describe the nature of the handicap in the charging document). It is also probably not improper to include that information if desired, though some individuals may not want public court records to contain detailed descriptions of their disabilities.

Sample Charge:

II. Solicitation of minor for prostitution

. . . unlawfully, willfully, and feloniously did solicit a minor, LaKisha Lewis, for the purpose of prostitution. The defendant was 18 years of age or older at the time of the solicitation.

AOC Forms for This Offense:
None.

Punishment:
Offense I is a Class 1 misdemeanor for a first offense and a Class H felony for a second or subsequent offense. Offense II is a Class G felony. Offense III is a Class E felony. A defendant convicted of any of these offenses is ineligible for a prayer for judgment continued (PJC). G.S. 14-205.1(a).

Introductory Comment:
Offenses I and II are felonies if they are the defendant's second or subsequent violation of G.S. 14-205.2. In such a case, substitute "unlawfully, willfully, and feloniously" for "unlawfully and willfully." An indictment or an information for a recidivist offense must comply with G.S. 15A-928, which requires that the defendant's prior convictions be alleged either (1) in a separate count of the indictment or information than the substantive offense or (2) in a separate indictment or information. In such a case, the separate count or separate indictment should set forth the date and court in which the prior conviction occurred. This requirement does not apply to arrest warrants or magistrates' orders, which still must allege the defendant's prior convictions but need not do so in a separate count or separate charging instrument. G.S. 15A-928 also requires that the name or title of an offense elevated by prior convictions must not make reference to such prior convictions.

Charging Language:

I. Sexual act with a prostitute **G.S. 14-205.2(a)(1)**

. . . unlawfully and willfully did engage in (*choose one or more*: vaginal intercourse; [*describe sexual act*], a sexual act as defined in G.S. 14-27.20; [*describe sexual contact*], sexual contact as defined in G.S. 14-27.20), for the purpose of sexual arousal and gratification with (*name prostitute, if known*), a prostitute who was not the defendant's spouse.

II. Entering or remaining in a place of prostitution **G.S. 14-205.2(a)(2)**

. . . unlawfully and willfully did (*choose one or both*: enter; remain in) (*describe place*), a place of prostitution, with intent to engage in (*choose one or more*: vaginal intercourse; [*describe sexual act*], a sexual act as defined in G.S. 14-27.20; [*describe sexual contact*], sexual contact as defined in G.S. 14-27.20), for the purpose of sexual arousal and gratification with (*name person, if known*), a person who was not the defendant's spouse.

Notes about Charging Language:

- Offenses I and II are felonies if the defendant is 18 years of age or older and the prostitute is a minor. In such a case, substitute "unlawfully, willfully, and feloniously" for "unlawfully and willfully" and add allegations that the defendant was 18 years of age or older and that the prostitute (or person, for Offense II) was a minor at the time of the offense.
- Offenses I and II are felonies if the prostitute has a severe or profound mental disability. In such a case, substitute "unlawfully, willfully, and feloniously" for "unlawfully and willfully" and add an allegation that the prostitute (or person, for Offense II) had a severe or profound mental disability. It is probably not necessary to describe the nature of the mental disability. *Cf.* State v. Collins, 221 N.C. App. 604 (2012) (holding, in the context of assault on a handicapped person, that it is not necessary to describe the nature of the handicap in the charging document). It is also probably not improper to include that information if desired.

Sample Charge:

I. Sexual act with a prostitute **G.S. 14-205.2(a)(1)**

. . . unlawfully and willfully did engage in vaginal intercourse for the purpose of sexual arousal and gratification with Trina Abrams, a prostitute who was not the defendant's spouse.

AOC Forms for This Offense:

None.

Punishment:

Offenses I and II are Class A1 misdemeanors for a first offense and Class G felonies for a second or subsequent offense. When the defendant is an adult and the prostitute is a minor, the offenses are Class F felonies. When the prostitute has a severe or profound mental disability, the offenses are Class D felonies.

G.S. 14-205.3
Promoting Prostitution
April 2024
Page 1 of 2

Introductory Comment:
Offenses I, II, III, and IV are punished more severely if the defendant has a qualifying prior conviction, as noted in the description of punishments below. An indictment or an information for a recidivist offense must comply with G.S. 15A-928, which requires that the defendant's prior convictions be alleged either (1) in a separate count of the indictment or information than the substantive offense or (2) in a separate indictment or information. In such a case, the separate count or separate indictment should set forth the date and court in which the prior conviction occurred. This requirement does not apply to arrest warrants or magistrates' orders, which still must allege the defendant's prior convictions but need not do so in a separate count or separate charging instrument. G.S. 15A-928 also requires that the name or title of an offense elevated by prior convictions must not make reference to such prior convictions.

Charging Language:

I. Advancing prostitution **G.S. 14-205.3(a)(1)**

. . . unlawfully, willfully, and feloniously did advance prostitution, as defined in G.S. 14-203, by (*describe conduct that constitutes advancing prostitution*).

II. Profiting from prostitution **G.S. 14-205.3(a)(2)**

. . . unlawfully, willfully, and feloniously did profit from prostitution by (*choose one or more*: compelling [*name person*] to become a prostitute; receiving a portion of the earnings from [*name person*], a prostitute, for [*choose one or both*: arranging; offering to arrange] a situation in which [*name person*] may practice prostitution; [*describe other means by which the defendant profited*]).

III. Advancing prostitution of a minor or a person with a mental disability **G.S. 14-205.3(b)(1)**

. . . unlawfully, willfully, and feloniously did advance prostitution, as defined in G.S. 14-203, by (*describe conduct that constitutes advancing prostitution*), where (*name person*), a (*choose one or more*: minor; person who has a severe mental disability; person who has a profound mental disability), engaged in prostitution.

IV. Profiting from prostitution of a minor or a person with a mental disability **G.S. 14-205.3(b)(2)**

. . . unlawfully, willfully, and feloniously did profit from the prostitution of (*name prostitute*) by (*describe means by which defendant profited*). At the time of the offense, (*name prostitute*) was a (*choose one or more*: minor; person with a severe mental disability; person with a profound mental disability).

V. Confining a minor or a person with a mental disability for prostitution **G.S. 14-205.3(b)(3)**

. . . unlawfully, willfully, and feloniously did confine (*name person*), a (*choose one or more*: minor; person with a severe mental disability; person with a profound mental disability), against (*choose one*: his; her) will, by (*choose one or more*: the infliction of great bodily harm; the infliction of permanent disability; the infliction of disfigurement; the threat of imminent infliction of great bodily harm; the threat of imminent infliction of permanent disability; the threat of imminent infliction of disfigurement; administering to [*choose one*: him; her], [*choose one or more*: without (*choose one*: his; her) consent; by threat; by deception], and for other than medical purposes, [*choose one or both and describe if possible*: an alcoholic intoxicant; a drug as defined in Article 5 of Chapter 90 of the General Statutes]) and did (*choose one or more*: compel [*name person*] to engage in prostitution; arrange a situation in which [*name person*] was able to practice prostitution; profit from prostitution by [*name person*]).

Notes about Charging Language:

- For Offense II, the catchall option of describing another means by which the defendant profited from prostitution should not be used if (1) the defendant is a minor engaged in prostitution or (2) "the practice of prostitution underlying the offense consists exclusively of the defendant's own acts of prostitution." G.S. 14-205.3(a)(2)(c).
- Offense III may be committed also by advancing prostitution where "any person engaged in prostitution in the place of prostitution is a minor or has a severe or profound mental disability at the time of the offense." In an appropriate case, modify the charging language accordingly.
- For offenses involving a person with a mental disability, it is probably not necessary to describe the nature of the mental disability. *Cf.* State v. Collins, 221 N.C. App. 604 (2012) (holding, in the context of assault on a handicapped person, that it is not necessary to describe the nature of the handicap in the charging document). It is also probably not improper to include that information if desired.

Sample Charge:

III. Advancing prostitution of a minor or a person with a mental disability G.S. 14-205.3(b)(1)

. . . unlawfully, willfully, and feloniously did advance prostitution, as defined in G.S. 14-203, by directing another, Eric Stevenson, to a place, 8108 Treetop Court, Zebulon, N.C., knowing the direction was for the purposes of prostitution, where Zoe Kipling, a person with a severe mental disability, engaged in prostitution.

AOC Forms for This Offense:

None.

Punishment:

Offenses I and II are Class F felonies for a first offense and Class E felonies if the defendant has a qualifying prostitution-related conviction as described in G.S. 14-205.3(c). Offenses III and IV are Class D felonies for a first offense and Class C felonies if the defendant has a qualifying prostitution-related conviction as described in G.S. 14-205.3(d). Offense V is a Class C felony.

G.S. 14-208.11
Failure to Register as a Sex Offender and Related Offenses
April 2024
Page 1 of 2

Introductory Comment:
Effective August 1, 2020, the General Assembly enacted a procedure for determining whether a North Carolina resident convicted of an out-of-state or federal sex offense is required to register as a sex offender in North Carolina. Generally, the sheriff must notify a person in these circumstances that they may be required to register, at which point the person has thirty days to file a petition seeking a judicial determination of the issue. During the thirty-day period, and during the pendency of any request for judicial determination, the person may not be charged with a failure to register. *See* G.S. 14-208.12B.

Charging Language:
. . . unlawfully, willfully, and feloniously did, as a person required by Article 27A of Chapter 14 of the General Statutes to register,
(*choose one or more*)

(1) fail to register (*describe facts of the failure to register*).
(2) fail to notify the last registering sheriff of a change of address as required by G.S. 14-208.9 (*describe facts of the change of address and the failure to notify*).
(3) fail to return a verification notice as required under G.S. 14-208.9A (*describe facts of failure to return notice*).
(4) (*choose one or both*: forge; submit) under false pretenses the (*choose one or both*: information; verification notices) required under Article 27A of General Statutes Chapter 14 (*describe facts*).
(5) fail to inform the registering sheriff of (*choose one or both*: enrollment; termination of enrollment) as a student (*describe facts*).
(6) fail to inform the registering sheriff of (*choose one or both*: employment; termination of employment) at an institution of higher education (*describe facts*).
(7) fail to report in person to the sheriff's office as required under (*choose one or more*: G.S. 14-208.7; G.S. 14-208.9; G.S. 14-208.9A).
(8) report (*choose one*: his; her) intent to reside in another (*choose one or both*: state; jurisdiction) but remain in North Carolina without reporting to the sheriff as required under G.S. 14-208.9.
(9) fail to notify the registering sheriff of out-of-county employment when temporary residence was established as required under G.S. 14-208.8A (*describe facts*).
(10) fail to notify the registering sheriff of (*choose one or both*: a new; changes to an existing) online identifier, (*describe identifier*), that the person (*choose one or both*: used; intended to use).

Notes about Charging Language:

- As used in G.S. 14-208.9(a) and -208.11(a)(2), "address" means the offender's "residence," the "actual place of abode where he or she lives, whether permanent or temporary" where "certain activities of life occur." State v. Abshire, 363 N.C. 322, 331, 332 (2009). In *Abshire*, the state supreme court held that a defendant changed her address when she slept at another house for five to six weeks, despite visiting the old house almost every day during that time to care for pets, wash clothes, and pick up mail. Every sex offender has an address of some sort, "even if it is a homeless shelter, a location under a bridge or some similar place." State v. Worsley, 198 N.C. App. 329 (2009).
- "Institution of higher education" is defined in G.S. 14-208.6(1h).
- "Online identifier" is defined in G.S. 14-208.6(1n).
- In *State v. Williams*, 368 N.C. 620, 626 (2016), the Supreme Court of North Carolina ruled that because the indictment contained substantially accurate language drawn from G.S. 14-208.11, specific "detail about the reporting requirement such as that found in [G.S.] 14-208.9 was neither needed nor required in the indictment."

Sample Charge:

. . . unlawfully, willfully, and feloniously did, as a person required by Article 27A of Chapter 14 of the General Statutes to register, fail to register in that the defendant, a Cary, N.C., resident, had been convicted of first-degree rape and did not register with the Sheriff of Wake County within three business days of his release from a penal institution.

AOC Forms for This Offense:

None.

Punishment:

Class F felony.

G.S. 14-208.16
Sex Offender Residency Restriction
April 2024

Introductory Comment:
None.

Charging Language:
. . . unlawfully, willfully, and feloniously did, as a person required by Article 27A of Chapter 14 of the General Statutes to register, knowingly reside (*choose one*: at a location; within a structure, [*describe structure*], a portion of which was) within 1,000 feet of any property line of a property on which a (choose one: school; child care center), (*name school or child care center*), is located.

Notes about Charging Language:
- The terms "school" and "child care center" are defined in G.S. 14-208.16(b).
- This offense does not apply to "child care centers that are located on or within 1,000 feet of the property of an institution of higher education where the registrant is a student or is employed." G.S. 14-206.16(c).
- Generally, when a property becomes a school or a child care center *after* a sex offender has established residency nearby, the sex offender has not committed this offense, as explained in G.S. 14-208.16(d). Additionally, the law does not apply to sex offenders who established residency before August 16, 2006.

Sample Charge:
. . . unlawfully, willfully, and feloniously did, as a person required by Article 27A of Chapter 14 of the General Statutes to register, knowingly reside within a structure, a one-story red brick house, a portion of which was within 1,000 feet of the property line of the property on which a school, Melvin Gipson Elementary School, is located.

AOC Forms for This Offense:
None.

Punishment:
Class G felony.

Sex Offender Unlawfully on Premises

Introductory Comment:

In two rulings, one in 2015 and the other in 2016, a federal judge determined that certain aspects of G.S. 14-208.18 were unconstitutional. During the 2016 legislative session, the General Assembly amended G.S. 14-208.18 in response to these rulings. The amendments are effective September 1, 2016, for offenses committed on or after that date. However, the legislation amending the statute provides that the amendments "shall be repealed" if the federal court's rulings are "stayed or overturned." S.L. 2016-102, § 2. To the contrary, however, the federal court's rulings have been affirmed by a panel of the Fourth Circuit Court of Appeals. Doe v. Cooper, 842 F.3d 833 (4th Cir. 2016). Therefore, this form is based on the 2016 amended version of the statute.

Charging Language:

. . . unlawfully, willfully, and feloniously was, as a person required to registered under Article 27A of Chapter 14 of the General Statutes, knowingly present at the following location:

(*choose one*)

(1) on the premises of (*name or describe place*), a place intended primarily for the (*choose one or more*: use; care; supervision) of minors. The defendant was required to register as a result of having previously committed (*choose one or more*: [*name prior offense*], an offense in Article 7B of Chapter 14 of the General Statutes; [*name prior offense*], a [*choose one*: federal offense; offense committed in another state] that is substantially similar to an offense in Article 7B of Chapter 14 of the General Statutes; [*name prior offense*], an offense where the victim of the offense was under the age of 18 years at the time of the offense; [*name prior offense*], an offense in violation of [*choose one*: G.S. 14-190.16; 14-190.17; 14-190.17A]; [*name prior offense*], a [*choose one*: federal offense; offense committed in another state] that is substantially similar to an offense in violation of [*choose one*: G.S. 14-190.16; 14-190.17; 14-190.17A]).

(2) within 300 feet of (*name or describe location*), a location intended primarily for the (*choose one or more*: use; care; supervision) of minors that is located on (*name or describe premises*), premises that are not intended primarily for the use, care, or supervision of minors. The defendant was required to register as a result of having previously committed (*choose one or more*: [*name prior offense*], an offense in Article 7B of Chapter 14 of the General Statutes, and a finding was made on or about [*date*] in [*name court*] that the defendant [*choose one*: presents; may present] a danger to minors under the age of 18; [*name prior offense*], a [*choose one*: federal offense; offense committed in another state] that is substantially similar to an offense in Article 7B of Chapter 14 of the General Statutes, and a finding was made on or about [*date*] in [*name court*] that the defendant [*choose one*: presents; may present] a danger to minors under the age of 18; [*name prior offense*], an offense where

the victim of the offense was under the age of 18 years at the time of the offense; [*name prior offense*], an offense in violation of [*choose one*: G.S. 14-190.16; 14-190.17; 14-190.17A]; [*name prior offense*], a [*choose one*: federal offense; offense committed in another state] that is substantially similar to an offense in violation of [*choose one*: G.S. 14-190.16; 14-190.17; 14-190.17A]).

(3) at (*name or describe place*), a place where minors frequently congregate, when minors were present. The defendant was required to register as a result of having previously committed (*choose one or more*: [*name prior offense*], an offense in Article 7B of Chapter 14 of the General Statutes; [*name prior offense*], a [*choose one*: federal offense; offense committed in another state] that is substantially similar to an offense in Article 7B of Chapter 14 of the General Statutes; [*name prior offense*], an offense where the victim of the offense was under the age of 18 years at the time of the offense); [*name prior offense*], an offense in violation of [*choose one*: G.S. 14-190.16; 14-190.17; 14-190.17A]; [*name prior offense*], a [*choose one*: federal offense; offense committed in another state] that is substantially similar to an offense in violation of [*choose one*: G.S. 14-190.16; 14-190.17; 14-190.17A]).

(4) on the (*choose one*)

  (1) State Fairgrounds during the period of time that the State Fair was being conducted.

  (2) Western North Carolina Agricultural Center grounds during the period of time that the Mountain State Fair was being conducted.

  (3) (*name or describe place*), a fairgrounds, during the period of time that an agricultural fair was being conducted.

  The defendant was required to register as a result of having previously committed (*choose one or more*: [*name prior offense*], an offense in Article 7B of Chapter 14 of the General Statutes; [*name prior offense*], a [*choose one*: federal offense; offense committed in another state] that is substantially similar to an offense in Article 7B of Chapter 14 of the General Statutes; [*name prior offense*], an offense where the victim of the offense was under the age of 18 years at the time of the offense; [*name prior offense*], an offense in violation of [*choose one*: G.S. 14-190.16; 14-190.17; 14-190.17A]; [*name prior offense*], a [*choose one*: federal offense; offense committed in another state] that is substantially similar to an offense in violation of [*choose one*: G.S. 14-190.16; 14-190.17; 14-190.17A]).

Notes about Charging Language:

- This offense does not apply to a parent or guardian of a minor in need of emergency medical care who takes the child to an appropriate location for treatment, G.S. 14-208.18(b); to a parent or guardian of a minor who is on school property for certain purposes and under certain conditions,

G.S. 14-208.18(d); to voters to the extent described in G.S. 14-208.18(e); to public school students if permitted to attend public school under G.S. 14-208.18(f); or to juveniles receiving medical or mental health treatment to the extent set forth in G.S. 14-208.18(g).

- The charging document should describe the place or location in a way that makes clear the connection between the place or location and children. For example, alleging that the defendant was *at the playground* at a specific park would be better than alleging only that the defendant was at the park, as it may be unclear whether a park is intended primarily for the use of minors. *Cf.* State v. Daniels, 224 N.C. App. 608 (2012) (holding the statute unconstitutional as applied to a defendant charged with being "kind of close to the parking lot area" of a park that contained youth sports fields, because a reasonable person would not be able to know whether being in that location would violate the statute).

Sample Charge:
. . . unlawfully, willfully, and feloniously was, as a person required to registered under Article 27A of Chapter 14 of the General Statutes, knowingly present at the following location: on the premises of the Kidspace Museum in Hometown, N.C., a place intended primarily for the use of minors. The defendant was required to register as a result of having previously committed second-degree forcible rape, an offense in Article 7B of Chapter 14 of the General Statutes.

AOC Forms for This Offense:
None.

Punishment:
Class H felony.

G.S. 14-209
Perjury
April 2024

Introductory Comment:
None.

Charging Language:
. . . unlawfully, willfully, corruptly, and feloniously did commit perjury upon the trial of an action in (*choose one*: district; superior) court in (*name county*) wherein (*if a criminal case, insert* the State of North Carolina; *if a civil case, insert the name of the plaintiff*) was the plaintiff and (*insert the name of the defendant*) was the defendant, by falsely asserting (*choose one*: under oath; upon solemn affirmation; in an unsworn declaration pursuant to G.S. 7A-98) that (*set out the statement or statements alleged to be false*), (*choose one of the following*)

(1) knowing the statement, which was material, to be false.

(2) knowing the statements, which were material, to be false.

(3) being ignorant whether or not the statement, which was material, was true.

(4) being ignorant whether or not the statements, which were material, were true.

Notes about Charging Language:
- G.S. 15-145 provides that the charging language set out above is sufficient to charge this offense. However, after the General Assembly simplified the perjury statute in S.L. 2019-243, § 3.(c), an alternative would be to track the new language of the statute, which provides that a person who "knowingly and intentionally makes a false statement under oath or affirmation in any suit, controversy, matter of cause, or in any unsworn declaration deemed sufficient pursuant to G.S. 7A-98 depending in any of the courts of the State; in any deposition or affidavit taken pursuant to law; in any oath or affirmation duly administered of or concerning any matter or thing where such person is lawfully required to be sworn" is guilty of perjury.
- G.S. 14-209 was amended effective December 1, 2021, to include the provision covering an unsworn declaration deemed sufficient under G.S. 7A-98, a statute which provides that certain matters to be evidenced or proved in writing under oath or affirmation may, if filed electronically in accordance with court rules, be proved instead "by an unsworn declaration in writing, subscribed by the declarant and dated, that the statement is true under penalty of perjury."

Sample Charge:
. . . unlawfully, willfully, corruptly, and feloniously did commit perjury upon the trial of an action in superior court in Wake County wherein the State of North Carolina was the plaintiff and Howard Jones was the defendant, by falsely asserting under oath that he was in Chicago with the defendant on the date of the offense being tried, knowing the statement, which was material, to be false.

AOC Forms for This Offense:
None.

Punishment:
Class F felony.

G.S. 14-210
Subornation of Perjury
April 2024

Introductory Comment:
None.

Charging Language:
. . . unlawfully, willfully, and feloniously did procure (*name person who committed perjury*) to commit willful and corrupt perjury as mentioned in G.S. 14-209. (*Name person who committed perjury*) did commit perjury upon the trial of an action in (*choose one*: district; superior) court in (*name county*) wherein (*if a criminal case, insert* the State of North Carolina; *if a civil case, insert the name of the plaintiff*) was the plaintiff and (*insert the name of the defendant*) was the defendant, by falsely asserting on (*choose one*: oath; solemn affirmation) (*set out the statement or statements alleged to be false*), (*choose one of the following*)

(1) knowing the statement, which was material, to be false.
(2) knowing the statements, which were material, to be false.
(3) being ignorant whether or not the statement, which was material, was true.
(4) being ignorant whether or not the statements, which were material, were true.

Notes about Charging Language:
- G.S. 15-146 sets out the requirements for charging this offense. This form sets out the charging language in more detail than may be required.

Sample Charge:
. . . unlawfully, willfully, and feloniously did procure Peter Falk to commit willful and corrupt perjury as mentioned in G.S. 14-209. Peter Falk did commit perjury upon the trial of an action in superior court in Wake County wherein the State of North Carolina was the plaintiff and Howard Jones was the defendant, by falsely asserting on oath that he was in Chicago with the defendant on the date of the offense being tried, knowing the statement to be false.

AOC Forms for This Offense:
None.

Punishment:
Class I felony.

G.S. 14-217, -218
Bribery of Public Official
April 2024
Page 1 of 2

Introductory Comment:
None.

Charging Language:

I. Official accepting bribe **G.S. 14-217(a)**

. . . unlawfully, willfully, and feloniously did, while holding the office of (*name official's office*), receive and consent to receive (*describe what was offered as the bribe*) from (*name person who offered the bribe*), with the understanding that the defendant would be influenced in (*choose one or both*: performing an official act; omitting to perform an official act) in that (*describe act to be performed or omitted to be performed as a result of the bribe*). This official act lay within the scope of the defendant's official authority and was connected with the discharge of the defendant's official and legal duties.

II. Offering bribe to official **G.S. 14-218**

. . . unlawfully, willfully, and feloniously did, with a corrupt intent, offer (*describe what was offered as the bribe*) to (*name public official*), a (*name the official's office*), knowing (*choose one*: him; her) to be a (*repeat the official's office*), to influence (*choose one*: him; her) in (*choose one or both*: performing an official act; omitting to perform an official act) in that (*describe act to be performed or omitted to be performed as a result of the bribe*). This official act lay within the scope of the official authority of (*repeat name of public official*) and was connected with the discharge of (*choose one*: his; her) official and legal duties.

Notes about Charging Language:

- As to Offense I, you may strike through either "receive" or "consent to receive" if one of those terms or phrases is not appropriate to the facts.
- The statute says that the bribe may be "anything of value or personal advantage, or the promise thereof." If nothing has exchanged hands, it is probably preferable to add "the promise of" in front of the description of the bribe.
- G.S. 14-217(c) requires specific charging language when alleging the offense of conspiracy to receive a bribe, including that the defendant and at least one other person intended at the time of the agreement that it be carried out and that they committed an overt act, which must be described, to carry out an object of the conspiracy.

Sample Charge:

I. Official accepting bribe **G.S. 14-217(a)**

. . . unlawfully, willfully, and feloniously did, while holding the office of Town Council member of Wayforth, N.C., receive and consent to receive $500 from Amos C. Krinkler with the understanding that the defendant would be influenced in performing an official act, in that he would vote in a Town Council meeting in favor of the Town of Wayforth to contract with Mr. Krinkler's company for sanitation services. This official act lay within the scope of the defendant's official authority and was connected with the discharge of the defendant's official and legal duties.

AOC Forms for This Offense:
None.

Punishment:
Class F felony.

G.S. 14-221.1
Altering, Destroying, or Stealing Criminal Evidence
April 2024

Introductory Comment:
None.

Charging Language:

I. Breaking or entering for the purpose of altering, etc., evidence

. . . unlawfully, willfully, and feloniously did (*choose one or both*: break; enter) a (*choose one or more and describe*: building; structure; compartment; vehicle; file; cabinet; drawer; enclosure) where evidence, (*describe*), relevant to (*choose one and describe*: a criminal offense; a court proceeding) was (*choose one or both*: kept; stored), with the purpose of (*choose one or more*: altering; destroying; stealing) such evidence.

II. Altering, etc., evidence

. . . unlawfully, willfully, and feloniously did (*choose one or more*: alter; destroy; steal) evidence, (*describe*), relevant to (*choose one and describe*: a criminal offense; a court proceeding).

Notes about Charging Language:

- G.S. 14-221.1 defines "evidence" as "any article or document in the possession of a law-enforcement officer or officer of the General Court of Justice being retained for the purpose of being introduced in evidence or having been introduced in evidence or being preserved as evidence."

Sample Charge:

II. Altering, etc., evidence

. . . unlawfully, willfully, and feloniously did steal evidence, two pounds of marijuana being held in the evidence locker of the Chapel Hill Police Department, relevant to a court proceeding, State v. Peter Smith, 19 CRS 8989, Orange County Superior Court.

AOC Forms for This Offense:
None.

Punishment:
Class I felony.

G.S. 14-221.2
Altering Court Document
April 2024

Introductory Comment:
None.

Charging Language:
. . . unlawfully, willfully, and feloniously did intentionally without lawful authority (*choose one or more*: enter a judgment on; materially alter; materially change) (*choose one or more and describe*: a criminal process; a civil process; a criminal pleading; a civil pleading; an official case record).

Notes about Charging Language:
None.

Sample Charge:
. . . unlawfully, willfully, and feloniously did intentionally without lawful authority materially alter an official case record by changing the judgment from "guilty" to "not guilty" in State v. Stanley Jones, 19 CR 1234, Durham County District Court, in which the defendant was charged with impaired driving.

AOC Forms for This Offense:
None.

Punishment:
Class H felony.

Resist, Delay, or Obstruct Public Officer

Introductory Comment:

This statute was amended effective December 1, 2021, to create two new offenses for resisting, delaying, or obstructing an officer that proximately causes injury to the officer.

Charging Language:

I. Resist, delay, or obstruct a public officer **G.S. 14-223(a)**

. . . unlawfully and willfully did resist, delay, and obstruct (*name public officer*), a public officer holding the office of (*name office*), by (*describe the defendant's conduct*). At the time, the officer was discharging and attempting to discharge an official duty, (*describe duty*).

II. Resist, delay, or obstruct a public officer causing serious injury **G.S. 14-223(b)**

. . . unlawfully, willfully, and feloniously did resist, delay, and obstruct (*name public officer*), a public officer holding the office of (*name office*), by (*describe the defendant's conduct*), thereby proximately causing serious injury to the officer. At the time, the officer was discharging and attempting to discharge an official duty, (*describe duty*).

III. Resist, delay, or obstruct a public officer causing serious bodily injury **G.S. 14-223(c)**

. . . unlawfully, willfully, and feloniously did resist, delay, and obstruct (*name public officer*), a public officer holding the office of (*name office*), by (*describe the defendant's conduct*), thereby proximately causing serious bodily injury to the officer. At the time, the officer was discharging and attempting to discharge an official duty, (*describe duty*).

Notes about Charging Language:

- The statute only requires proof that the defendant resisted, delayed, *or* obstructed an officer. You may delete any of those terms that are inappropriate.
- The statute does not provide a definition of "public officer." See the discussion of the meaning of public officer under this offense in Jessica Smith, *North Carolina Crimes: A Guidebook on the Elements of Crime* 460 (UNC School of Government, 7th ed. 2012).
- The statute only requires proof that the officer was discharging *or* attempting to discharge an official duty. You may delete one of those terms if appropriate.
- Alleging the duty that the public officer was discharging is required (e.g., "attempting to place the defendant under arrest"). State v. Smith, 262 N.C. 472 # (1964). However, it is not necessary to further allege the specific basis for that duty (e.g., "arresting the defendant for possession of marijuana"), nor is it a fatal variance if such a basis is alleged and it differs from the evidence at trial. *See* State v. Tarlton, 279 N.C. App. 249 (2021).
- For Offense II, the phrase "serious injury" is not defined by the statute, but it is generally interpreted to mean physical or bodily injury of real consequence, or such physical injury as causes great pain and suffering. It may also include severe mental injury. State v. Everhardt, 326 N.C. 777 (1990). The nature of the serious injury need not be alleged. State v. Gregory, 223 N.C. 415 (1943); State v. Lanford, 225 N.C. App. 189 (2013); State v. Ebron, 173 N.C. App. 642 (2005) (unpublished).

- For Offense III, the phrase "serious bodily injury" is defined by G.S. 14-223(d) as "bodily injury that creates a substantial risk of death, or that causes serious permanent disfigurement, coma, a permanent or protracted condition that causes extreme pain, or permanent or protracted loss or impairment of the function of any bodily member or organ, or that results in prolonged hospitalization."

Sample Charge:

Offense II. Resist, delay, or obstruct a public officer causing serious injury G.S. 14-223(b)

. . . unlawfully, willfully, and feloniously did resist, delay, and obstruct Lt. Oscar Sims, a public officer holding the office of Lieutenant in the Hartley, N.C., Police Department, by biting the officer and snatching a summons from his hand, thereby causing serious injury. At the time, the officer was discharging and attempting to discharge an official duty, serving on the defendant a summons for assault on a female.

AOC Forms for This Offense:
AOC-J-324 (Juvenile Petition)

Punishment:
Offense I is a Class 2 misdemeanor. Offense II is a Class I felony. Offense III is a Class F felony.

G.S. 14-225
False Report to Law Enforcement Officer or Agency
April 2024

Introductory Comment:
None.

Charging Language:
. . . unlawfully and willfully did (*choose one or both*: make; cause to be made) to a (*choose one or both and describe*: law enforcement officer; law enforcement agency) a (*choose one or more and describe*: false report; deliberately misleading report; unfounded report) [*choose one or both*: for the purpose of interfering with the operation of the law enforcement agency; to hinder and obstruct the law enforcement officer in the performance of (*choose one*: his; her) duty (*describe duty*)].

Notes about Charging Language:
This offense is a Class H felony if the false report "relates to a law enforcement investigation involving the disappearance of a child as that term is defined in G.S. 14-318.5 or child victim of a Class A, B1, B2 or C felony offense." G.S. 14-225(b). In such a case, allege "unlawfully, willfully, and feloniously" instead of "unlawfully and willfully" and add an allegation at the end of the charging language regarding the relationship to a child disappearance or child victim matter.

Sample Charge:
. . . unlawfully and willfully did make to a law enforcement officer, Sally Smith of the Orangeville Police Department, Orangeville, N.C., a false report, stating that his brother, Dean Ellis, was at home with him on the night of February 8, 2009, when in fact Dean Ellis was not at home that night, to hinder and obstruct the law enforcement officer in the performance of her duty, investigating Dean Ellis's involvement in a series of burglaries.

AOC Forms for This Offense:
None.

Punishment:
Class 2 misdemeanor, except when it is a Class H felony as described above.

G.S. 14-226
Intimidating Witnesses
April 2024

Introductory Comment:
There are several related offenses that should be considered when a witness has been asked or instructed to behave inappropriately, including this offense, subornation of perjury, G.S. 14-210, and common law obstruction of justice.

Charging Language:

I. Intimidating a witness

. . . unlawfully, willfully, and feloniously did by threats (*choose one or more*: intimidate; attempt to intimidate) (*name witness*), who was (*choose one or more*: summoned; acting) as a witness in (*name court and case in question*). The intimidation consisted of (*describe threats*).

II. Deterring appearance by a witness

. . . unlawfully, willfully, and feloniously did by threats (*choose one or more*: deter; attempt to deter; prevent; attempt to prevent) (*name witness*) from attending court by (*describe threats and manner of preventing or deterring attendance*). (*Repeat name of witness*) was (*choose one or more*: summoned; acting) as a witness in (*name court and case in question*).

Notes about Charging Language:
- The statute prohibits intimidation by use of "threats, menaces or in any other manner." Substitute other language for "threats" if appropriate.
- The statute does not define what it means to be "acting" as a witness, but in some cases, a witness who is not under subpoena may nonetheless fall within the scope of the statute. *See* Jessica Smith, North Carolina Crimes: A Guidebook on the Elements of Crime 559 (UNC School of Government, 7th ed. 2012).
- The statute appears to encompass situations in which a witness is intimidated with respect to out-of-court behavior, as when a defendant pressures a witness to ask a prosecutor to dismiss a charge.
- The statute applies only to witnesses in proceedings in state court, not federal court.

Sample Charge:

I. Intimidating a witness

. . . unlawfully, willfully, and feloniously did by threats intimidate Susan Smith, who was summoned as a witness in the case of State v. John Smith, 19 CR 1235, Assault on a Female, in Randolph County District Court. The intimidation consisted of threatening to assault Susan Smith if she failed to ask the prosecutor to dismiss the charge against the defendant.

AOC Forms for This Offense:
None.

Punishment:
Class G felony.

G.S. 14-226.3
Interfering with Electronic Monitoring Device
April 2024

Introductory Comment:
This offense does not apply to persons who are being monitored by an electronic monitoring device pursuant to Article 27A of Chapter 14 of the General Statutes (sex offenders) or Chapter 7B of the General Statutes (juveniles). G.S. 14-226.3(d).

Charging Language:
. . . unlawfully and willfully (*if felony offense is being charged add*: and feloniously) did knowingly and without authority (*choose all that apply*: remove; destroy; circumvent the operation of) an electronic monitoring device that was being used for the purpose of monitoring a person, (*name person*), who was (*choose one*: complying with a house arrest program; wearing an electronic monitoring device as a condition of bond or pretrial release; wearing an electronic monitoring device as a condition of probation; wearing an electronic monitoring device as a condition of parole; wearing an electronic monitoring device as a condition of post-release supervision).

Notes about Charging Language:
- G.S. 14-226.3(a) defines an "electronic monitoring device" to include "any electronic device that is used to track the location of a person."
- As noted below, this offense may be a felony or a misdemeanor, depending on the reason the person was wearing the monitoring device. If the offense is a felony, be sure to include "and feloniously" in the charging language.
- G.S. 14-226.3(c) defines the separate offense of requesting or soliciting another to remove, destroy, etc., an electronic monitoring device.

Sample Charge:
. . . unlawfully, willfully, and feloniously did knowingly and without authority remove and destroy an electronic monitoring device that was being used for the purpose of monitoring a person, Nancy Adams, who was wearing an electronic monitoring device as a condition of post-release supervision.

AOC Forms for This Offense:
None.

Punishment:
G.S. 14-226.3(e) provides as follows with respect to the punishment for this offense:
Violation of this section by a person who is required to comply with electronic monitoring as a result of a conviction for a criminal offense is a felony one class lower than the most-serious underlying felony, or a misdemeanor one class lower than the most-serious underlying misdemeanor, except that, if the most-serious underlying felony is a Class I felony, then violation of this section is a Class A1 misdemeanor. Violation of this section by a person who is required to comply with electronic monitoring as a condition of bond or pretrial release is a Class 1 misdemeanor. Violation of this section by any other person is a Class 2 misdemeanor.

Common Law
Obstructing Justice
April 2024

Introductory Comment:
The common law offense of obstructing justice consists of any act that prevents, obstructs, impedes, or hinders public or legal justice and may take a variety of forms. For a discussion of the scope of the offense, see Jessica Smith, *North Carolina Crimes: A Guidebook on the Elements of Crime* 557 (UNC School of Government, 7th ed. 2012).

Charging Language:
. . . unlawfully, willfully, and feloniously did obstruct justice by (*describe conduct involved in obstructing justice*). (*To allege this offense as a felony, if appropriate, choose one or more*: This offense was done with deceit and intent to defraud; This offense was done in secrecy and malice; This offense was infamous.)

Notes about Charging Language:
- The common law offense of obstructing justice is a misdemeanor. If charged as a misdemeanor, strike through the words "and feloniously."
- Under G.S. 14-3(b), a misdemeanor for which a specific punishment is not prescribed—such as obstructing justice—is a Class H felony if it is (1) done with deceit and intent to defraud, (2) done in secrecy and malice, or (3) infamous. A criminal pleading that alleges one or more of these charges is a felony. *See* State v. Clemmons, 100 N.C. App. 286 (1990); State v. Preston, 73 N.C. App. 174 (1985).
- The North Carolina Court of Appeals has held that an indictment for felony obstruction of justice was insufficient that failed to allege the defendant's actions were done to subvert a potential subsequent investigation or legal proceeding. State v. Coffey, ___ N.C. App. ___, 898 S.E.2d 359, *temp. stay allowed*, ___ N.C. ___, 897 S.E.2d 672 (2024).

Sample Charge:
. . . unlawfully, willfully, and feloniously did obstruct justice by pleading guilty to impaired driving in Guilford County District Court in State v. Sam R. Jones, 09 CR 14566, falsely representing to the court that he was Sam R. Jones, when in fact his name is Albert C. Pickens. This offense was done with deceit and intent to defraud.

AOC Forms for This Offense:
None.

Punishment:
Class 1 misdemeanor or Class H felony, as discussed above.

G.S. 14-230
Willfully Failing to Discharge Duties
April 2024

Introductory Comment:
None.

Charging Language:
. . . unlawfully and willfully did, as a (*name public office*), (*choose one or more*: omit; neglect; refuse) to discharge a duty of (*choose one*: his; her) office, (*describe duty and how defendant omitted, neglected, or refused to discharge it*), and did thereby cause injury to the public.

Notes about Charging Language:
- Public officials covered by this statute include a "clerk of any court of record, sheriff, magistrate, school board member, county commissioner, county surveyor, coroner, treasurer, or official of any of the State institutions, or of any county, city or town." G.S. 14-230(a).
- The State is not legally required to specify the duty that the defendant failed to discharge. State v. Birdsong, 325 N.C. 418 (1989); State v. Rhome, 120 N.C. App. 278 (1995). This form nonetheless asks for that information.
- Although the statute does not refer to injury to the public as an element of the offense, this form includes an allegation regarding injury to the public because case law indicates that such an injury may be an element. *Birdsong*, 325 N.C. 418 (citing State v. Anderson, 196 N.C. 771 (1929)); *Rhome*, 120 N.C. App. 278.

Sample Charge:
. . . unlawfully and willfully did, as a magistrate of Essex County, omit, neglect, and refuse to discharge a duty of her office by collecting cash bond monies for secured bonds and willfully and corruptly failing to turn over those monies, as required, to the Clerk of Superior Court of Essex County, and did thereby cause injury to the public.

AOC Forms for This Offense:
None.

Punishment:
Class 1 misdemeanor. G.S. 14-230 also provides that as part of the punishment for this offense, the sentencing judge may remove the official from office.

G.S. 14-254
Malfeasance of Corporate Officer
April 2024

Introductory Comment:
None.

Charging Language:
. . . unlawfully, willfully, and feloniously did, as the (*choose one or more*: president; director; cashier; teller; clerk; agent) of a corporation, (*name corporation*), (*choose one or more*)

(1) (*choose one or more*: embezzle; abstract; willfully misapply) moneys of the corporation in the amount of (*give amount*),

(2) without authority from the directors,
(*choose one or more*)
 (a) issue a certificate of deposit, (*describe*),
 (b) draw (*choose one or both and describe*: an order; a bill of exchange),
 (c) make an acceptance, (*describe*),
 (d) assign a (*choose one or more and describe*: note; bond; draft; bill of exchange; mortgage; judgment; decree),

(3) make a false entry in a (*choose one or more and describe*: book; report; statement) of the corporation,

with the intent to injure, defraud, and deceive a person, (*name or describe person*).

Notes about Charging Language:

- In option (1), "funds" or "credits" may be included instead of "moneys" if more appropriate.
- Although this form states that the defendant had the intent to injure, defraud, *and* deceive, the statute only requires proof of intent to injure *or* defraud *or* deceive. You may delete any inappropriate words.
- The "person" the defendant intends to defraud may be a natural person, association, consortium, corporation, body politic, partnership, or other group, entity, or organization. G.S. 14-254(b).

Sample Charge:
. . . unlawfully, willfully, and feloniously did, as the president of a corporation, XYZ Corporation, Selma, N.C., embezzle moneys of the corporation in the amount of $110,000, with the intent to injure, defraud, and deceive a person, the stockholders of the XYZ Corporation.

AOC Forms for This Offense:
None.

Punishment:
Class H felony.

G.S. 14-256
Escape from Local Jail or Officer
April 2024

Introductory Comment:
This offense applies when the defendant escapes from a county or municipal jail. Escape from the state prison system is covered by G.S. 148-45.

Charging Language:
. . . unlawfully, willfully, and feloniously did escape from (*choose one*)

(1) lawful confinement in the (*name jail or lockup*), a jail maintained by (*name city or county*).

(2) the lawful custody of (*name person from whose custody the prisoner escaped*), a (*choose one*: superintendent; guard; officer) of the (*name jail or lockup*), a jail maintained by (*name city or county*).

If applicable, allege any of the following: The defendant had been charged with (*name felony*), a felony, and had been committed to the aforementioned facility pending trial; the defendant had been convicted of (*name felony*), a felony, and had been committed to the aforementioned facility pending transfer to the state prison system; the defendant was serving a sentence imposed upon conviction of (*name felony*), a felony. *If none of the preceding apply, explain briefly why the defendant was in custody.*

Notes about Charging Language:
- Escape is a felony if the defendant is charged with a felony and is in custody awaiting trial, or if the defendant was convicted of a felony and is in custody serving a sentence or awaiting transfer to prison. Otherwise, it is a misdemeanor. If it is a misdemeanor, omit "and feloniously" from the charging document.
- To charge misdemeanor escape, it may not be necessary to allege why the defendant was in custody. However, because old cases like *State v. Jones*, 247 N.C. 253 (1878), call for that information, this form asks for it.

Sample Charge:
. . . unlawfully and willfully did escape from lawful confinement in the Orange County Jail, Hillsborough, N.C., a jail maintained by Orange County. The defendant was in custody awaiting trial on assault on a female in case number 19 CR 22398.

AOC Forms for This Offense:
None.

Punishment:
Misdemeanor escape is a Class 1 misdemeanor. Felony escape is a Class H felony.

G.S. 14-258.1
Providing Contraband to Inmate
April 2024
Page 1 of 2

Introductory Comment:
G.S. 14-258.1 addresses providing contraband to inmates. This form covers the felony offenses set forth in subsection (a), concerning the provision of weapons, ammunition, drugs, and poison; subsection (d), concerning the provision of mobile phones and wireless devices; and subsection (g), concerning the possession of mobile phones and wireless devices. It does not cover the misdemeanor offenses set forth in the statute concerning alcohol, tobacco, and vapor products.

Charging Language:

I. Providing weapon, ammunition, drugs, or poison **G.S. 14-258.1(a)**

. . . unlawfully, willfully, and feloniously did (*choose one*: give; sell) (*choose one or more*)

(1) a deadly weapon, a (*describe weapon*),
(2) ammunition for a firearm, (*describe ammunition*),
(3) a controlled substance, (*name substance*), which is included in Schedule (*state schedule number*) of the Controlled Substances Act,
(4) a poisonous substance, (*name substance*),

to (*name the inmate the contraband was given or sold to*), who was at the time an inmate of (*name the institution*), which is a (*choose one*: penal institution; local confinement facility; mental institution; charitable institution).

II. Providing mobile phone or wireless device **G.S. 14-258.1(d)**

. . . unlawfully, willfully, and feloniously did knowingly (*choose one*: give; sell) a (*choose one or more*: mobile telephone; wireless communications device; component of a mobile telephone; component of a wireless communications device) to (*name inmate/juvenile*), who was at the time (*choose one*)

(1) an inmate in the custody of the Division of Adult Correction and Juvenile Justice of the Department of Public Safety.
(2) a delinquent juvenile in the custody of the Juvenile Justice Section of the Division of Adult Correction and Juvenile Justice of the Department of Public Safety.
(3) an inmate in the custody of (name facility), a local confinement facility, when such provision of the device was not approved by the official in charge of that facility.

III. Possession of mobile phone or wireless device **G.S. 14-258.1(g)**

. . . unlawfully, willfully, and feloniously did possess a (*choose one or more*: mobile telephone; wireless communications device; component of a mobile telephone; component of a wireless communications device) while an inmate in the custody of (*choose one*: the Division of Adult Correction of the Department of Public Safety; (*name facility*), a local confinement facility, when such possession was not approved by the official in charge of that facility).

Notes about Charging Language:

- As to Offense I, the statute also prohibits conspiring with, aiding, abetting, soliciting, advising, or encouraging others to provide the contraband. If the defendant did not actually give or sell the contraband himself or herself, choose the proper wording from the statute.
- As to Offense I, in alternative (1), if the weapon is considered a deadly weapon only because of the way it was used, describe how it was used to show that it was a deadly weapon.
- Offense II applies when the juvenile in question is in a "youth development center or a detention facility as defined in G.S. 7B-1501, and shall include transportation of a juvenile to or from confinement." G.S. 14-258.1(d).
- As to Offense II, when the person to whom the phone or device was given or sold is a juvenile, it may be appropriate to identify that person by his or her initials rather than by his or her full name. Using the person's full name might run afoul of the juvenile confidentiality provisions in G.S. 7B-3100(b).
- As to Offense II, the statute also makes it unlawful to knowingly give or sell a covered item to a person who is not an inmate for delivery to an inmate. In an appropriate case, modify the charging language accordingly.
- S.L. 2020-74 added subsection (h) to G.S. 14-258.1, which provides the exception for mobile telephones and similar devices provided with approval of the official in charge of a local confinement facility as modeled in the charging language for Offenses II and III. No North Carolina appellate case has decided whether lack of the official's approval is an element of the offense or whether existence of the official's approval is an affirmative defense. The charging language takes the conservative approach of requiring an allegation of lack of approval as if it is an element of the offense.

Sample Charge:

I. Providing weapon, ammunition, drugs, or poison **G.S. 14-258.1(a)**

. . . unlawfully, willfully, and feloniously did give a controlled substance, marijuana, which is included in Schedule VI of the Controlled Substances Act, to Hansen G. Willingham, who was at the time an inmate of the Mecklenburg County Jail, a local confinement facility.

AOC Forms for This Offense:

None.

Punishment:

Offenses I, II, and III are Class H felonies. As to Offense I, if the defendant is an officer or employee of any state institution or local confinement facility, the defendant must be dismissed from his or her employment upon conviction.

G.S. 14-258.2(a)
Possession of Dangerous Weapon in Prison or Confinement Facility
April 2024

Introductory Comment:
In addition to the offense of possession of a dangerous weapon while in prison or a local confinement facility described in this form, G.S. 14-258.2(a) also defines Class F felonies related to assaults and escapes involving such weapons. This form does not provide charging language for those Class F felonies, nor does it provide charging language for the offenses defined in G.S. 14-258.2(b) regarding persons who assist in escape attempts.

Charging Language:
. . . unlawfully, willfully, and feloniously did, while in the custody of (*choose one*: the Section of Prisons of the Division of Adult Correction and Juvenile Justice; [*name facility*,] a local confinement facility), (*choose one or more*: fabricate; create; possess without permission or authorization) (*describe weapon*), a weapon capable of inflicting serious bodily injuries or death.

Notes about Charging Language:
- G.S. 14-258.2(a) cross references G.S. 153A-217 for the definition of a "local confinement facility." That statute provides as follows:
  - "Local confinement facility" includes a county or city jail, a local lockup, a regional or district jail, a juvenile detention facility, a detention facility for adults operated by a local government, and any other facility operated by a local government for confinement of persons awaiting trial or serving sentences except that it shall not include a county satellite jail/work release unit governed by Part 3 of Article 10 of G.S. 153A.
- Although G.S. 14-258.2(a) does not define "serious bodily injury", that term is defined in the assault context as "bodily injury that creates a substantial risk of death, or that causes serious permanent disfigurement, coma, a permanent or protracted condition that causes extreme pain, or permanent or protracted loss or impairment of the function of any bodily member or organ, or that results in prolonged hospitalization." G.S. 14-32.4(a).

Sample Charge:
. . . unlawfully, willfully, and feloniously did, while in the custody of the Columbus County Jail, a local confinement facility, fabricate and possess without permission or authorization a metal shank, a weapon capable of inflicting serious bodily injuries or death.

AOC Forms for This Offense:
None.

Punishment:
Class H felony.

G.S. 14-258.4
Malicious Conduct by Prisoner
April 2024

Introductory Comment:
This statute was substantially revised by S.L. 2018-67, effective December 1, 2018, for offenses committed on or after that date.

Charging Language:
I. Throwing bodily fluids and other substances **G.S. 14-258.4(a)**

. . . unlawfully, willfully, and feloniously did, while a prisoner, knowingly and willfully (*choose one*: throw; emit; cause to be used as a projectile) (*choose one*: a bodily fluid; excrement; an unknown substance) at (*name employee*), an employee, while (*name employee*) was in the performance of his or her duties.

II. Exposing genitalia **G.S. 14-258.4(b)**

. . . unlawfully, willfully, and feloniously did, while a prisoner, knowingly and willfully expose (*choose one*: his; her) genitalia to (*name employee*), an employee, while (*name employee*) was in the performance of his or her duties.

Notes about Charging Language:
- G.S. 14-254.5 defines an "employee" as "[a]ny person who is hired or contracted to work for the State or a local government."
- G.S. 14-254.5 defines a "prisoner" as "[a]ny person in the custody of (i) the Division of Adult Correction and Juvenile Justice of the Department of Public Safety, (ii) any law enforcement officer, or (iii) any local confinement facility as defined in G.S. 153A-217 or G.S. 153A-230.1, including persons pending trial, appellate review, or presentence diagnostic evaluation."
- Per G.S. 14-258.4(c), "[t]he provisions of this section apply to violations committed inside or outside of the prison, jail, detention center, or other confinement facility."
- For Offense I, this form does not call for further specificity regarding the substance in question, but such information could be added as follows if desired: "blood, a bodily fluid."
- For Offenses I and II, this form does not call for further specificity regarding the entity for which the employee works, or regarding the duties the employee was performing at the time of the offense. Such information could be added if desired.

Sample Charge:
II. Exposing genitalia **G.S. 14-258.4(b)**

. . . unlawfully, willfully, and feloniously did, while a prisoner, knowingly and willfully expose his genitalia to Leroy Saxon, an employee, while Leroy Saxon was in the performance of his duties.

AOC Forms for this Offense:
None.

Punishment:
Offense I is a Class F felony. Offense II is a Class I felony. The statute provides that a sentence for these offenses "shall run consecutively to and shall commence at the expiration of any sentence being served by the person."

G.S. 14-269
Carrying a Concealed Weapon
April 2024

Introductory Comment:
A second or subsequent conviction of carrying a concealed gun is a felony. If the defendant is being charged with the felony offense, use the words "unlawfully, willfully, and feloniously" instead of "unlawfully and willfully." An indictment or an information for a recidivist offense must comply with G.S. 15A-928, which requires that the defendant's prior convictions be alleged either (1) in a separate count of the indictment or information than the substantive offense or (2) in a separate indictment or information. In such a case, the separate count or separate indictment should set forth the date and court in which the prior conviction occurred. This requirement does not apply to arrest warrants or magistrates' orders, which still must allege the defendant's prior convictions but need not do so in a separate count or separate charging instrument. G.S. 15A-928 also requires that the name or title of an offense elevated by prior convictions must not make reference to such prior convictions.

Charging Language:
. . . unlawfully and willfully did intentionally carry concealed about the defendant's person while off the defendant's own premises a (*choose one:* gun; deadly weapon), (*describe the gun or weapon*).

Notes about Charging Language:
- The statute applies to a range of weapons other than firearms but does not apply to an "ordinary pocket knife" carried in a closed position. G.S. 14-269(d) (defining "ordinary pocket knife" as a small knife, designed for carrying in a pocket or purse, which has its cutting edge and point entirely enclosed by its handle and may not be opened by a throwing, explosive, or spring action).
- The statute contains several exemptions, including for certain military personnel, law enforcement officers, and holders of concealed-handgun permits. A permit holder who carries a concealed handgun outside the scope of the permit violates this section, except that "[a] violation . . . punishable under G.S. 14-415.21(a) [which makes it an infraction to carry a concealed handgun without one's permit in one's possession or to fail to disclose a concealed handgun and permit to a law enforcement officer] is not punishable under this section." G.S. 14-269(c).

Sample Charge:
. . . unlawfully and willfully did carry concealed about the defendant's person while off the defendant's own premises a gun, a Ruger 9mm pistol.

AOC Forms for This Offense:
AOC-J-325 (Juvenile Petition)

Punishment:
Class 2 misdemeanor. However, a second conviction of carrying a concealed gun is a Class H felony.

G.S. 14-269.2
Weapon on Campus or Other Educational Property
April 2024
Page 1 of 2

Introductory Comment:
Amendments effective December 1, 2023, added subsections (1c) (defining school operating hours) and (k1) (creating an exemption for certain persons with a handgun on certain property outside of school operating hours) to the statute.

Charging Language:

I. Misdemeanor possession of a weapon other than firearm **G.S. 14-269.2(d)**

. . . unlawfully and willfully did possess a (*choose one and describe item*: BB gun; stun gun; air rifle; air pistol; bowie knife [*see other weapons listed in statute*]) on educational property, (*describe educational property*).

II. Misdemeanor possession of a firearm **G.S. 14-269.2(f)**

. . . unlawfully and willfully did knowingly possess a (*choose one and describe item*: gun; rifle; pistol; firearm) on educational property, (*describe educational property*).

III. Felony possession of a firearm **G.S. 14-269.2(b)**

. . . unlawfully, willfully, and feloniously did knowingly possess a (*choose one and describe item*: gun; rifle; pistol; firearm) on educational property, (*describe educational property*).

IV. Felony discharging a firearm **G.S. 14-269.2(b)**

. . . unlawfully, willfully, and feloniously did discharge a firearm, (*describe firearm*), on educational property, (*describe educational property*).

V. Felony involving a bomb or other powerful explosive **G.S. 14-269.2(b1)**

. . . unlawfully, willfully, and feloniously did possess a (*choose one and describe item*: dynamite cartridge; bomb; grenade; mine; powerful explosive as defined in G.S. 14-284.1) on educational property, (*describe educational property*).

Notes about Charging Language:

- The statute applies whether the weapon in question is possessed openly or concealed.
- It ordinarily is a Class I felony to possess a firearm on educational property. G.S. 14-269.2(b). However, it is a Class 1 misdemeanor, rather than a Class I felony, for certain persons to possess a firearm on educational property when the firearm is unloaded and locked in a container or rack inside a vehicle. G.S. 14-269.2(f). When the misdemeanor provision applies, use Offense II, above. When the felony provision applies, use Offense III.
- Fireworks are not explosives for purposes of Offense V but are, rather, among the weapons listed in the statute to which Offense I would apply.
- "Educational property" is defined in G.S. 14-269.2(a)(1). Note that Offenses II, III, and V, above, may be committed at a curricular or extracurricular activity sponsored by a school, even if the activity is not located on educational property. In such a case, modify the charging language accordingly.

- When describing the educational property, it generally is sufficient to provide the name of the educational institution to which the property pertains. Listing the street address of the property is not required. *See* State v. Huckelba, 240 N.C. App. 544, 567 ("We agree with the State that the physical address for High Point University listed in the indictment is surplusage because the indictment already described the 'educational property' element as 'High Point University.' "), *rev'd in part on other grounds*, 368 N.C. 569 (2015).
- G.S. 14-269.2(c), (c1), and (e) set out specific provisions for people who aid and abet a minor under 18 to commit felony and misdemeanor violations.
- The following people, among others, are exempted from the statute while they are discharging official duties: law enforcement officers, firefighters, emergency service personnel, private police employed by educational institutions, and military personnel. The statute also exempts weapons used solely for educational or school-sanctioned ceremonial purposes. G.S. 14-269.2(g).

Sample Charge:

III. Felony possession of a firearm **G.S. 14-269.2(b)**

. . . unlawfully, willfully, and feloniously did knowingly possess a gun, a Smith and Wesson .45-caliber handgun, on educational property, Jamestown High School, Jamestown, N.C.

AOC Forms for This Offense:

AOC-J-316 (Juvenile Petition)

Punishment:

Offenses I and II are Class 1 misdemeanors. Offense III is a Class I felony. Offense IV is a Class F felony. Offense V is a Class G felony.

G.S. 14-269.3
Carrying Gun into Assembly or Alcoholic Beverage Establishment
April 2024

Introductory Comment:
None.

Charging Language:

I. Carrying gun into an assembly for which an admission fee is charged

. . . unlawfully and willfully did carry a (*choose one and describe*: gun; rifle; pistol) into (*name the assembly into which the gun was carried*), an assembly for which an admission fee was charged.

II. Carrying gun into an establishment where alcoholic beverages are sold and consumed

. . . unlawfully and willfully did carry a (*choose one and describe*: gun; rifle; pistol) into (*name the establishment into which the gun was carried*), an establishment in which alcoholic beverages are sold and consumed.

Notes about Charging Language:
- As an example of the scope of Offense II, above, an establishment with a permit for the on-premises sale of beer or wine would be one where an alcoholic beverage is sold and consumed. An ABC store, however, would not be such an establishment, since liquor is sold there but not consumed.
- This offense does not apply to (1) law enforcement officers and others exempted from the provisions of G.S. 14-269, (2) the owner or lessee of the premises, (3) certain persons who have the permission of the owner or lessee, (4) registered security guards hired by the owner or lessee, and (5) certain persons with valid concealed handgun permits or who are exempt from obtaining such a permit, unless a notice is posted prohibiting concealed carry. G.S. 14-269.3(b).

Sample Charge:

I. Carrying gun into an assembly for which an admission fee is charged

. . . unlawfully and willfully did carry a pistol, a Smith and Wesson .38-caliber revolver, into the Charlotte Motor Speedway during a stock car race, an assembly for which an admission fee was charged.

AOC Forms for This Offense:
None.

Punishment:
Offenses I and II are Class 1 misdemeanors.

G.S. 14-269.7
Minor Possessing Handgun
April 2024

Introductory Comment:
None.

Charging Language:
. . . unlawfully and willfully did intentionally, as a minor, (*choose one or both:* possess; carry) a handgun, (*describe handgun*).

Notes about Charging Language:
- A "minor" is defined by the statute as a person under 18 years of age. G.S. 14-269.7(c)(2).
- A "handgun" is defined by the statute as a firearm with a short stock and designed to be fired by using a single hand, or any combination of parts from which such a firearm can be assembled. G.S. 14-269.7(c)(1).
- The statute contains several exemptions, including for certain military personnel, certain supervised minors, certain emancipated minors, and certain minors engaged in hunting and trapping activities. G.S. 14-269.7(b).

Sample Charge:
. . . unlawfully and willfully did intentionally, as a minor, possess a handgun, a .22-caliber Kimber pistol.

AOC Forms for This Offense:
None.

Punishment:
Class 1 misdemeanor.

G.S. 14-277(a)–(d)
Impersonating Law Enforcement Officer
April 2024
Page 1 of 2

Introductory Comment:
This form only applies to the impersonation of sworn law enforcement officers. However, G.S. 14-277(e) criminalizes, in some circumstances, the impersonation of other government officials.

Charging Language:

I. Misdemeanor impersonating officer **G.S. 14-277(a)(1)–(a)(3)**

. . . unlawfully and willfully did falsely represent to (*name person*) that the defendant was a sworn law enforcement officer by (*choose one or more)*

(1) verbally informing (*name person*) that the defendant was a sworn law enforcement officer.

(2) displaying to (*name person*) a (*choose one or both*: badge; identification) signifying to a reasonable person that the defendant was a law enforcement officer.

(3) unlawfully operating a vehicle, (*describe vehicle*), on a (*choose one or more and describe*: public street; public highway; public vehicular area) with an operating red light as defined in G.S. 20-130.1(a).

II. Felony impersonating officer **G.S. 14-277(a)(4)**

. . . unlawfully, willfully, and feloniously did falsely represent to (*name person*) that the defendant was a sworn law enforcement officer by unlawfully operating a vehicle, (*describe vehicle*), on a (*choose one or more and describe*: public street; public highway; public vehicular area) with an operating blue light as defined in G.S. 20-130.1(c).

III. Misdemeanor acting as officer **G.S. 14-277(b)(1)–(b)(4)**

. . . unlawfully and willfully did, while falsely representing to (*name person*) that the defendant was a sworn law enforcement officer, carry out the following act in accordance with the authority granted to a law enforcement officer: (*choose one or more*)

(1) ordering (*name person*) to (*choose one or both*: remain at; leave from) a particular (*choose one or both and describe*: place; area).

(2) (*choose one or both*: detaining; arresting) (*name person*).

(3) searching a (*choose one or more and describe*: vehicle; building; premises) (*choose one*: with; without) (*choose one or both*: a search warrant; an administrative inspection warrant).

(4) unlawfully operating a vehicle on a (*choose one or more and describe*: public street; public highway; public vehicular area) with an operating (*choose one or both*: red light; siren) in such a manner as to cause a reasonable person to (*choose one or both*: yield the right-of-way; stop one's vehicle) in obedience to such (*choose one or both*: red light; siren).

IV. Felony acting as officer **G.S. 14-277(b)(5)**

. . . unlawfully, willfully, and feloniously did, while falsely representing to (*name person*) that the defendant was a sworn law enforcement officer, carry out the following act in accordance with the authority granted to a law enforcement officer: unlawfully operating a vehicle on a (*choose one or more and describe*: public street; public highway; public vehicular area) equipped with an operating blue light in such a manner as to cause a reasonable person to (*choose one or both*: yield the right-of-way; stop one's vehicle) in obedience to such blue light.

Notes about Charging Language:

- In Offense I, neither the verbal representation described in (1) nor the badge or identification described in (2) need refer to a specific agency.

Sample Charge:

II. Felony impersonating officer **G.S. 14-277(a)(4)**

. . . unlawfully, willfully, and feloniously did falsely represent to Susan Blackwelder that the defendant was a sworn law enforcement officer by unlawfully operating a vehicle, a 2004 blue Ford Taurus, on a public highway, U.S. 70 in Durham, N.C., with an operating blue light as defined in G.S. 20-130.1(c).

AOC Forms for This Offense:

None.

Punishment:

Offense I is a Class 1 misdemeanor. Offense II is a Class I felony. Offense III is a Class 1 misdemeanor, for which intermediate punishment is allowed even if it would not otherwise be authorized under structured sentencing. Offense IV is a Class H felony.

G.S. 14-277.1
Communicating Threats
April 2024

Introductory Comment:
G.S. 14-277.1 already requires that the threat be one which a reasonable person would believe was likely to be carried out, and which the threatened person did believe would be carried out. Since the effect of this statute is to criminalize a particular type of speech, the "true threat" doctrine under the First Amendment likely also requires the State to prove that the alleged threat was "an objectively threatening statement communicated by a party which possesses the subjective intent to threaten a listener or identifiable group." *See* State v. Taylor, 379 N.C. 589 (2021).

Charging Language:
. . . unlawfully and willfully did threaten to (*choose one or more*)

(1) physically injure the person of (*name the person threatened*).

(2) damage the property of (*name the person threatened*).

(3) physically injure the person of (*name the person to whom the threat was made*)'s (*choose one*: child; sibling; spouse; dependent), (*name the child, sibling, spouse, or dependent*).

The threat was communicated to (*name the person to whom the threat was made*) by (*describe how the threat was communicated*), the threat was made in a manner and under circumstances which would cause a reasonable person to believe that the threat was likely to be carried out, and the person threatened believed that the threat would be carried out.

Notes about Charging Language:
- As to threats that are communicated indirectly through a third party, see Jessica Smith, *North Carolina Crimes: A Guidebook on the Elements of Crime* 129 (UNC School of Government, 7th ed. 2012).
- It is probably not legally necessary to include the exact words used to communicate a threat. *Cf.* State v. Elliott, 193 N.C. App. 455 (2008) (unpublished) (finding no fatal defect where a warrant alleged certain specific words but the evidence at trial was of different words). However, in some cases it may be helpful to include the words, if known. *See In re* S.R.S., 180 N.C. App. 151 (2006) (finding that the inclusion of the specific words resolved some ambiguity regarding the nature of the alleged threat).

Sample Charge:
. . . unlawfully and willfully did threaten to physically injure the person of John Cashwell's child, Susan Cashwell. The threat was communicated to John Cashwell by orally stating it to John Cashwell, the threat was made in a manner and under circumstances which would cause a reasonable person to believe that the threat was likely to be carried out, and the person threatened believed that the threat would be carried out.

AOC Forms for This Offense:
AOC-J-314 (Juvenile Petition)

Punishment:
Class 1 misdemeanor.

G.S. 14-277.3A
Stalking
April 2024
Page 1 of 2

Introductory Comment:
A second or subsequent offense of stalking is a felony. If the defendant is being charged with the felony recidivist offense, use the words "unlawfully, willfully, and feloniously" instead of "unlawfully and willfully." An indictment or an information for a recidivist offense must comply with G.S. 15A-928, which requires that the defendant's prior convictions be alleged either (1) in a separate count of the indictment or information than the substantive offense or (2) in a separate indictment or information. In such a case, the separate count or separate indictment should set forth the date and court in which the prior conviction occurred. This requirement does not apply to arrest warrants or magistrates' orders, which still must allege the defendant's prior convictions but need not do so in a separate count or separate charging instrument. G.S. 15A-928 also requires that the name or title of an offense elevated by prior convictions must not make reference to such prior convictions.

Charging Language:
. . . unlawfully and willfully did, without legal purpose, (*choose one or both*)

(1) on more than one occasion harass (*name victim*) by (*briefly describe harassment*).

(2) engage in a course of conduct directed at (*name victim*) by (*briefly describe course of conduct*).

The defendant knew and should have known that the (*choose one or both*: harassment; course of conduct) would cause a reasonable person to (*choose one or both*)

(1) fear for the person's safety or the safety of the person's (*choose one or both*: immediate family; close personal associates).

(2) suffer substantial emotional distress by placing that person in fear of (*choose one or more*: death; bodily injury; continued harassment).

Notes about Charging Language:
- "Course of conduct" is defined in the statute as two or more acts, typically involving following, threatening, or interfering with a person.
- "Harassment" is defined in the statute as knowing conduct "directed at a specific person that torments, terrorizes, or terrifies that person and that serves no legitimate purpose."
- Under the statute, emotional distress may be "substantial" without requiring medical treatment or counseling.
- Stalking is a Class H felony when done in violation of a court order. To charge felony stalking in violation of a court order, use the charging language above, add "and feloniously" after "willfully," allege that the defendant's conduct violated a court order, and provide the date, county, file number, and general type of order in question.

Sample Charge:
. . . unlawfully and willfully did, without legal purpose, on more than one occasion harass Debbie Smith by repeatedly contacting her by telephone, despite being told to stop, and threatening to "get" her if she did not have a relationship with him. The defendant knew and should have known that the harassment would cause a reasonable person to suffer substantial emotional distress by placing that person in fear of death, bodily injury, and continued harassment.

AOC Forms for This Offense:
None.

Punishment:
Class A1 misdemeanor. As noted above, habitual stalking is a Class F felony, and stalking in violation of a court order is a Class H felony.

Making a False Report Concerning Mass Violence on Educational Property

Introductory Comment:
None.

Charging Language:

I. False report concerning mass violence on educational property G.S. 14-277.5(b)

. . . unlawfully, willfully, and feloniously did make a report, knowing and having reason to know that the report was false, that an act of mass violence was going to occur (*choose all that apply*: on educational property; at a curricular activity sponsored by a school; or at an extracurricular activity sponsored by a school). (*Describe the report as well as the person or persons to whom the report was directed or the person or persons who saw or received the report*).

Notes about Charging Language:

- The report may be made "by any means of communication to any person or groups of persons." G.S. 14-277.5(b). This form asks for a description of the report and for identification of the person or persons who saw or received it because that information appears to be required under *In re D.W.L.B*, 267 N.C. App. 392 (2019) (holding that a juvenile petition for this offense was defective because it failed to allege this information).
- This offense may be committed by a person who knows *or who has reason to know* that the report is false. In an appropriate case, remove the words "knowing and" from the charging language.
- G.S. 14-277.5 defines "educational property" by cross reference to G.S. 14-269.2. That statute defines the term as "[a]ny school building or bus, school campus, grounds, recreational area, athletic field, or other property owned, used, or operated by any board of education or school board of trustees, or directors for the administration of any school."
- G.S. 14-277.5 defines "school" by cross reference to G.S. 14-269.2. That statute defines the term as "[a] public or private school, community college, college, or university."
- G.S. 14-277.5 defines "mass violence" as "[p]hysical injury that a reasonable person would conclude could lead to permanent injury (including mental or emotional injury) or death to two or more people."
- It may be helpful to include a brief description of the act of mass violence that was reported, e.g., "a shooting." However, it is not clear that such a description is legally required.
- It may be helpful to identify the activity and school in question, e.g., "at a curricular activity sponsored by a school, namely, at a field trip to the North Carolina Zoo sponsored by Doolittle Elementary School." However, it is not clear that such a description is legally required.

Sample Charge:

I. False report concerning mass violence on educational property G.S. 14-277.5(b)

. . . unlawfully, willfully, and feloniously did make a report, knowing and having reason to know that the report was false, that an act of mass violence was going to occur on educational property. (*Defendant's name*) sent an email to Terry Tisch, a teacher at Stoney Brook Middle School, stating that there would be a shooting at the school the following day. Tisch received this email and notified authorities.

G.S. 14-277.5
Making a False Report Concerning Mass Violence on Educational Property
April 2024
Page 2 of 2

AOC Forms for This Offense:
None.

Punishment:
Class H felony. A person convicted of this offense may be ordered to pay restitution pursuant to Article 81C of Chapter 15A of the General Statutes. G.S. 14-277.5(c).

G.S. 14-277.6
Communicating a Threat of Mass Violence on Educational Property
April 2024

Introductory Comment:
Pursuant to *State v. Taylor*, 379 N.C. 589 (2021), the State must prove that the threat alleged under this statute was a "true threat," which is defined "as an objectively threatening statement communicated by a party which possesses the subjective intent to threaten a listener or identifiable group." *See also In re* Z.P., 280 N.C. App. 442 (2021) (applying "true threat" analysis to this offense).

Charging Language:
. . . unlawfully, willfully, and feloniously did threaten to commit an act of mass violence (*choose all that apply*: on educational property; at a curricular activity sponsored by a school; at an extracurricular activity sponsored by a school). (*Describe the threat that was made, as well as the person or persons to whom the threat was directed and the means by which the threat was communicated*).

Notes about Charging Language:
- The threat may be made "by any means of communication to any person or groups of persons." G.S. 14-277.6(a).
- G.S. 14-277.6(b) states that the definitions found in G.S. 14-277.5 apply to this offense.
- G.S. 14-277.5 defines "educational property" by cross reference to G.S. 14-269.2. That statute defines the term as "[a]ny school building or bus, school campus, grounds, recreational area, athletic field, or other property owned, used, or operated by any board of education or school board of trustees, or directors for the administration of any school."
- G.S. 14-277.5 defines "school" by cross reference to G.S. 14-269.2. That statute defines the term as "[a] public or private school, community college, college, or university."
- G.S. 14-277.5 defines "mass violence" as "[p]hysical injury that a reasonable person would conclude could lead to permanent injury (including mental or emotional injury) or death to two or more people."
- It may be helpful to include a brief description of the act of mass violence that was threatened, e.g., "a shooting." However, it is not clear that such a description is legally required.
- It may be helpful to identify the activity and school in question, e.g., "at a curricular activity sponsored by a school, namely, at a field trip to the North Carolina Zoo sponsored by Doolittle Elementary School." However, it is not clear that such a description is legally required.

Sample Charge:
. . . unlawfully, willfully, and feloniously did threaten to commit an act of mass violence on educational property. (*Defendant's name*) sent a text message to James Smith, a football coach at George Washington High School, stating that he was going to bring a gun to practice after school and shoot the whole team. Smith received this text message and contacted law enforcement.

AOC Forms for This Offense:
None.

Punishment:
Class H felony.

G.S. 14-286.1
Making False Ambulance Request
April 2024

Introductory Comment:
None.

Charging Language:
. . . unlawfully and willfully did (*choose one*: summon an ambulance; report that an ambulance was needed), (*describe what occurred*), when the defendant did not have good cause to believe that the services of an ambulance were needed.

Notes about Charging Language:
None.

Sample Charge:
. . . unlawfully and willfully did summon an ambulance, calling 911 in Monroe, N.C., and falsely stating that he was sick and needed an ambulance to take him to the hospital, when the defendant did not have good cause to believe that the services of an ambulance were needed.

AOC Forms for This Offense:
None.

Punishment:
Class 3 misdemeanor.

G.S. 14-288.2(a)
Misdemeanor Riot
April 2024

Introductory Comment:
None.

Charging Language:
. . . unlawfully and willfully did assemble with at least two other persons, (*if the names of the others are known, state the names of at least two of them; if not, state* "whose names are not known"), and riot by engaging in a public disturbance, (*indicate the nature of the public disturbance and indicate in which public place it occurred*). This disorderly and violent conduct resulted in (*choose one or both*: injury to persons; damage to property), including (*describe the injury to persons or damage to property*).

Notes about Charging Language:
- If many people participated in the riot, name several and then use the phrase "and many others."
- By statute, a public disturbance is "[a]ny annoying, disturbing or alarming act or condition exceeding the bounds of social toleration normal for the time and place in question which occurs in, affects persons in, or is likely to affect persons in a place to which the public or a substantial group has access. The places covered by this definition shall include, but not be limited to, highways, transport facilities, schools, prisons, apartment houses, places of business or amusement, or any neighborhood." G.S. 14-288.1(8).
- A riot also occurs if there is an "imminent threat" of disorderly and violent conduct, even if it has not yet taken place, and if there is a "clear and present danger" of injury or damage to persons or property. If either of the foregoing applies, make appropriate alterations to the charging language.

Sample Charge:
. . . unlawfully and willfully did assemble with at least two other persons, including Delfor McIntosh, Alice Kay Mitchell, Florence Trueheart, and many others, and engage in a public disturbance by throwing rocks and bottles, jumping on automobiles, and yelling obscenities at and threatening drivers of automobiles in the 400 block of Oldman Street in Charlotte, N.C. This disorderly and violent conduct resulted in damage to property, including dents and broken windshields to the automobiles of Walter Clement, Edward Neal Childress, and David Simpson Felwell.

AOC Forms for This Offense:
None.

Punishment:
Class 1 misdemeanor.

G.S. 14-288.2(c)
Felony Riot
April 2024
Page 1 of 2

Introductory Comment:
Riot was a misdemeanor at common law, and it was prosecuted in North Carolina as such until well into the twentieth century. Following certain civil disorders that occurred in this state during April 1968, the General Assembly enacted G.S. 14-288.2 in 1969. The North Carolina Supreme Court upheld the statute against constitutional challenge in *State v. Brooks*, 287 N.C. 392, 401 (1975). Amendments effective December 1, 2023, increased the penalty for rioting that causes property damage in excess of $2,500, serious bodily injury, or death.

Charging Language:
. . . unlawfully, willfully, and feloniously did assemble with at least two other persons, (*if the names of the others are known, state the names of at least two of them; if not, state* "whose names are not known"), and riot by engaging in a public disturbance, (*indicate the nature of the public disturbance and indicate in which public place it occurred*). (*Choose one or more of the following*)

(1) The riot included disorderly and violent conduct. In the course of the riot, the defendant caused property damage in excess of $2,500, including (*describe the damage and value of it*).

(2) The riot included disorderly and violent conduct. In the course of the riot, the defendant caused serious bodily injury, including (*describe the injury*), inflicted on (*name the person injured*).

(3) This disorderly and violent conduct resulted in (*choose one or both*: injury to persons; damage to property), including (*describe the injury to persons or damage to property*), and during the riot the defendant brandished a (*describe the dangerous weapon*), a dangerous weapon, or used a dangerous substance (*identify substance*).

(4) This disorderly and violent conduct resulted in (*choose one or both*: injury to persons; damage to property), including (*describe the injury to persons or damage to property*), and during the riot the defendant caused the death of (*name victim*).

Notes about Charging Language:
- If many people participated in the riot, name several and then use the phrase "and many others."
- By statute, a public disturbance is "[a]ny annoying, disturbing or alarming act or condition exceeding the bounds of social toleration normal for the time and place in question which occurs in, affects persons in, or is likely to affect persons in a place to which the public or a substantial group has access. The places covered by this definition shall include, but not be limited to, highways, transport facilities, schools, prisons, apartment houses, places of business or amusement, or any neighborhood." G.S. 14-288.1(8).
- A riot also occurs if there is an "imminent threat" of disorderly and violent conduct, even if it has not yet taken place, and if there is a "clear and present danger" of injury or damage to persons or property. If either of the foregoing applies, make appropriate alterations to the charging language.

- For option (3) above, the statute also prohibits the use of a dangerous substance. Dangerous weapon or substance is defined as "[a]ny deadly weapon, ammunition, explosive, incendiary device, or any instrument or substance designed for a use that carries a threat of serious bodily injury or destruction of property; or any instrument or substance that is capable of being used to inflict serious bodily injury, when the circumstances indicate a probability that such instrument or substance will be so used; or any part or ingredient in any instrument or substance included above, when the circumstances indicate a probability that such part or ingredient will be so used." G.S. 14-288.1(2).
- Mere presence alone without an overt act is not sufficient to sustain a conviction pursuant to this statute. G.S. 14-288.2(g).

Sample Charge:
. . . unlawfully, willfully, and feloniously did assemble with at least two other persons, including Wilfred McDonald, Charles Owens Greenberg, Fowler K. Tremont, and many others, and riot by engaging in a public disturbance by breaking windows; overturning garbage cans; carrying knives, clubs, and guns; setting fire to stores; and assaulting police officers and other citizens in the 1700 and 1800 blocks of S. Main Street, Quailville, N.C. The riot included disorderly and violent conduct. In the course of the riot the defendant caused property damage in excess of $2,500, including the burning of the Young and Brissel Hardware Store at 1720 S. Main Street, Quailville, N.C., at an estimated damage of $27,000. During the riot the defendant brandished a .22-caliber rifle and a knife with a ten-inch blade, dangerous weapons.

AOC Forms for This Offense:
None.

Punishment:
Offenses 1 and 2 are Class F felonies.
Offense 3 is a Class H felony.
Offense 4 is a Class E felony.

G.S. 14-288.2(d), (e)
Inciting to Riot
April 2024
Page 1 of 2

Introductory Comment:
See Introductory Comment to G.S. 14-288.2(c). Amendments effective December 1, 2023, deleted the phrase "or urges" as an alternative to "incites" and increased the penalty for inciting a riot that causes property damage in excess of $2,500, serious bodily injury, or death. S.L. 2023-6, § 1; S.L. 2023-71, § 4(a).

Charging Language:

I. Inciting a misdemeanor riot **G.S. 14-288.2(d)**

. . . unlawfully and willfully did incite (*name person incited who engaged in riot*) to engage in a riot by (*indicate statements or other means by which person was incited*). As a result of that inciting, (*name person incited*) unlawfully and willfully did assemble with at least two other persons, (*if the names of the others are known, state the names of at least two of them; if not, state* "whose names are not known"), and riot by engaging in a public disturbance, (*indicate the nature of the public disturbance, the public place in which it occurred, and, if necessary, the date*). This disorderly and violent conduct resulted in (*choose one or both*: injury to persons; damage to property), including (*describe the injury to persons or damage to property*).

II. Inciting a felony riot **G.S. 14-288.2(e) & (e1)**

. . . unlawfully, willfully, and feloniously did incite (*name person incited who engaged in riot*) to engage in a riot by (*indicate statements or other means by which person was incited*). That inciting was a contributing cause to a riot in that (*name person incited*) unlawfully, willfully, and feloniously did assemble with at least two other persons, (*if the names of the others are known, state the names of at least two of them; if not, state* "whose names are not known"), and riot by engaging in a public disturbance, (*indicate the nature of the public disturbance and the public place in which it occurred*). (*Choose one or more of the following*)

(1) The riot included disorderly and violent conduct. In the course of the riot and as a result of it, there was property damage in excess of $2,500, including (*describe the damage and value of it*).

(2) The riot included disorderly and violent conduct. In the course of the riot and as a result of it, there was serious bodily injury, including (*describe the injury*), inflicted on (*name the person injured*).

(3) The riot included disorderly and violent conduct. In the course of the riot and as a result of it, there was a death, namely that of (*name victim*).

Notes about Charging Language:

- If many people participated in the riot, name several and then use the phrase "and many others."
- By statute, a public disturbance is "[a]ny annoying, disturbing or alarming act or condition exceeding the bounds of social toleration normal for the time and place in question which occurs in, affects persons in, or is likely to affect persons in a place to which the public or a substantial group has access. The places covered by this definition shall include, but not be limited to, highways, transport facilities, schools, prisons, apartment houses, places of business or amusement, or any neighborhood." G.S. 14-288.1(8).
- A riot also occurs if there is an "imminent threat" of disorderly and violent conduct, even if it has not yet taken place, and if there is a "clear and present danger" of injury or damage to persons or property. If either of the foregoing applies, make appropriate alterations to the charging language.
- Inciting a riot also occurs if the inciting is directly and imminently likely to produce a riot. If that circumstance applies, make appropriate alterations to the charging language.
- Mere presence alone without an overt act is not sufficient to sustain a conviction pursuant to this statute. G.S. 14-288.2(g).

Sample Charge:

I. Inciting a misdemeanor riot **G.S. 14-288.2(d)**

. . . unlawfully and willfully did incite Howard Davis to engage in a riot by telling him it is time to tear up downtown Millersville. As a result of that inciting, Howard Davis unlawfully and willfully did assemble with at least two other persons, including Sally Davis and Peter Porter, and riot by engaging in a public disturbance by overturning cars on Main Street in downtown Millersville, N.C. This disorderly and violent conduct resulted in damage to property, including several broken windows on three cars.

AOC Forms for This Offense:

None.

Punishment:

Offense I is a Class A1 misdemeanor.
Offense II (1) & (2) are Class E felonies.
Offense II (3) is a Class D felony.

G.S. 14-288.4
Disorderly Conduct
April 2024
Page 1 of 2

Introductory Comment:
The disorderly conduct statute sets forth eight separate types of behavior that constitute disorderly conduct. This form includes charging language for the first two types of behavior, which are the most frequently charged.

Charging Language:

I. Violent conduct **G.S. 14-288.4(a)(1)**

. . . unlawfully and willfully did intentionally cause a public disturbance at (*identify the place where the public disturbance took place so as to indicate its public nature*), by engaging in (*choose one or more*: fighting; violent conduct; conduct creating the threat of imminent fighting and violence). This conduct consisted of (*describe the conduct sufficiently to show its violent nature or how it created the threat of immediate violence*).

II. Speech likely to provoke violence **G.S. 14-288.4(a)(2)**

. . . unlawfully and willfully did intentionally cause a public disturbance at (*identify the place where the public disturbance took place so as to indicate its public nature*), by (*choose one or more*: making utterances; making gestures; making displays; using abusive language), intended and plainly likely to provoke immediate violent retaliation and thereby cause a breach of the peace. The acts of the defendant were directed toward (*name the person subjected to the abuse*) and consisted of (*describe the abuse sufficiently to show why it was likely to provoke retaliation; use exact words if known*).

Notes about Charging Language:

- The statute defines a public disturbance as "[a]ny annoying, disturbing, or alarming act or condition exceeding the bounds of social toleration normal for the time and place in question which occurs in a public place or which occurs in, affects persons in, or is likely to affect persons in a place to which the public or a substantial group has access. The places covered by this definition shall include, but not be limited to, highways, transport facilities, schools, prisons, apartment houses, places of business or amusement, or any neighborhood." G.S. 14-288.1(8).
- The North Carolina Supreme Court has held that a juvenile petition sufficiently alleged a violation of G.S. 14-288.4(a)(1) where it alleged that the juvenile threw a chair towards another person but did not specifically cite subdivision (a)(1) of the statute as the basis of the charge. The court reasoned that the alleged act of throwing a chair at another person placed the juvenile "in the category of any person . . . who [e]ngages in fighting or other violent conduct or in conduct creating the threat of imminent fighting or other violence." *In re* T.T.E., 372 N.C. 413 (2019).

Sample Charge:

II. Speech likely to provoke violence **G.S. 14-288.4(a)(2)**

. . . unlawfully and willfully did intentionally cause a public disturbance at the 5400 block of Washington Drive, Freedom, N.C., by making utterances and gestures and using abusive language intended and plainly likely to provoke immediate violent retaliation and thereby cause a breach of the peace. The acts of the defendant were directed toward Mary Louise Melville and her date, Thomas Forrest, and consisted of the defendant moving his hips in a manner to imitate sexual intercourse and saying in a loud, lewd, and provocative manner that Mary Louise Melville looked "like she could really do it in bed" and would be "a good lay" and that Thomas Forrest was an "ugly, skinny, pimply bastard" who could not satisfy Ms. Melville's sexual desires and "couldn't punch his way out of a paper bag."

AOC Forms for This Offense:
AOC-J-326 (Juvenile Petition, Disorderly Conduct at School in violation of G.S. 14-288.4(a)(6))

Punishment:
Class 2 misdemeanor. Note that a second or subsequent violation of G.S. 14-288.4(a)(8), which concerns disrupting a military funeral, is subject to enhanced penalties. For those penalties to apply, the defendant's prior convictions must properly be alleged in the charging document; if an enhanced penalty version of the offense is to be prosecuted in superior court, be sure to charge it in compliance with G.S. 15A-928.

G.S. 14-288.8
Possession of Weapon of Mass Death and Destruction
April 2024

Introductory Comment:
None.

Charging Language:
. . . unlawfully, willfully, and feloniously did possess a weapon of mass death and destruction, (*describe the weapon*).

Notes about Charging Language:

- Although the charging language above focuses on possession of a weapon of mass death and destruction, the statute also provides that it is unlawful to manufacture, assemble, store, transport, sell, offer to sell, purchase, offer to purchase, deliver or give to another, or acquire such a weapon. Modify the charge when appropriate.
- The definition of a "weapon of mass death and destruction" is set forth in G.S. 14-288.8(c). Consult this subsection when deciding whether to charge this offense. Generally, the definition includes explosives, large-bore firearms, fully automatic firearms, shortened rifles and shotguns, and silenced firearms.
- G.S. 14-288.8(b) contains a list of those people who are exempt from this statute. Again, consult this subsection before charging this offense.

Sample Charge:
. . . unlawfully, willfully, and feloniously did possess a weapon of mass death and destruction, a Browning shotgun that was modified so it had a barrel of less than eighteen inches in length.

AOC Forms for This Offense:
None.

Punishment:
Class F felony.

G.S. 14-292
Gambling
April 2024

Introductory Comment:
None.

Charging Language:

I. Playing at a game of chance

. . . unlawfully and willfully did play at (*name or describe the game*), a game of chance at which money was bet.

II. Operating a game of chance

. . . unlawfully and willfully did operate a game of (*name or describe the game*), a game of chance at which money was bet.

III. Betting on a game of chance

. . . unlawfully and willfully did bet on (*name or describe the game*), a game of chance.

Notes about Charging Language:

- A game of chance is one in which the element of chance determines the outcome, outweighing any element of skill. Thus a card game is a game of chance but golf is not. Something that is a game of skill to the participants may be a game of chance to others who bet on it. Thus it is lawful for the players in a basketball game to bet on the outcome since it is a game of skill for them, but it is unlawful for others to bet on that game since it is a game of chance for them. State v. Brown, 221 N.C. 301 (1942).
- If something of value other than money was bet, modify the charging language accordingly.
- Participation in the state-run lottery is expressly permitted by G.S. 14-292.

Sample Charge:

III. Betting on a game of chance

. . . unlawfully and willfully did bet on craps, a dice game that was a game of chance.

. . . unlawfully and willfully did bet on the UNC vs. N.C. State basketball game, which was for the defendant a game of chance.

AOC Forms for This Offense:
None.

Punishment:
Class 2 misdemeanor.

Prohibited Electronic Machines and Devices for Sweepstakes

Introductory Comment:
None.

Charging Language:

I. First offense

. . . unlawfully and willfully did (*choose one or both*: operate; place into operation) an electronic (*choose one or both*: machine; device), (*describe machine or device generally and identify its location*), for the purpose of (*choose one or both*)

(1) conducting a sweepstakes through the use of an entertaining display, including the entry process and the reveal of a prize.

(2) promoting a sweepstakes that is conducted through the use of an entertaining display, including the entry process and the reveal of a prize.

II. Second or subsequent offense

A. Charging language for an arrest warrant or magistrate's order

. . . unlawfully, willfully, and feloniously did (*choose one or both*: operate; place into operation) an electronic (*choose one or both*: machine; device), (*describe machine or device generally and identify its location*), for the purpose of (*choose one or both*)

(1) conducting a sweepstakes through the use of an entertaining display, including the entry process and the reveal of a prize.

(2) promoting a sweepstakes that is conducted through the use of an entertaining display, including the entry process and the reveal of a prize.

The defendant was previously convicted of (*choose one or both as appropriate to describe the prior offense*: conducting; promoting) a sweepstakes on the _____ day of ________________, _____, in the ____________ Court, ______________ County. (*Add additional prior convictions in a like manner.*)

B. Charging language for an indictment or information

First count of indictment or information

. . . unlawfully, willfully, and feloniously did (*choose one or both*: operate; place into operation) an electronic (*choose one or both*: machine; device), (*describe machine or device generally and identify its location*), for the purpose of (*choose one or both*)

(1) conducting a sweepstakes through the use of an entertaining display, including the entry process and the reveal of a prize.

(2) promoting a sweepstakes that is conducted through the use of an entertaining display, including the entry process and the reveal of a prize.

Second count of indictment or information

The defendant was previously convicted of (*choose one or both as appropriate to describe the prior offense*: conducting; promoting) a sweepstakes on the _____ day of ________________, _____, in the ____________ Court, ______________ County. (*Add additional prior convictions as additional counts in a like manner.*)

Notes about Charging Language:

- G.S. 14-306.4(a) defines many of the terms used in the charging language above.
- G.S. 14-306.4(a)(4) defines the term "prize" to mean "any gift, award, gratuity, good, service, credit or anything else of value." In *Crazie Overstock Promotions, LLC v. State of North Carolina*, 377 N.C. 391, 404 (2021), the North Carolina Supreme Court held that "reward points" awarded as a result of a random drawing conducted by an electronic machine were a "thing of value" under the statutory definition because the number of reward points a player possessed increased the dollar value of prizes that the player was entitled to win in a subsequent conjoined game known as the "dexterity test."
- G.S. 14-306.4(a)(5) defines the term "sweepstakes" to mean "any game, advertising scheme or plan, or other promotion, which, with or without payment of any consideration, a person may enter to win or become eligible to receive any prize, the determination of which is based upon chance." In *Crazie Overstock Promotions*, 377 N.C. 391, 403, the North Carolina Supreme Court held that when a game involves a mix of skill and chance, the "relevant test" in determining whether it violates the statute is "whether, viewed in its entirety, the results produced by [the electronic machine or device] in terms of whether the player wins or loses and the relative amount of the player's winnings or losses varies primarily with the vagaries of chance or the extent of the player's skill and dexterity." *See also* Gift Surplus, LLC v. State of North Carolina, 380 N.C. 1 (2022).
- An indictment or an information for a second or subsequent offense must comply with G.S. 15A-928, which requires that the defendant's prior convictions be alleged in either (1) a count of the indictment or information separate from the substantive offense or (2) a separate indictment or information. This requirement does not apply to arrest warrants or magistrates' orders, which explains why two sets of charging language appear above.
- G.S. 14-306.4(e) provides that "each violation of this section is considered a separate offense."

Sample Charge:

I. Conducting or promoting a sweepstakes

. . . unlawfully and willfully did operate and place into operation an electronic machine and device, a Mega Winner 5000 arcade machine located at 200 West Birch Street, Weaverville, N.C., for the purpose of conducting a sweepstakes through the use of an entertaining display, including the entry process and the reveal of a prize.

AOC Forms for This Offense:

None.

Punishment:

A first offense is a Class 1 misdemeanor, a second offense is a Class H felony, and a third or subsequent offense is a Class G felony.

G.S. 14-315.1
Failing to Store Firearm to Protect Minor
April 2024

Introductory Comment:
None.

Charging Language:
. . . unlawfully and willfully did, as a person who resides in the same premises, (*give address*), as a minor, (*name minor*), (*choose one or both*: store; leave) a firearm, (*describe firearm*), (*choose one or both*: owned; possessed) by the defendant, in a condition that the firearm could be discharged and in a manner that the defendant (*choose one or both*: knew; should have known) that an unsupervised minor would be able to gain access to the firearm, and the minor gained access to the firearm without the lawful permission of [*choose one and give name(s)*: the minor's parents; the person having charge of the minor], and the minor (*choose one or more*)

(1) possessed it in violation of G.S. 14-269.2(b), (*describe violation*).

(2) exhibited it in a public place, (*name place*), in a (*choose one or more*: careless; angry; threatening) manner.

(3) caused (*choose one or both*: personal injury; death) to (*name victim*) with the firearm and acted not in self-defense.

(4) used it in the commission of a crime, (*describe crime*).

Notes about Charging Language:
- A minor is defined in the statute as a person under 18 years old who is not emancipated.
- The statute does not apply if the minor obtained the firearm as a result of an unlawful entry by any person.
- G.S. 14-315.1 does not prohibit carrying a firearm on the body or keeping it in such proximity that it can be used as easily as a firearm carried on the body.

Sample Charge:
. . . unlawfully and willfully did, as a person who resides in the same premises, 28 Main Street, Burgest, N.C., as a minor, John Secrest, leave a firearm, a .22-caliber pistol, owned by the defendant, in a condition that the firearm can be discharged and in a manner that the defendant knew and should have known that an unsupervised minor would be able to gain access to the firearm, and the minor gained access to the firearm without the lawful permission of the minor's parents, Peter and Sally Secrest, and the minor possessed it in violation of G.S. 14-269.2(b) at the Smith Middle School, Haverford, N.C.

AOC Forms for This Offense:
None.

Punishment:
Class 1 misdemeanor.

G.S. 14-316.1

Contributing to the Delinquency or Other Condition of a Minor

April 2024

Page 1 of 2

Introductory Comment:

None.

Charging Language:

. . . unlawfully and willfully did knowingly, while at least 18 years of age, cause, encourage, and aid (*name juvenile*), age (*state juvenile's age*), a juvenile within the jurisdiction of the court, to (*choose one or more*)

(1) be in a place, (*describe place*),

(2) be in a condition, (*describe condition*),

(3) commit an act, (*describe act*),

whereby that juvenile could be adjudicated (*choose one or more*: delinquent; undisciplined; abused; neglected).

Notes about Charging Language:

- For offenses committed on or after December 1, 2019, the minimum age of the defendant was raised from 16 to 18. S.L. 2017-57, §§ 16D.4.(p) (substantive provision), 16D.4.(jj) (effective date provision). For offenses before that date, modify the charging language accordingly.
- The statute makes it unlawful to either "knowingly" or "willfully" cause the delinquency. If one of these terms is inappropriate, it may be deleted, though it likely is not error to leave an unneeded term in place as surplusage.
- The statute makes it unlawful to cause *or* encourage *or* aid the delinquency, etc., of a minor. If any of those terms is inappropriate, it may be deleted, though it likely is not error to leave an unneeded term in place as surplusage.
- The statute specifies that an adult may be prosecuted for contributing to the delinquency, etc., of a minor, even if the juvenile has not been adjudicated delinquent, etc.
- G.S. 7B-1501(7) defines "delinquent juvenile" as a juvenile under 16 years old but at least 6 years old who has committed a crime or an infraction. Effective December 1, 2019, G.S. 7B-1501(7)(b) expands the definition of "delinquent juvenile" to also include a juvenile who is at least 16 but under 18 and who has committed a crime or an infraction "excluding violation of the motor vehicle laws." S.L. 2017-57, §§ 16D.4.(a) (substantive provision), 16D.4(jj) (effective date provision).
- Also effective December 1, 2019, G.S. 7B-2200.5 provides for mandatory transfer to superior court of cases in which 16- and 17-year-old juveniles are charged with Class A through G felonies. As a practical matter, therefore, such juveniles cannot be adjudicated delinquent for such offenses, and persons who aid or encourage such juveniles probably should not be charged with contributing to the delinquency of a juvenile. In appropriate circumstances, persons who aid or encourage such juveniles may be charged with aiding and abetting or similar offenses.
- See G.S. 7B-1501(27) for the definition of "undisciplined juvenile", 7B-101(1) for the definition of "abused juvenile", and 7B-101(15) for the definition of "neglected juvenile."

Sample Charges:

. . . unlawfully and willfully did knowingly, while at least 18 years of age, cause, encourage, and aid Freddie D. Myers, age 15, a juvenile within the jurisdiction of the court, to be in a condition, truant from school for one week, whereby that juvenile could be adjudicated undisciplined.

. . . unlawfully and willfully did knowingly, while at least 18 years of age, cause, encourage, and aid Wilma C. Wesselham, age 14, a juvenile within the jurisdiction of the court, to commit an act, feloniously breaking into Sanders' Quick Grocery, 1140 Hamilton Road, Greensboro, N.C., with the intent to commit larceny, whereby that juvenile could be adjudicated delinquent.

AOC Forms for This Offense:

None.

Punishment:

Class 1 misdemeanor.

G.S. 14-318.2
Misdemeanor Child Abuse
April 2024
Page 1 of 2

Introductory Comment:
None.

Charging Language:

I. Inflicting physical injury

. . . unlawfully and willfully did, being [*choose one*: the parent; a person providing care and supervision because of (*describe relationship*)] of (*name child*), who was a child less than 16 years of age, inflict physical injury, (*describe injury*), on that child. The physical injury was inflicted by other than accidental means.

II. Allowing physical injury to be inflicted

. . . unlawfully and willfully did, being [*choose one*: the parent; a person providing care and supervision because of (*describe relationship*)] of (*name child*), who was a child less than 16 years of age, allow (*name person who inflicted injury*) to inflict physical injury, (*describe injury*), upon that child by: (*describe circumstances under which injury was inflicted*). The physical injury was inflicted by other than accidental means.

III. Creating risk of physical injury

. . . unlawfully and willfully did, being [*choose one*: the parent; a person providing care and supervision because of (*describe relationship*)] of (*name child*), who was a child less than 16 years of age, create and allow a substantial risk of physical injury upon that child by other than accidental means by (*describe how defendant created or allowed substantial risk of injury*).

Notes about Charging Language:

- This form calls for a description of the relationship between the child and the person, other than a parent, providing care to and supervision of the child because of the suggestion in *State v. Carrilo*, 149 N.C. App. 543 (2002), that only "caretakers" or those who stand "in loco parentis" may be prosecuted under G.S. 14-318.2. In *State v. Chambers*, 278 N.C. App. 474 (2021), the court found sufficient evidence that the defendant was a caretaker of the victim where he stayed with the victim and the victim's mother most nights, helped get the victim ready for bed, helped potty train the victim, and cooked and did yard work around the victim's home.

Sample Charges:

I. Inflicting physical injury

. . . unlawfully and willfully did, being a person providing care and supervision because of her relationship as the baby-sitter of Rachel Ross, who was a child less than 16 years of age, inflict physical injury, bruising on the arms and legs, on that child. The physical injury was inflicted by other than accidental means.

II. Allowing physical injury to be inflicted

. . . unlawfully and willfully did, being the parent of Thomas Wayne Smith, who was a child less than 16 years of age, allow James Robert Harrison to inflict physical injury, lacerations on the back, upon that child by: the defendant was present in the room while James Robert Harrison, the defendant's boyfriend, inflicted the injury to her child by striking him with a belt and did not attempt to stop James Robert Harrison from inflicting the injury. The physical injury was inflicted by other than accidental means.

AOC Forms for This Offense:
None.

Punishment:
Class A1 misdemeanor.

G.S. 14-318.4
Felony Child Abuse
April 2024
Page 1 of 3

Introductory Comment:
None.

Charging Language:

I. Inflicting serious physical injury **G.S. 14-318.4(a)**

. . . unlawfully, willfully, and feloniously did [*choose one* or both: intentionally inflict; intentionally commit an assault on (*name child*) that resulted in] serious physical injury, (*describe injury*), (*choose proper word*: on; to) (*name child*), who was (*state child's age*) years old and thus under 16 years of age. At the time the defendant inflicted the injury, the defendant was (*choose one*)

(1) the child's parent.
(2) providing care for the child as (*describe the defendant's relationship to the child*).
(3) supervising the child as (*describe the defendant's relationship to the child*).

II. Inflicting serious bodily injury **G.S. 14-318.4(a3)**

. . . unlawfully, willfully, and feloniously did (*choose one or more*)

(1) intentionally inflict serious bodily injury, (*describe injury*), on (*name child*), who was (*state child's age*) years old and thus under 16 years of age.
(2) intentionally commit an assault that resulted in serious bodily injury, (*describe injury*), on (*name child*), who was (*state child's age*) years old and thus under 16 years of age.
(3) intentionally commit an assault that resulted in (*choose one or both*: permanent; protracted) (*choose one or both*: loss; impairment) of a (*choose one or both*: mental; emotional) function of (*name child*), who was (*state child's age*) years old and thus under 16 years of age.

At the time the defendant inflicted the injury the defendant was (*choose one*)

(1) the child's parent.
(2) providing care for the child as (*describe the defendant's relationship to the child*).
(3) supervising the child as (*describe the defendant's relationship to the child*).

III. Prostitution of child **G.S. 14-318.4(a1)**

. . . unlawfully, willfully, and feloniously did (*choose one or more*: commit; permit; encourage) an act of prostitution (*choose appropriate word*: with; by) (*name child*), who was (*state child's age*) and thus under 16 years of age. The act of prostitution (describe what occurred and the parties involved, if known). At the time the defendant committed the offense, the defendant was (*choose one*)

(1) the child's parent.
(2) providing care for the child as (*describe the defendant's relationship to the child*).
(3) supervising the child as (*describe the defendant's relationship to the child*).

IV. Sexual act upon child **G.S. 14-318.4(a2)**

. . . unlawfully, willfully, and feloniously did (*choose one*: allow; commit) a sexual act, (*describe act, such as sexual intercourse, fellatio, etc., and name any third parties involved, if known*), upon (*name child*), who was (*state child's age*) and thus under 16 years of age. At the time the defendant committed the offense, the defendant was the (*choose one*: parent; guardian) of the child.

V. Reckless disregard for life/serious bodily injury **G.S. 14-318.4(a4)**

. . . unlawfully, willfully, and feloniously did show a reckless disregard for human life by (*choose one or both*)

(1) committing a willful act, (*describe act*), in the care of (*name child*), who was (*state child's age*) and thus under 16 years of age.

(2) committing a grossly negligent omission, (*describe omission*), in the care of (*name child*), who was (*state child's age*) and thus under 16 years of age.

The defendant's (*choose one*: act; omission) resulted in serious bodily injury, (*describe injury*), to the child. At the time the defendant committed the offense, the defendant was (*choose one*)

(1) the child's parent.

(2) providing care for the child as (*describe the defendant's relationship to the child*).

(3) supervising the child as (*describe the defendant's relationship to the child*).

VI. Reckless disregard for life/serious physical injury **G.S. 14-318.4(a5)**

. . . unlawfully, willfully, and feloniously did show a reckless disregard for human life by (*choose one or both*)

(1) committing a willful act, (*describe act*), in the care of (*name child*), who was (*state child's age*) and thus under 16 years of age.

(2) committing a grossly negligent omission, (*describe omission*), in the care of (*name child*), who was (*state child's age*) and thus under 16 years of age.

The defendant's (*choose one*: act; omission) resulted in serious physical injury, (*describe injury*), to the child. At the time the defendant committed the offense, the defendant was (*choose one*)

(1) the child's parent.

(2) providing care for the child as (*describe the defendant's relationship to the child*).

(3) supervising the child as (*describe the defendant's relationship to the child*).

Notes about Charging Language:

- This form calls for a description of the relationship between the child and the person, other than a parent, providing care to and supervision of the child because of the suggestion in *State v. Carrilo*, 149 N.C. App. 543 (2002), that only "caretakers" or those who stand "in loco parentis" may be prosecuted under G.S. 14-318.2. In *State v. Chambers*, 278 N.C. App. 474 (2021), the court found sufficient evidence that the defendant was a caretaker of the victim where he stayed with the victim and the victim's mother most nights, helped get the victim ready for bed, helped potty train the victim, and cooked and did yard work around the victim's home.
- "Serious bodily injury" is defined in G.S. 14-318.4(d)(1) as bodily injury that creates a substantial risk of death; that causes serious permanent disfigurement, coma, a permanent or protracted condition that causes extreme pain, or permanent or protracted loss or impairment of the function of any bodily member or organ; or that results in prolonged hospitalization.
- "Serious physical injury" is defined in G.S. 14-318.4(d)(2) as physical injury that causes great pain or suffering. The statute states that "[t]he term includes serious mental injury."
- "Sexual act" is not defined but probably includes sexual intercourse and all sexual acts included within first- and second-degree sexual offense.
- The term "grossly negligent omission" includes the failure to report a child as missing to law enforcement as provided in G.S. 14-318.5(b). G.S. 14-318.4(a6).

Sample Charges:

I. Inflicting serious physical injury **G.S. 14-318.4(a)**

. . . unlawfully, willfully, and feloniously did intentionally inflict serious physical injury, two broken arms, on Emily Radford, who was 9 years old and thus under 16 years of age. At the time the defendant inflicted the injury, the defendant was the child's parent.

V. Reckless disregard for life/serious bodily injury **G.S. 14-318.4(a4)**

. . . unlawfully, willfully, and feloniously did show a reckless disregard for human life by committing a grossly negligent omission, allowing the child to play unattended in a busy parking lot, in the care of Steven Saunders, who was 6 years old and thus under 16 years of age. The defendant's omission resulted in serious physical injury, being hit by a car and losing his left leg at the knee, to the child. At the time the defendant committed the offense, the defendant was providing care for the child as the live-in boyfriend of the child's mother.

AOC Forms for This Offense:
None.

Punishment:
Offense I is a Class D felony. Offense II is a Class B2 felony. Offense III is a Class D felony. Offense IV is a Class D felony. Offense V is a Class E felony. Offense VI is a Class G felony.

G.S. 14-320.1
Transporting or Keeping Child Out of State in Violation of Custody Order
April 2024

Introductory Comment:
None.

Charging Language:

I. Taking out of state unlawfully

. . . unlawfully, willfully, and feloniously did take (*name child*), a child under the age of 16, from (*name city or geographic area*), North Carolina, to (*name place taken outside of North Carolina*), with the intent to violate a custody order issued by (*name federal or state court that issued order*).

II. Keeping out of state unlawfully

. . . unlawfully, willfully, and feloniously did keep (*name child*), a child under the age of 16, outside of the State of North Carolina, with the intent to violate a custody order issued by (*name federal or state court that issued order*).

Notes about Charging Language:
- The statute is not limited to custody orders issued by North Carolina courts but applies as well to orders issued by federal and other state courts.
- A defendant also violates the statute if he or she "cause[s]" a child under 16 to be taken out of state with the intent to violate a custody order, even if the defendant does not personally take the child. If that is the case, modify the charging language appropriately.
- The statute provides that keeping a child out of state in violation of a court order for more than seventy-two hours is prima facie evidence of intent to violate the order.

Sample Charge:
. . . unlawfully, willfully, and feloniously did take John Jefferson, a child under the age of 16, from Durham, N.C., to New York City, N.Y., with the intent to violate a custody order issued by the District Court, Orange County, N.C.

AOC Forms for This Offense:
None.

Punishment:
Class I felony.

G.S. 14-321.2
Unlawful Transfer of Custody
April 2024
Page 1 of 2

Introductory Comment:
None.

Charging Language:

I. Unlawful transfer of custody **G.S. 14-321.2(a)(1)**

. . . unlawfully and willfully did, as a parent of (*name child*), a minor child, (*choose one*: effect; attempt to effect) an unlawful transfer of custody of the child to (*name person to whom custody was to be transferred, if known, or state*: "an unknown person").

II. Accepting unlawful transfer of custody **G.S. 14-321.2(a)(2)**

. . . unlawfully and willfully did (*choose one*: accept; attempt to accept) custody pursuant to an unlawful transfer of custody of (*name child*), a minor child.

III. Soliciting the unlawful transfer of custody **G.S. 14-321.2(a)(3)**

. . . unlawfully and willfully did (*choose one or more*: advertise; recruit; solicit) the unlawful transfer of custody of a minor child (*name child, if known*).

Notes about Charging Language:

- The statute defines several pertinent terms, including "unlawful transfer of custody", which means "the transfer of physical custody of a minor child, in willful violation of applicable adoption law or by grossly negligent omission in the care of the child, by the child's parent, without a court order or other authorization under law, to a person other than a relative or another individual having a substantial relationship with the child." G.S. 14-321.2(b)(4). The statute also lists a number of actions that do not fall within the concept of unlawful transfer of custody.
- For Offense II, there is an exception for "a person to receive custody of a child from a parent who intends to effect an unlawful transfer of custody of that parent's minor child if the person promptly notifies law enforcement or child protective services . . . and promptly makes the child available to law enforcement or child protective services." G.S. 14-321.2(a)(2).
- This form calls for the name of the minor. The Court of Appeals of North Carolina has approved of the use of the victim's initials in at least one sexual assault case. State v. McKoy, 196 N.C. App. 650 (2009) (use of initials provided adequate notice to the defendant where the defendant admitted that he knew the victim and did not claim that the use of initials made it difficult to prepare his defense). It is unclear whether it would be permissible to use initials to identify the minor in the offenses set forth in this form. In another sexual assault case, the North Carolina Supreme Court held that an indictment was facially invalid where it identified the victim using the generic description "Victim #1." State v. White, 372 N.C. 248 (2019).
- Offense III may also be committed by aiding, abetting, conspiring with, or seeking the assistance of another to advertise, recruit, or solicit an unlawful transfer. In an appropriate case, alter the charging language to so reflect.

- Offenses I, II, and III are felonies if the conduct in question results in serious physical injury to the child. In such a case, replace "unlawfully and willfully" with "unlawfully, willfully, and feloniously" and add a sentence at the end of the charging language as follows: "This resulted in serious physical injury to the child." Serious physical injury is not defined in the statute. The nature of the injury likely need not be alleged, *cf.* State v. Gregory, 223 N.C. 415 (1943), but it is not improper to include that information if desired.

Sample Charge:

I. Unlawful transfer of custody **G.S. 14-321.2(a)(1)**

. . . unlawfully and willfully did, as a parent of Taylor Spinks, a minor child, attempt to effect an unlawful transfer of custody of Taylor Spinks to Alexis Sevier.

AOC Forms for This Offense:

None.

Punishment:

Offenses I, II, and III are Class A1 misdemeanors, unless the child suffered serious physical injury as a result of the defendant's conduct. In that case, the offenses are Class G felonies.

G.S. 14-322
Abandonment or Nonsupport of Dependent Spouse or Child

April 2024
Page 1 of 2

Introductory Comment:
A second or subsequent offense of abandonment or nonsupport of a dependent spouse or child is punished as a Class 1, rather than a Class 2, misdemeanor. An indictment or an information for a recidivist offense must comply with G.S. 15A-928, which requires that the defendant's prior convictions be alleged either (1) in a separate count of the indictment or information than the substantive offense or (2) in a separate indictment or information. In such a case, the separate count or separate indictment should set forth the date and court in which the prior conviction occurred. This requirement does not apply to arrest warrants or magistrates' orders, which still must allege the defendant's prior convictions but need not do so in a separate count or separate charging instrument. Also note that in situations where a conviction for a recidivist offense is appealed from district to superior court for trial de novo, G.S. 15A-922(h) and -928(d) require the State to replace the pleading in the case with superseding statements of charges separately alleging the substantive offense and any prior convictions. G.S. 15A-928 also requires that the name or title of an offense elevated by prior convictions must not make reference to such prior convictions.

Charging Language:

I. Abandonment of a dependent spouse — **G.S. 14-322(b)**

. . . unlawfully and willfully did, being a supporting spouse, abandon (*choose one*: his; her) dependent spouse, (*name spouse*), without providing (*choose one*: him; her) with adequate support.

II. Nonsupport of a dependent spouse — **G.S. 14-322(c)**

. . . unlawfully and willfully did, while being a supporting spouse and living with (*choose one*: his, her) dependent spouse, (*name spouse*), neglect to provide adequate support for (*choose one*: him, her).

III. Nonsupport of a child — **G.S. 14-322(d)**

. . . unlawfully and willfully did (*choose one or both*: neglect; refuse) to provide adequate support for (*choose one*: his; her) (*choose one*: child; children), (*give name(s) and age(s) of child or children*).

Notes about Charging Language:

- "Supporting spouse" means a spouse, whether husband or wife, on whom the other spouse is actually substantially dependent or from whom such other spouse is substantially in need of maintenance and support.
- "Dependent spouse" means a spouse, whether husband or wife, who is actually substantially dependent on the other spouse for his or her maintenance and support or is substantially in need of maintenance and support from the other spouse.
- "Child" refers to a minor less than 18 years of age. For purposes of this statute, the term refers to natural children born within wedlock and adopted children. State v. Gardner, 219 N.C. 331 (1941); State v. Caudill, 68 N.C. App. 268 (1984). If the mother or father fails to support a child born out of wedlock, the offense must be charged under G.S. 49-2.
- G.S. 14-325.1 states that the offense of willful neglect or refusal to support and maintain a child is considered to have been committed in the state of North Carolina whenever the child is living here at the time of the willful neglect or refusal to support and maintain the child.

- Under G.S. 14-322(d), nonsupport of a child is a "continuing offense and shall not be barred by any statute of limitations until the youngest living child of the parent shall reach the age of 18 years."
- G.S. 14-322.3 exempts a parent from prosecution under this section when he or she voluntarily delivers an infant under 7 days of age pursuant to G.S. 7B-500(b) or (d) and does not express an intent to return for the infant.

Sample Charge:

I. Abandonment of a dependent spouse **G.S. 14-322(b)**

. . . unlawfully and willfully did, being a supporting spouse, abandon his dependent spouse, Jennifer Smith Douglas, without providing her with adequate support.

AOC Forms for This Offense:

None.

Punishment:

Class 2 misdemeanor. A second or subsequent offense is a Class 1 misdemeanor. Under G.S. 14-322(e), upon a defendant's conviction, the court may make certain orders to provide for the support of the dependent spouse or child(ren) in question.

G.S. 14-322.1
Abandonment and Nonsupport of Child for Six Months
April 2024

Introductory Comment:
None.

Charging Language:
. . . unlawfully, willfully, and feloniously did without just cause or provocation abandon (*choose one*: his; her) (*choose one*: child; children), (*give name and age of child or children*), for a period of six months from (*give date*) to (*give date*). During the period of six months, the defendant willfully failed and refused to provide adequate means of support for the above-named (*choose one*: child; children) and attempted to conceal (*choose one*: his; her) whereabouts from the (*choose one*: child; children) with the intent of escaping (*choose one*: his; her) lawful obligation to support such (*choose one*: child; children).

Notes about Charging Language:
- "Child" refers to a minor less than 18 years of age. It is not clear whether the term refers only to natural and adopted legitimate children, which is how the term has been interpreted for purposes of G.S. 14-322. State v. Gardner, 219 N.C. 331 (1941); State v. Caudill, 68 N.C. App. 268 (1984).
- G.S. 14-322.3 exempts a parent from prosecution under this section when he or she voluntarily delivers an infant under 7 days of age pursuant to G.S. 7B-500(b) or (d) and does not express an intent to return for the infant.

Sample Charge:
. . . unlawfully, willfully, and feloniously did without just cause or provocation abandon his children, Samuel Patrick Greene, age 10, and Mary Elizabeth Greene, age 6, for a period of six months from January 30, 2019, to July 30, 2019. During the period of six months, the defendant willfully failed and refused to provide adequate means of support for the above-named children and attempted to conceal his whereabouts from the children with the intent of escaping his lawful obligation to support such children.

AOC Forms for This Offense:
None.

Punishment:
Class I felony.

G.S. 14-360
Cruelty to Animals
April 2024

Introductory Comment:
None.

Charging Language:

I. Misdemeanor cruelty **G.S. 14-360(a)**

. . . unlawfully and willfully did intentionally (*choose one or more and describe act*: overdrive; overload; wound; injure; torment; kill; deprive of necessary sustenance) an animal, (*describe animal and owner, if known*).

II. Felony malicious starvation **G.S. 14-360(a1)**

. . . unlawfully, willfully, and feloniously did maliciously kill an animal, (*describe animal and owner, if known*), by intentionally depriving the animal of necessary sustenance.

III. Felony cruelty **G.S. 14-360(b)**

. . . unlawfully, willfully, and feloniously did maliciously (*choose one or more and describe act*: torture; mutilate; maim; cruelly beat; disfigure; poison; kill) an animal, (*describe animal and owner, if known*).

Notes about Charging Language:

- The statute also prohibits a person from causing or procuring the acts described in each of the three charges above. If the defendant caused or procured the acts in question, add appropriate language to the charge.
- A definition of "animal" and definitions of several other terms used in the statute appear in G.S. 14-360(c).
- In *State v. Watkins*, 101 N.C. 702 (1888), the court ruled that an indictment alleging the overloading, injuring, or tormenting of an animal must allege "the facts that give special character and significance to the acts charged," i.e., that constitute the crime. Although the continuing validity of *Watkins* is not clear given subsequent statutory changes, this form requests a description of the acts underlying the charge.
- The name of the animal "is not an essential element" of an animal cruelty offense. State v. Lawson, 285 N.C. App. 404, *review denied*, ___ N.C. ___, 881 S.E.2d 314 (2022).

Sample Charge:

I. Misdemeanor cruelty **G.S. 14-360(a)**

. . . unlawfully and willfully did intentionally injure, by shooting it with a BB gun, an animal, a dog named Spot owned by Peter Jones.

AOC Forms for This Offense:
None.

Punishment:
Offense I is a Class 1 misdemeanor. Offense II is a Class H felony. Offense III is a Class H felony.

G.S. 14-362
Cockfighting
April 2024

Introductory Comment:
None.

Charging Language:
. . . unlawfully, willfully, and feloniously [*choose one or more*: did instigate; did promote; did conduct; was employed at; allowed property under (*choose one*: his; her) ownership to be used for; allowed property under (*choose one*: his; her) control to be used for; did participate as a spectator at; did profit from] an exhibition featuring the fighting of a cock.

Notes about Charging Language:
- In some cases, it may be helpful to add a brief description of the property that was used or of the exhibition itself. Such a description can be added as shown in the sample charge below.

Sample Charge:
. . . unlawfully, willfully, and feloniously allowed property under her control to be used for an exhibition featuring the fighting of a cock. The defendant allowed the barn at her home, 18 Sawgrass Way, Maxton, N.C., to be used as a venue for several cockfights.

AOC Forms for This Offense:
None.

Punishment:
Class I felony. Note that a person from whom animals are seized in connection with this offense may under some circumstances be required to pay for the cost of the animals' care during the pendency of the case. G.S. 19A-70.

G.S. 14-362.1
Animal Fighting and Baiting
April 2024
Page 1 of 2

Introductory Comment:
This offense applies to all animal fighting and baiting except cockfighting, which is criminalized under G.S. 14-362, and dog fighting and dog baiting, which are criminalized under G.S. 14-362.2.

Offense I is a felony if the defendant has been convicted within the previous three years of any offense defined in G.S. 14-362.1. In such a case, allege "unlawfully, willfully, and feloniously" instead of "unlawfully and willfully." An indictment or an information for the recidivist offense must comply with G.S. 15A-928, which requires that the defendant's prior convictions be alleged either (1) in a separate count of the indictment or information than the substantive offense or (2) in a separate indictment or information. In such a case, the separate count or separate indictment should set forth the date and court in which the prior conviction occurred. This requirement does not apply to arrest warrants or magistrates' orders, which still must allege the defendant's prior convictions but need not do so in a separate count or separate charging instrument. G.S. 15A-928 also requires that the name or title of an offense elevated by prior convictions must not make reference to such prior convictions.

Charging Language:

I. Instigating, promoting, etc., animal fighting **G.S. 14-362.1(a)**

. . . unlawfully and willfully [*choose one or more*: did instigate; did promote; did conduct; was employed at; did provide an animal for; did allow property under (*choose one*: his; her) ownership to be used for; did allow property under (*choose one*: his; her) control to be used for; did profit from] an exhibition featuring the (*choose one or both*: fighting; baiting) of an animal, (*describe animal, which may not be a dog or a cock*).

II. Possession of animal with intent to fight **G.S. 14-362.1(b)**

. . . unlawfully and willfully did (*choose one or more*: own; possess; train) an animal, (*describe animal, which may not be a dog or a cock*), with the intent that the animal be used in an exhibition featuring the (*choose one or both*: fighting; baiting) of [*choose one or both*: that animal; another animal (*describe animal*)].

III. Participating in animal fighting as a spectator **G.S. 14-362.1(c)**

. . . unlawfully and willfully did participate as a spectator at an exhibition featuring the (*choose one or both*: fighting; baiting) of an animal, (*describe animal, which may not be a dog or a cock*).

Notes about Charging Language:

- In some cases, it may be helpful to add a brief description of the property that was used or of the exhibition itself.

Sample Charge:

II. Possession of animal with intent to fight **G.S. 14-362(b)**

. . . unlawfully and willfully did possess an animal, a wild hog, with the intent that the animal be used in an exhibition featuring the baiting of another animal, a dog.

AOC Forms for This Offense:
None.

Punishment:
All offenses are Class 2 misdemeanors, except that Offense I may be elevated to a felony under the circumstances described above. Note that a person from whom animals are seized in connection with this offense may under some circumstances be required to pay for the cost of the animals' care during the pendency of the case. G.S. 19A-70.

G.S. 14-362.2
Dog Fighting and Baiting
April 2024

Introductory Comment:
None.

Charging Language:

I. Instigating, promoting, etc., dog fighting **G.S. 14-362.2(a)**

. . . unlawfully, willfully, and feloniously [*choose one or more*: did instigate; did promote; did conduct; was employed at; did provide a dog for; did allow property under (*choose one*: his; her) ownership to be used for; did allow property under (*choose one*: his; her) control to be used for; did gamble on; did profit from] an exhibition featuring the (*choose one or more*: baiting of a dog; fighting of a dog with another dog; fighting of a dog with another animal).

II. Possession of dog with intent to fight **G.S. 14-362.2(b)**

. . . unlawfully, willfully, and feloniously did (*choose one or more*: own; possess; train) a dog with the intent that the dog be used in an exhibition featuring the (*choose one or more*: baiting of that dog; fighting of that dog with another dog; fighting of that dog with another animal).

III. Participating in dog fighting as a spectator **G.S. 14-362.2(c)**

. . . unlawfully, willfully, and feloniously did participate as a spectator at an exhibition featuring the (*choose one or more*: baiting of a dog; fighting of a dog with another dog; fighting of a dog with another animal).

Notes about Charging Language:

- In some cases, it may be helpful to add a brief description of the property that was used or of the exhibition itself. Such a description can be added as shown in the sample charge below.

Sample Charge:

I. Instigating, promoting, etc., dog fighting **G.S. 14-362.2(a)**

. . . unlawfully, willfully, and feloniously did promote an exhibition featuring the fighting of a dog with another dog, by handing out flyers advertising "Dog Warz," a dog-fighting exhibition.

AOC Forms for This Offense:
None.

Punishment:
Class H felony.

G.S. 14-399
Littering
April 2024
Page 1 of 2

Introductory Comment:
This form provides charging language for felony and misdemeanor littering. Littering may also be charged as an infraction, with no requirement that the littering be intentional or reckless. *See* G.S. 14-399(a1), (c1), (d1), and (e1).

Charging Language:

I. Misdemeanor littering (15 pounds or less) **G.S. 14-399(a), (c)**

. . . unlawfully and willfully did intentionally and recklessly (*choose one or more*: throw; scatter; spill; place; dispose of) litter (*choose one and describe*: on property not owned by the defendant; in the waters of North Carolina), not into a litter receptacle as defined in G.S. 14-399(a)(2), and not on property designated by the State or a political subdivision thereof for the disposal of garbage and refuse with authorization to use the property for that purpose.

II. Aggravated misdemeanor littering (over 15 pounds but not over 500 pounds) **G.S. 14-399(a), (d)**

. . . unlawfully and willfully did intentionally and recklessly (*choose one or more*: throw; scatter; spill; place; dispose of) litter (*choose one and describe*: on property not owned by the defendant; in the waters of North Carolina), not into a litter receptacle as defined in G.S. 14-399(a)(2), and not on property designated by the State or a political subdivision thereof for the disposal of garbage and refuse with authorization to use the property for that purpose. The amount of the litter exceeded 15 pounds but did not exceed 500 pounds.

III. Felony littering **G.S. 14-399(a), (e)**

. . . unlawfully, willfully, and feloniously did intentionally and recklessly (*choose one or more*: throw; scatter; spill; place; dispose of) litter (*choose one and describe*: on property not owned by the defendant; in the waters of North Carolina), not into a litter receptacle as defined in G.S. 14-399(a)(2), and not on property designated by the State or a political subdivision thereof for the disposal of garbage and refuse with authorization to use the property for that purpose.
(*choose one or more*)

(1) The amount of litter exceeded 500 pounds.
(2) The littering was done for a commercial purpose.
(3) The litter discarded was hazardous waste.

Notes about Charging Language:

- "Litter" is defined in G.S. 14-399(i)(4).
- The statute only requires proof of intentionally *or* recklessly throwing, scattering, etc., the litter. Therefore, you may delete either "intentionally" or "recklessly" from the charging language above if appropriate in a particular case.
- The statute also prohibits a person from causing the litter to be thrown, scattered, etc. Add appropriate language if necessary in a particular case.
- The statute makes it a crime to litter, "except . . . [w]hen the property is designated by the State or political subdivision thereof for the disposal of garbage and refuse, and the person is authorized to use the property for this purpose." In *State v. Rankin*, 371 N.C. 885 (2018), the state supreme court ruled that this provision is an element of the crime, not a defense, so it must be alleged and proven by the State.
- The statute prohibits littering on both public and private property, except property owned by the defendant.
- The "waters of North Carolina" include lakes, rivers, and the ocean.
- For misdemeanor littering of 15 pounds or less, G.S. 14-399(c) increases the fine for a second or subsequent misdemeanor offense occurring within three years of the date of a prior offense. In such a case, allege the date of the prior offense, the date of the prior conviction, and the court in which the conviction occurred.
- For felony littering, "commercial purpose" is defined in G.S. 14-399(i)(2a), and "hazardous waste" is defined in G.S. 130A-290.

Sample Charge:

I. Misdemeanor littering (15 pounds or less) **G.S. 14-399(a), (c)**

. . . unlawfully and willfully did intentionally and recklessly throw litter on property not owned by the defendant, Interstate 40 in Winston-Salem, N.C., not into a litter receptacle as defined in G.S. 14-399(a)(2), and not on property designated by the State or a political subdivision thereof for the disposal of garbage and refuse with authorization to use the property for that purpose.

AOC Forms for This Offense:

None.

Punishment:

Misdemeanor littering is a Class 3 misdemeanor punishable by a fine of not less than $250 but not more than $1,000 for a first offense. Aggravated misdemeanor littering is a Class 3 misdemeanor punishable by a fine of not less than $500 but not more than $2,000. Felony littering is a Class I felony.

G.S. 14-401.14
Ethnic Intimidation
April 2024

Introductory Comment:
Before charging a defendant under this statute, it may be worth considering G.S. 14-3, which elevates the punishment for misdemeanors committed because of the victim's race, color, religion, nationality, or country of origin.

Charging Language:

. . . unlawfully and willfully did (*choose one or more*)

(1) assault (*name person assaulted*);

(2) damage the property of (*name owner or possessor of property*);

(3) deface the property of (*name owner or possessor of property*);

because of (*choose one*: his; her) (*choose one or more*: race; color; religion; nationality; country of origin).

Notes about Charging Language:
- The statute also prohibits a person from threatening to do any of the acts listed in the charging language above. If appropriate in a particular case, add "threaten to" before the relevant verb.
- The statute does not require that the *victim's* race, color, religion, nationality, or country of origin be the reason for the criminal act. For example, a defendant may violate the statute by assaulting one spouse because of the race of the other spouse. In such a case, delete "his" or "her" from the charging language.

Sample Charge:
. . . unlawfully and willfully did assault Nancy Smith because of her race.

AOC Forms for This Offense:
None.

Punishment:
Class 1 misdemeanor.

G.S. 14-408.1(b)–(c)
Unlawful Solicitation of, or Providing False Information to, Firearms Dealer or Seller
April 2024

Introductory Comment:
None.

Charging Language:

I. Unlawful solicitation of firearms dealer or seller **G.S. 14-408.1(b)**

. . . unlawfully, willfully, and feloniously did knowingly (*choose one or more*: solicit; persuade; encourage; entice) (*name dealer or seller*), a (*choose one*: licensed dealer; private seller) of (*choose one or more*: firearms; ammunition), to transfer (*choose one or more and describe*: a firearm; firearms; ammunition) under circumstances that the defendant knew would violate the laws of (*choose one or both*: North Carolina; the United States), (*describe circumstances of transfer*).

II. Providing false information to firearms dealer or seller **G.S. 14-408.1(c)**

. . . unlawfully, willfully, and feloniously did provide to (*name dealer or seller*), a (*choose one*: licensed dealer; private seller) of (*choose one or more*: firearms; ammunition), information that the defendant knew to be materially false, (*describe information*), with the intent to deceive the (*choose one*: dealer; seller) about the legality of a transfer of (*choose one or more and describe*: a firearm; firearms; ammunition).

Notes about Charging Language:
- A person who willfully procures another to engage in either offense is a principal.

Sample Charge:

I. Unlawful solicitation of firearms dealer or seller **G.S. 14-408.1(b)**

. . . unlawfully, willfully, and feloniously did encourage Dan Barrett, a licensed dealer of firearms and ammunition, to transfer a firearm, a Glock 9mm pistol, under circumstances that the defendant knew would violate the laws of North Carolina and the United States, in that the defendant encouraged Mr. Barrett to transfer the firearm to Joe Smithers, a convicted felon.

AOC Forms for This Offense:
None.

Punishment:
Class F felony.

G.S. 14-415.1
Possession of Firearm by Convicted Felon
April 2024

Introductory Comment:
None.

Charging Language:
. . . unlawfully, willfully, and feloniously did (*choose one or more*: possess; purchase; own; have in the defendant's custody; have in the defendant's care; have in the defendant's control) a (*describe the weapon*), which is a [*choose one*: firearm; weapon of mass death and destruction as defined in G.S. 14-288.8(c)]. The defendant had previously been convicted of the felony of (*name felony*), which was punishable by (*give maximum punishment and classification of felony, if classified*). This felony was committed on (*give date of offense*), and the defendant (*choose one*: pled guilty to; pled no contest to; was convicted of) the felony on (*give date of conviction*), in (*name court and state in which the court is located*) and was sentenced to (*give sentence imposed for the conviction*).

Notes about Charging Language:
- The statute defines a "firearm" as (1) any weapon, including a starter gun, which will or is designed to or may readily be converted to expel a projectile by the action of an explosive, or its frame or receiver, or (2) any firearm muffler or firearm silencer.
- If the statute is to be applied against a person who was convicted of a felony in another state or in federal court, that felony must be substantially similar to a North Carolina felony and must be punishable where committed by imprisonment for more than 1 year.
- This offense should not be charged if, pursuant to the law of the jurisdiction in which the felony conviction occurred, the defendant has been pardoned or has had his or her firearm rights restored if such restoration of rights could also be granted under North Carolina law. G.S. 14-415.1(d).
- An indictment charging this offense must be separate from an indictment charging the defendant "with other offenses related to or giving rise to a charge under this section." G.S. 14-415.1(c). Failure to comply with this provision does not, however, render an indictment fatally defective. State v. Newborn, 384 N.C. 656, 661 (2023).

Sample Charge:
. . . unlawfully, willfully, and feloniously did possess a Smith and Wesson .45-caliber pistol, which is a firearm. The defendant had previously been convicted of the felony of felonious breaking and entering, which was punishable as a Class H felony with a maximum punishment of 10 years. This felony was committed on September 15, 1992, and the defendant was convicted of the felony on January 18, 1993, in Wayne County Superior Court and was sentenced to 3 years of imprisonment.

AOC Forms for This Offense:
None.

Punishment:
Class G felony.

G.S. 14-415.21
Concealed Handgun Permit Violations
April 2024

Introductory Comment:
G.S. 14-415.21 creates several different offenses involving violation of the concealed handgun permit laws. Three are set out below.

Charging Language:

I. Carrying a concealed handgun without a permit in possession **G.S. 14-415.21(a)**

. . . unlawfully and willfully did, having been issued a valid concealed handgun permit by the sheriff of (*name county*), carry a concealed handgun, (*describe handgun*), without the permit in the defendant's possession.

II. Failure to disclose permit and weapon to officer **G.S. 14-415.21(a)**

. . . unlawfully and willfully did, having been issued a valid concealed handgun permit by the sheriff of (*name county*), carry a concealed handgun, (*describe handgun*), without disclosing to (*name officer*), a law enforcement officer of (*name department*) who had (*choose one or both*: approached; addressed) the defendant, that the defendant held a valid concealed handgun permit and was carrying a concealed handgun, in violation of G.S. 14-415.11.

III. Other violations of concealed handgun statutes **G.S. 14-415.21(b)**

. . . unlawfully and willfully did violate the provisions of Article 54B of Chapter 14 of the North Carolina General Statutes by (*describe violation*).

Notes about Charging Language:

- The statute also creates offenses for permit holders who carry concealed handguns on private property where they are prohibited (G.S. 14-415.21(a), an infraction with a fine of up to $500) and for permit holders who consume alcohol while carrying a firearm (G.S. 14-415.21(a1), a Class 1 misdemeanor). Modify the charging language as appropriate in such a case.

Sample Charge:

I. Carrying a concealed handgun without a permit in possession **G.S. 14-415.21(a)**

. . . unlawfully and willfully did, having been issued a valid concealed handgun permit by the sheriff of Warren County, carry a concealed handgun, a .22-caliber pistol, without the permit in the defendant's possession.

AOC Forms for This Offense:
None.

Punishment:
Offenses I and II are infractions punished under G.S. 14-3.1. However, the statute provides that in lieu of paying the penalty for the infraction, the defendant may surrender his or her permit. Offense III is a Class 2 misdemeanor.

G.S. 14-444
Drunk and Disruptive
April 2024

Introductory Comment:
None.

Charging Language:
. . . unlawfully and willfully did appear intoxicated in a public place, (*name or describe the public place in which the defendant was found*), and was disruptive in that the defendant did (*choose one or more*)

(1) (*choose one or both*: block; interfere) with traffic on (*name the street, highway, or public vehicular area*), a (*choose one*: highway; public vehicular area).
(2) (*choose one or both*: block; lie across; prevent passage across; interfere with passage across; prevent access to; interfere with access to) (*choose one or both*: a sidewalk; an entrance to a building).
(3) (*choose one or more*: grab; shove; push) (*name person grabbed, shoved or pushed, if known; otherwise, state* "a person whose name is not known at this time").
(4) fight with (*name person defendant fought with, if known*).
(5) challenge (*name person, if known*) to a fight.
(6) (*choose one or more*: curse, shout at; rudely insult) others by using the following words: (*describe what defendant said and name who it was said to, if known*).
(7) beg for money and other property.

Notes about Charging Language:
- "Public place" is defined in G.S. 14-443(3) as a place open to the public, whether publicly or privately owned.
- Alcoholism is a defense to this charge. G.S. 14-445.

Sample Charge:
. . . unlawfully and willfully did appear intoxicated in a public place, the 600 block of Greensboro Boulevard, Sawyer, N.C., and was disruptive in that he did block, lie across, and interfere with passage across a sidewalk.

AOC Forms for This Offense:
None.

Punishment:
Class 3 misdemeanor.

G.S. 14-454
Accessing a Computer
April 2024
Page 1 of 2

Introductory Comment:
None.

Charging Language:

I. Misdemeanor fraudulent access **G.S. 14-454(a)**

. . . unlawfully and willfully did access a (*choose one or more and describe*: computer; computer program; computer system; computer network) for the purpose of (*choose one or both*)

(1) devising and executing a scheme and artifice to defraud, (*describe scheme*).

(2) obtaining (*choose one or both and describe*: property; services) by means of a false and fraudulent pretense, representation, and promise, (*describe false and fraudulent pretense, etc.*).

II. Felony fraudulent access **G.S. 14-454(a)**

. . . unlawfully, willfully, and feloniously did access a (*choose one or more and describe*: computer; computer program; computer system; computer network) for the purpose of (*choose one or both*)

(1) devising and executing a scheme and artifice to defraud, (*describe scheme*).

(2) obtaining (*choose one or both and describe*: property; services) by means of a false and fraudulent pretense, representation, and promise, (*describe false and fraudulent pretense, etc.*).

The violation (*choose one or both*: resulted in damage of more than $1,000; resulted in obtaining property and services of more than $1,000.)

III. Misdemeanor unauthorized access **G.S. 14-454(b)**

. . . unlawfully and willfully did without authorization access a (*choose one or more and describe unauthorized act*: computer; computer program; computer system; computer network).

Notes about Charging Language:

- G.S. 14-453 defines many of the terms used in the charging language above.
- Each of the offenses above can be committed by a person who "cause[s]" a computer, etc., to be accessed, even if the person does not himself or herself access the computer. Modify the charging language accordingly if appropriate.
- Each of the offenses above can be committed by a person who accesses a "part of" a computer, etc. Modify the charging language accordingly if appropriate.
- For Offenses I and II, the statute only requires proof of devising *or* executing a scheme or artifice to defraud. Delete unnecessary words if appropriate.
- For Offenses I and II, the statute only requires proof of a false or fraudulent pretense, representation, *or* promise. Delete unnecessary words if appropriate.
- For Offense II, the statute requires only that property *or* services be obtained. If one of these terms is inappropriate, delete it.

- With respect to Offense III, in *Van Buren v. United States*, 593 U.S. 374 (2021), the United States Supreme Court interpreted the similar federal Computer Fraud and Abuse Act's prohibition on intentionally accessing a computer "without authorization" as not covering a situation where a police officer "plainly flouted his department's policy" by running a license-plate search in a law enforcement computer database in exchange for money and for a non–law enforcement purpose. The Court reasoned that while the officer acted with an improper purpose, he did not violate the statute because, in contrast to an outside hacker acting without any permission at all, the officer was authorized to access the database.
- The statute provides that the fraudulent purpose requirement of Offenses I and II is not met when the object of the scheme or false or fraudulent pretense, representation, etc., is to obtain educational testing material or to falsify educational testing scores or academic or vocational grades. If this is the case, it is typically appropriate to charge Offense III.

Sample Charge:

II. Felony fraudulent access **G.S. 14-454(a)**

. . . unlawfully, willfully, and feloniously did access a computer system, a set of computers of the First Savings Bank, Wilson, N.C., for the purpose of devising and executing a scheme and artifice to defraud the bank by causing the computers in the bank to print twenty checks in the amount $100 each, payable to the defendant, when the defendant was not entitled to receive these checks. The violation resulted in obtaining property and services of more than $1,000.

AOC Forms for This Offense:

None.

Punishment:

Offenses I and III are Class 1 misdemeanors. Offense II is a Class G felony.

G.S. 14-454.1
Accessing a Government Computer
April 2024
Page 1 of 2

Introductory Comment:
None.

Charging Language:

I. Misdemeanor unauthorized access **G.S. 14-454.1(c)**

. . . unlawfully and willfully and without authorization did access (*choose one or both*)

(1) educational testing material, (*describe*),

(2) (*choose one or more and describe*: academic testing scores; academic testing grades; vocational testing scores; vocational testing grades)

that (*choose one*: was; were) in a government computer of (*name entity of state or local government*).

II. Felony unauthorized access **G.S. 14-454.1(b)**

. . . unlawfully, willfully, and feloniously and without authorization did access a government computer of (*name entity of state or local government*) for the following purpose: (*name purpose*).

III. Felony fraudulent access **G.S. 14-454.1(a)**

. . . unlawfully, willfully, and feloniously did access a government computer of (*name entity of state or local government*) for the purpose of (*choose one or both*)

(3) devising and executing a scheme and artifice to defraud, (*describe scheme*).

(4) obtaining (*choose one or both and describe*: property; services) by means of a false and fraudulent pretense, representation, and promise, (*describe false and fraudulent pretense, etc.*).

Notes about Charging Language:

- G.S. 14-453 defines many of the terms used in the charging language above.
- Each of the offenses above can be committed by a person who "cause[s]" a computer, etc., to be accessed, even if the person does not himself or herself access the computer. Modify the charging language accordingly if appropriate.
- With respect to Offenses I and II, in *Van Buren v. United States*, 593 U.S. 374 (2021), the United States Supreme Court interpreted the similar federal Computer Fraud and Abuse Act's prohibition on intentionally accessing a computer "without authorization" as not covering a situation where a police officer "plainly flouted his department's policy" by running a license-plate search in a law enforcement computer database in exchange for money and for a non–law enforcement purpose. The Court reasoned that while the officer acted with an improper purpose, he did not violate the statute because, in contrast to an outside hacker acting without any permission at all, the officer was authorized to access the database.
- For Offense III, the statute only requires proof of devising *or* executing a scheme or artifice to defraud. Delete unnecessary words if appropriate.
- For Offense III, the statute requires only that property *or* services be obtained. If one of these terms is inappropriate, delete it.
- For Offense III, the statute only requires proof of a false or fraudulent pretense, representation, *or* promise. Delete unnecessary words if appropriate.

Sample Charge:

III. Felony fraudulent access **G.S. 14-454.1(a)**

. . . unlawfully, willfully, and feloniously did access a government computer of the City of Smallville, N.C., for the purpose of devising and executing a scheme and artifice to defraud, to change a billing to the defendant so the defendant financially benefited from doing so.

AOC Forms for This Offense:

None.

Punishment:

Offense I is a Class 1 misdemeanor. Offense II is a Class H felony. Offense III is a Class F felony.

G.S. 14-455
Damaging a Computer
April 2024

Introductory Comment:
None.

Charging Language:

I. Misdemeanor damaging computer **G.S. 14-455(a)**

. . . unlawfully and willfully did without authorization (*choose one or more*: alter; damage; destroy) a (*choose one or more and describe*: computer; computer program; computer system; computer network).

II. Felony damaging computer in excess of $1,000 **G.S. 14-455(a)**

. . . unlawfully, willfully, and feloniously did without authorization (*choose one or more*: alter; damage; destroy) a (*choose one or more and describe*: computer; computer program; computer system; computer network). The violation caused damage in excess of $1,000.

III. Felony damaging government computer **G.S. 14-455(a1)**

. . . unlawfully, willfully, and feloniously did without authorization (*choose one or more and describe*: alter; damage; destroy) a government computer of (*name entity of state or local government*).

Notes about Charging Language:

- G.S. 14-453 defines many of the terms used in the charging language above.
- G.S. 14-455(b) provides that the statute applies to the alteration, damage, or destruction effectuated by introducing a computer program (including a self-replicating or a self-propagating computer program) into a computer, computer system, or computer network.

Sample Charges:

II. Felony damaging computer in excess of $1,000 **G.S. 14-455(a)**

. . . unlawfully, willfully, and feloniously did without authorization damage a computer network at ABC Trucking Company, Medina, N.C., by introducing a virus into the network. The violation caused damage in excess of $1,000.

III. Felony damaging government computer **G.S. 14-455(a1)**

. . . unlawfully, willfully, and feloniously did without authorization damage a government computer of the City of Durham, N.C., by striking the computer with his fist.

AOC Forms for This Offense:
None.

Punishment:
Offense I is a Class 1 misdemeanor. Offense II is a Class G felony. Offense III is a Class F felony.

G.S. 14-458
Computer Trespass
April 2024
Page 1 of 2

Introductory Comment:
None.

Charging Language:
. . . unlawfully and willfully did without authority use a (*choose one or both*: computer; computer network) with the intent to (*choose one or more*)

(1) (*choose one*: temporarily; permanently) (*choose one or more*: remove; halt; disable) (*choose one or more*: computer data; a computer program; computer software) from a (*choose one or more and describe*: computer; computer network).
(2) cause a computer (*describe computer*) to malfunction.
(3) (*choose one or both*: alter; erase) (*choose one or more and describe*: computer data; a computer program; computer software).
(4) cause physical injury to the property of (*name owner, if known, and describe property*).
(5) (*choose one*: make; cause to be made) an unauthorized copy of (*choose one or more*: computer data; a computer program; computer software) (*choose one or more*: residing in; communicated by; produced by) a (*choose one or both and describe*: computer; computer network).
(6) [*choose one or both*: falsely identify with the intent to deceive and defraud the recipient; forge commercial electronic mail transmission information (*add if appropriate*: and other routing information)] in connection with the transmission of unsolicited bulk commercial electronic mail (*choose one or both*: through; into) the computer network of [*choose one or both*: an electronic mail service provider, (*name provider*); the subscribers of an electronic mail service provider, (*name provider*)].

[*To charge an aggravated misdemeanor, add the following language*: This violation caused damage to the property of another, (*name person or organization*), in an amount less than $2,500.] [*To charge a felony, replace "unlawfully and willfully" with "unlawfully, willfully, and feloniously" and add the following language*: This violation caused damage to the property of another, (*name person or organization*), in an amount of $2,500 or more.]

Notes about Charging Language:
- G.S. 14-453 defines many of the terms used in the charging language above.
- G.S. 14-458(a) defines "without authority."

Sample Charge:

[Felony computer trespass]

. . . unlawfully, willfully, and feloniously did without authority use a computer with the intent to permanently remove computer data from a computer network of Big Auto Parts Store, Inc., Monticello, N.C. This violation caused damage to the property of Big Auto Parts Store, Inc., in an amount of $2,500 or more.

AOC Forms for This Offense:

None.

Punishment:

A violation without any monetary damage is a Class 3 misdemeanor. A violation with monetary damage less than $2,500 is a Class 1 misdemeanor. A violation with monetary damage of $2,500 or more is a Class I felony.

G.S. 15A-1340.16A
Firearm or Deadly Weapon Enhancement
April 2024

Introductory Comment:
This charging form is to be used in preparing a bill of indictment or a criminal information—not an arrest warrant or the like—that alleges that the defendant is subject to an enhanced sentence under G.S. 15A-1340.16A. That statute, under certain circumstances, increases the minimum term of imprisonment when a defendant is convicted of a felony that the defendant committed by using, displaying, or threatening the use or display of a firearm or deadly weapon.

Charging Language:
The defendant committed the felony (*substitute* felonies *for* felony *if more than one felony is subject to the firearm enhancement*) alleged in this (*choose one*: bill of indictment; criminal information) by using, displaying, or threatening the use or display of a (*choose one*: firearm; deadly weapon), and the defendant did actually possess the (*choose one*: firearm; deadly weapon) about the defendant's person.

Notes about Charging Language:
- G.S. 15A-1340.16A(d) provides that the charging language set out above is sufficient to allege a firearm enhancement, and one pleading is sufficient for all qualifying felonies that are tried at a single trial.
- For the procedure used in proving a firearm enhancement, see G.S. 15A-1340.16A(e).

Sample Charge:
The defendant committed the felony alleged in this bill of indictment by using, displaying, or threatening the use or display of a firearm, and the defendant did actually possess the firearm about the defendant's person.

AOC Forms for This Offense:
None.

Punishment:
For Class A through E felonies, this enhancement increases the defendant's minimum term of imprisonment by 72 months and increases the defendant's maximum term by a corresponding amount. G.S. 15A-1340.16A(c)(1). For Class F and G felonies, this enhancement increases the defendant's minimum term of imprisonment by 36 months and increases the defendant's maximum term by a corresponding amount. G.S. 15A-1340.16A(c)(2). For Class H and I felonies, this enhancement increases the defendant's minimum term of imprisonment by 12 months and increases the defendant's maximum term by a corresponding amount. G.S. 15A-1340.16A(c)(3).

G.S. 15A-1340.16E
Criminal Gang Activity Enhancement
April 2024
Page 1 of 2

Introductory Comment:
This charging form is to be used in preparing a bill of indictment or a criminal information—not an arrest warrant or the like—that alleges that the defendant is subject to an enhanced sentence under G.S. 15A-1340.16E. That statute, under certain circumstances, increases the felony class level of the principal felony for which the person is convicted in cases where the offense was committed as part of criminal gang activity as defined in G.S. 14-50.16A(2).

Charging Language:
The defendant committed the felony (*substitute* felonies *for* felony *if more than one felony is subject to the criminal gang activity enhancement*) alleged in this (*choose one*: bill of indictment; criminal information) as part of criminal gang activity as defined in G.S. 14-50.16A(2). (*Describe the facts that indicate that the offense was committed as part of criminal gang activity*). (*If applicable, continue by alleging as follows*: The defendant is a criminal gang leader or organizer as defined in G.S. 14-50.16A(3).)

Notes about Charging Language:

- Several pertinent terms are defined in G.S. 14-50.16A. "Criminal gang activity" means "[t]he commission of, attempted commission of, or solicitation, coercion, or intimidation of another person to commit (i) any offense under Article 5 of Chapter 90 of the General Statutes or (ii) any offense under Chapter 14 of the General Statutes except Article 9, 22A, 40, 46, or 59 thereof, and further excepting G.S. 14-82, 14-145, 14-183, 14-184, 14-186, 14-190.9, 14-247, 14-248, or 14-313 thereof, and either of the following conditions is met: a. The offense is committed with the intent to benefit, promote, or further the interests of a criminal gang or for the purposes of increasing a person's own standing or position within a criminal gang. b. The participants in the offense are identified as criminal gang members acting individually or collectively to further any criminal purpose of a criminal gang."
- This punishment enhancement does not apply to Class A, B1, or B2 felonies. G.S. 15A-1340.16E(a).
- This punishment enhancement does not apply to any gang offense included under Article 13A of Chapter 14 of the General Statutes. G.S. 15A-1340.16E(f).
- One pleading alleging this punishment enhancement is sufficient for all felonies that are tried at a single trial. G.S. 15A-1340.16E(d).

Sample Charge:
The defendant committed the felony alleged in this bill of indictment as part of criminal gang activity as defined in G.S. 14-50.16A(2). The defendant committed the felony for the purposes of increasing his standing and position within a criminal gang.

AOC Forms for This Offense:
None.

Punishment:
If it is found that a principal felony was committed as part of criminal gang activity, the defendant shall be sentenced at a felony class level one class higher than would otherwise apply to the principal felony. G.S. 15A-1340.16E(a). If the defendant additionally is found to be a criminal gang leader or organizer, the defendant shall be sentenced at a felony level two classes higher than would otherwise apply to the principal felony. G.S. 15A-1340.16E(b).

No defendant sentenced pursuant to this punishment enhancement shall be sentenced at a level higher than a Class C felony. G.S. 15A-1340.16E(c). Any sentence imposed pursuant to this punishment enhancement shall run consecutively with and shall commence at the expiration of any sentence being served by the defendant. *Id.*

Important Definitions Concerning Alcoholic Beverages

April 2024

To understand the North Carolina alcoholic beverage law and to properly use these charging forms, it is essential to understand the terms used in Chapter 18B of the General Statutes for the different categories of alcoholic beverages.

Many of the charges in this publication are applicable only to fortified wine and spirituous liquor. Generally, malt beverages and unfortified wine may be possessed, consumed, and transported, except as restricted by Chapter 18B, while fortified wine, spirituous liquor, and mixed beverages may be possessed, consumed, and transported only as allowed by Chapter 18B.

Alcoholic beverage: beverage containing at least one-half of 1 percent (0.5%) alcohol by volume, including malt beverages, unfortified wine, fortified wine, spirituous liquor, and mixed beverages. G.S. 18B-101(4).

Malt beverage: beer, lager, malt liquor, ale, porter, and any other brewed or fermented beverage except unfortified or fortified wine containing at least one-half of 1 percent (0.5%) and not more than 15 percent (15%) of alcohol by volume. G.S. 18B-101(9).

Unfortified wine: any wine of 16 percent (16%) or less alcohol by volume made by fermentation from grapes, fruits, berries, rice, or honey; or by the addition of pure cane, beet, or dextrose sugar; or by the addition of pure brandy from the same type of grape, fruit, berry, rice, or honey that is contained in the base wine and produced in accordance with the regulations of the United States. G.S. 18B-101(15).

Fortified wine: any wine, of more than 16 percent (16%) and no more than 24 percent (24%) alcohol by volume, made by fermentation from grapes, fruits, berries, rice, or honey; or by the addition of pure cane, beet, or dextrose sugar; or by the addition of pure brandy from the same type of grape, fruit, berry, rice, or honey that is contained in the base wine and produced in accordance with the regulations of the United States. G.S. 18B-101(7).

Spirituous liquor: distilled spirits or ethyl alcohol, including spirits of wine, whiskey, rum, brandy, gin, and all other distilled spirits, including mixtures of cordials, liqueur, and pre-mixed cocktails, in closed containers for beverage use regardless of their dilution. G.S. 18B-101(14).

Mixed beverage: (1) a drink composed in whole or in part of spirituous liquor and served in a quantity less than the quantity contained in a closed package or (2) a pre-mixed cocktail served from a closed package containing only one serving. G.S. 18B-101(10).

G.S. 18B-111
Possession, Sale, or Transportation of Nontaxpaid Alcoholic Beverages
April 2024

Introductory Comment:
None.

Charging Language:
. . . unlawfully and willfully did [*choose one*: possess; sell to (*name person to whom sold*); transport] (*name or otherwise indicate kind of nontaxpaid alcoholic beverage; although not required, you may state the amount of the beverage*), an alcoholic beverage on which the taxes imposed by the (*choose one or both*: United States; State of North Carolina) had not been paid.

Notes about Charging Language:
- Since a court might rule that possession, sale, and transportation are separate offenses that must be separately charged (which is required with some drug offenses), it would be prudent to charge these three acts as separate offenses.
- The definition of "nontaxpaid alcoholic beverage" in G.S. 18B-101(11) includes an alcoholic beverage on which the United States tax, North Carolina tax, or tax of "any other territorial jurisdiction in which the alcoholic beverage was purchased" has not been paid. If the failure to pay tax arises from the purchase of an alcoholic beverage in "[an]other territorial jurisdiction," substitute that jurisdiction's name for "United States" or "State of North Carolina" and indicate that that jurisdiction is where the alcoholic beverage was purchased.

Sample Charge:
. . . unlawfully and willfully did possess seventeen gallons of whiskey, an alcoholic beverage on which the taxes imposed by the United States and by the State of North Carolina had not been paid.

AOC Forms for This Offense:
None.

Punishment:
Class 1 misdemeanor.

G.S. 18B-300/Local Ordinance
Public Possession or Consumption of Malt Beverage or Unfortified Wine
April 2024

G.S. 18B-300(c) provides that a city or county may by ordinance:

(1) Regulate or prohibit the consumption of malt beverages and unfortified wine on the public streets in that city or county by persons who are not occupants of motor vehicles and on property owned, occupied, or controlled by that city or county;

(2) Regulate or prohibit the possession of open containers of malt beverages and unfortified wine on public streets in that city or county by persons who are not occupants of motor vehicles and on property owned, occupied, or controlled by that city or county; and

(3) Regulate or prohibit the possession of malt beverages and unfortified wine on public streets, alleys, or parking lots which are temporarily closed to regular traffic for special events.

When charging a violation of a local ordinance enacted pursuant to this statute, carefully charge all the words of the ordinance and insert explanatory information such as the type of beverage (malt beverage or unfortified wine) and the name of the public street where the offense occurred. Be sure to include the citation and caption of the local ordinance, as is required by G.S. 160A-79.

AOC Forms for This Offense:
None.

Punishment:
Class 3 misdemeanor under G.S. 14-4.

G.S. 18B-300(b)
Consumption of Malt Beverages or Unfortified Wine on Premises with Off-Premises Permit Only
April 2024

Introductory Comment:
None.

Charging Language:

I. Consumption of malt beverage or unfortified wine

. . . unlawfully and willfully did consume (*choose one or both*: malt beverages; unfortified wine) on (*name premises*), premises having only an off-premises permit for the kind of alcoholic beverage being consumed.

II. Permittee allowing consumption of malt beverage or unfortified wine

. . . unlawfully and willfully did, as a permittee, allow [*name person(s) who consumed or state*: "person unknown" *or* "persons unknown"] to consume (*choose one or both*: malt beverages; unfortified wine) on (*name premises*), premises having only an off-premises permit for the kind of alcoholic beverage being consumed.

Notes about Charging Language:
None.

Sample Charge:

I. Consumption of malt beverage or unfortified wine

. . . unlawfully and willfully did consume malt beverages on Circle C convenience store grounds, Fairfield, N.C., premises having only an off-premises permit for the kind of alcoholic beverage being consumed.

AOC Forms for This Offense:
None.

Punishment:
Class 1 misdemeanor.

G.S. 18B-301(f)(1)
Consumption of Fortified Wine, Spirituous Liquor, or Mixed Beverages on Public Street or Highway
April 2024

Introductory Comment:
None.

Charging Language:
. . . unlawfully and willfully did (*choose one*: consume; offer to another person [*name person, if known*]) a (*choose one and describe*: fortified wine; spirituous liquor; mixed beverage), (*name or otherwise indicate kind of beverage*), while on a public (*choose one*: highway; street; road; sidewalk), (*name the highway, street, etc.*).

Notes about Charging Language:
It is not unlawful to consume fortified wine, spirituous liquor, or mixed beverages, or to offer such beverages to another person, on a public road, street, highway, or sidewalk when a consumer tasting authorized by G.S. 18B-1114.7 is being conducted. *See* G.S. 18B-301(f)(1)c. This appears to create a defense, so the nonexistence of an authorized consumer tasting is not an element of the offense that must be included in the charging document.

Sample Charge:
. . . unlawfully and willfully did consume a spirituous liquor, Jack Daniels bourbon, while on a public highway, U.S. 70 in Durham, N.C.

AOC Forms for This Offense:
None.

Punishment:
Class 1 misdemeanor. *See* G.S. 18B-102(b).

G.S. 18B-301(f)(2)
Public Display of Fortified Wine, Spirituous Liquor, or Mixed Beverages at Athletic Contest
April 2024

Introductory Comment:
None.

Charging Language:
. . . unlawfully and willfully did publicly display a (*insert appropriate term, such as* bottle *or* can) of (*name or otherwise indicate kind of beverage*), a (*choose one*: fortified wine; spirituous liquor; mixed beverage), while at an athletic contest, (*name or otherwise indicate what athletic contest*).

Notes about Charging Language:
None.

Sample Charge:
. . . unlawfully and willfully did publicly display a bottle of I.W. Harper bourbon, a spirituous liquor, while at an athletic contest, a football game between N.C. State and Wake Forest, in Raleigh, N.C.

AOC Forms for This Offense:
None.

Punishment:
Class 1 misdemeanor. *See* G.S. 18B-102(b).

G.S. 18B-301(f)(3), (4)

Possession or Consumption of Fortified Wine, Spirituous Liquor, or Mixed Beverages on Unauthorized Premises

April 2024

Page 1 of 2

Introductory Comment:

None.

Charging Language:

I. Possession or consumption **G.S. 18B-301(f)(4)**

. . . unlawfully and willfully did (*choose one or both*: possess; consume) a (*choose one*: fortified wine; spirituous liquor; mixed beverage) while on the premises at (*give address or other identification of premises*), where such (*choose one or both*: possession; consumption) is not authorized by law.

II. Permitting possession or consumption **G.S. 18B-301(f)(3)**

. . . unlawfully and willfully did permit (*name person who actually possessed or consumed the beverage*) to (*choose one or both*: possess; consume) a (*choose one*: fortified wine; spirituous liquor; mixed beverage) on the premises at (*give address or other identification of the premises*), where such (*choose one or both*: possession; consumption) is not authorized by Chapter 18B of the General Statutes.

Notes about Charging Language:

- Possession and consumption of spirituous liquor and fortified wine is permitted by G.S. 18B-301 in the following places: (1) a person's residence or the residence of another person with that person's consent; (2) a person's temporary residence, such as a hotel room; (3) other property not primarily used for commercial purposes and not open to the public when the alcoholic beverage is possessed, when possession and consumption is allowed by the owner or other person in charge of the property; (4) a private club with the appropriate permit from the State ABC Commission; (5) a restaurant or hotel having an appropriate permit; and (6) any other commercial establishment having a special-occasion permit from the State ABC Commission. The amount that may be possessed by a person is limited to 8 liters, unless that person is in his or her own home or a temporary residence or unless there is a private special occasion for which the person is the host. The owner and employees of a business with a mixed beverage permit may possess alcoholic beverages on those premises for resale as mixed beverages.
- As to Offense I, the statute also prohibits possession or consumption on premises where it would otherwise be permitted but where the owner or person in charge has forbidden possession or consumption. If that is the case, strike the words "is not authorized by law" and substitute "has been forbidden by" and name the person who did so and state whether that person is the owner or someone else in charge of the premises.
- Offense II will ordinarily be charged only against the owner or other person in charge of the premises where the possession or consumption took place.

Sample Charge:

I. Possession or consumption **G.S. 18B-301(f)(4)**

. . . unlawfully and willfully did possess and consume a spirituous liquor while on the premises at Harry's All-Nite Diner, 600 W. Jones Street, Wilmington, N.C., where such possession and consumption is not authorized by law.

AOC Forms for This Offense:
None.

Punishment:
Class 1 misdemeanor. *See* G.S. 18B-102(b).

G.S. 18B-301(f)(7)

Possession or Consumption of Malt Beverages or Unfortified Wine on Property Owned or Leased by a Local School Board

April 2024

Introductory Comment:
None.

Charging Language:
. . . unlawfully and willfully did (*choose one or both*: possess on the defendant's person; consume) a (*choose one and describe*: malt beverage; unfortified wine) at (*describe or give address of property*), property (*choose one*: owned; leased) by the (*name the board of education*), a local board of education, and used by that local board of education for school purposes.

Notes about Charging Language:
None.

Sample Charge:
. . . unlawfully and willfully did possess on the defendant's person a malt beverage, one 12-ounce can of Budweiser beer, at 1605 Old Oxford Road, Raleigh, N.C., property owned by the Wake County Board of Education, a local board of education, and used by that local board of education for school purposes.

AOC Forms for This Offense:
None.

Punishment:
Class 1 misdemeanor. *See* G.S. 18B-102(b).

G.S. 18B-302(a)(1), (a1)(1), (b)(1), (b)(3), (c)
Underage Offenses Involving Malt Beverages or Unfortified Wine
April 2024
Page 1 of 2

Introductory Comment:
None.

Charging Language:

I. Sale or giving to person under 21 **G.S. 18B-302(a)(1), (a1)(1)**

. . . unlawfully and willfully did (*choose one*: sell; give) (*describe alcoholic beverage sold or given*), a (*choose one*: malt beverage; unfortified wine), to (*name person to whom the beverage was sold or given*), who was at the time under 21 years of age.

II. Purchase, possession, or consumption by person under 21 **G.S. 18B-302(b)(1), (b)(3)**

. . . unlawfully and willfully did, while under 21 years of age, namely, (*give age*), (*choose one*: purchase; attempt to purchase; possess; consume) (*describe beverage bought*), a (*choose one*: malt beverage; unfortified wine) [*if alleging a purchase or an attempted purchase add the following*: from (*name person from whom or store where the beverage was bought*)].

III. Aiding or abetting while under 21 **G.S. 18B-302(c)(1)**

. . . unlawfully and willfully did, while under 21 years of age, aid and abet (*name person aided or abetted*) in (*insert charging language for the offense aided and abetted, such as*: while under 21, possessing a 40-ounce bottle of King Cobra, a malt beverage). The defendant did (*state the way in which defendant aided and abetted*).

IV. Aiding or abetting while over 21 **G.S. 18B-302(c)(2)**

. . . unlawfully and willfully did, while being 21 years of age or over, aid and abet (*name person aided or abetted*) in (*insert charging language for the offense aided and abetted, such as*: while under 21, possessing a 40-ounce bottle of King Cobra, a malt beverage). The defendant did (*state the way in which defendant aided and abetted*).

Notes about Charging Language:

- As to Offense I, there is no requirement that the State prove that a sale of a malt beverage or unfortified wine to an underage person was made knowingly. However, it is a defense if the seller can prove that he or she was presented with certain forms of identification, listed in G.S. 18B-302(d). The separate offense of fraudulently loaning or using a driver's license or other identification to make an underage purchase, in violation of G.S. 18B-302(e), is covered by a separate charging form provided in this publication.
- G.S. 18B-302(h) permits an underage person to possess, sell, etc., alcoholic beverages in the course of employment if that person's employment is otherwise lawful.

Sample Charge:

I. Sale or giving to person under 21 **G.S. 18B-302(a)(1), (a1)(1)**

. . . unlawfully and willfully did sell one bottle of Pabst Blue Ribbon beer, a malt beverage, to James Evans Montgomery, who was at the time under 21 years of age.

AOC Forms for This Offense:
None.

Punishment:
Offense II is a Class 3 misdemeanor if committed by a person who is 19 or 20 years old. *See* G.S. 18B-302(i). Offense III is a Class 2 misdemeanor. All other offenses are Class 1 misdemeanors. In some instances, special sentencing and driver's license penalties are required by the statute. *See generally* G.S. 18B-302.1; -302(g).

Introductory Comment:
None.

Charging Language:

I. Sale or giving to person under 21 **G.S. 18B-302(a)(2), (a1)(2)**

. . . unlawfully and willfully did (*choose one*: sell; give) (*describe alcoholic beverage sold or given*), a (*choose one*: fortified wine; spirituous liquor), to (*name person to whom the beverage was sold or given*), who was at the time under 21 years of age.

II. Purchase, possession, or consumption by person under 21 **G.S. 18B-302(b)(2), (b)(3)**

. . . unlawfully and willfully did, while under 21 years of age, namely, (*give age*), (*choose one*: purchase; attempt to purchase; possess; consume) (*describe beverage bought*), a (*choose one*: fortified wine; spirituous liquor) [*if alleging a purchase or an attempted purchase add the following*: from (*name person from whom or store where the beverage was bought*)].

III. Aiding or abetting while under 21 **G.S. 18B-302(c)(1)**

. . . unlawfully and willfully did, while under 21 years of age, aid and abet (*name person aided or abetted*) in (*insert charging language for the offense aided and abetted, such as*: while under 21 years of age, namely, 18 years old, possessing one pint of Wild Turkey bourbon, a spirituous liquor). The defendant did (*state the way in which defendant aided and abetted*).

IV. Aiding or abetting while over 21 **G.S. 18B-302(c)(2)**

. . . unlawfully and willfully did, while being 21 years of age or over, aid and abet (*name person aided or abetted*) in (*insert charging language for the offense aided and abetted, such as*: while under 21 years of age, namely, 18 years old, possessing one pint of Wild Turkey bourbon, a spirituous liquor). The defendant did (*state the way in which defendant aided and abetted*).

Notes about Charging Language:

- As to Offense I, there is no requirement that the State prove that a sale of a fortified wine or spirituous liquor to an underage person was made knowingly. However, it is a defense if the seller can prove that he or she was presented with certain forms of identification, listed in G.S. 18B-302(d). The separate offense of fraudulently loaning or using a driver's license or other identification to make an underage purchase, in violation of G.S. 18B-302(e), is covered by a separate charging form provided in this publication.
- G.S. 18B-302(h) permits an underage person to possess, sell, etc., alcoholic beverages in the course of employment if that person's employment is otherwise lawful.

Sample Charge:

IV. Aiding or abetting while over 21 **G.S. 18B-302(c)(2)**

. . . unlawfully and willfully did, while being 21 years of age or over, aid and abet Trina Spinks in, while under 21 years of age, namely, 18 years old, purchasing one 750-milliter bottle of Wild Irish Rose, a fortified wine. The defendant did drive Trina Spinks to an AM/PM mini market to purchase the fortified wine.

AOC Forms for This Offense:

None.

Punishment:

Offense II is a Class 3 misdemeanor if committed by a person who is 19 or 20 years old. *See* G.S. 18B-302(i). Offense III is a Class 2 misdemeanor. All other offenses are Class 1 misdemeanors. In some instances, special sentencing and driver's license penalties are required by the statute. *See generally* G.S. 18B-302.1; -302(g).

G.S. 18B-302(a)(2), (a1)(2), (b)(2), (b)(3), (c)
Underage Offenses Involving Mixed Beverages
April 2024
Page 1 of 2

Introductory Comment:
None.

Charging Language:

I. Sale or giving to person under 21 **G.S. 18B-302(a)(2), (a1)(2)**

. . . unlawfully and willfully did (*choose one*: sell; give) a (*describe drink sufficiently to establish its character as a mixed beverage*), a mixed beverage, to (*name person to whom the beverage was sold or given*), who was at the time under 21 years of age.

II. Purchase, possession, or consumption by person under 21 **G.S. 18B-302(b)(2), (b)(3)**

. . . unlawfully and willfully did, while under 21 years of age, namely, (*give age*), (*choose one*: purchase; attempt to purchase; possess; consume) a (*describe drink sufficiently to establish its character as a mixed beverage*), a mixed beverage, [*if alleging a purchase or an attempted purchase add the following*: from (*name person from whom or store where the beverage was bought*)].

III. Aiding or abetting while under 21 **G.S. 18B-302(c)(1)**

. . . unlawfully and willfully did, while under 21 years of age, aid and abet (*name person aided or abetted*) in (*insert charging language for the offense aided and abetted, such as*: while under 21 years of age, namely, 18 years old, possessing one rum and Coke cocktail, a mixed beverage). The defendant did (*state the way in which defendant aided and abetted*).

IV. Aiding or abetting while over 21 **G.S. 18B-302(c)(2)**

. . . unlawfully and willfully did, while being 21 years of age or over, aid and abet (*name person aided or abetted*) in (*insert charging language for the offense aided and abetted, such as*: while under 21 years of age, namely, 18 years old, possessing one rum and Coke cocktail, a mixed beverage). The defendant did (*state the way in which defendant aided and abetted*).

Notes about Charging Language:

- As to Offense I, there is no requirement that the State prove that a sale of a mixed beverage to an underage person was made knowingly. However, it is a defense if the seller can prove that he or she was presented with certain forms of identification, listed in G.S. 18B-302(d). The separate offense of fraudulently loaning or using a driver's license or other identification to make an underage purchase, in violation of G.S. 18B-302(e), is covered by a separate charging form provided in this publication.
- G.S. 18B-302(h) permits an underage person to possess, sell, etc., alcoholic beverages in the course of employment if that person's employment is otherwise lawful.

Sample Charge:

III. Aiding or abetting while under 21 **G.S. 18B-302(c)(1)**

. . . unlawfully and willfully did, while under 21 years of age, aid and abet Frankie Titelbaum in, while under 21 years of age, namely, 18 years old, possessing one Long Island iced tea cocktail containing vodka, tequila, rum, and other ingredients, a mixed beverage. The defendant did permit Frankie Titelbaum to store the mixed beverage in the defendant's car.

AOC Forms for This Offense:
None.

Punishment:
Offense II is a Class 3 misdemeanor if committed by a person who is 19 or 20 years old. *See* G.S. 18B-302(i). Offense III is a Class 2 misdemeanor. All other offenses are Class 1 misdemeanors. In some instances, special sentencing and driver's license penalties are required by the statute. *See generally* G.S. 18B-302.1; -302(g).

G.S. 18B-302(e), (f)
Fraudulent Use or Loan of Identification to Commit Underage Offense
April 2024

Introductory Comment:
None.

Charging Language:

I. Use of identification **G.S. 18B-302(e)**

. . . unlawfully and willfully did (*choose one*: use; attempt to use) a [*choose one*: fraudulent or altered driver's license; driver's license issued to another person; fraudulent or altered identification document other than a driver's license; identification document other than a driver's license issued to another person, (*name person whose identification was used and describe identification if it is other than a driver's license*); form or means of identification that indicates or symbolizes that the person is not prohibited from purchasing or possessing alcoholic beverages, (*describe form or means of identification*)] to (*choose one*: purchase; attempt to purchase) (*state kind and amount of the alcoholic beverage*), a (*choose one*: malt beverage; unfortified wine; fortified wine; spirituous liquor; mixed beverage), while under the age of 21, from (*state person and place making the sale*).

II. Allowing use of identification **G.S. 18B-302(f)**

. . . unlawfully and willfully did permit the use of the defendant's [(*choose one*: driver's license; form of identification issued or given to the defendant, (*describe the form if it is anything other than a driver's license*)], by (*name the person*), who at the time was under 21 years of age, to (*choose one*: purchase; attempt to purchase) (*state kind and amount of alcoholic beverage*), a (*choose one*: malt beverage; unfortified wine; fortified wine; spirituous liquor; mixed beverage), from (*state person and place making the sale*).

Notes about Charging Language:

- A person who loans his or her driver's license or other identification document for the purpose of facilitating an underage purchase can also be charged under the aiding or abetting provisions of G.S. 18B-302(c).

Sample Charge:

II. Allowing use of identification **G.S. 18B-302(f)**

. . . unlawfully and willfully did permit the use of the defendant's driver's license by Michael Byrd Smith, who at the time was under 21 years of age, to attempt to purchase one bottle of Pabst Blue Ribbon beer, a malt beverage, from Wanda LaFlore at A & F Grocery in Eastgate Shopping Center, Chapel Hill, N.C.

AOC Forms for This Offense:
None.

Punishment:
Class 1 misdemeanor. A conviction also requires revocation of the defendant's driver's license under G.S. 20-17.3.

G.S. 18B-303
Sale of More Alcoholic Beverage Than Allowed
April 2024

Introductory Comment:
None.

Charging Language:
. . . unlawfully and willfully did, while employed at and while on the premises of (*name licensed premises*), premises licensed for the sale of (*choose one or more*: malt beverages; unfortified wine; fortified wine; spirituous liquor), sell to (*name person to whom sale was made*) (*indicate kind and amount of alcoholic beverage sold or delivered*), which was [*choose one*: more than 80 liters of malt beverages, not in kegs; more than 50 liters of unfortified wine; more than 8 liters of spirituous liquor; more than 8 liters of fortified wine; more than 8 liters of spirituous liquor and fortified wine combined; more than the amount of (*give amount*) of (*name type of alcoholic beverages permitted by permit*) permitted by a purchase-transportation permit issued under (*choose one*: G.S. 18B-403; G.S. 18B-403.1)].

Notes about Charging Language:

- This statute also makes it a violation to purchase alcoholic beverages over the amount allowed. Modify this charging form if an illegal purchase is to be charged.
- Amounts greater than those listed above may be purchased with a purchase-transportation permit under G.S. 18B-403.
- Under G.S. 18B-303(d), a "mixed beverage permittee, or an employee of a mixed beverage permittee, may purchase and transport any amount of fortified wine or spiritous liquor for use by the mixed beverage permittee without obtaining a purchase-transportation permit."
- Draft malt beverages sold in kegs to a permittee for on-premises consumption may be sold in unlimited quantities. G.S. 18B-303(a)(2). Such beverages sold in kegs for off-premises consumption are subject to the limits contained in the permit required by G.S. 18B-403.1(a).

Sample Charge:
. . . unlawfully and willfully did, while employed at and while on the premises of Food Goods Grocery Store, premises licensed for the sale of malt beverages, sell to Howard Jones more than 100 liters of Budweiser beer, which was more than 80 liters of malt beverages, not in kegs.

AOC Forms for This Offense:
None.

Punishment:
Class 1 misdemeanor.

G.S. 18B-304

Sale of Alcoholic Beverage without a Permit or License

April 2024

Introductory Comment:

None.

Charging Language:

. . . unlawfully and willfully did (*choose one*: possess for sale; sell) an alcoholic beverage, (*describe the alcoholic beverage and the amount, if desired*), without first obtaining the applicable (*choose one or both*: ABC permit; revenue licenses).

Notes about Charging Language:

- The statute provides that a prima facie case of possession for unlawful sale is established by showing that the person possessed more than 8 liters of spirituous liquor, more than 80 liters of malt beverages (other than draft malt beverages in kegs), or any amount of nontaxpaid alcoholic beverages. (The statute does not establish amounts to establish prima facie evidence for possessing fortified or unfortified wine.) It is unnecessary to allege an amount in a criminal pleading to use the prima facie evidence rule at trial.
- This form may also be used in charging a permit holder for sale of a kind of alcoholic beverage for which he or she is not licensed.
- G.S. 18B-111 prohibits the possession or sale of nontaxpaid alcoholic beverages, except as authorized by Chapter 18B or Chapter 105 (the revenue laws). A form for charging that offense is contained in this manual.

Sample Charge:

. . . unlawfully and willfully did possess for sale an alcoholic beverage, 9 liters of Jack Daniels bourbon, without first obtaining the applicable ABC permit and revenue licenses.

AOC Forms for This Offense:

None.

Punishment:

Class 1 misdemeanor.

G.S. 18B-305(a)
Sale to Intoxicated Person
April 2024

Introductory Comment:
None.

Charging Language:
. . . unlawfully and willfully did, while employed at and while on the premises of (*name licensed premises*), premises licensed for the retail sale of (*choose one or more*: malt beverages; unfortified wine; fortified wine; spirituous liquor; mixed beverages), knowingly sell (*indicate kind and amount of alcoholic beverage sold*), a (*choose one*: malt beverage; unfortified wine; fortified wine; spirituous liquor; mixed beverage) to (*name intoxicated person to whom beverage was sold*), who was intoxicated at the time of the sale.

Notes about Charging Language:
- If the person making the sale is the permit holder rather than an employee, make the appropriate change in language.
- The statute also is violated when a person gives an alcoholic beverage to an intoxicated person. If so, substitute "give" for the word "sell."

Sample Charge:
. . . unlawfully and willfully did, while employed at and on the premises of Old Towne Tavern, premises licensed for the retail sale of malt beverages, knowingly sell four bottles of Budweiser, a malt beverage, to Joseph Talley, who was intoxicated at the time of sale.

AOC Forms for This Offense:
None.

Punishment:
Class 1 misdemeanor.

G.S. 18B-307(b)
Manufacturing Alcoholic Beverage
April 2024

Introductory Comment:
A second or subsequent offense under this section is a felony rather than a misdemeanor. In such a case, state "unlawfully, willfully, and feloniously" rather than "unlawfully and willfully." An indictment or an information for the recidivist offense must comply with G.S. 15A-928, which requires that the defendant's prior convictions be alleged either (1) in a separate count of the indictment or information than the substantive offense or (2) in a separate indictment or information. In such a case, the separate count or separate indictment should set forth the date and court in which the prior conviction occurred. This requirement does not apply to arrest warrants or magistrates' orders, which still must allege the defendant's prior convictions but need not do so in a separate count or separate charging instrument. G.S. 15A-928 also requires that the name or title of an offense elevated by prior convictions must not make reference to such prior convictions.

Charging Language:
. . . unlawfully and willfully did manufacture (*choose one or more*: spirituous liquor; fortified wine; unfortified wine; malt beverage), an alcoholic beverage, without first obtaining the applicable ABC permit and revenue licenses.

Notes about Charging Language:
- G.S. 18B-307(b) excepts from this offense the manufacture of an alcoholic beverage with a Brew on Premises permit issued under G.S. 18B-1001(14) or a Winemaking on Premises permit issued under G.S. 18B-1001(17).
- It is likewise not a violation of this section to manufacture, under the conditions specified in G.S. 18B-306, native wines and malt beverages for one's own use and the use of one's family and guests.

Sample Charge:
. . . unlawfully and willfully did manufacture spirituous liquor, an alcoholic beverage, without first obtaining the applicable ABC permit and revenue licenses.

AOC Forms for This Offense:
None.

Punishment:
Class 1 misdemeanor. A second offense is a Class I felony.

G.S. 18B-401, -406
Unlawful Transportation of Spirituous Liquor or Fortified Wine
April 2024
Page 1 of 2

Introductory Comment:
None.

Charging Language:

I. Transporting more than allowed by law **G.S. 18B-406**

. . . unlawfully and willfully did transport in the defendant's motor vehicle (*indicate amount of beverage transported*) of (*name or indicate kind of beverage transported*), a (*choose one*: fortified wine; spirituous liquor), which transportation was not authorized by law.

II. Transporting open container in passenger area **G.S. 18B-401(a)**

. . . unlawfully and willfully did transport (*choose one*: fortified wine; spirituous liquor) in the passenger area of a motor vehicle in other than the manufacturer's unopened original container.

III. Transportation by taxi without passenger **G.S. 18B-401(b)**

. . . unlawfully and willfully did transport (*choose one*: fortified wine; spirituous liquor) in a (*describe the taxi*), a for-hire passenger vehicle that the defendant was operating at the time, without the owner of that beverage as a paying passenger.

Notes about Charging Language:

- For Offense I, the statute does not require that the transportation must be by motor vehicle, although that is the most likely means. If some other form of transportation was used, strike "in the defendant's motor vehicle" and either add another appropriate phrase or simply do not allege the form of transportation.
- For Offense I, G.S. 18B-303 and -400 only allow transportation of up to 8 liters of spirituous liquor or fortified wine, or any combination of the two (or 40 liters with the proper permit, *see* G.S. 18B-403). The 8-liter limit applies regardless of the number of people in the vehicle. A greater amount may be transported by a mixed beverage permit holder with a purchase-transportation permit. If the restrictions of such a permit are not followed, this form could be used to charge that unlawful transportation.
- For Offense II, no minimum quantity is required.
- For Offense II, G.S. 18B-401(c) states that a container of alcoholic beverages is considered "opened" if the container's seal has been broken. Thus, transporting the beverage with a broken seal on the original container is unlawful, as is transporting the beverage in any container, open or closed, other than the manufacturer's original container.
- For Offense III, G.S. 20-4.01(27)f. defines "for-hire passenger vehicles."

Sample Charge:

I. Transporting more than allowed by law **G.S. 18B-406**

. . . unlawfully and willfully did transport in the defendant's motor vehicle 8.75 liters of Beefeaters gin (five 1.75-liter bottles), a spirituous liquor, which transportation was not authorized by law.

AOC Forms for This Offense:
None.

Punishment:
Offenses I and III are Class 1 misdemeanors. Offense II is a Class 3 misdemeanor.

G.S. 18B-401(a)
Consumption of Malt Beverage or Unfortified Wine by Driver of Motor Vehicle
April 2024

Introductory Comment:
None.

Charging Language:
. . . unlawfully and willfully did, while driving a motor vehicle, (*describe the vehicle*), on a (*choose one*: highway; public vehicular area), (*indicate the location where the violation occurred*), consume in that vehicle's passenger area a (*choose one*: malt beverage; unfortified wine), (*name or indicate kind of beverage consumed*).

Notes about Charging Language:
None.

Sample Charge:
. . . unlawfully and willfully did, while driving a motor vehicle, a 2004 Ford pickup truck, on a highway, U.S. 70 in Raleigh, N.C., consume in that vehicle's passenger area a malt beverage, a Budweiser beer.

AOC Forms for This Offense:
None.

Punishment:
Class 3 misdemeanor.

G.S. 18B-1004

Sale of Malt Beverages, Wine, or Mixed Beverages Outside Permitted Hours

April 2024

Page 1 of 2

Introductory Comment:

None.

Charging Language:

I. Sale between 2:00 a.m. and 7:00 a.m. **G.S. 18B-1004(a)**

. . . unlawfully and willfully did sell a (*choose one*: malt beverage; unfortified wine; fortified wine; mixed beverage) to (*name person to whom the beverage was sold*) between the hours of 2:00 a.m. and 7:00 a.m. in a place, (*name place*), that has been issued a permit under G.S. 18B-1001.

II. Sale before 12:00 noon on Sunday **G.S. 18B-1004(c)**

. . . unlawfully and willfully did sell a (*choose one*: malt beverage; unfortified wine; fortified wine; mixed beverage) to (*name person to whom the beverage was sold*) between 2:00 a.m., the time at which the sale of alcoholic beverages must cease on Sunday morning, (*give date*), and 12:00 noon, that same Sunday, in a licensed premise, (*name place*).

III. Local ordinance prohibiting Sunday sales **G.S. 18B-1004(d)**

. . . unlawfully and willfully did [*if a city ordinance was violated, insert here*: within the city limits of (*name city*)] sell at retail a (*choose one*: malt beverage; unfortified wine; fortified wine) to (*name person to whom the beverage was sold*) between the hour of 12:00 noon on Sunday (*give date*) and the hour of 7:00 a.m. on the following Monday, in violation of (*give citation and caption of local ordinance prohibiting sale*).

Notes about Charging Language:

- For Offense I, the statute also prohibits consumption of these alcoholic beverages between 2:30 a.m. and 7:00 a.m. Make appropriate changes to the charging language if charging such an offense.
- For Offense II, the statute also prohibits consumption of these alcoholic beverages from the time consumption must cease on Sunday morning, 2:30 a.m., until 12:00 noon on Sunday. Make appropriate changes to the charging language if charging such an offense.
- For Offense III, G.S. 160A-79(a) requires that both the section number and caption of the local ordinance be included.
- For Offense III, note that if the sale takes place after 2:00 a.m. on Monday morning, charge I could be used instead. As indicated below, the punishment is greater for charge I than for charge III.
- For Offense II, under G.S. 18B-112(b1), 153A-145.7, and 160A-205.3, the Eastern Band of Cherokee Indians, counties, and cities may adopt ordinances allowing for the sale of these alcoholic beverages beginning at 10:00 a.m. on Sunday.

G.S. 18B-1004
Sale of Malt Beverages, Wine, or Mixed Beverages Outside Permitted Hours
April 2024
Page 2 of 2

Sample Charge:

I. Sale between 2:00 a.m. and 7:00 a.m. **G.S. 18B-1004(a)**

. . . unlawfully and willfully did sell a malt beverage to Peter Jenkins between the hours of 2:00 a.m. and 7:00 a.m. in a place, Joe's Bar & Grill, Manic, N.C., that has been issued a permit under G.S. 18B-1001.

AOC Forms for This Offense:
None.

Punishment:
Offenses I and II are Class 1 misdemeanors. Offense III is a Class 3 misdemeanor under G.S. 14-4.

G.S. 20-71(a)
Altering or Forging Certificate of Title, Registration Card, or Application
April 2024

Introductory Comment:
This form contains charging language for cases involving the forging, counterfeiting, or fraudulent alteration of motor vehicle titles and registration cards. In addition to these offenses, G.S. 20-71(a) also criminalizes the falsification or forgery of assignments of title and the knowing use of certain forged, altered, or falsified documents. This form does not contain charging language for those offenses or for the offenses regarding blank motor vehicle titles set forth in G.S. 20-71(b).

Charging Language:
I. Altering certificate of title or registration card

. . . unlawfully, willfully, and feloniously did with fraudulent intent alter (*choose one*: a certificate of title; a registration card issued by the North Carolina Division of Motor Vehicles; an application for a certificate of title; an application for a registration card issued by the North Carolina Division of Motor Vehicles) by (*describe way in which the document was altered*).

II. Forging or counterfeiting certificate of title or registration card

. . . unlawfully, willfully, and feloniously did with fraudulent intent (*choose one*: forge; counterfeit) (*choose one*: a certificate of title; a registration card) purported to have been issued by the North Carolina Division of Motor Vehicles under the provisions of Article 3 of Chapter 20 of the North Carolina General Statutes by (*describe forgery or counterfeiting*).

Sample Charge:
I. Altering certificate of title or registration card

. . . unlawfully, willfully, and feloniously did with fraudulent intent alter a registration card issued by the North Carolina Division of Motor Vehicles by making it appear as if it had been issued for a 2008 Toyota Camry having the VIN 123456 when in fact the registration card was issued for a 2006 Toyota Camry having the VIN 654321.

AOC Forms for This Offense:
None.

Punishment:
G.S. 20-71(a) provides that a person who commits any of these offenses "shall be guilty of a felony and upon conviction thereof shall be punished in the discretion of the court." Pursuant to G.S. 20-177, that means that the person shall be punished as a Class I felon.

G.S. 20-130.1
Use of Red or Blue Lights
April 2024

Introductory Comment:
None.

Charging Language:
. . . unlawfully and willfully did (*choose one or more*: install; activate; operate) a [*choose one or both*: red light, within the meaning of G.S. 20-130.1(a); blue light, within the meaning of G.S. 20-130.1(c)], (*choose one*: in; on) a vehicle, (*describe vehicle*).

Notes about Charging Language:
- The statute also makes it illegal to possess a blue light. In an appropriate case, modify the charging language accordingly.
- The statute contains a list of exceptions, that is, a list of permitted uses of red and blue lights. G.S. 20-130.1(b), (c1).

Sample Charge:
. . . unlawfully and willfully did activate a blue light, within the meaning of G.S. 20-130.1(c), on a vehicle, a 1993 Chevrolet Caprice.

AOC Forms for This Offense:
None.

Punishment:
Class 1 misdemeanor.

G.S. 20-138.1
Impaired Driving
April 2024

Introductory Comment:
None.

Charging Language:
. . . unlawfully and willfully did drive a vehicle on (*name or describe highway or public vehicular area*), a (*choose one*: highway; public vehicular area), while subject to an impairing substance.

Notes about Charging Language:
- The charging language above is specifically authorized by G.S. 20-138.1(c), which states that "the pleading is sufficient if it states the time and place of the alleged offense in the usual form and charges that the defendant drove a vehicle on a highway or public vehicular area while subject to an impairing substance" Alleging the date on which the offense took place is a sufficient statement of the "time" of the offense. *See* State v. Friend, 219 N.C. App. 338, 347 (2012) (concluding that "the date of the offense is a sufficient allegation of time").
- "Vehicle" is defined in G.S. 20-4.01(49). However, G.S. 20-138.1(e) provides, in effect, that this offense is not applicable to a horse.
- "Highway" is defined in G.S. 20-4.01(13).
- "Public vehicular area" is defined in G.S. 20-4.01(32).
- "Impairing substance" is defined in G.S. 20-4.01(14a).

Sample Charge:
. . . unlawfully and willfully did drive a vehicle on U.S. 70 in Durham, N.C., a highway, while subject to an impairing substance.

AOC Forms for This Offense:
None.

Punishment:
Misdemeanor, punishable at one of six sentencing levels depending on the existence of grossly aggravating, aggravating, and mitigating factors determined at a sentencing hearing. See G.S. 20-179 for each of the six sentencing levels.

G.S. 20-138.2
Impaired Driving in Commercial Vehicle
April 2024

Introductory Comment:
None.

Charging Language:
. . . unlawfully and willfully did drive a commercial motor vehicle on (*name or describe highway or public vehicular area*), a (*choose one*: highway; public vehicular area), while subject to an impairing substance.

Notes about Charging Language:
- The charging language above is specifically authorized by G.S. 20-138.2(c).
- "Commercial motor vehicle" is defined in G.S. 20-4.01(3d).
- "Highway" is defined in G.S. 20-4.01(13).
- "Public vehicular area" is defined in G.S. 20-4.01(32).
- "Impairing substance" is defined in G.S. 20-4.01(14a).

Sample Charge:
. . . unlawfully and willfully did drive a commercial motor vehicle on Interstate 40 in Asheville, N.C., a highway, while subject to an impairing substance.

AOC Forms for This Offense:
None.

Punishment:
Misdemeanor, punishable at one of five sentencing levels depending on the existence of grossly aggravating, aggravating, and mitigating factors determined at a sentencing hearing. See G.S. 20-179 for each of the five sentencing levels.

G.S. 20-138.5
Habitual Impaired Driving
April 2024
Page 1 of 2

Introductory Comment:
An indictment or an information for this offense must comply with G.S. 15A-928, which requires that the defendant's prior convictions be alleged either (1) in a separate count of the indictment or information than the substantive offense or (2) in a separate indictment or information. This requirement does not apply to arrest warrants or magistrates' orders, which explains why two sets of charging language appear below.

G.S. 15A-928 also requires that an "improvised name or title" be used so that the title of the indictment or information does not refer to the defendant's prior convictions. Therefore, an indictment or information charging habitual impaired driving should be captioned "impaired driving under G.S. 20-138.5" or something similar.

Charging Language:

I. Charging language for an arrest warrant or a magistrate's order

. . . unlawfully, willfully, and feloniously did drive a vehicle on (*name or describe highway or public vehicular area*), a (*choose one*: highway; public vehicular area), while subject to an impairing substance and, within ten years of the date of this offense, has been convicted of three or more offenses involving impaired driving. The defendant has been previously convicted on (1) (*give date of conviction, offense, and court in which conviction occurred*); (2) (*give date of conviction, offense, and court in which conviction occurred*); and (3) (*give date of conviction, offense, and court in which conviction occurred*).

II. Charging language for an indictment or information

First count in indictment or information

. . . unlawfully, willfully, and feloniously did drive a vehicle on (*name or describe highway or public vehicular area*), a (*choose one*: highway; public vehicular area), while subject to an impairing substance.

Second count in indictment or information

Within ten years of the date of the offense charged above, the defendant has been convicted of three or more offenses involving impaired driving. The defendant has been previously convicted on (1) (*give date of conviction, offense, and court in which conviction occurred*); (2) (*give date of conviction, offense, and court in which conviction occurred*); and (3) (*give date of conviction, offense, and court in which conviction occurred*).

Notes about Charging Language:

- The charging language used above to charge the current impaired driving offense is specifically authorized by G.S. 20-138.1(c).
- The misdemeanor offense of impaired driving, G.S. 20-138.1, is a lesser-included offense of habitual impaired driving. Therefore, it is not necessary to charge the misdemeanor offense when charging habitual impaired driving.
- "Vehicle" is defined in G.S. 20-4.01(49).
- "Highway" is defined in G.S. 20-4.01(13).
- "Public vehicular area" is defined in G.S. 20-4.01(32).

- "Impairing substance" is defined in G.S. 20-4.01(14a).
- "Offense involving impaired driving" is defined in G.S. 20-4.01(24a).
- "Conviction" is defined in G.S. 20-4.01(4a). It includes, for example, out-of-state convictions. A conviction must have occurred within ten years of the date of the impaired driving offense.
- More than three prior convictions may be alleged. It may be useful to do so because if the State is unable to prove a particular prior conviction at trial, it may still be able to prove three other prior convictions alleged in the criminal pleading.

Sample Charges:

I. Sample arrest warrant or magistrate's order

. . . unlawfully, willfully, and feloniously did drive a vehicle on U.S. 70 in Raleigh, N.C., a highway, while subject to an impairing substance and, within ten years of the date of this offense, has been convicted of three or more offenses involving impaired driving. The defendant has been previously convicted on (1) April 1, 2015, of impaired driving in Durham County District Court; (2) March 6, 2017, of felony death by vehicle in Wake County Superior Court; and (3) January 4, 2018, of impaired driving in Durham County District Court.

II. Sample indictment or information

First count in indictment or information

. . . unlawfully, willfully, and feloniously did drive a vehicle on U.S. 70 in Raleigh, N.C., a highway, while subject to an impairing substance.

Second count in indictment or information

Within ten years of the offense charged above, the defendant has been convicted of three or more offenses involving impaired driving. The defendant has been previously convicted on (1) April 1, 2015, of impaired driving in Durham County District Court; (2) March 6, 2017, of felony death by vehicle in Wake County Superior Court; and (3) January 4, 2018, of impaired driving in Durham County District Court.

AOC Forms for This Offense:

AOC-CR-154 (Indictment)

Punishment:

Class F felony, with additional sentencing requirements set forth in G.S. 20-138.5(b).

G.S. 20-138.7
Transporting Open Container of Alcoholic Beverage After Consuming Alcohol
April 2024

Introductory Comment:
None.

Charging Language:
. . . unlawfully and willfully did drive a motor vehicle on (*name or describe highway or the right-of-way of a highway*), a (*choose one*: highway; right-of-way of a highway) with an open container of alcoholic beverage after drinking.

Notes about Charging Language:
- G.S. 20-138.7(g) provides that the language above is sufficient to charge this offense.
- "Motor vehicle" is defined in G.S. 20-4.01(23).
- "Highway" is defined in G.S. 20-4.01(13).
- A second or subsequent violation of this statute is subject to elevated punishment. An indictment or an information for the recidivist offense must comply with G.S. 15A-928, which requires that the defendant's prior convictions be alleged either (1) in a separate count of the indictment or information than the substantive offense or (2) in a separate indictment or information. In such a case, the separate count or separate indictment should set forth the date and court in which the prior conviction occurred. This requirement does not apply to arrest warrants or magistrates' orders, which still must allege the defendant's prior convictions but need not do so in a separate count or separate charging instrument. Also note that in situations where a conviction for the recidivist offense is appealed from district to superior court for trial de novo, G.S. 15A-922(h) and -928(d) require the State to replace the pleading in the case with superseding statements of charges separately alleging the substantive offense and any prior convictions. G.S. 15A-928 also requires that the name or title of an offense elevated by prior convictions must not make reference to such prior convictions.

Sample Charge:
. . . unlawfully and willfully did drive a motor vehicle on U.S. 64 in Raleigh, N.C., a highway, with an open container of alcoholic beverage after drinking.

AOC Forms for This Offense:
None.

Punishment:
Class 3 misdemeanor. For a second or subsequent offense, Class 2 misdemeanor.

G.S. 20-141.3
Racing
April 2024

Introductory Comment:
None.

Charging Language:

I. Prearranged racing **G.S. 20-141.3(a)**

. . . unlawfully and willfully did operate a motor vehicle, (*describe vehicle*), on (*name highway*), a highway, in a prearranged speed competition with another motor vehicle, (*give description of other vehicle and driver's name, if known*).

II. Willful racing **G.S. 20-141.3(b)**

. . . unlawfully and willfully did operate a motor vehicle, (*describe vehicle*), on (*name highway*), a highway, in a speed competition with another motor vehicle, (*give description of other vehicle and driver's name, if known*).

III. Authorizing use of vehicle in prearranged racing **G.S. 20-141.3(c)**

. . . unlawfully and willfully did (*choose one or both*: authorize; knowingly permit) (*describe defendant's vehicle*), a motor vehicle (*choose one or both*: owned by the defendant; under the defendant's control) to be operated on a highway in a prearranged speed competition with another motor vehicle, as follows: (*briefly describe race and circumstances and give names of drivers; if unknown, give description of vehicles*).

IV. Betting or wagering on race **G.S. 20-141.3(c)**

. . . unlawfully and willfully did [*choose one*: place a bet of (*give amount*) on; receive (*describe thing of value*) from] the outcome of a prearranged speed competition between motor vehicles on a highway, as follows: (*briefly describe race and bet or thing of value*).

Notes about Charging Language:

- For Offense III, if the defendant was present at the race, include that information at the end of the charging language above.

Sample Charge:

I. Prearranged racing **G.S. 20-141.3(a)**

. . . unlawfully and willfully did operate a motor vehicle, a 1999 Chevrolet Corvette, N.C. License 2FS T4U, on State Road 1512, a highway, in a prearranged speed competition with another motor vehicle, a 1998 Chevrolet Camaro driven by James Jones.

AOC Forms for This Offense:
None.

Punishment:
Offenses I, III, and IV are Class 1 misdemeanors. Offense II is a Class 2 misdemeanor.

G.S. 20-141.4
Death or Serious Injury by Vehicle
April 2024
Page 1 of 4

Introductory Comment:
An indictment or an information for the recidivist offenses defined in G.S. 20-141.4(a4), -141.4(a5), and -141.4(a6) and illustrated as Offense IV, Offense V, and Offense VI below must comply with G.S. 15A-928, which requires that the defendant's prior convictions be alleged either (1) in a separate count of the indictment or information than the substantive offense or (2) in a separate indictment or information. This requirement does not apply to arrest warrants or magistrates' orders, which explains why two sets of charging language appear below. G.S. 15A-928 also requires in indictments or informations that the name or title of an offense elevated by prior convictions must not make reference to such prior convictions. Thus, it may be advisable to use an improvised title when charging the recidivist offenses.

Charging Language:

I. Felony death by vehicle **G.S. 20-141.4(a1)**

. . . unlawfully, willfully, and feloniously did unintentionally cause the death of (*name person*) while engaged in the offense of impaired driving under G.S. 20-138.1, in that the defendant unlawfully and willfully did drive a vehicle on (*name and describe highway or public vehicular area*), a (*choose one*: highway; public vehicular area), while subject to an impairing substance. The impaired driving offense was the proximate cause of the death.

II. Misdemeanor death by vehicle **G.S. 20-141.4(a2)**

. . . unlawfully and willfully did unintentionally cause the death of (*name person*) while engaged in a violation of [*choose one*: G.S. 20-(*give number*); Section (*give number of the local ordinance violated by the defendant and name the city or county*)], applying to the operation and use of a vehicle and to the regulation of traffic, in that the defendant unlawfully and willfully did drive a vehicle on (*name and describe highway or public vehicular area*), a (*choose one*: highway; public vehicular area), (*state elements of traffic offense and, if ordinance, set out the caption*). This violation was the proximate cause of the death.

III. Felony serious injury by vehicle **G.S. 20-141.4(a3)**

. . . unlawfully, willfully, and feloniously did unintentionally cause serious injury to (*name person*) while engaged in the offense of impaired driving under G.S. 20-138.1, in that the defendant unlawfully and willfully did drive a vehicle on (*name and describe highway or public vehicular area*), a (*choose one*: highway; public vehicular area), while subject to an impairing substance. The impaired driving offense was the proximate cause of the serious injury.

IV. Aggravated felony serious injury by vehicle **G.S. 20-141.4(a4)**

A. Charging language for an arrest warrant or magistrate's order

. . . unlawfully, willfully, and feloniously did unintentionally cause serious injury to (*name person*) while engaged in the offense of impaired driving under G.S. 20-138.1, in that the defendant unlawfully and willfully did drive a vehicle on (*name and describe highway or public vehicular area*), a (*choose one*: highway; public vehicular area), while subject to an impairing substance. The impaired driving offense was the proximate cause of the serious injury. The defendant has a previous conviction involving impaired driving within seven years of this offense, having been convicted of (*name offense*) on (*name date of conviction*), in (*name court in which conviction occurred*).

B. Charging language for an indictment or information

First count of indictment or information

. . . unlawfully, willfully, and feloniously did unintentionally cause serious injury to (*name person*) while engaged in the offense of impaired driving under G.S. 20-138.1, in that the defendant unlawfully and willfully did drive a vehicle on (*name and describe highway or public vehicular area*), a (*choose one*: highway; public vehicular area), while subject to an impairing substance. The impaired driving offense was the proximate cause of the serious injury.

Second count of indictment or information

The defendant has a previous conviction involving impaired driving within seven years of the offense charged above, having been convicted of (*name offense*) on (*name date of conviction*), in (*name court in which conviction occurred*).

V. Aggravated felony death by vehicle **G.S. 20-141.4(a5)**

A. Charging language for an arrest warrant or magistrate's order

. . . unlawfully, willfully, and feloniously did unintentionally cause the death of (*name person*) while engaged in the offense of impaired driving under G.S. 20-138.1, in that the defendant unlawfully and willfully did drive a vehicle on (*name and describe highway or public vehicular area*), a (*choose one*: highway; public vehicular area), while subject to an impairing substance. The impaired driving offense was the proximate cause of the death. The defendant has a previous conviction involving impaired driving within seven years of this offense, having been convicted of (*name offense*) on (*name date of conviction*), in (*name court in which conviction occurred*).

B. Charging language for an indictment or information

First count of indictment or information

. . . unlawfully, willfully, and feloniously did unintentionally cause the death of (*name person*) while engaged in the offense of impaired driving under G.S. 20-138.1, in that the defendant unlawfully and willfully did drive a vehicle on (*name and describe highway or public vehicular area*), a (*choose one*: highway; public vehicular area), while subject to an impairing substance. The impaired driving offense was the proximate cause of the death.

Second count of indictment or information

The defendant has a previous conviction involving impaired driving within seven years of the offense charged above, having been convicted of (*name offense*) on (*name date of conviction*), in (*name court in which conviction occurred*).

VI. Repeat felony death by vehicle **G.S. 20-141.4(a6)**

Charge felony death by vehicle or aggravated felony death by vehicle as indicated above, and then add the following to the arrest warrant or magistrate's order, or add as a third count in the indictment or information.

The defendant has a previous conviction under (*choose one*)

(1) G.S. 20-141.4(a1),

(2) G.S. 20-141.4(a5),

(3) G.S. 14-17, and the basis of the conviction was the unintentional death of another person while engaged in the offense of impaired driving under (*choose one*: G.S. 20-138.1; G.S. 20-138.2),

(4) G.S. 14-18, and the basis of the conviction was the unintentional death of another person while engaged in the offense of impaired driving under (*choose one*: G.S. 20-138.1; G.S. 20-138.2),

having been convicted of (*name offense*) on (*name date of conviction*), in (*name court in which conviction occurred*).

Notes about Charging Language:

- Several of the terms used in the charging language above, including "vehicle", "highway", "public vehicular area", and "impairing substance", are defined in G.S. 20-4.01.
- Offenses I, III, IV, V, and VI may also be based on impaired driving in a commercial vehicle in violation of G.S. 20-138.2. In such a case, modify the charging language appropriately.
- Before charging Offense II based on a death in a public vehicular area, make sure that the underlying motor vehicle violation can be committed in a public vehicular area.
- The motor vehicle violation in Offense II cannot be impaired driving. In such a case, Offense I should be charged.
- When charging Offense II based on a local ordinance violation, you may include the caption or title of the ordinance. This information is required when charging a violation of a local ordinance as a stand-alone offense. G.S. 153A-50, 160A-79. It does not appear to be required when charging Offense II, but you may include it if desired.
- When charging Offenses III and IV, the nature of the serious injury likely need not be alleged. *Cf.* State v. Gregory, 223 N.C. 415 (1943). It is not improper to include that information if desired.

Sample Charge:

I. Felony death by vehicle **G.S. 20-141.4(a1)**

. . . unlawfully, willfully, and feloniously did unintentionally cause the death of Samuel Goss while engaged in the offense of impaired driving under G.S. 20-138.1, in that the defendant unlawfully and willfully did drive a vehicle on U.S. 70 in Raleigh, N.C., a highway, while subject to an impairing substance. The impaired driving offense was the proximate cause of the death.

AOC Forms for This Offense:

None.

Punishment:

Offense I is a Class D felony with special sentencing provisions. Offense II is a Class A1 misdemeanor. Offense III is a Class F felony. Offense IV is a Class E felony. Offense V is a Class D felony with special sentencing provisions. Offense VI is a Class B2 felony. G.S. 20-141.4(b).

G.S. 20-141.5
Speeding to Elude Arrest
April 2024
Page 1 of 2

Introductory Comment:
Although the statutory title of this offense is "speeding to elude arrest," the offense may be committed without the defendant violating the speeding laws.

Charging Language:

I. Misdemeanor speeding to elude arrest **G.S. 20-141.5(a)**

. . . unlawfully and willfully did operate a motor vehicle on a (*choose one*: street; highway; public vehicular area), (*give location*), while (*choose one or both*: fleeing; attempting to elude) a law enforcement officer, (*name officer*), in the lawful performance of the officer's duties.

II. Felony speeding to elude arrest **G.S. 20-141.5(b)**

. . . unlawfully, willfully, and feloniously did operate a motor vehicle on a (*choose one*: street; highway; public vehicular area), (*give location*), while (*choose one or both*: fleeing; attempting to elude) a law enforcement officer, (*name officer*), in the lawful performance of the officer's duties. At the time of the violation, (*choose any of the following that apply, but at least two*)

(1) the defendant was speeding in excess of 15 miles per hour over the legal speed limit;
(2) there was gross impairment of the defendant's faculties while driving due to (*choose one or both*: consumption of an impairing substance; a blood alcohol concentration of 0.14 or more within a relevant time after driving);
(3) the defendant was driving recklessly in violation of G.S. 20-140;
(4) the defendant was driving negligently, leading to an accident causing (*choose one or both*: property damage in excess of $1,000; personal injury);
(5) the defendant was driving while the defendant's driver's license was revoked;
(6) the defendant was driving in excess of the posted speed limit [*choose one or more*: on school property in violation of G.S. 20-141(e1); in an area designated as a school zone under G.S. 20-141.1 during the days and hours when the posted limit was in effect; in a highway work zone as defined in G.S. 20-141(j2)];
(7) the defendant passed a stopped school bus as proscribed in G.S. 20-217;
(8) the defendant was driving with a child under 12 years of age in the vehicle.

Notes about Charging Language:

- If Offense I is a proximate cause of the death of any person, it becomes a felony. G.S. 20-141.5(b1). In such a case, allege "unlawfully, willfully, and feloniously" rather than "unlawfully and willfully" and add the following to the charging language: "The foregoing was a proximate cause of the death of (*name victim*)."
- If Offense II is a proximate cause of the death of any person, it becomes a more serious felony.
- G.S. 20-141.5(b1). In such a case, add the following to the charging language: "The foregoing was a proximate cause of the death of (*name victim*)."

- The state court of appeals has held that it is not necessary to state the specific duty or duties the officer was performing. State v. McVay, 287 N.C. App. 293, 298 (2022); State v. Teel, 180 N.C. App. 446 (2006). Because the state supreme court has held otherwise with respect to the charge of resisting a public officer, *see, e.g.*, State v. Dunston, 256 N.C. 203 (1962), a very cautious prosecutor may wish to include that information.

Sample Charges:

I. Misdemeanor speeding to elude arrest **G.S. 20-141.5(a)**

. . . unlawfully and willfully did operate a motor vehicle on a highway, U.S. 70 in Durham County, while attempting to elude a law enforcement officer, City of Durham police officer Sally Jones, in the lawful performance of the officer's duties.

II. Felony speeding to elude arrest **G.S. 20-141.5(b)**

. . . unlawfully, willfully, and feloniously did operate a motor vehicle on a highway, Interstate 40 in Forsyth County, while attempting to elude a law enforcement officer, State Highway Patrol officer Peter Smith, in the lawful performance of the officer's duties, stopping the defendant's vehicle for the offense of impaired driving. At the time of the violation, there was gross impairment of the defendant's faculties while driving due to a blood alcohol concentration of 0.14 or more within a relevant time after driving, and the defendant was driving while the defendant's driver's license was revoked.

AOC Forms for This Offense:
None.

Punishment:
Offense I is a Class 1 misdemeanor, and a Class H felony if death results. Offense II is a Class H felony, and a Class E felony if death results.

G.S. 20-141.10
Street Takeover
April 2024
Page 1 of 2

Introductory Comment:
G.S. 20-141.10 applies to offenses committed on or after December 1, 2023. *See* Shea Denning, *Recent Legislation Outlaws Street Takeovers*, N.C. CRIM. L.: A UNC SCH. OF GOV'T BLOG (Aug 10, 2023), nccriminallaw.sog.unc.edu/recent-legislation-outlaws-street-takeovers/.

Charging Language:

I. Misdemeanor street takeover **G.S. 20-141.10(b) & (c)**

. . . unlawfully and willfully did (*choose one*: operate a motor vehicle in; knowingly participate in; coordinate through social media or otherwise (*specify*); commit an overt act (*specify*) in furtherance of; facilitate (*specify*)) a street takeover. The street takeover occurred at (*describe location*), a portion of a (*choose one:* highway; street; public vehicular area), and involved the unauthorized blocking or impeding of the regular flow of traffic with a motor vehicle to perform a motor vehicle (*choose one*: stunt (*specify*); contest; exhibition).

II. Felony street takeover **G.S. 20-141.10(b) & (e)**

. . . unlawfully, willfully, and feloniously did operate a motor vehicle in a street takeover. The street takeover occurred at (*describe location*), a portion of a (choose one: highway; street; public vehicular area), and involved the unauthorized blocking or impeding of the regular flow of traffic with a motor vehicle to perform a motor vehicle (*choose one*: stunt; contest; exhibition). In addition, the defendant

(1) operated a motor vehicle in another street takeover within the last twenty-four-month period; or

(2) (*choose*: assaulted; knowingly and willfully threatened) a law enforcement officer, (*name officer*).

Notes about Charging Language:

- "Stunt" is defined as "a *burnout, doughnut, wheelie, drifting,* or other dangerous motor vehicle activity." G.S. 20-141.10(a)(9) (emphasis added). Each of the italicized terms is defined in the statute. G.S 20-141.10(a) Stunts should be identified with particularity.
- It is not clear from the statute whether coordinating, committing an act in furtherance of, or facilitating requires that a street takeover occurred. If it did not, the language should be modified accordingly.
- An indictment charging street takeover elevated to a felony due to a prior conviction must comply with G.S. 15A-928, requiring the prior conviction to be alleged in a separate count. *See* G.S. 15A-928.

Sample Charges:

I. Misdemeanor street takeover **G.S. 20-141.10(b)**

. . . . . unlawfully and willfully did operate a motor vehicle in a street takeover. The street takeover occurred on U.S. 70 in Durham County, a portion of a highway, and involved the unauthorized blocking or impeding of the regular flow of traffic with a motor vehicle to perform a motor vehicle contest.

II. Felony street takeover **G.S. 20-141.10(b)**

. . . unlawfully, willfully, and feloniously did operate a motor vehicle in a street takeover. The street takeover occurred on U.S. 70 in Durham County, a portion of a highway, and involved the unauthorized blocking or impeding of the regular flow of traffic with a motor vehicle to perform a motor vehicle contest. In addition, the defendant assaulted a law enforcement officer, Lieutenant Robert Peel of the Durham County Sheriff's Office.

AOC Forms for This Offense:

None.

Punishment:

Offense I is a Class A1 misdemeanor. Offense II is a Class H felony.

G.S. 20-157(a)
Failure to Heed Light or Siren of Emergency Vehicle

April 2024
Page 1 of 2

Introductory Comment:
Although other subsections of G.S. 20-157 contain prohibitions against, for example, following a fire truck too closely and driving over a fire hose, this form is limited to G.S. 20-157(a), failure to stop for an emergency vehicle. The statute does not apply to vehicles on the opposite side of a divided highway from an emergency vehicle.

Charging Language:
. . . unlawfully and willfully did, while driving a vehicle, upon the approach of a (*choose one*: law enforcement vehicle; fire department vehicle; public ambulance; private ambulance; rescue squad emergency service vehicle) giving warning signal by appropriate light and by (*choose one*: bell; siren; exhaust whistle), audible under normal conditions from a distance of not less than 1,000 feet, fail to (*choose one or more*)

(1) drive (*choose one*: his; her) vehicle to a position as near as possible and parallel to the right-hand (*choose one*: edge; curb), clear of any intersection of streets or highways.
(2) stop (*choose one*: his; her) vehicle.

Notes about Charging Language:
- The statute also applies when a driver initially pulls over and stops but fails to "remain in such position" until the emergency vehicle passes or the driver is otherwise instructed by a law enforcement officer or a traffic officer. In an appropriate case, alter the charging language accordingly.
- This statute also applies to failures to stop for vehicles operated by the Division of Marine Fisheries of the Department of Environmental Quality, the Division of Parks and Recreation of the Department of Natural and Cultural Resources, or the North Carolina Forest Service of the Department of Agriculture and Consumer Services when traveling in response to a fire alarm or other emergency response purpose and giving warning signals as required by the statute. In an appropriate case, alter the charging language accordingly.
- G.S. 20-157.1(h) and (i) set forth aggravated versions of this offense, which may apply in cases resulting in property damage, injuries, or death. In an appropriate case, alter the charging language to allege the additional circumstances required by those subsections. Also allege that the defendant acted "unlawfully, willfully, and feloniously" when charging the felony aggravated version of the offense.

Sample Charge:
. . . unlawfully and willfully did, upon the approach of a fire department vehicle giving warning signal by appropriate light and by siren, audible under normal conditions from a distance of not less than 1,000 feet, fail to stop his vehicle.

AOC Forms for This Offense:
None.

Punishment:
Class 2 misdemeanor. The aggravated versions of this offense referenced above are a Class 1 misdemeanor and a Class F felony.

G.S. 20-166(a), (a1)
Felonious Hit and Run
April 2024
Page 1 of 2

Introductory Comment:
None.

Charging Language:

I. Failure to stop

. . . unlawfully, willfully, and feloniously did fail to immediately stop the vehicle the defendant was driving at the scene of a crash in which the defendant was involved. This crash occurred (*give location of accident*) and resulted in (*choose one*: injury; serious bodily injury; death) to (*name victim*). The defendant knew and reasonably should have known that the vehicle which the defendant was operating was involved in the crash and that the crash had resulted in (*choose one*: injury; serious bodily injury; death) to (*name victim*).

II. Failure to remain at scene

. . . unlawfully, willfully, and feloniously did fail to remain at the scene of a crash in which the defendant was involved until a law enforcement officer completed an investigation of the crash and authorized the defendant to leave. This crash occurred (*give location of accident*) and resulted in (*choose one*: injury; serious bodily injury; death) to (*name victim*). The defendant knew and reasonably should have known that the vehicle he or she was operating was involved in the crash and that the crash had resulted in (*choose one*: injury; serious bodily injury; death) to (*name victim*).

III. Failure to return to scene after seeking assistance

. . . unlawfully, willfully, and feloniously did fail to return within a reasonable period of time to the scene of a crash in which the defendant was involved after the defendant left the scene to [*choose one or more*: call for a law enforcement officer; call for medical assistance and treatment; remove (*choose one or more*: himself; herself; another) from significant risk of injury]. The defendant knew and reasonably should have known that the vehicle which the defendant was operating was involved in the crash and that the crash, which occurred (*give location of accident*), resulted in (*choose one*: injury; serious bodily injury; death) to (*name victim*).

Notes about Charging Language:

- The statute requires that the defendant knew or reasonably should have known of the crash and that injury, serious bodily injury, or death resulted. If there is no evidence that the defendant knew, delete the words "knew and."
- "Serious bodily injury" is defined in G.S. 14-32.4.
- The classification of the above offenses is higher if the crash resulted in death or serious bodily injury than if the crash resulted only in injury. Do not allege, for example, "injury and death," as that might create confusion about the proper classification of the offense.

Sample Charge:

I. Failure to stop

. . . unlawfully, willfully, and feloniously did fail to immediately stop the vehicle the defendant was driving at the scene of a crash in which the defendant was involved. This crash occurred on Main Street in Durham, N.C., and resulted in injury to Thelma Barnes. The defendant knew and reasonably should have known that the vehicle the defendant was operating was involved in the crash and that the crash had resulted in injury to Thelma Barnes.

AOC Forms for This Offense:
None.

Punishment:
If injury resulted from the crash, Class H felony. If death or serious bodily injury resulted, Class F felony.

G.S. 20-166(b), (c), (c1)
Misdemeanor Hit and Run
April 2024
Page 1 of 2

Introductory Comment:
None.

Charging Language:

I. Failure to give information or assistance when injury or death results from a crash **G.S. 20-166(b)**

. . . unlawfully and willfully did, at the scene of a crash occurring (*give location of accident*), in which the vehicle driven by the defendant was involved, fail to (*choose one or both of the following*)

(1) give the defendant's name, address, driver's license number, and license plate number to the (*choose one or more and name person or persons*: person struck; driver of the vehicle collided with; occupants of the vehicle collided with) who (*choose one*: was; were) physically and mentally capable of receiving the information.

(2) render reasonable assistance to (*name injured person*), who was injured as a result of the crash.

The defendant knew and reasonably should have known that the vehicle the defendant was operating was involved in the crash and that the crash had resulted in (*choose one*: injury; serious bodily injury; death) to (*name victim*).

II. Failure to stop when a crash results in property damage **G.S. 20-166(c)**

. . . unlawfully and willfully did fail to immediately stop the vehicle the defendant was driving at the scene of a crash in which the defendant was involved. This crash occurred (*give location of accident*) and resulted in (*choose one or both*)

(1) property damage (*describe damage*).

(2) (*choose one*: injury; death) to (*name victim*) that the defendant did not know of and did not have reason to know of.

The defendant knew and reasonably should have known that the vehicle the defendant was operating was involved in the crash.

III. Failure to give information when a crash results in property damage **G.S. 20-166(c1)**

. . . unlawfully and willfully did at the scene of a crash occurring (*give location of accident*), in which the vehicle driven by the defendant was involved, fail to give the defendant's name, address, driver's license number, and license plate number to the (*choose one or more and name person or persons*: driver of another vehicle involved in the crash; occupants of another vehicle involved in the crash; person whose property was damaged in the crash). The defendant knew and reasonably should have known that the vehicle the defendant was operating was involved in the crash. The crash had resulted in (*choose one or both*)

(1) property damage (*describe damage*).

(2) (*choose one*: injury; death) to (*name victim*) that the defendant did not know of and did not have reason to know of.

Notes about Charging Language:

- For Offense I, the words "person struck" would be used when a pedestrian was hit.
- The statute requires that the defendant knew or reasonably should have known of the crash. If there is no evidence that the defendant knew, delete the words "knew and."
- Cases in which the driver strikes an unattended vehicle or certain unattended items are addressed in subsection (c1) of the statute. In such a case, make appropriate alterations to the charging language for Offense III, above.
- "Crash" is defined in G.S. 20-4.01(4c).

Sample Charge:

I. Failure to give information or assistance when injury or death results from a crash **G.S. 20-166(b)**

. . . unlawfully and willfully did at the scene of a crash occurring at Fayetteville Street in Raleigh, N.C., in which the vehicle driven by the defendant was involved, fail to give the defendant's name, address, driver's license number, and license plate number to the driver, Peter Norman, of the vehicle collided with, who was physically and mentally capable of receiving the information. The defendant knew and reasonably should have known that the vehicle the defendant was operating was involved in the crash and that the crash had resulted in injury to Peter Norman.

AOC Forms for This Offense:
None.

Punishment:
Class 1 misdemeanor.

G.S. 20-166.1(a)
Hit and Run: Failure to Notify Authorities
April 2024

Introductory Comment:
None.

Charging Language:
. . . unlawfully and willfully did fail by the quickest means of communication to immediately notify (*name the law enforcement agency that was to be notified*), the appropriate law enforcement agency, of a reportable accident in which the vehicle driven by the defendant was involved. The accident occurred (*give location of accident*) and caused [*choose one or more*: personal injury to (*name victim*); death to (*name victim*); property damage of $1,000 or more to (*describe property or properties that were damaged*)].

Notes about Charging Language:
- The statute provides that the "appropriate law enforcement agency" is the city police department if the accident occurred within the city limits. If the accident occurred outside a city, the statute provides that any of the following agencies are appropriate: the sheriff's department, State Highway Patrol, or other qualified county rural police—for example, county police.
- Because "crash" and "accident" mean the same thing for purposes of the motor vehicle laws, G.S. 20-4.01(4c), a "reportable accident" is the same as a "reportable crash", which is defined as an accident or collision involving a motor vehicle that results in either of the following: (1) death or injury to a human being or (2) total property damage of $1,000 or more or property damage of any amount to a vehicle seized pursuant to G.S. 20-28.3. *See* G.S. 20-4.01(33b).

Sample Charge:
. . . unlawfully and willfully did fail by the quickest means of communication to immediately notify Durham City Police Department, the appropriate law enforcement agency, of a reportable accident in which the vehicle driven by the defendant was involved. The accident occurred on Washington Street in Durham, N.C., and caused personal injury to Sally Smith.

AOC Forms for This Offense:
None.

Punishment:
Class 2 misdemeanor.

G.S. 49-2
Nonsupport of Child Born Out of Wedlock
April 2024

Introductory Comment:
None.

Charging Language:
. . . unlawfully and willfully did neglect and refuse to provide adequate support and to maintain (*name child*), (*choose one*: his; her) child born out of wedlock to (*if charging mother, state* her; *if charging father, name mother*) on (*date*), in that (*choose one*: he; she) (*briefly state facts showing the failure to support and maintain the child*). The neglect and refusal to provide adequate support continued after due notice and demand was made upon (*choose one*: him; her) by (*name person with interest in child's welfare who made the demand*).

Notes about Charging Language:
- "Child" as used in G.S. 49-2 refers to a person less than 18 years of age and any person whom either parent might be required under North Carolina law to support and maintain if such a child were the legitimate child of such a parent.
- G.S. 49-2 is a special statute of limitations for this offense.
- In order for a father to be convicted of this offense, the State must prove that the mother, or in some cases, a public official, demanded support from the father. *See* G.S. 49-5; State v. Ellis, 262 N.C. 446 (1964). Out of an abundance of caution, this is included in the last sentence of the above charging language, although its inclusion is probably not required.
- G.S. 14-325.1 states: "The offense of willful neglect or refusal of a parent to support and maintain a child, and the offense of willful neglect or refusal to support and maintain one's child born out of wedlock, shall be deemed to have been committed in this State whenever the child is living in this State at the time of such willful neglect or refusal to support and maintain such child."

Sample Charge:
. . . unlawfully and willfully did neglect and refuse to provide adequate support and to maintain Paul Harold Davis, his child born out of wedlock to Sarah Graham Jones on August 1, 2014, in that he did not provide financial support for the child, even after notice and demand was made upon him on September 1, 2014, by Sarah Graham Jones.

AOC Forms for This Offense:
None.

Punishment:
Class 2 misdemeanor.

G.S. 50B-4.1
Violating Civil Domestic Violence Protective Order
April 2024
Page 1 of 3

Introductory Comment:
An indictment or an information for Offense II must comply with G.S. 15A-928, which requires that the defendant's prior convictions be alleged either (1) in a separate count of the indictment or information than the substantive offense or (2) in a separate indictment or information. This requirement does not apply to arrest warrants or magistrates' orders, which explains why two sets of charging language appear below.

G.S. 15A-928 also requires that an "improvised name or title" be used so that the title of the indictment or information does not refer to the defendant's prior convictions. Therefore, an indictment or information charging Offense II should be captioned "violating a domestic violence protective order under G.S. 50B-4.1(f)" or something similar.

Charging Language:

I. Violating a domestic violence protective order **G.S. 50B-4.1(a)**

. . . unlawfully and willfully did knowingly violate a valid protective order entered pursuant to [*choose one*: Chapter 50B of the General Statutes; a court of another state, (*name court and state*); a court of an Indian tribe, *(name tribe)*]. The defendant violated a valid protective order issued by (*insert as much of the following information as available*: *name of judicial official issuing order, official's title, court, and date of order*) by (*describe defendant's conduct that violated order*).

II. Habitual violating a domestic violence protective order **G.S. 50B-4.1(f)**

A. Charging language for an arrest warrant or magistrate's order

. . . unlawfully, willfully, and feloniously did knowingly violate a valid protective order entered pursuant to [*choose one*: Chapter 50B of the General Statutes; a court of another state, (*name court and state*); a court of an Indian tribe, *(name tribe)*]. The defendant violated a valid protective order issued by (*insert as much of the following information as available*: *name of judicial official issuing order, official's title, court, and date of order*) by (*describe defendant's conduct that violated order*). The defendant has previously been convicted of two offenses under Chapter 50B of the General Statutes, namely: (*give name of offense, statutory citation, and date and court of conviction of the two offenses*).

B. Charging language for an indictment or information

First count in indictment or information

. . . unlawfully, willfully, and feloniously did knowingly violate a valid protective order entered pursuant to [*choose one*: Chapter 50B of the General Statutes; a court of another state, (*name court and state*); a court of an Indian tribe, *(name tribe)*. The defendant violated a valid protective order issued by (*insert as much of the following information as available*: *name of judicial official issuing order, official's title, court, and date of order*) by (*describe defendant's conduct that violated order*).

Second count in indictment or information

At the time of the offense charged above, the defendant had previously been convicted of two offenses under Chapter 50B of the General Statutes, namely: (*give name of offense, statutory citation, and date and court of conviction of the two offenses*).

III. Violating a domestic violence protective order while in possession of a deadly weapon **G.S. 50B-4.1(g)**

. . . unlawfully, willfully, and feloniously did knowingly violate a valid protective order entered pursuant to [*choose one*: Chapter 50B of the General Statutes; a court of another state, (*name court and state*); a court of an Indian tribe, (*name tribe*)]. The defendant violated a valid protective order issued by (*insert as much of the following information as available*: *name of judicial official issuing order, official's title, court, and date of order*) by failing to stay away from a (*choose one or both*: place; person) as directed under the terms of the order (*briefly identify the place or person and describe the defendant's failure to stay away*). At the time of the violation, the defendant possessed a deadly weapon, (*name deadly weapon and, if necessary, describe the characteristics that make it a deadly weapon*), (*choose one*: on and about the defendant's person; within close proximity to the defendant's person).

IV. Entering a domestic violence safe house **G.S. 50B-4.1(gl)**

. . . unlawfully, willfully, and feloniously did, while subject to a valid protective order entered pursuant to [*choose one*: Chapter 50B of the General Statutes; a court of another state, (*name court and state*); a court of an Indian tribe, (*name tribe*)], enter (*give address or describe property*), a property operated as a (*choose one or both*: safe house; haven) for victims of domestic violence. At that time, (*name person*), a person protected under the protective order, was residing at the (*choose one or both*: safe house; haven).

V. Upgrading punishment for another felony **G.S. 50B-4.1(d), (e)**

[*Add the following sentences at the end of the count alleging the felony to be upgraded under G.S. 50B-4.1(d), (e).*]

The defendant committed this felony at a time when the defendant knew that the behavior was prohibited by a valid protective order entered pursuant to [*choose one*: Chapter 50B of the General Statutes; a court of another state, (*name court and state*); a court of an Indian tribe, (*name tribe*)]. The behavior was prohibited by a valid protective order issued by (*insert as much of the following information as available*: *name of judicial official issuing order, official's title, court, and date of order*) by (*describe defendant's conduct that violated order*). The defendant knowingly violated this protective order in the course of conduct constituting this felony.

Notes about Charging Language:

- Offense V is not a stand-alone offense, but rather a means of increasing the penalty for a crime that also amounts to a protective order violation.

Sample Charge:

I. Violating a domestic violence protective order **G.S. 50B-4.1(a)**

. . . unlawfully and willfully did knowingly violate a valid protective order entered pursuant to Chapter 50B of the General Statutes. The defendant violated a valid protective order issued by Julia Smythe, District Court Judge, Fourteenth District Court District, on December 3, 2019, by entering the premises of Katrina Cantwell, 2305 South Main Street, Livingston, N.C., when he had been ordered excluded from those premises.

AOC Forms for This Offense:

None.

Punishment:

Offense I is a Class A1 misdemeanor. Offense II is a Class H felony. Offense III is a Class H felony. Offense IV is a Class H felony. Offense V is a felony one class higher than the underlying felony.

G.S. 58-2-161
Insurance Fraud
April 2024

Introductory Comment:
Amendments effective December 1, 2023, added subsection (c), increasing the punishment if the amount of the claim for payment or other benefit is one hundred thousand dollars ($100,000) or more.

Charging Language:
. . . unlawfully, willfully, and feloniously did, with the intent to (*choose one or more*: injure; defraud; deceive) an (*choose one*: insurer; insurance claimant), (*name insurer or insurance claimant*), present a (*choose one or both*: written; oral) statement (*choose one or more*: as part of; in support of; in opposition to) a [*choose one*: claim for payment; claim for benefit (*describe benefit)*] pursuant to an insurance policy, (*describe insurance policy*), knowing that the statement contained (*choose one or both*: false; misleading) information, (*describe false or misleading information*). The statement concerned a fact and matter material to the claim. The amount of the claim for payment or other benefit was (*choose one*: one hundred thousand dollars ($100,000) or more; less than one hundred thousand dollars ($100,000).)

Notes about Charging Language:
- "Insurer" is defined in G.S. 58-2-161(a)(1), and "statement" is defined in G.S. 58-2-161(a)(2).
- The statute makes it illegal to "present" or "cause to be presented" any false statement. If appropriate, replace "present" in the language above with "cause to be presented."
- The statute also makes it illegal to assist, abet, solicit, or conspire with another person to prepare or make a false statement. If appropriate, modify the language accordingly.
- The statute refers to any fact *or* matter material to the claim. You may delete one of these words if appropriate.

Sample Charge:
. . . unlawfully, willfully, and feloniously did, with the intent to defraud an insurer, BlueCross BlueShield of North Carolina, present a written statement in support of a claim for payment pursuant to an insurance policy, policy no. 87698, owned by the defendant, knowing that the statement contained false information, a statement that the defendant had paid Dr. Susan Smith $2,010 for services when actually the defendant had only paid $200. The statement concerned a fact and matter material to the claim.

AOC Forms for This Offense:
None.

Punishment:
Class H felony if the amount of the claim for payment or other benefit is less than $100,000.
Class C felony if the amount of the claim for payment or other benefit is $100,000 or more.

G.S. 75A-10(b1)
Boating While Impaired
April 2024

Introductory Comment:
None.

Charging Language:
. . . unlawfully and willfully did operate a vessel on the waters of North Carolina, namely, (*name or describe body of water*),
(*choose one or both*)
(1) while under the influence of an impairing substance.
(2) after having consumed sufficient alcohol such that the defendant had, at a relevant time after the boating, an alcohol concentration of 0.08 or more.

Notes about Charging Language:
- The charging language above is somewhat different from the charging language for driving while impaired because G.S. 20-138.1(c) specifically provides that certain language be used in charging driving while impaired. G.S. Chapter 75A has no analogous provision.
- "Impairing substance" is defined in G.S. 20-4.01(14a). Under G.S. 75A-10(b2), that definition is applicable to boating cases as well.

Sample Charge:
. . . unlawfully and willfully did operate a vessel on the waters of North Carolina, namely, Jordan Lake, while under the influence of an impairing substance.

AOC Forms for This Offense:
None.

Punishment:
Class 2 misdemeanor. The statute provides that the defendant shall be fined at least $250 "in addition to any other penalty imposed." G.S. 75A-10(b4).

G.S. 75A-10.3
Death or Serious Injury by Impaired Boating
April 2024
Page 1 of 4

Introductory Comment:
These offenses were enacted by the General Assembly in 2016 and are effective for offenses committed on or after December 1, 2016. These offenses parallel the impaired driving death or serious injury offenses in G.S. 20-141.4.

An indictment or an information for the recidivist offenses defined in G.S. 75A-10.3(c), -10.3(d), and -10.4(e) illustrated as Offense III, Offense IV, and Offense V, below, must comply with G.S. 15A-928, which requires that the defendant's prior convictions be alleged either (1) in a separate count of the indictment or information than the substantive offense or (2) in a separate indictment or information. This requirement does not apply to arrest warrants or magistrates' orders, which explains why two sets of charging language appear below. G.S. 15A-928 also requires in indictments or informations that the name or title of an offense elevated by prior convictions must not make reference to such prior convictions. Thus, it may be advisable to use an improvised title when charging the recidivist offenses.

Charging Language:

I. Felony death by impaired boating **G.S. 75A-10.3(a)**

. . . unlawfully, willfully, and feloniously did unintentionally cause the death of (*name person*) while engaged in the offense of impaired boating under G.S. 75A-10(b1), in that the defendant unlawfully and willfully did operate a vessel on the waters of North Carolina, namely, (*name and/or describe body of water*), while (*choose one or both*: under the influence of an impairing substance; after having consumed sufficient alcohol such that the defendant had, at a relevant time after the boating, an alcohol concentration of 0.08 or more). The impaired boating offense was the proximate cause of the death.

II. Felony serious injury by impaired boating **G.S. 75A-10.3(b)**

. . . unlawfully, willfully, and feloniously did unintentionally cause serious injury to (*name person*) while engaged in the offense of impaired boating under G.S. 75A-10(b1), in that the defendant unlawfully and willfully did operate a vessel on the waters of North Carolina, namely, (*name and/or describe body of water*), while (*choose one or both*: under the influence of an impairing substance; after having consumed sufficient alcohol such that the defendant had, at a relevant time after the boating, an alcohol concentration of 0.08 or more). The impaired boating offense was the proximate cause of the serious injury.

III. Aggravated felony serious injury by impaired boating **G.S. 75A-10.3(c)**

A. Charging language for an arrest warrant or magistrate's order

. . . unlawfully, willfully, and feloniously did unintentionally cause serious injury to (*name person*) while engaged in the offense of impaired boating under G.S. 75A-10(b1), in that the defendant unlawfully and willfully did operate a vessel on the waters of North Carolina, namely, (*name and/or describe body of water*), while (*choose one or both:* under the influence of an impairing substance; after having consumed sufficient alcohol such that the defendant had, at a relevant time after the boating, an alcohol concentration of 0.08 or more). The impaired boating offense was the proximate cause of the serious injury. The defendant has a previous conviction involving impaired boating within seven years of this offense, having been convicted of (*name offense*) on (*name date of conviction*), in *(name court in which conviction occurred*).

B. Charging language for an indictment or information

First count in indictment or information

. . . unlawfully, willfully, and feloniously did unintentionally cause serious injury to (*name person*) while engaged in the offense of impaired boating under G.S. 75A-10(b1), in that the defendant unlawfully and willfully did operate a vessel on the waters of North Carolina, namely, (*name and/or describe body of water*), while (*choose one or both:* under the influence of an impairing substance; after having consumed sufficient alcohol such that the defendant had, at a relevant time after the boating, an alcohol concentration of 0.08 or more). The impaired boating offense was the proximate cause of the serious injury.

Second count in indictment or information

. . . The defendant has a previous conviction of impaired boating under G.S. 75A-10(b1) within seven years of this offense, having been convicted of (*name offense*) on (*name date of conviction*), in *(name court in which conviction occurred*).

IV. Aggravated felony death by impaired boating **G.S. 75A-10.3(d)**

A. Charging language for an arrest warrant or magistrate's order

. . . unlawfully, willfully, and feloniously did unintentionally cause the death of (*name person*) while engaged in the offense of impaired boating under G.S. 75A-10(b1), in that the defendant unlawfully and willfully did operate a vessel on the waters of North Carolina, namely, (*name and/or describe body of water*), while (*choose one or both*: under the influence of an impairing substance; after having consumed sufficient alcohol such that the defendant had, at a relevant time after the boating, an alcohol concentration of 0.08 or more). The impaired boating offense was the proximate cause of the death. The defendant has a previous conviction involving impaired boating within seven years of this offense, having been convicted of (*name offense*) on (*name date of conviction*), in (*name court in which conviction occurred*).

B. Charging language for an indictment or information

First count in indictment or information

. . . unlawfully, willfully, and feloniously did unintentionally cause the death of (*name person*) while engaged in the offense of impaired boating under G.S. 75A-10(b1), in that the defendant unlawfully and willfully did operate a vessel on the waters of North Carolina, namely, (*name and/or describe body of water*), while (*choose one or both*: under the influence of an impairing substance; after having consumed sufficient alcohol such that the defendant had, at a relevant time after the boating, an alcohol concentration of 0.08 or more). The impaired boating offense was the proximate cause of the death.

Second count in indictment or information

. . . The defendant has a previous conviction of impaired boating under G.S. 75A-10(b1) within seven years of this offense, having been convicted of (*name offense*) on (*name date of conviction*), in (*name court in which conviction occurred*).

V. Repeat felony death by impaired boating **G.S. 75A-10.3(e)**

Charge felony death by impaired boating or aggravated felony death by impaired boating as indicated above, and then add the following to the arrest warrant or magistrate's order or as an additional count in the indictment or information.

The defendant has a previous conviction under
(*choose one*):

(1) G.S. 75A-10.3(a),
(2) G.S. 75A-10.3(d),
(3) G.S. 14-17, and the basis of the conviction was the unintentional death of another person while engaged in the offense of impaired boating under G.S. 75A-10(b1),
(4) G.S. 14-18, and the basis of the conviction was the unintentional death of another person while engaged in the offense of impaired boating under G.S. 75A-10(b1),

having been convicted of (*name offense*) on (*name date of conviction*), in (*name court in which conviction occurred*).

Notes about Charging Language:

- The charging language above is somewhat different from the charging language for the parallel impaired driving offenses because G.S. 20-138.1(c) specifically provides that certain language be used in charging driving while impaired. G.S. Chapter 75A has no analogous provision.
- "Impairing substance" is defined in G.S. 20-4.01(14a). Under G.S. 75A-10(b2), that definition is applicable to boating cases as well.

Sample Charge:

I. Felony death by impaired boating **G.S. 75A-10.3(a)**

. . . unlawfully, willfully, and feloniously did unintentionally cause the death of Riley McKirahan while engaged in the offense of impaired boating under G.S. 75A-10(b1), in that the defendant unlawfully and willfully did operate a vessel on the waters of North Carolina, namely, Lake Norman, while under the influence of an impairing substance. The impaired boating offense was the proximate cause of the death.

AOC Forms for This Offense:
None.

Punishment:
Offense I is a Class D felony. Offense II is a Class F felony. Offense III is a Class E felony. Offense IV is a Class D felony and requires sentencing in the aggravated range. Offense V is a Class B2 felony. When charging Offenses II and III, the nature of the serious injury likely need not be alleged. *Cf.* State v. Gregory, 223 N.C. 415 (1943). It is not improper to include that information if desired. The statute provides: "No person who has been placed in jeopardy upon a charge of death by impaired boating may be prosecuted for the offense of manslaughter arising out of the same death; and no person who has been placed in jeopardy upon a charge of manslaughter may be prosecuted for death by impaired boating arising out of the same death." G.S. 75A-10.3(g).

G.S. 90-88
Rescheduling of Substance by Commission
April 2024

Although G.S. 90-89 through -94 list the controlled substances in six schedules, the Commission for Mental Health, Developmental Disabilities, and Substance Abuse Services is given authority in G.S. 90-88 to reschedule substances and to add new substances to the schedules in the statutes. If a substance has been scheduled in a manner other than what appears in the statutes, the criminal pleading should indicate the proper schedule and should allege the action of the commission, as set out below.

(*To be added at the end of the charging language*:)
The controlled substance named above is included in Schedule (*give schedule number*) of the North Carolina Controlled Substances Act pursuant to an order of the Commission for Mental Health, Developmental Disabilities, and Substance Abuse Services dated (*give date of order and any other identifying characteristics that may be useful*). The order was issued pursuant to the North Carolina Controlled Substances Act.

G.S. 90-95(a)(1)
Manufacture of a Controlled Substance
April 2024
Page 1 of 2

Introductory Comment:
None.

Charging Language:
. . . unlawfully, willfully, and feloniously did manufacture (*identify the substance*), a controlled substance included in Schedule (*give schedule number*) of the North Carolina Controlled Substances Act. The manufacturing consisted of (*describe the process in accordance with the statute*).

Notes about Charging Language:
- When identifying the controlled substance, do so "by its chemical name as it appears in [the controlled substance schedules]." State v. Turshizi, 175 N.C. App. 783 (2006).
- G.S. 90-87(15) defines "manufacture" as "the production, preparation, propagation, compounding, conversion or processing of a controlled substance by any means, whether directly or indirectly, artificially or naturally, or by extraction from substances of a natural origin, or independently by means of chemical synthesis, or by a combination of extraction and chemical synthesis; and 'manufacture' further includes any packaging or repackaging of the substance or labeling or relabeling of its container, except that this term does not include the preparation or compounding of a controlled substance by an individual for his own use or the preparation, compounding, packaging, or labeling of a controlled substance:
    a. By a practitioner as an incident to his administering or dispensing of a controlled substance in the course of his professional practice, or
    b. By a practitioner, or by his authorized agent under his supervision, for the purpose of, or as an incident to research, teaching, or chemical analysis and not for sale."
- If the manufacturing consists of preparing or compounding a controlled substance, it may be necessary to allege an intent to distribute. *See* G.S. 90-87(15) (stating that manufacturing "does not include the preparation or compounding of a controlled substance by an individual for his own use"); State v. Brown, 310 N.C. 563, 568 (1984) ("[T]he offense of manufacturing a controlled substance does not require an intent to distribute unless the activity constituting manufacture is preparation or compounding."). *But cf.* State v. Lofton, 372 N.C. 216, 222 (2019) (holding that an indictment alleging manufacturing by production, propagation, processing, and preparation was not defective on its face for failing to allege an intent to distribute, as "the indictment at issue in this case alleged that defendant manufactured marijuana in four different ways, one of which required a showing of an 'intent to distribute' in order for the State to obtain a conviction and three of which did not").
- Schedule VI includes tetrahydrocannabinols "except for tetrahydrocannabinols found in a product with a delta-9 tetrahydrocannabinol concentration of not more than three-tenths of one percent (0.3%) on a dry weight basis." G.S. 90-94(b)(2). Is it sufficient to allege that the substance at issue is "a tetrahydrocannabinol"? Perhaps so, on the theory that whether the substance falls under the exception in the statute is in the nature of a defense rather than an element. Under a prior statutory regime, the North Carolina Court of Appeals ruled in *State v. Teague*, 286 N.C. App. 160, 180, 181 (2022), that "the concentration of THC is not an element of the offense of possession with intent to sell or deliver THC," but rather is an "exception." However, as of this

writing, the state supreme court may review *Teague*, and the law regarding marijuana, hemp, and related substances is changing quickly. Therefore, a cautious prosecutor may wish to allege more than *Teague* requires, perhaps along the lines of "a tetrahydrocannabinol contained in a product with a delta-9 tetrahydrocannabinol concentration greater than 0.3% on a dry weight basis."

Sample Charges:

. . . unlawfully, willfully, and feloniously did manufacture marijuana, a controlled substance included in Schedule VI of the North Carolina Controlled Substances Act. The manufacturing consisted of packaging and repackaging the marijuana.

. . . unlawfully, willfully, and feloniously did manufacture marijuana, a controlled substance included in Schedule VI of the North Carolina Controlled Substances Act. The manufacturing consisted of growing marijuana in pots in the defendant's house and growing marijuana in a field near his house.

AOC Forms for This Offense:

AOC-CR-151 (Indictment)

Punishment:

If the controlled substance is in Schedule I or II, the manufacture is a Class H felony. However, the manufacture of methamphetamine (a Schedule II controlled substance) is a Class C felony, unless the offense involves packaging or repackaging methamphetamine or labeling or relabeling the methamphetamine container, in which case its manufacture is a Class H felony. If the controlled substance is included in Schedule III through VI, the manufacture is a Class I felony.

G.S. 90-95(a)(1)

Possession of Controlled Substance with Intent to Manufacture, Sell, or Deliver

April 2024

Page 1 of 2

Introductory Comment:

Possession with intent to manufacture, possession with intent to deliver, and possession with intent to sell, when arising from the same act of possession, are one offense and should not be charged separately. State v. Moore, 327 N.C. 378 (1990). However, a defendant may be convicted and punished for both (1) sale and delivery of a controlled substance and (2) possession with intent to sell and deliver the same controlled substance. State v. Stoner, 59 N.C. App. 656 (1982).

Charging Language:

. . . unlawfully, willfully, and feloniously did possess with intent to (*choose one or more*: manufacture; sell; deliver) a controlled substance, namely, (*specify the amount*) of (*identify substance*), which is included in Schedule (*give schedule number*) of the North Carolina Controlled Substances Act.

Notes about Charging Language:

- It is not essential to specify the amount for this offense. However, such an allegation may be helpful, at least when the severity of the punishment for a lesser offense of simple possession depends on the amount possessed and the allegation will permit a jury instruction on the lesser offense. State v. Perry, 84 N.C. App. 309 (1987). For example, the possession of more than 100 tablets of a Schedule II controlled substance is a felony and the possession of less than 100 tablets is a misdemeanor.
- If there is evidence of the intent to sell or deliver, this charge would be appropriate regardless of how small a quantity was involved. A large quantity, by itself, is indicative of the intent to sell or deliver. State v. Morgan, 329 N.C. 654 (1991).
- When identifying the controlled substance, do so "by its chemical name as it appears in [the controlled substance schedules]." State v. Turshizi, 175 N.C. App. 783, 785 (2006).
- Schedule VI includes tetrahydrocannabinols "except for tetrahydrocannabinols found in a product with a delta-9 tetrahydrocannabinol concentration of not more than three-tenths of one percent (0.3%) on a dry weight basis." G.S. 90-94(b)(2). Is it sufficient to allege that the substance at issue is "a tetrahydrocannabinol"? Perhaps so, on the theory that whether the substance falls under the exception in the statute is in the nature of a defense rather than an element. Under a prior statutory regime, the North Carolina Court of Appeals ruled in *State v. Teague*, 286 N.C. App. 160, 180, 181 (2022), that "the concentration of THC is not an element of the offense of possession with intent to sell or deliver THC," but rather is an "exception." However, as of this writing, the state supreme court may review *Teague*, and the law regarding marijuana, hemp, and related substances is changing quickly. Therefore, a cautious prosecutor may wish to allege more than *Teague* requires, perhaps along the lines of "a tetrahydrocannabinol contained in a product with a delta-9 tetrahydrocannabinol concentration greater than 0.3% on a dry weight basis."

Sample Charge:

. . . unlawfully, willfully, and feloniously did possess with intent to deliver a controlled substance, namely, 500 tablets, capsules, and dosage units of amphetamine, which is included in Schedule II of the North Carolina Controlled Substances Act.

AOC Forms for This Offense:
AOC-CR-151 (Indictment)
AOC-J-328 (Juvenile Petition)

Punishment:
If the controlled substance is in Schedule I or II, this offense is a Class H felony. If the controlled substance is in Schedule III through VI, this offense is a Class I felony.

G.S. 90-95(a)(1)
Sale or Delivery of a Controlled Substance
April 2024
Page 1 of 2

Introductory Comment:
Before charging this offense, consider whether to charge the defendant under G.S. 90-95(e)(5) (sale or delivery to a person under 16 or to a pregnant person) or under G.S. 90-95(e)(8) or (e)(10) (drug offenses within 1,000 feet of a child care center, park, and similar locations).

Note that a sale and delivery arising from a single transaction constitute one offense; therefore, do not charge sale and delivery as separate offenses. State v. Moore, 327 N.C. 378 (1990).

Charging Language:
. . . unlawfully, willfully, and feloniously did (*choose one or both*: sell; deliver) to (*identify buyer or recipient of substance, if known, or state* "an unknown person") a controlled substance, (*identify substance*), which is included in Schedule (*give schedule number*) of the North Carolina Controlled Substances Act.

Notes about Charging Language:
- G.S. 90-87(7) defines "deliver" as "the actual, constructive, or attempted transfer from one person to another of a controlled substance, whether or not there is an agency relationship." Delivering would include all instances of selling; but if there is an exchange of money, use the word "sell" in addition to or instead of "deliver." As noted below, the punishment for sale is greater than the punishment for delivery.
- Under G.S. 90-95(b)(2), the transfer of less than 5 grams of marijuana for no remuneration does not constitute a delivery in violation of G.S. 90-95(a)(1). If charging delivery of marijuana because there was no sale, the better practice is to allege the amount of marijuana delivered if greater than the threshold quantity. See the sample charge, below.
- The case law requires the charging document to identify the buyer or recipient of the substance, if known. When a law enforcement officer uses an intermediary and the defendant sells or delivers the controlled substance to the intermediary without knowing that the officer was buying or taking delivery of the controlled substance, the name of the intermediary, not the name of the law enforcement officer, normally must be alleged. State v. Wall, 96 N.C. App. 45 (1989).
- When identifying the controlled substance, do so "by its chemical name as it appears in [the controlled substance schedules]." State v. Turshizi, 175 N.C. App. 783, 785 (2006).
- Schedule VI includes tetrahydrocannabinols "except for tetrahydrocannabinols found in a product with a delta-9 tetrahydrocannabinol concentration of not more than three-tenths of one percent (0.3%) on a dry weight basis." G.S. 90-94(b)(2). Is it sufficient to allege that the substance at issue is "a tetrahydrocannabinol"? Perhaps so, on the theory that whether the substance falls under the exception in the statute is in the nature of a defense rather than an element. Under a prior statutory regime, the North Carolina Court of Appeals ruled in *State v. Teague*, 286 N.C. App. 160, 180, 181 (2022), that "the concentration of THC is not an element of the offense of possession with intent to sell or deliver THC," but rather is an "exception." However, as of this writing, the state supreme court may review *Teague*, and the law regarding marijuana, hemp, and related substances is changing quickly. Therefore, a cautious prosecutor may wish to allege more than *Teague* requires, perhaps along the lines of "a tetrahydrocannabinol contained in a product with a delta-9 tetrahydrocannabinol concentration greater than 0.3% on a dry weight basis."

G.S. 90-95(a)(1)
Sale or Delivery of a Controlled Substance
April 2024
Page 2 of 2

Sample Charges:
. . . unlawfully, willfully, and feloniously did sell to Leslie Jones a controlled substance, heroin, which is included in Schedule I of the North Carolina Controlled Substances Act.

. . . unlawfully, willfully, and feloniously did deliver to James Monroe a controlled substance, 12 grams of marijuana, which is included in Schedule VI of the North Carolina Controlled Substances Act.

AOC Forms for This Offense:
- AOC-CR-151 (Indictment) (use only when charging both sale or delivery of, and possession with the intent to manufacture, sell, or deliver, the same substance)
- AOC-J-327 (Juvenile Petition)

Punishment:
If the controlled substance is in Schedule I or II, sale is a Class G felony and delivery is a Class H felony. If the controlled substance is in Schedule III through VI, sale is a Class H felony and delivery is a Class I felony, unless the delivery falls under the exception for less than 5 grams of marijuana as described above.

G.S. 90-95(a)(2)
Sale or Delivery of Counterfeit Controlled Substance
April 2024

Introductory Comment:
None.

Charging Language:
. . . unlawfully, willfully, and feloniously did (*choose one or both*: sell; deliver) to (*identify purchaser or recipient of substance*), a counterfeit controlled substance, (*identify substance and describe how it is counterfeit*).

Notes about Charging Language:
- It also is a violation of G.S. 90-95(a)(2) to create, or to possess with intent to sell or deliver, a counterfeit controlled substance. To charge one of these offenses, modify this form using charging language similar to the language used to charge the manufacture of a controlled substance or the possession with intent to sell or deliver a controlled substance.
- G.S. 90-87(6) defines a "counterfeit controlled substance" as follows:
  a. A controlled substance which, or the container or labeling of which, without authorization, bears the trademark, trade name, or other identifying mark, imprint, number, or device, or any likeness thereof, of a manufacturer, distributor, or dispenser other than the person or persons who in fact manufactured, distributed, or dispensed such substance and which thereby falsely purports, or is represented to be the product of, or to have been distributed by, such other manufacturer, distributor, or dispenser or
  b. Any substance which is by any means intentionally represented as a controlled substance. It is evidence that the substance has been intentionally misrepresented as a controlled substance if the following factors are established:
     1. The substance was packaged or delivered in a manner normally used for the illegal delivery of controlled substances.
     2. Money or other valuable property has been exchanged or requested for the substance, and the amount of that consideration was substantially in excess of the reasonable value of the substance.
     3. The physical appearance of the tablets, capsules, or other finished product containing the substance is substantially identical to a specified controlled substance.
- There is no requirement that the defendant know that the substance is counterfeit. State v. Bivens, 204 N.C. App. 350 (2010).

Sample Charge:
. . . unlawfully, willfully, and feloniously did sell and deliver to James Monroe a counterfeit controlled substance, which the defendant intentionally and falsely represented was marijuana, which is included in Schedule VI of the North Carolina Controlled Substances Act. The counterfeit controlled substance was in fact oregano packaged in a Ziploc bag.

AOC Forms for This Offense:
None.

Punishment:
Class I felony.

G.S. 90-95(a)(3)
Simple Possession of Schedule I Controlled Substance
April 2024

Introductory Comment:
None.

Charging Language:
. . . unlawfully, willfully, and feloniously did possess a controlled substance, (*identify the substance*), which is included in Schedule I of the North Carolina Controlled Substances Act.

Notes about Charging Language:
- When identifying the controlled substance, do so "by its chemical name as it appears in [the controlled substance schedules]." State v. Turshizi, 175 N.C. App. 783, 785 (2006).
- G.S. 90-95(d)(1) provides that if the controlled substance is MDPV and the quantity of the MDPV is 1 gram or less, the offense is punishable as a Class 1 misdemeanor. In such a case, allege "unlawfully and willfully" rather than "unlawfully, willfully, and feloniously."

Sample Charge:
. . . unlawfully, willfully, and feloniously did possess a controlled substance, mescaline, which is included in Schedule I of the North Carolina Controlled Substances Act.

AOC Forms for This Offense:
AOC-J-329 (Juvenile Petition)

Punishment:
Class I felony, unless the controlled substance is MDPV and the quantity of the MDPV is 1 gram or less, in which case the offense is a Class 1 misdemeanor.

Introductory Comment:
The seriousness of this offense depends on the type of substance and the quantity of the substance that the defendant possessed. Be sure to use the appropriate charge for the type and quantity in your case. Also, note that possession of any quantity of fentanyl or carfentanil became a felony, as described below, effective December 1, 2021, for offenses committed on or after that date. *See* S.L. 2021-155. Offenses prior to that date should be charged as misdemeanors.

Charging Language:

I. Misdemeanor simple possession

. . . unlawfully and willfully did possess (*identify substance*), a controlled substance that is included in Schedule (*choose one*: II; III; IV) of the North Carolina Controlled Substances Act.

II. Felonious simple possession of any quantity of methamphetamine, amphetamine, phencyclidine, cocaine, fentanyl, or carfentanil

. . . unlawfully, willfully, and feloniously did possess (*choose one*: methamphetamine, amphetamine, phencyclidine, cocaine, fentanyl, or carfentanil), a controlled substance that is included in Schedule II of the North Carolina Controlled Substances Act.

III. Felonious simple possession of over 4 dosage units of hydromorphone or over 100 dosage units of any other substance

. . . unlawfully, willfully, and feloniously did possess (*choose one*: more than 100 tablets; more than 100 capsules; more than 100 dosage units; *or, if hydromorphone, choose one*: more than 4 tablets; more than 4 capsules; more than 4 dosage units) of (*identify substance*), a controlled substance that is included in Schedule (*choose one*: II; III; IV) of the North Carolina Controlled Substances Act.

Notes about Charging Language:

- When identifying the controlled substance, do so "by its chemical name as it appears in [the controlled substance schedules]." State v. Turshizi, 175 N.C. App. 783, 785 (2006).
- Do not charge Offense I in a case involving methamphetamine, amphetamine, phencyclidine, cocaine, fentanyl, or carfentanil. Simple possession of those substances is a felony, and there is no misdemeanor possession offense for those substances.
- Offense II also applies to various cocaine-related substances, including salts and isomers thereof; see the statute for a complete listing.
- For Offense III, if the substance possessed is in a form not distinguishable by individual dosage units, such as in powder or liquid form, a felony can still be charged if the substance could be converted into more than 100 dosage units (or 4 units, for hydromorphone); that is, if the form of the substance is the equivalent of more than 100 dosage units even though some packaging or other processing would be necessary to convert it into recognizable dosage units. In such a case, state "a quantity equivalent to more than 100 dosage units of . . ."

Sample Charge:

I. Misdemeanor simple possession

. . . unlawfully and willfully did possess phenobarbital, a controlled substance that is included in Schedule IV of the North Carolina Controlled Substances Act.

AOC Forms for This Offense:
AOC-J-330 (Juvenile Petition)

Punishment:
Offense I is a Class 1 misdemeanor. Offenses II and III are Class I felonies.

G.S. 90-95(a)(3)
Simple Possession of Schedule V Controlled Substance
April 2024

Introductory Comment:
Many substances included in Schedule V are available over the counter in drugstores. In cases involving such substances, this offense should not be charged unless there is clear evidence that the substance involved is being used for unlawful purposes.

Charging Language:
. . . unlawfully and willfully did possess (*identify the substance*), a controlled substance included in Schedule V of the North Carolina Controlled Substances Act.

Notes about Charging Language:
- When identifying the controlled substance, do so "by its chemical name as it appears in [the controlled substance schedules]." State v. Turshizi, 175 N.C. App. 783, 785 (2006).

Sample Charge:
. . . unlawfully and willfully did possess pyrovalerone, a controlled substance included in Schedule V of the North Carolina Controlled Substances Act.

AOC Forms for This Offense:
None.

Punishment:
Class 2 misdemeanor.

G.S. 90-95(a)(3)
Simple Possession of Schedule VI Controlled Substance
April 2024
Page 1 of 2

Introductory Comment:
Schedule VI of the North Carolina Controlled Substances Act consists exclusively of marijuana and certain tetrahydrocannabinols. It does not include synthetic cannabinoids, which were rescheduled to Schedule I, effective December 1, 2017. S.L. 2017-115. The seriousness of this offense depends on the exact type of the substance and the quantity of the substance that the defendant possessed. Be sure to use the appropriate charge for the type and quantity in your case.

Charging Language:

I. Simple misdemeanor possession (one-half of an ounce of marijuana or one-twentieth of an ounce of hashish, or less; any quantity of covered tetrahydrocannabinols)

. . . unlawfully and willfully did possess (*choose one*: marijuana; the extracted resin of marijuana, commonly known as hashish; tetrahydrocannabinols), a controlled substance that is included in Schedule VI of the North Carolina Controlled Substances Act.

II. Aggravated misdemeanor possession (over one-half of an ounce of marijuana but not more than one and one-half ounces, or over one-twentieth of an ounce of hashish but not more than three-twentieths of an ounce)

. . . unlawfully and willfully did possess (*choose one*: more than one-half of an ounce of marijuana but not more than one and one-half ounces of marijuana; more than one-twentieth of an ounce of the extracted resin of marijuana, commonly known as hashish, but not more than three-twentieths of an ounce of hashish), a controlled substance that is included in Schedule VI of the North Carolina Controlled Substances Act.

III. Felonious simple possession (over one and one-half ounces of marijuana, three-twentieths of an ounce of hashish, or any quantity of synthetic tetrahydrocannabinols or tetrahydrocannabinols isolated from the resin or marijuana)

. . . unlawfully, willfully, and feloniously did possess (*choose one*: more than one and one-half ounces of marijuana; more than three-twentieths of an ounce of the extracted resin of marijuana, commonly known as hashish; synthetic tetrahydrocannabinols; tetrahydrocannabinols isolated from the resin of marijuana), a controlled substance that is included in Schedule VI of the North Carolina Controlled Substances Act.

Notes about Charging Language:

- Schedule VI includes tetrahydrocannabinols "except for tetrahydrocannabinols found in a product with a delta-9 tetrahydrocannabinol concentration of not more than three-tenths of one percent (0.3%) on a dry weight basis." G.S. 90-94(b)(2). Is it sufficient to allege that the substance at issue is "a tetrahydrocannabinol"? Perhaps so, on the theory that whether the substance falls under the exception in the statute is in the nature of a defense rather than an element. Under a prior statutory regime, the North Carolina Court of Appeals ruled in *State v. Teague*, 286 N.C. App. 160, 180, 181 (2022), that "the concentration of THC is not an element of the offense of possession with intent to sell or deliver THC," but rather is an "exception." However, as of this writing, the state supreme court may review *Teague*, and the law regarding marijuana, hemp, and related substances is changing quickly. Therefore, a cautious prosecutor may wish to allege more than *Teague* requires, perhaps along the lines of "a tetrahydrocannabinol contained in a product with a delta-9 tetrahydrocannabinol concentration greater than 0.3% on a dry weight basis."

- G.S. 90-95(d)(4) makes it a felony to possess any amount of Schedule VI "synthetic tetrahydrocannabinols" or "tetrahydrocannabinols isolated from the resin of marijuana." It may be difficult to differentiate between these substances. Additionally, some may argue that such substances do not fall within Schedule VI—and so are not unlawful to possess—if they are contained in a product with a delta-9 THC concentration of less not more than 0.3% on a dry-weight basis. Finally, although it is perhaps possible to argue that a synthetic tetrahydrocannabinol fits within the definition of a "synthetic cannabinoid" under G.S. 90-89(7) and so should be classified as a Schedule I substance rather than a Schedule VI substance, the specific inclusion of "tetrahydrocannabinols" in Schedule VI, *see* G.S. 90-94(b)(2), and the fact that the chemical structures listed as examples in G.S. 90-89(7) are all very different from tetrahydrocannabinols, seem to indicate that synthetic tetrahydrocannabinols are best addressed under Schedule VI. Because the law and chemistry in this area are complex and evolving, before charging a felony involving "synthetic tetrahydrocannabinols" or "tetrahydrocannabinols isolated from the resin of marijuana," a prosecutor may wish to consult an expert in drug chemistry.

Sample Charge:

I. Simple misdemeanor possession (one-half of an ounce of marijuana or one-twentieth of an ounce of hashish, or less)

. . . unlawfully and willfully did possess marijuana, a controlled substance that is included in Schedule VI of the North Carolina Controlled Substances Act.

AOC Forms for This Offense:

AOC-J-331 (Juvenile Petition)

Punishment:

Offense I is a Class 3 misdemeanor, with special sentencing provisions set forth in the statute. Offense II is a Class 1 misdemeanor. Offense III is a Class I felony.

G.S. 90-95(d1)
Possession of Immediate Precursor Chemical

April 2024
Page 1 of 2

Introductory Comment:
For a list of immediate precursor chemicals, see G.S. 90-95(d2). Note that the precursor chemicals designated under G.S. 90-88 are incorporated into the list by reference.

Charging Language:

I. Possession with intent to manufacture immediate precursor chemical (not involving methamphetamine) **G.S. 90-95(d1)(1)**

. . . unlawfully, willfully, and feloniously did possess an immediate precursor chemical, (*name chemical*), with the intent to manufacture a controlled substance, (*name controlled substance*).

II. Possession with intent to manufacture immediate precursor chemical (involving methamphetamine) **G.S. 90-95(d1)(2)**

. . . unlawfully, willfully, and feloniously did possess an immediate precursor chemical, (*name chemical*), with the intent to manufacture methamphetamine, a controlled substance.

III. Possession or distribution of immediate precursor chemical (not involving methamphetamine) **G.S. 90-95(d1)(1)**

. . . unlawfully, willfully, and feloniously did (*choose one or both*: possess; distribute) an immediate precursor chemical, (*name chemical*), (*choose one or both*: knowing; having reasonable cause to believe) that the immediate precursor chemical would be used to manufacture a controlled substance, (*name controlled substance*).

IV. Possession or distribution of immediate precursor chemical (involving methamphetamine) **G.S. 90-95(d1)(2)**

. . . unlawfully, willfully, and feloniously did (*choose one or both*: possess; distribute) an immediate precursor chemical, (*name chemical*), (*choose one or both*: knowing; having reasonable cause to believe) that the immediate precursor chemical would be used to manufacture methamphetamine, a controlled substance.

V. Possession of pseudoephedrine by person with prior methamphetamine conviction **G.S. 90-95(d1)(1)c.**

. . . unlawfully, willfully, and feloniously did possess (*name or describe product*), a pseudoephedrine product. The defendant had a prior conviction for (*choose one or more*: possession of methamphetamine; possession with intent to sell or deliver methamphetamine; selling or delivering methamphetamine; trafficking methamphetamine; possession of an immediate precursor chemical; manufacture of methamphetamine). Specifically, the defendant was convicted of (*name offense*) on or about (*date*), in (*court*).

Notes about Charging Language:

- The prior conviction discussed in Offense V may be from "any jurisdiction within the United States." G.S. 90-95(d1)(1)c. Provide appropriate detail about the court in which the conviction took place, such as the county and—at least if it is not North Carolina—the state the court serves.
- It is not clear whether Offense V may be charged when a defendant's only pertinent prior conviction is for possession of an immediate precursor chemical and the chemical is used in the manufacture of a controlled substance other than methamphetamine.

Sample Charge:

I. **Possession with intent to manufacture immediate precursor chemical (not involving methamphetamine)** **G.S. 90-95(d1)(1)**

. . . unlawfully, willfully, and feloniously did possess an immediate precursor chemical, sulfuric acid, with the intent to manufacture a controlled substance, heroin.

AOC Forms for This Offense:
None.

Punishment:
Offenses I, III, and V are Class H felonies. Offenses II and IV are Class F felonies.

G.S. 90-95(e)
Prior Drug Convictions
April 2024
Page 1 of 2

Introductory Comment:
G.S. 90-95(e) contains several provisions increasing the punishment for defendants who commit misdemeanor drug violations after already having been convicted of a drug offense. Under G.S. 90-95(e)(3), if a defendant is charged with a Class 1 misdemeanor and a prior drug conviction is alleged in the criminal pleading and proven at trial, the crime is punished as a Class I felony. Under G.S. 90-95(e)(4), if the defendant is charged with a Class 2 misdemeanor and a prior drug conviction is alleged in the criminal pleading and proven at trial, the crime is punished as a Class 1 misdemeanor. Under G.S. 90-95(e)(7), if the defendant is charged with a misdemeanor whose punishment requires a suspended sentence, see G.S. 90-95(d)(4), and a prior drug conviction is alleged in the criminal pleading and proven at trial, the crime is punished as a Class 2 misdemeanor. The prior drug convictions may be misdemeanors or felonies and include convictions in other states or in federal court as long as the drug violation would be punishable under North Carolina's Controlled Substances Act. Remember, however, that G.S. 90-95(e)(6) provides that prior drug convictions occurring at one trial count only as one prior drug conviction.

An indictment or an information for the recidivist offense must comply with G.S. 15A-928, which requires that the defendant's prior convictions be alleged either (1) in a separate count of the indictment or information than the substantive offense or (2) in a separate indictment or information. This requirement does not apply to arrest warrants or magistrates' orders, which still must allege the defendant's prior convictions but need not do so in a separate count or separate charging instrument. Also note that in situations where a conviction for a recidivist offense is appealed from district to superior court for trial de novo, G.S. 15A-922(h) and -928(d) require the State to replace the pleading in the case with superseding statements of charges separately alleging the substantive offense and any prior convictions. G.S. 15A-928 also requires that the name or title of an offense elevated by prior convictions must not make reference to such prior convictions.

Charging Language:
(*For arrest warrants and magistrates' orders, add the following at the end of the charge; for indictments and informations, set out the following as a separate count or in a separate charging instrument*:)
The defendant has previously been convicted of (*identify the offense*), an offense punishable (*when appropriate, add the words* "as a felony") under the North Carolina Controlled Substances Act. The conviction was on (*give date*), in the (*identify the court*) Court, (*name county*) County, (*name city and state*).

Notes about Charging Language:
- If an offense that would otherwise be a misdemeanor is a felony as a result of the defendant's prior conviction, include "and feloniously" after "willfully" in the charging language for the offense.

Sample Charge:
The defendant has previously been convicted of distribution of heroin, an offense punishable as a felony under the North Carolina Controlled Substances Act. The conviction was on March 14, 2014, in the United States District Court for the Western District of North Carolina, Asheville, N.C.

AOC Forms for This Offense:
None.

Punishment:
See above.

G.S. 90-95(e)(5)
Selling or Delivering a Controlled Substance to a Person under 16 or to a Pregnant Woman
April 2024
Page 1 of 2

Introductory Comment:
None.

Charging Language:

I. Selling or delivering a controlled substance to a person under 16 but over 13 by a person 18 or older

. . . unlawfully, willfully, and feloniously did violate G.S. 90-95(a)(1) by (*select one or both*: selling; delivering) a controlled substance, (*name substance*), which is included in Schedule (*give schedule number*) of the North Carolina Controlled Substances Act, to (*name person*), a person under 16 years old but more than 13 years old, namely, (*give age*). The defendant was at least 18 years old or older at the time of this offense, namely, (*give age*).

II. Selling or delivering a controlled substance to a person 13 or younger by a person 18 or older

. . . unlawfully, willfully, and feloniously did violate G.S. 90-95(a)(1) by (*select one or both*: selling; delivering) a controlled substance, (*name substance*), which is included in Schedule (*give schedule number*) of the North Carolina Controlled Substances Act, to (*name person*), a person 13 years old or younger, namely, (*give age*). The defendant was at least 18 years old or older at the time of this offense, namely, (*give age*).

III. Selling or delivering a controlled substance to a pregnant woman by a person 18 or older

. . . unlawfully, willfully, and feloniously did violate G.S. 90-95(a)(1) by (*select one or both*: selling; delivering) a controlled substance, (*name substance*), which is included in Schedule (*give schedule number*) of the North Carolina Controlled Substances Act, to (*name person*), a female who was pregnant at the time. The defendant was at least 18 years old or older at the time of this offense, namely, (*give age*).

Notes about Charging Language:

- G.S. 90-87(7) defines "deliver" as "the actual, constructive, or attempted transfer from one person to another of a controlled substance, whether or not there is an agency relationship." Delivering would include all instances of selling; but if there is an exchange of money, use the word "sell" in addition to or instead of "deliver." As noted below, the punishment for sale is greater than the punishment for delivery.
- The case law requires the charging document to identify the buyer or recipient of the substance, if known.
- When identifying the controlled substance, do so "by its chemical name as it appears in [the controlled substance schedules]." State v. Turshizi, 175 N.C. App. 783, 785 (2006).
- Schedule VI includes tetrahydrocannabinols "except for tetrahydrocannabinols found in a product with a delta-9 tetrahydrocannabinol concentration of not more than three-tenths of one percent (0.3%) on a dry weight basis." G.S. 90-94(b)(2). Is it sufficient to allege that the substance at issue is "a tetrahydrocannabinol"? Perhaps so, on the theory that whether the substance falls

under the exception in the statute is in the nature of a defense rather than an element. Under a prior statutory regime, the North Carolina Court of Appeals ruled in *State v. Teague*, 286 N.C. App. 160, 180, 181 (2022), that "the concentration of THC is not an element of the offense of possession with intent to sell or deliver THC," but rather is an "exception." However, as of this writing, the state supreme court may review *Teague*, and the law regarding marijuana, hemp, and related substances is changing quickly. Therefore, a cautious prosecutor may wish to allege more than *Teague* requires, perhaps along the lines of "a tetrahydrocannabinol contained in a product with a delta-9 tetrahydrocannabinol concentration greater than 0.3% on a dry weight basis."

Sample Charge:

I. Selling or delivering a controlled substance to a person under 16 but over 13 by a person 18 or older

. . . unlawfully, willfully, and feloniously did violate G.S. 90-95(a)(1) by selling and delivering a controlled substance, cocaine, which is included in Schedule II of the North Carolina Controlled Substances Act, to Johnny Jones, a person under 16 years old but more than 13 years old, namely, 14 years old. The defendant was at least 18 years old or older at the time of this offense, namely, 20 years old.

AOC Forms for This Offense:
None.

Punishment:
Offenses I and III are Class D felonies. Offense II is a Class C felony. G.S. 90-95(e)(5) provides that the fact that the defendant was mistaken about the buyer's age or whether the buyer was pregnant is no defense to this offense.

G.S. 90-95(e)(8)
Selling, Delivering, etc., Controlled Substance Near School
April 2024

Introductory Comment:
Note that the transfer of less than 5 grams of marijuana for no remuneration does not constitute a delivery in violation of G.S. 90-95(a)(1). An appellate court interpreting a similar federal law ruled that the distance required for a violation of this statute is measured in a straight line from the school's property line to the place of the drug transaction, not by the pedestrian route of travel. United States v. Watson, 887 F.2d 980 (9th Cir. 1989). Middle schools and high schools are secondary schools. This offense would apply to all elementary and secondary schools, both private and public. The drug transaction need not involve school children for this offense to be committed. United States v. Rowe, 911 F.2d 50 (8th Cir. 1990) (interpreting a similar federal law). There is also no requirement that the defendant must have intended to distribute the controlled substance within the proscribed number of feet from the school. United States v. Wake, 948 F.2d 1422 (5th Cir. 1991) (interpreting a similar federal law).

Charging Language:
. . . unlawfully, willfully, and feloniously did commit an offense under G.S. 90-95(a)(1) (*incorporate proper charging language for underlying offense*) (*choose one*: on property used for; within 1,000 feet of the boundary of real property used for) (*choose one*: an elementary school; a secondary school), (*name school*). The defendant was 21 years of age or older, namely, (*give defendant's age*), at the time of this offense.

Notes about Charging Language:
None.

Sample Charge:
. . . unlawfully, willfully, and feloniously did commit an offense under G.S. 90-95(a)(1) by selling a controlled substance, cocaine, which is included in Schedule II of the North Carolina Controlled Substances Act, to Peter Jones within 1,000 feet of the boundary of real property used for an elementary school, Marshall Elementary School, Millburn, N.C. The defendant was 21 years old or older, namely, 30 years old, at the time of this offense.

AOC Forms for This Offense:
None.

Punishment:
Class E felony.

G.S. 90-95(e)(8)
Selling, Delivering, etc., Controlled Substance Near Child Care Center
April 2024

Introductory Comment:
Note that the transfer of less than 5 grams of marijuana for no remuneration does not constitute a delivery in violation of G.S. 90-95(a)(1). The distance required for a violation of this statute would likely be measured in a straight line from the child care center's property line to the place of the drug transaction, not by the pedestrian route of travel. *See* United States v. Watson, 887 F.2d 980 (9th Cir. 1989) (concerning a federal law involving a drug transaction near a school and ruling that the distance is measured from the school's property line to the place of the drug transaction). There is no requirement that the defendant must have intended to distribute the controlled substance within the proscribed number of feet from the child care center. *Cf.* United States v. Wake, 948 F.2d 1422 (5th Cir. 1991) (interpreting a similar federal law).

Charging Language:
. . . unlawfully, willfully, and feloniously did commit an offense under G.S. 90-95(a)(1) (*incorporate proper charging language for underlying offense*) (*choose one*: on property used for; within 1,000 feet of the boundary of real property used for) a child care center, (*name child care center and give location*). The defendant was 21 years of age or older, namely, (*give defendant's age*), at the time of this offense.

Notes about Charging Language:
- G.S. 90-95(e)(8) provides that a "child care center" is as defined in G.S. 110-86(3)a. and licensed by the Secretary of the Department of Health and Human Services.

Sample Charge:
. . . unlawfully, willfully, and feloniously did commit an offense under G.S. 90-95(a)(1) by selling a controlled substance, cocaine, which is included in Schedule II of the North Carolina Controlled Substances Act, to Peter Jones within 1,000 feet of the boundary of real property used for a child care center, Little Children's Center, Oakdale, N.C. The defendant was 21 years of age or older, namely, 22 years old, at the time of this offense.

AOC Forms for This Offense:
None.

Punishment:
Class E felony.

G.S. 90-95(e)(9)
Possessing Controlled Substance in Prison or Jail
April 2024

Introductory Comment:
This offense applies to any person who possesses a controlled substance on the premises of a penal institution or local confinement facility, including prisoners, inmates, employees, and visitors. The scope of the statute includes areas that are not secured and accessible only to officers. State v. Moncree, 188 N.C. App. 221 (2008).

Charging Language:
. . . unlawfully, willfully, and feloniously did violate G.S. 90-95(a)(3) by possessing (*name controlled substance*), a controlled substance that is included in Schedule (*give schedule number*) of the North Carolina Controlled Substances Act, on the premises of a (*choose one and name institution or facility*: penal institution; local confinement facility).

Notes about Charging Language:
None.

Sample Charge:
. . . unlawfully, willfully, and feloniously did violate G.S. 90-95(a)(3) by possessing marijuana, a controlled substance that is included in Schedule VI of the North Carolina Controlled Substances Act, on the premises of a local confinement facility, the Durham County Jail.

AOC Forms for This Offense:
None.

Punishment:
Class H felony.

G.S. 90-95(e)(10)
Selling, Delivering, etc., Controlled Substance Near Public Park
April 2024

Introductory Comment:
Note that the transfer of less than 5 grams of marijuana for no remuneration does not constitute a delivery in violation of G.S. 90-95(a)(1). The distance required for a violation of this statute would likely be measured in a straight line from the park's property line to the place of the drug transaction, not by the pedestrian route of travel. *See* United States v. Watson, 887 F.2d 980 (9th Cir. 1989) (concerning a federal law involving a drug transaction near a school and ruling that the distance is measured from the school's property line to the place of the drug transaction). There is no requirement that the defendant must have intended to distribute the controlled substance within the proscribed number of feet from the park. *Cf.* United States v. Wake, 948 F.2d 1422 (5th Cir. 1991) (interpreting a similar federal law).

Charging Language:
. . . unlawfully, willfully, and feloniously did commit an offense under G.S. 90-95(a)(1) (*incorporate proper charging language for underlying offense*) (*choose one*: on; within 1,000 feet of the boundary of) real property that is a public park, (*name park and give location*). The defendant was 21 years of age or older, namely, (*give defendant's age*), at the time of this offense.

Notes about Charging Language:
None.

Sample Charge:
. . . unlawfully, willfully, and feloniously did commit an offense under G.S. 90-95(a)(1) by selling a controlled substance, cocaine, which is included in Schedule II of the North Carolina Controlled Substances Act, to Peter Jones within 1,000 feet of the boundary of real property that is a public park, James Peters Park, Charlotte, N.C. The defendant was 21 years of age or older, namely, 31 years old, at the time of this offense.

AOC Forms for This Offense:
None.

Punishment:
Class E felony.

Introductory Comment:
None.

Charging Language:

I. Trafficking in drugs **G.S. 90-95(h)**

. . . unlawfully, willfully, and feloniously did [*choose only one*: sell to (*name purchaser of controlled substance*); deliver to (*name person to whom controlled substance was delivered*); manufacture; transport; possess] (*insert appropriate statutory minimum and maximum amount, listed under "Punishment," below*) of [*choose one*: marijuana; synthetic cannabinoids; methaqualone; cocaine; methamphetamine; amphetamine; (*name substance*), a substituted cathinone as defined in G.S. 90-89(5)(j); heroin; opium; (*name substance*), an opiate; (*name substance*), an opioid; lysergic acid diethylamide; 3,4-methylene- dioxyamphetamine (MDA); 3,4- methylenedioxymethamphetamine (MDMA)].

II. Conspiracy to traffic in drugs **G.S. 90-95(i)**

. . . unlawfully, willfully, and feloniously did conspire with (*name persons with whom conspired and/ or write* "persons unknown") to commit the felony of trafficking by [*choose one or more*: sale (*if known, insert to whom defendants conspired to sell*); delivery (*if known, insert to whom defendants conspired to deliver*); manufacture; transportation; possession] of (*insert appropriate statutory minimum and maximum amount, listed under "Punishment," below*) of [*choose one*: marijuana; synthetic cannabinoids; methaqualone; cocaine; methamphetamine; amphetamine; (*name substance*), a substituted cathinone as defined in G.S. 90-89(5)(j); heroin; opium; (*name substance*), an opiate; (*name substance*), an opioid; lysergic acid diethylamide; 3,4-methylenedioxyamphetamine (MDA); 3,4-methylenedioxy- methamphetamine (MDMA)].

Notes about Charging Language:

- For Offense I, each act (sell, deliver, manufacture, transport, possess) is a separate offense, State v. Perry, 316 N.C. 87 (1986), and must be charged separately, State v. Diaz, 317 N.C. 545 (1986).
- G.S. 90-95(h)(1a) refers to "dosage units of a synthetic cannabinoid or any mixture containing such substance." In a case involving a mixture, although probably not legally required, insert the words "a mixture containing synthetic cannabinoid" in the pleading. A dosage unit is 3 grams of synthetic cannabinoid or any mixture containing synthetic cannabinoid.
- G.S. 90-95(h)(2) refers to methaqualone contained in "tablets, capsules, or other dosage units, or the equivalent quantity . . . or any mixture containing such substance." In a case involving a mixture, although probably not legally required, insert the words "a mixture containing methaqualone" in the pleading.
- G.S. 90-95(h)(3) also applies to the weight of any mixture containing cocaine or any salt, isomer, etc., thereof. In such a case, although probably not legally required, insert the words "a mixture containing cocaine" in the pleading.

- G.S. 90-95(h)(3b) also applies to the weight of any mixture containing methamphetamine. In such a case, although probably not legally required, insert "a mixture containing methamphetamine" in the pleading.
- G.S. 90-95(h)(3c) also applies to the weight of any mixture containing amphetamine. In such a case, although probably not legally required, insert "a mixture containing amphetamine" in the pleading.
- G.S. 90-95(h)(3d) also applies to the weight of any mixture containing a substituted cathinone. In such a case, although probably not legally required, insert "a mixture containing a substituted cathinone" in the pleading.
- G.S. 90-95(h)(4) also applies to the weight of any mixture containing heroin, opium, an opiate, or an opioid. In such a case, although probably not legally required, insert "a mixture containing heroin (or, as appropriate, opium, an opiate, or an opioid)" in the pleading.
- G.S. 90-95(h)(4a) refers to lysergic acid diethylamide contained in "tablets, capsules, or other dosage units, or the equivalent quantity . . . or any mixture containing such substance." In a case involving a mixture, although probably not legally required, insert the words "a mixture containing lysergic acid diethylamide" in the pleading.
- G.S. 90-95(h)(4b) refers (1) to the substance in a quantity of "tablets, capsules, or other dosage units"; (2) to the substance by weight in grams; or (3) to any mixture containing the substance. In a case involving a mixture, although probably not legally required, insert "a mixture containing (*name the substance*)" in the pleading.
- For Offense II, when only one agreement encompasses a conspiracy to sell, deliver, manufacture, transport, and possess, only one trafficking conspiracy charge can be brought, and all the intended acts (sale, manufacture, etc.) of the conspiracy should be alleged in one conspiracy charge. State v. Worthington, 84 N.C. App. 150 (1987). However, if, for example, there is an agreement to transport drugs and a later separate agreement is made to sell the drugs, two separate conspiracy charges could be brought.

Sample Charges:

I. Trafficking in drugs **G.S. 90-95(h)**

. . . unlawfully, willfully, and feloniously did sell to Alice B. Toklas more than 10 pounds but less than 50 pounds of marijuana.

. . . unlawfully, willfully, and feloniously did sell to Harold Jones 14 grams or more but less than 28 grams of a mixture containing heroin.

. . . unlawfully, willfully, and feloniously did sell to Marsha Tolson 500 or more but less than 1,000 dosage units of lysergic acid diethylamide.

II. Conspiracy to traffic in drugs **G.S. 90-95(i)**

. . . unlawfully, willfully, and feloniously did conspire with Samuel Smith, Jennifer Robin, and others unknown to commit the felony of trafficking by possession and transportation of 5,000 or more but less than 10,000 dosage units of methaqualone.

. . . unlawfully, willfully, and feloniously did conspire with Peter Jones, Albert Hall, and John Miller to commit the felony of trafficking by sale to Arthur Baltos of 10,000 pounds or more of marijuana.

AOC Forms for This Offense:
None.

Punishment:
The following sentences are mandatory, regardless of a defendant's prior record level. A judge may not suspend a sentence or place the defendant on probation, except when the defendant has provided substantial assistance as described in G.S. 90-95(h)(5). The sentence must run consecutively with any sentences being served by the defendant.

For sentences imposed on or after December 1, 2020, G.S. 90-95(h)(5a) now allows the judge to depart from these mandatory sentencing provisions and impose a sentence consistent with the normal structured sentencing rules under G.S. 15A-1340.17, but only if the court finds after a hearing that certain conditions are satisfied. Otherwise, the offense must be sentenced as summarized below.

Marijuana:
- *More than 10 pounds but less than 50 pounds*: Class H felony, punishable by imprisonment for a minimum term of 25 months and a maximum term of 39 months and a fine of not less than $5,000.
- *50 pounds or more but less than 2,000 pounds*: Class G felony, punishable by imprisonment for a minimum term of 35 months and a maximum term of 51 months and a fine of not less than $25,000.
- *2,000 pounds or more but less than 10,000 pounds*: Class F felony, punishable by imprisonment for a minimum term of 70 months and a maximum term of 93 months and a fine of not less than $50,000.
- *10,000 pounds or more*: Class D felony, punishable by imprisonment for a minimum term of 175 months and a maximum term of 222 months and a fine of not less than $200,000.

Synthetic Cannabinoids:
- *More than 50 but less than 250 dosage units*: Class H felony, punishable by imprisonment for a minimum term of 25 months and a maximum term of 39 months and a fine of not less than $5,000.
- *250 or more but less than 1,250 dosage units*: Class G felony, punishable by imprisonment for a minimum term of 35 months and a maximum term of 51 months and a fine of not less than $25,000.
- *1,250 or more but less than 3,750 dosage units*: Class F felony, punishable by imprisonment for a minimum term of 70 months and a maximum term of 93 months and a fine of not less than $50,000.
- *3,750 or more dosage units*: Class D felony, punishable by imprisonment for a minimum term of 175 months and a maximum term of 222 months and a fine of not less than $200,000.

Methaqualone:
- *1,000 or more but less than 5,000 dosage units*: Class G felony, punishable by imprisonment for a minimum term of 35 months and a maximum term of 51 months and a fine of not less than $25,000.

- *5,000 or more but less than 10,000 dosage units*: Class F felony, punishable by imprisonment for a minimum term of 70 months and a maximum term of 93 months and a fine of not less than $50,000.
- *10,000 or more dosage units*: Class D felony, punishable by imprisonment for a minimum term of 175 months and a maximum term of 222 months and a fine of not less than $200,000.

Cocaine:

- *28 grams or more but less than 200 grams*: Class G felony, punishable by imprisonment for a minimum term of 35 months and a maximum term of 51 months and a fine of not less than $50,000.
- *200 grams or more but less than 400 grams*: Class F felony, punishable by imprisonment for a minimum term of 70 months and a maximum term of 93 months and a fine of not less than $100,000.
- *400 grams or more*: Class D felony, punishable by imprisonment for a minimum term of 175 months and a maximum term of 222 months and a fine of not less than $250,000.

Methamphetamine:

- *28 grams or more but less than 200 grams*: Class F felony, punishable by imprisonment for a minimum term of 70 months and a maximum term of 93 months and a fine of not less than $50,000.
- *200 grams or more but less than 400 grams*: Class E felony, punishable by imprisonment for a minimum term of 90 months and a maximum term of 120 months and a fine of not less than $100,000.
- *400 grams or more*: Class C felony, punishable by imprisonment for a minimum term of 225 months and a maximum term of 282 months and a fine of not less than $250,000.

Amphetamine:

- *28 grams or more but less than 200 grams*: Class H felony, punishable by imprisonment for a minimum term of 25 months and a maximum term of 39 months and a fine of not less than $5,000.
- *200 grams or more but less than 400 grams*: Class G felony, punishable by imprisonment for a minimum term of 35 months and a maximum term of 51 months and a fine of not less than $25,000.
- *400 grams or more*: Class E felony, punishable by imprisonment for a minimum term of 90 months and a maximum term of 120 months and a fine of not less than $100,000.

Substituted Cathinones:

- *28 grams or more but less than 200 grams*: Class F felony, punishable by imprisonment for a minimum term of 70 months and a maximum term of 93 months and a fine of not less than $50,000.
- *200 grams or more but less than 400 grams*: Class E felony, punishable by imprisonment for a minimum term of 90 months and a maximum term of 120 months and a fine of not less than $100,000.
- *400 grams or more*: Class C felony, punishable by imprisonment for a minimum term of 225 months and a maximum term of 282 months and a fine of not less than $250,000.

Heroin, Opium, Opiates, and Opioids:

- *4 grams or more but less than 14 grams*: Class F felony, punishable by imprisonment for a minimum term of 70 months and a maximum term of 93 months and a fine of $500,000 if the controlled substance is heroin, fentanyl, or carfentanil, or any salt, compound, derivative, or preparation thereof, or any mixture containing any of these substances, and not less than $50,000 for any other controlled substance described in G.S. 90-95(h)(4).
- *14 grams or more but less than 28 grams*: Class E felony, punishable by imprisonment for a minimum term of 90 months and a maximum term of 120 months and a fine of $750,000 if the controlled substance is heroin, fentanyl, or carfentanil, or any salt, compound, derivative, or preparation thereof, or any mixture containing any of these substances, and not less than $100,000 for any other controlled substance described in G.S. 90-95(h)(4).
- *28 grams or more*: Class C felony, punishable by imprisonment for a minimum term of 225 months and a maximum term of 282 months and a fine of $1,000,000 if the controlled substance is heroin, fentanyl, or carfentanil, or any salt, compound, derivative, or preparation thereof, or any mixture containing any of these substances, and not less than $500,000 for any other controlled substance described in G.S. 90-95(h)(4).

Lysergic acid diethylamide:

- *100 or more but less than 500 dosage units*: Class G felony, punishable by imprisonment for a minimum term of 35 months and a maximum term of 51 months and a fine of not less than $25,000.
- *500 or more but less than 1,000 dosage units*: Class F felony, punishable by imprisonment for a minimum term of 70 months and a maximum term of 93 months and a fine of not less than $50,000.
- *1,000 or more dosage units*: Class D felony, punishable by imprisonment for a minimum term of 175 months and a maximum term of 222 months and a fine of not less than $200,000.

3,4-methylenedioxyamphetamine (MDA) and 3,4-methylenedioxymethamphetamine (MDMA):

- *100 or more but less than 500 dosage units, or 28 grams or more but less than 200 grams*: Class G felony, punishable by imprisonment for a minimum term of 35 months and a maximum term of 51 months and a fine of not less than $25,000.
- *500 or more but less than 1,000 dosage units, or 200 grams or more but less than 400 grams*: Class F felony, punishable by imprisonment for a minimum term of 70 months and a maximum term of 93 months and a fine of not less than $50,000.
- *1,000 or more dosage units or 400 grams or more*: Class D felony, punishable by imprisonment for a minimum term of 175 months and a maximum term of 222 months and a fine of not less than $250,000.

G.S. 90-95.1
Continuing Criminal Enterprise
April 2024
Page 1 of 2

Introductory Comment:
Enacted in 1979, this statute was construed by a state appellate court for the first time in *State v. Guffey*, ___ N.C. App. ___, 897 S.E.2d 144 (2024); *cf.* G.S. 14-7.20.

Charging Language:
. . . unlawfully, willfully, and feloniously did engage in a continuing criminal enterprise by violating (*name felony offense or offenses in Article 5 of G.S. Chapter 90*). The (*choose one*: violation was; violations were) part of a continuing series of violations of Article 5 of Chapter 90 of the General Statutes. The violations included the following: (*enumerate series of Chapter 90, Article 5 violations with dates*). The defendant undertook these violations in concert with (*choose one*: five; more than five) other persons, (*name persons, if known, or state* "whose names are not known"), with respect to whom the defendant occupied a (*choose one or more*: position of organizer; supervisory position; management position) and from which the defendant obtained substantial income and resources.

Notes about Charging Language:

- An indictment charging continuing criminal enterprise (CCE) is invalid unless it specifies the acts alleged to have constituted the enterprise itself. *See Guffey*, ___ N.C. App. at ___, 897 S.E.2d at 149 (indictment was fatally defective that alleged that the defendant aided and abetted two named co-conspirators in a CCE by violating G.S. 90-95(h)(3b) by trafficking in methamphetamine, and that the violation was part of a continuing series of violations of G.S. Chapter 90, Article 5, undertaken in concert with more than five others and from which the co-conspirators obtained substantial income, etc., but failed to allege that the enterprise engaged in any specific conduct.)
- For a case upholding a federal indictment's charging language for the federal offense of continuing criminal enterprise, which is similar to G.S. 90-95.1, see *United States v. Amend*, 791 F.2d 1120 (4th Cir. 1986).

Sample Charge:
. . . unlawfully, willfully, and feloniously did engage in a continuing criminal enterprise by violating G.S. 90-95(h)(3) by trafficking in cocaine and by violating G.S. 90-95(a)(1) by selling heroin. The violations were part of a continuing series of violations of Article 5 of Chapter 90 of the General Statutes. These violations included the following:

(1) possessing more than 28 but less than 200 grams of cocaine on or about January 1, 2024;
(2) selling heroin, a Schedule I controlled substance, to Abe Brady on or about January 3, 2024; and
(3) selling heroin, a Schedule I controlled substance, to Cal Daniels on or about January 4, 2024.

The defendant undertook these violations in concert with more than five other persons, including Julius Smith, Harvey Smeltzer, Howard Peters, Gerry Jones, Sally Means, and Cynthia Walker, with respect to whom the defendant occupied a position of organizer and a supervisory position and from which the defendant obtained substantial income and resources.

AOC Forms for This Offense:
None.

Punishment:
Class C felony. The statute also provides for forfeiture of certain assets connected to the criminal enterprise.

G.S. 90-95.4
Employing Minor to Commit Drug Offense
April 2024
Page 1 of 2

Introductory Comment:
None.

Charging Language:

I. Person at least 18 years old but under 21 years old hiring minor under 18 years old but more than 13 years old **G.S. 90-95.4(a)(1)**

. . . unlawfully, willfully, and feloniously did (*choose one or both*: hire; intentionally use) a minor, (*name minor*), a person under 18 years old but more than 13 years old, namely, (*give age*), to violate G.S. 90-95(a)(1) (*briefly describe violation*). The defendant was at least 18 years old but under 21 years old at the time of this offense, namely, (*give age*).

II. Person at least 18 years old but under 21 years old hiring minor 13 years old or younger **G.S. 90-95.4(a)(2)**

. . . unlawfully, willfully, and feloniously did (*choose one or both*: hire; intentionally use) a minor, (*name minor*), a person 13 years old or younger, namely, (*give age*), to violate G.S. 90-95(a)(1) (*briefly describe violation*). The defendant was at least 18 years old but under 21 years old at the time of this offense, namely, (*give age*).

III. Person 21 years old or older hiring minor under 18 years old but more than 13 years old **G.S. 90-95.4(b)(1)**

. . . unlawfully, willfully, and feloniously did (*choose one or both*: hire; intentionally use) a minor, (*name minor*), a person under 18 years old but more than 13 years old, namely, (*give age*), to violate G.S. 90-95(a)(1) (*briefly describe violation*). The defendant was 21 years old or older at the time of this offense, namely, (*give age*).

IV. Person 21 years old or older hiring minor 13 years old or younger **G.S. 90-95.4(b)(2)**

. . . unlawfully, willfully, and feloniously did (*choose one or both*: hire; intentionally use) a minor, (*name minor*), who was 13 years old or younger, namely, (*give age*), to violate G.S. 90-95(a)(1) (*briefly describe violation*). The defendant was 21 years old or older at the time of this offense, namely, (*give age*).

Notes about Charging Language:

- G.S. 90-95(a)(1) makes it unlawful to manufacture, sell, or deliver, or to possess with intent to manufacture, sell, or deliver, a controlled substance.

Sample Charge:

I. Person at least 18 years old but under 21 years old hiring minor under 18 years old but more than 13 years old **G.S. 90-95.4(a)(1)**

. . . unlawfully, willfully, and feloniously did hire a minor, Susan Connor, a person under 18 years old but more than 13 years old, namely, 14 years old, to violate G.S. 90-95(a)(1) by delivering to Peter Jones a controlled substance, heroin, which is included in Schedule I of the North Carolina Controlled Substances Act. The defendant was at least 18 years old but under 21 years old at the time of this offense, namely, 19 years old.

AOC Forms for This Offense:

None.

Punishment:

- Offense I is punishable as one class more severe than the violation of G.S. 90-95(a)(1) for which the minor was hired. Thus, if that violation is a Class H felony, then the offense is punishable as a Class G felony.
- Offense II is punishable as two classes more severe than the violation of G.S. 90-95(a)(1) for which the minor was hired. Thus, if that violation is a Class H felony, then the offense is punishable as a Class F felony.
- Offense III is punishable as three classes more severe than the violation of G.S. 90-95(a)(1) for which the minor was hired. Thus, if that violation is a Class H felony, then the offense is punishable as a Class E felony.
- Offense IV is punishable as four classes more severe than the violation of G.S. 90-95(a)(1) for which the minor was hired. Thus, if that violation is a Class H felony, then the offense is punishable as a Class D felony.
- G.S. 90-95.4(c) provides that the fact that the defendant mistakenly believed that the minor was a certain age is no defense to this offense.

G.S. 90-95.6
Promoting Drug Sales by Minor
April 2024

Introductory Comment:
None.

Charging Language:
. . . unlawfully, willfully, and feloniously did knowingly (*choose one or more*: entice; force; encourage; facilitate) a minor, (*name minor*), who was (*give age*), to violate G.S. 90-95(a)(1) (*briefly describe violation*) and did (*choose one or more*: supervise; support; advise; protect) that minor in violating G.S. 90-95(a)(1). The defendant was 21 years of age or older at the time of this offense, namely, (*give age*).

Notes about Charging Language:
- It is not clear whether this offense requires proof of both subdivisions (a)(1) and (a)(2) of G.S. 90-95.6 or just one of the subdivisions. The charging language takes the cautious approach and alleges both.
- G.S. 90-95(a)(1) makes it unlawful to manufacture, sell, or deliver, or to possess with intent to manufacture, sell, or deliver, a controlled substance.
- A minor is a person under 18 years old.

Sample Charge:
. . . unlawfully, willfully, and feloniously did knowingly entice and encourage a minor, Brad Jones, who was 16 years old, to violate G.S. 90-95(a)(1) by selling heroin to Paula Smith and did supervise that minor in violating G.S. 90-95(a)(1). The defendant was 21 years of age or older at the time of this offense, namely, 22 years old.

AOC Forms for This Offense:
None.

Punishment:
Class D felony. G.S. 90-95.6(b) provides that the fact that the defendant mistakenly believed that the minor was a certain age is no defense to this offense.

G.S. 90-95.7
Participating in Drug Violation by Minor
April 2024

Introductory Comment:
None.

Charging Language:
. . . unlawfully, willfully, and feloniously did (*choose one or both*: purchase; receive) a controlled substance, (*name substance*), from (*name minor*), a minor 13 years of age or younger, namely, (*give age*), who (*choose one or more*: possessed; sold; delivered) the controlled substance in violation of G.S. 90-95(a)(1). The defendant was 21 years of age or older at the time of this offense, namely, (*give age*).

Notes about Charging Language:

- G.S. 90-95(a)(1) makes it unlawful to manufacture, sell, or deliver, or to possess with intent to manufacture, sell, or deliver, a controlled substance.
- Schedule VI includes tetrahydrocannabinols "except for tetrahydrocannabinols found in a product with a delta-9 tetrahydrocannabinol concentration of not more than three-tenths of one percent (0.3%) on a dry weight basis." G.S. 90-94(b)(2). Is it sufficient to allege that the substance at issue is "a tetrahydrocannabinol"? Perhaps so, on the theory that whether the substance falls under the exception in the statute is in the nature of a defense rather than an element. Under a prior statutory regime, the North Carolina Court of Appeals ruled in *State v. Teague*, 286 N.C. App. 160, 180, 181 (2022), that "the concentration of THC is not an element of the offense of possession with intent to sell or deliver THC," but rather is an "exception." However, as of this writing, the state supreme court may review *Teague*, and the law regarding marijuana, hemp, and related substances is changing quickly. Therefore, a cautious prosecutor may wish to allege more than *Teague* requires, perhaps along the lines of "a tetrahydrocannabinol contained in a product with a delta-9 tetrahydrocannabinol concentration greater than 0.3% on a dry weight basis."

Sample Charge:
. . . unlawfully, willfully, and feloniously did purchase a controlled substance, cocaine, from Robert Stephens, a minor 13 years of age or younger, namely, 11 years old, who sold the controlled substance in violation of G.S. 90-95(a)(1). The defendant was 21 years of age or older at the time of this offense, namely, 23 years old.

AOC Forms for This Offense:
None.

Punishment:
Class G felony. G.S. 90-95.7(b) provides that the fact that the defendant mistakenly believed that the minor was a certain age is no defense to this offense.

G.S. 90-108(a)(2)
Practitioner and Others Unlawfully Dispensing a Controlled Substance
April 2024

Introductory Comment:
None.

Charging Language:
. . . unlawfully, willfully, and feloniously did intentionally distribute and dispense (*name substance*), a controlled substance included in Schedule (*give number*) of the North Carolina Controlled Substances Act, to (*name person*) in violation of (*choose one or both*: G.S. 90-105; G.S. 90-106) by (*describe how G.S. 90-105 and/or G.S. 90-106 were violated*). The defendant was (*choose one*: a practitioner; subject to the requirements of G.S. 90-101) at the time the defendant distributed and dispensed the controlled substance.

Notes about Charging Language:
- The statute provides that this offense is a felony if it is alleged and specifically found that it was committed intentionally. G.S. 90-108(b). It would seem that this particular violation would almost always have to be committed intentionally. However, if it is appropriate to charge a misdemeanor instead, allege "unlawfully and willfully did" rather than "unlawfully, willfully, and feloniously did intentionally."
- The statute prohibits both distributing and dispensing. If only one of these occurred, delete the inappropriate word.
- G.S. 90-87 defines the following: "dispense", "distribute", and "practitioner."

Sample Charge:
. . . unlawfully, willfully, and feloniously did intentionally dispense Secobarbitol, a controlled substance included in Schedule II of the North Carolina Controlled Substances Act, to Howard Smith in violation of G.S. 90-106 by dispensing the Secobarbitol without the written prescription of a practitioner. The defendant was a practitioner at the time he dispensed the controlled substance.

AOC Forms for This Offense:
None.

Punishment:
If done intentionally, a Class I felony. Otherwise, a Class 1 misdemeanor.

G.S. 90-108(a)(7)
Maintaining a Place for Using, Keeping, or Selling Controlled Substances
April 2024
Page 1 of 2

Introductory Comment:
None.

Charging Language:
. . . unlawfully, willfully, and feloniously did knowingly and intentionally keep and maintain a (*choose one*: dwelling house; building; warehouse; store; shop; vehicle; boat; aircraft; *name other type of place*) (*briefly describe place*) (*choose one or both*)

(1) that was used for keeping and selling controlled substances, (*name substance or substances*), in violation of the North Carolina Controlled Substances Act.

(2) that was resorted to by persons using controlled substances, (*name substance or substances*), in violation of the North Carolina Controlled Substances Act, for the purpose of using such substances.

Notes about Charging Language:
- The statute provides that this offense is a felony if it is alleged and specifically found that it was committed intentionally. G.S. 90-108(b). The language above charges a felony offense. To charge a misdemeanor instead, allege "unlawfully and willfully did" rather than "unlawfully, willfully, and feloniously did intentionally." The North Carolina Court of Appeals has recognized that a misdemeanor offense exists under this statute. State v. Bright, 78 N.C. App. 239 (1985).
- For option (1), above, the statute only requires proof of keeping *or* selling. Delete one of these words if inappropriate.
- Schedule VI includes tetrahydrocannabinols "except for tetrahydrocannabinols found in a product with a delta-9 tetrahydrocannabinol concentration of not more than three-tenths of one percent (0.3%) on a dry weight basis." G.S. 90-94(b)(2). Is it sufficient to allege that the substance at issue is "a tetrahydrocannabinol"? Perhaps so, on the theory that whether the substance falls under the exception in the statute is in the nature of a defense rather than an element. Under a prior statutory regime, the North Carolina Court of Appeals ruled in *State v. Teague*, 286 N.C. App. 160, 180, 181 (2022), that "the concentration of THC is not an element of the offense of possession with intent to sell or deliver THC," but rather is an "exception." However, as of this writing, the state supreme court may review *Teague*, and the law regarding marijuana, hemp, and related substances is changing quickly. Therefore, a cautious prosecutor may wish to allege more than *Teague* requires, perhaps along the lines of "a tetrahydrocannabinol contained in a product with a delta-9 tetrahydrocannabinol concentration greater than 0.3% on a dry weight basis."

Sample Charge:
. . . unlawfully, willfully, and feloniously did knowingly and intentionally keep and maintain a dwelling house, the defendant's home at 124 Perkins Place, Washburn, N.C., that was used for keeping and selling controlled substances, heroin and cocaine, in violation of the North Carolina Controlled Substances Act.

AOC Forms for This Offense:
None.

Punishment:
If done intentionally, a Class I felony. Otherwise, a Class 1 misdemeanor.

G.S. 90-108(a)(10)
Obtaining Controlled Substance by Fraud or Forgery
April 2024

Introductory Comment:
None.

Charging Language:
. . . unlawfully, willfully, and feloniously did intentionally acquire and obtain possession of (*name substance*), a controlled substance included in Schedule (*give number*) of the North Carolina Controlled Substances Act, from (*name person from whom substance acquired*) by (*choose one or more*: misrepresentation; fraud; forgery; deception; subterfuge) in that (*describe the acts that are the basis of the charge*).

Notes about Charging Language:
- Generally, a defendant obtains a controlled substance by forgery when the defendant forges a prescription by signing a provider's name to it. The remaining terms in the statute—misrepresentation, fraud, deception, and subterfuge—are very similar. In many cases, as when a defendant falsely claims to have certain symptoms in order to convince a provider to prescribe a controlled substance, any of the remaining terms could probably be used.
- The statute provides that this offense is a felony if it is alleged and specifically found that it was committed intentionally. G.S. 90-108(b). In *State v. Church*, 73 N.C. App. 645 (1985), the North Carolina Court of Appeals ruled that there is no misdemeanor offense under this statute. Therefore, always charge a felony by alleging that the act was committed intentionally.

Sample Charges:
. . . unlawfully, willfully, and feloniously did intentionally acquire and obtain possession of Trinol (sulfonethylmethane), a controlled substance included in Schedule III of the North Carolina Controlled Substances Act, from George Manchester of Robin's Pharmacy, 1110 Wayland Avenue, Greensboro, N.C., by forgery, in that defendant presented a prescription for that substance dated March 3, 2019, on which defendant had forged the name of A. C. Davis, M.D., and had forged the DEA registration number 77243265.

. . . unlawfully, willfully, and feloniously did intentionally acquire and obtain possession of Demerol (pethidine), a controlled substance included in Schedule II of the North Carolina Controlled Substances Act, from Lloyd Wells of CVS, Inc., West Village Shopping Center, Harvest, N.C., by misrepresentation, fraud, deception, and subterfuge, in that defendant presented a prescription for that substance dated February 12, 2018, and signed by Raymond Fowler, M.D., issued to Seaman Boyd, Jr., when in fact he was not Seaman Boyd, Jr., and had only made a photocopy of the prescription.

AOC Forms for This Offense:
None.

Punishment:
Class I felony.

G.S. 90-108(a)(12)–(12a)
Equipment for Manufacturing a Controlled Substance or Counterfeit Controlled Substance
April 2024

Introductory Comment:
G.S. 90-108(a)(12) and (12a) apply to offenses committed on or after December 1, 2023.

Charging Language:

I. Equipment for manufacturing a substance **G.S. 90-108(a)(12)a. & (12a)**

. . . unlawfully, willfully, and feloniously did intentionally (*choose one or more*: possess; manufacture; distribute; export; import) any (*choose one or more*: three-neck round-bottom flask; tableting machine; encapsulating machine; gelatin capsule; equipment; chemical; product; material (*identify if necessary*)), which may be used to (*choose one*: manufacture a controlled substance; create a counterfeit controlled substance) (*identify the controlled substance*) knowing, intending, or having reasonable cause to believe that it will be used to (*choose one*: manufacture a controlled substance; create a counterfeit controlled substance).

II. Device for imprinting a false label **G.S. 90-108(a)(12)b.**

. . . unlawfully, willfully, and feloniously did intentionally (*choose one or more*: make; distribute; possess) any (*choose one or more*: punch; die; plate; stone; other thing (*identify if necessary*)) designed to print, imprint, or reproduce the trademark; tradename; or other identifying mark, imprint, or device of another or any likeness of the foregoing, (*identify the mark*), upon any (*choose one*: drug; container; label) so as to render such drug a counterfeit controlled substance, knowing, intending, or having reasonable cause to believe it will be used to create a counterfeit controlled substance.

Notes about Charging Language:

- With regard to counterfeit controlled substances, these offenses are felonies only if it is alleged and specifically found that they were committed intentionally. G.S. 90-108(b). (Violation with regard to a controlled substance is a felony in any event. G.S. 90-108(b)(1a).) In the rare event that it is appropriate to charge a misdemeanor instead, allege "unlawfully and willfully did" rather than "unlawfully, willfully, and feloniously did intentionally."

Sample Charge:
. . . unlawfully, willfully, and feloniously did intentionally possess a three-neck round-bottom flask, which may be used to manufacture a controlled substance, methamphetamine, knowing, intending, or having reasonable cause to believe that it will be used to manufacture a controlled substance.

AOC Forms for This Offense:
None.

Punishment:
Violation pertaining to a controlled substance is a Class E felony. *See* G.S. 90-108(b)(1a).
Violation pertaining to a counterfeit controlled substance is a Class I felony.

G.S. 90-108(a)(14)
Embezzlement of a Controlled Substance
April 2024
Page 1 of 2

Introductory Comment:
None.

Charging Language:

I. Embezzlement of a controlled substance **G.S. 90-108(a)(14)**

. . . unlawfully and willfully (*if felony offense is being charged add*: and feloniously intentionally) did, being (*choose one*: a registrant; a practitioner; an employee of a registrant who had access to and was authorized to possess controlled substances by virtue of employment; an employee of a practitioner who had access to and was authorized to possess controlled substances by virtue of employment), (*choose one or more and modify as appropriate*:)

- embezzle;
- fraudulently misapply;
- knowingly and willfully misapply;
- fraudulently divert to [*choose one:* his own use; her own use; an unauthorized and illegal use];
- knowingly and willfully divert to [*choose one:* his own use; her own use; an unauthorized and illegal use];
- [*choose one or more:* take; make away with; secrete] with intent to embezzle;
- [*choose one or more:* take; make away with; secrete] with intent to fraudulently misapply;
- [*choose one or more:* take; make away with; secrete] with intent to knowingly and willfully misapply;
- [*choose one or more:* take; make away with; secrete] with intent to fraudulently divert to [*choose one:* his own use; her own use; an unauthorized and illegal use];
- [*choose one or more:* take; make away with; secrete] with intent to knowingly and willfully divert to [*choose one:* his own use; her own use; an unauthorized and illegal use]

(name controlled substance), a controlled substance included in Schedule (give number) of the North Carolina Controlled Substances Act, which came (*choose one or more*: into his possession; into her possession; under his care; under her care).

Notes about Charging Language:

- When identifying the controlled substance, do so "by its chemical name as it appears in [the controlled substance schedules]." State v. Turshizi, 175 N.C. App. 783, 785 (2006).
- G.S. 90-108(b) provides that this offense is a Class G felony rather than a misdemeanor when the pleading alleges that the violation was committed intentionally and that fact is specifically found at trial.
- G.S. 90-108(b) further provides that this offense is a Class E felony when committed intentionally and where the offender diverts a controlled substance by means of "dilution" or "substitution" or both. The statute defines "dilution" as "[t]he act of diluting or the state of being diluted; the act

of reducing the concentration of a mixture or solution." It defines "substitution" as "[t]o take the place of or replace." In an appropriate case, charge the felony version of this offense and add an allegation that the offense was committed by dilution and/or substitution.
- G.S. 90-87 defines a "registrant" as "a person registered by the Commission [for Mental Health, Developmental Disabilities, and Substance Abuse Services] to manufacture, distribute, or dispense any controlled substance as required by [Article 5 of Chapter 90 of the General Statutes, the North Carolina Controlled Substances Act]."
- G.S. 90-87 defines a "practitioner" as follows:
    - A physician, dentist, optometrist, veterinarian, scientific investigator, or other person licensed, registered or otherwise permitted to distribute, dispense, conduct research with respect to or to administer a controlled substance so long as such activity is within the normal course of professional practice or research in this State.
    - A pharmacy, hospital or other institution licensed, registered, or otherwise permitted to distribute, dispense, conduct research with respect to or to administer a controlled substance so long as such activity is within the normal course of professional practice or research in this State.

Sample Charge:

I. Embezzlement of a controlled substance **G.S. 90-108(a)(14)**

. . . unlawfully, willfully, and feloniously intentionally did, being an employee of a practitioner who had access to and was authorized to possess controlled substances by virtue of employment, knowingly and willfully divert to her own use oxycodone, a controlled substance included in Schedule II of the North Carolina Controlled Substances Act, which came under her care.

AOC Forms for This Offense:

None.

Punishment:

Class 1 misdemeanor. This offense is a Class G felony when the pleading alleges that the violation was committed intentionally and that fact is specifically found at trial. G.S. 90-108(b)(2). This offense is a Class E felony when committed intentionally and where the offender diverts a controlled substance by means of "dilution" or "substitution" or both. G.S. 90-108(b)(3).

G.S. 90-113.22
Possession of Drug Paraphernalia
April 2024

Introductory Comment:
In the 2014 legislative session, the General Assembly amended this statute to exclude marijuana-related paraphernalia. At the same time, it enacted G.S. 90-113.22A to address marijuana-related paraphernalia, but at a lower punishment level. In the 2015 legislative session, the General Assembly expanded the nonprosecution provision in G.S. 90-113.22(c). The provision now states: "If there is a hypodermic needle or other sharp object on [a] person, on the person's premises, or in the person's vehicle and the person alerts [an] officer of that fact prior to [a] search, the person shall not be charged with or prosecuted for possession of drug paraphernalia for the needle or sharp object, or for residual amounts of a controlled substance contained in the needle or sharp object." In the 2019 legislative session, the General Assembly added a new subsection (d) to the statute to exempt the possession and use of "testing equipment for identifying or analyzing the strength, effectiveness, or purity" of a controlled substance. S.L. 2019-159.

Charging Language:
. . . unlawfully and willfully did knowingly possess with intent to use drug paraphernalia, (*describe paraphernalia*), to (*choose one or more*: plant; propagate; cultivate; grow; harvest; manufacture; compound; convert; produce; process; prepare; test; analyze; package; repackage; store; contain; conceal; introduce into the body) a controlled substance other than marijuana which it would be unlawful to possess.

Notes about Charging Language:
- "Drug paraphernalia" is defined in G.S. 90-113.21.
- G.S. 90-113.22(a) makes it unlawful to "use, or to possess with intent to use" the specified paraphernalia. Because it is improbable, if not impossible, to use paraphernalia without possessing it with the intent to use it, this form simplifies the charging language by alleging only possession with intent to use. If, in a particular case, there is some reason to include an allegation of use in addition to or instead of the allegation of possession with intent to use, modify the charging language accordingly.

Sample Charge:
. . . unlawfully and willfully did knowingly possess with intent to use drug paraphernalia, two miniature cocaine spoons, to introduce into the body a controlled substance other than marijuana which it would be unlawful to possess.

AOC Forms for This Offense:
AOC-J-332 (Juvenile Petition)

Punishment:
Class 1 misdemeanor.

G.S. 90-113.22A
Possession of Marijuana Drug Paraphernalia
April 2024

Introductory Comment:
In the 2014 legislative session, the General Assembly amended G.S. 90-113.22, the general drug paraphernalia statute, to exclude marijuana-related paraphernalia. At the same time, it created this statute to address marijuana-related paraphernalia, but at a lower punishment level. In the 2019 legislative session, the General Assembly added a new subsection (c) to the statute to exempt the possession and use of "testing equipment for identifying or analyzing the strength, effectiveness, or purity" of a controlled substance. S.L. 2019-159.

Charging Language:
. . . unlawfully and willfully did knowingly possess with intent to use drug paraphernalia, (*describe paraphernalia*), to (*choose one or more*: plant; propagate; cultivate; grow; harvest; manufacture; compound; convert; produce; process; prepare; test; analyze; package; repackage; store; contain; conceal; introduce into the body) marijuana.

Notes about Charging Language:
- "Drug paraphernalia" is defined in G.S. 90-113.21.
- The statute makes it unlawful to "use or possess with intent to use" the specified paraphernalia. Because it is improbable, if not impossible, to use paraphernalia without possessing it with the intent to use it, this form simplifies the charging language by alleging only possession with intent to use. If, in a particular case, there is some reason to include an allegation of use in addition to or instead of the allegation of possession with intent to use, modify the charging language accordingly.

Sample Charge:
. . . unlawfully and willfully did knowingly possess with intent to use drug paraphernalia, a metal pipe, to introduce into the body marijuana.

AOC Forms for This Offense:
None.

Punishment:
Class 3 misdemeanor.

G.S. 90-113.23
Manufacture or Delivery of Drug Paraphernalia
April 2024

Introductory Comment:
None.

Charging Language:
. . . unlawfully and willfully did [*choose one*: deliver to (*name person to whom paraphernalia was delivered*); manufacture with intent to deliver; possess with intent to deliver] drug paraphernalia, (*describe paraphernalia*), knowing that it would be used to (*choose one or more*: plant; propagate; cultivate; grow; harvest; manufacture; compound; convert; produce; process; prepare; test; analyze; package; repackage; store; contain; conceal; introduce into the body) a controlled substance which it would be unlawful to possess.

Notes about Charging Language:
- "Drug paraphernalia" is defined in G.S. 90-113.21.

Sample Charge:
. . . unlawfully and willfully did deliver to Monroe Snipes drug paraphernalia, 10 pounds of quinine and a set of scales and balances, knowing that they would be used to process and prepare a controlled substance which it is unlawful to possess.

AOC Forms for This Offense:
None.

Punishment:
Class 1 misdemeanor.

G.S. 90-113.23
Delivery of Drug Paraphernalia to a Minor
April 2024

Introductory Comment:
None.

Charging Language:
. . . unlawfully, willfully, and feloniously did deliver to (*name person to whom paraphernalia was delivered and give age*), a person under the age of 18, drug paraphernalia, (*describe paraphernalia*), knowing that it would be used to (*choose one or more*: plant; propagate; cultivate; grow; harvest; manufacture; compound; convert; produce; process; prepare; test; analyze; package; repackage; store; contain; conceal; introduce into the body) a controlled substance which it would be unlawful to possess. At the time of the delivery, the defendant was over the age of 18, namely, (*give age*), and at least three years older than (*name person to whom paraphernalia was delivered*).

Notes about Charging Language:
- "Drug paraphernalia" is defined in G.S. 90-113.21.

Sample Charge:
. . . unlawfully, willfully, and feloniously did deliver to Monroe Snipes, age 16, a person under the age of 18, drug paraphernalia, a hypodermic syringe and twelve needles, knowing that it would be used to introduce into the body a controlled substance which it would be unlawful to possess. At the time of the delivery, the defendant was over the age of 18, namely, 25 years old, and at least three years older than Monroe Snipes.

AOC Forms for This Offense:
None.

Punishment:
Class I felony.

G.S. 90-113.24
Advertisement of Drug Paraphernalia
April 2024

Introductory Comment:
None.

Charging Language:
. . . unlawfully and willfully did procure an advertisement (*choose one*: in; on) a (*choose one*: newspaper; magazine; handbill; publication; billboard; sign; outdoor display), (*name publication or describe display*), knowing that the purpose of the advertisement was to promote the sale of objects intended for use as drug paraphernalia, namely, (*describe paraphernalia*).

Notes about Charging Language:
- "Drug paraphernalia" is defined in G.S. 90-113.21.

Sample Charge:
. . . unlawfully and willfully did procure an advertisement in a newspaper, the Durham High Roller, knowing that the purpose of the advertisement was to promote the sale of objects intended for use as drug paraphernalia, namely, ceramic pipes.

AOC Forms for This Offense:
None.

Punishment:
Class 2 misdemeanor.

G.S. 90-113.53
Pseudoephedrine Transaction Limits
April 2024
Page 1 of 2

Introductory Comment:
Neither the daily nor the thirty-day limit applies to products dispensed under a valid prescription. Certain liquid, gel, and pediatric products are generally exempted from the daily and thirty-day limits. *See* G.S. 90-113.53(c).

Offenses I and II both are misdemeanors for a first offense, but second and subsequent offenses are subject to elevated punishment as described below. An indictment or an information for a recidivist offense must comply with G.S. 15A-928, which requires that the defendant's prior convictions be alleged either (1) in a separate count of the indictment or information than the substantive offense or (2) in a separate indictment or information. In such a case, the separate count or separate indictment should set forth the date and court in which the prior conviction occurred. This requirement does not apply to arrest warrants or magistrates' orders, which still must allege the defendant's prior convictions but need not do so in a separate count or separate charging instrument. Also note that in situations where a conviction for a recidivist offense is appealed from district to superior court for trial de novo, G.S. 15A-922(h) and -928(d) require the State to replace the pleading in the case with superseding statements of charges separately alleging the substantive offense and any prior convictions. G.S. 15A-928 also requires that the name or title of an offense elevated by prior convictions must not make reference to such prior convictions.

Charging Language:

I. Exceeding daily limit **G.S. 90-113.53(a)**

. . . unlawfully and willfully did [*choose one or more*: deliver at retail to (*name person*); attempt to deliver at retail to (*name person*); purchase at retail; attempt to purchase at retail] more than 3.6 grams of pseudoephedrine products in a single calendar day. (*Add if appropriate*: The defendant was a retailer within the meaning of G.S. 90-113.51.)

II. Exceeding thirty-day limit **G.S. 90-113.53(b)**

. . . unlawfully and willfully did purchase at retail more than 9 grams of pseudoephedrine products within the thirty-day period from (*start date*) to (*end date*). (*Add if appropriate*: The defendant was a retailer within the meaning of G.S. 90-113.51.)

Notes about Charging Language:
- If charging a felony recidivist offense, allege "unlawfully, willfully, and feloniously" rather than "unlawfully and willfully."

Sample Charge:

I. Exceeding daily limit **G.S. 90-113.53(a)**

. . . unlawfully, willfully, and feloniously did attempt to purchase at retail more than 3.6 grams of pseudoephedrine products in a single calendar day.

AOC Forms for This Offense:
None.

Punishment:
Offenses I and II are punished in the same manner: For a retailer, the offenses are Class A1 misdemeanors for a first offense and Class I felonies for a second or subsequent offense. For a purchaser or an employee, they are Class 1 misdemeanors for a first offense, Class A1 misdemeanors for a second offense, and Class I felonies for a third or subsequent offense.

G.S. 108A-39
Welfare Fraud
April 2024

Introductory Comment:
This statute is in Part 2 of Article 2 of G.S. Chapter 108A; that Part deals only with the Work First program. It is possible, but not certain, that the statute also would be held to apply to fraud concerning the State-County Special Assistance for Adults program and the Foster Care and Adoption Assistance Payments program, which are also "programs of public assistance" under G.S. 108A-25. Fraud in connection with those programs might, of course, constitute another criminal offense, such as obtaining property by false pretenses.

Charging Language:
. . . unlawfully, willfully, and feloniously did knowingly and with the intent to deceive (*choose one or more*: make a false statement; make a false representation; fail to disclose a material fact) and, as a result, (*either write* "the defendant" *or name the other person who received the public assistance*) (*choose one or more*: obtained; attempted to obtain; continued to receive) public assistance to which (*either write* "the defendant" *or name the other person who received the public assistance*) was not entitled in the amount of (*state amount*) from the (*name assistance program*) program, from (*give date*), to (*give date*). The (*choose one or more*: false statement; false representation; failure to disclose a material fact) consisted of (*state the contents of the false statement or other misrepresentation, including when it was given and to whom and in what way it was false*).

Notes about Charging Language:
- If the amount of welfare received was not more than $400, this offense is a misdemeanor. In that case, allege "unlawfully and willfully" instead of "unlawfully, willfully, and feloniously."

Sample Charge:
. . . unlawfully, willfully, and feloniously did knowingly and with the intent to deceive make a false statement and, as a result, the defendant obtained and continued to receive public assistance to which the defendant was not entitled in the amount of $2,500 from the Work First program from July 15, 2018, to October 19, 2018. The false statement consisted of a statement made July 8, 2018, to Sandra Farmer of the Orange County Department of Social Services that Robert Ross, the father of Thomas Lynn Hayes, the defendant's child, was not providing any support to that child when in fact Ross was providing support in the amount of $100 each month.

AOC Forms for This Offense:
None.

Punishment:
If the assistance unlawfully received was not more than $400, the offense is a Class 1 misdemeanor. If the assistance received was more than $400, the offense is a Class I felony.

G.S. 108A-53
Food and Nutrition Benefit Fraud
April 2024
Page 1 of 2

Introductory Comment:
None.

Charging Language:

I. Obtaining benefit by fraud **G.S. 108A-53(a)**

. . . unlawfully, willfully, and feloniously did knowingly (*choose one*: obtain; attempt to obtain) from the Food and Nutrition Services program of the (*name county*) Department of Social Services an electronic food and nutrition benefit in the amount of (*give amount*), to which the defendant was not entitled, by (*choose one or more*)

(1) making the following willfully false (*choose one or both*: statement; representation): (*give the contents of the false statement or representation, including the date it was made and to whom and in what way it was false*).

(2) impersonating (*name the person the defendant impersonated*).

(3) failing to disclose the following material facts: [*state what material fact(s) the defendant failed to disclose*].

II. Transferring benefit **G.S. 108A-53(a)**

. . . unlawfully, willfully, and feloniously did knowingly, without authority, and with the intent to defraud transfer to (*name person to whom transferred*) an electronic food and nutrition benefit in the amount of (*give amount*) from the Food and Nutrition Services program of the (*name county*) Department of Social Services, to which the defendant was not entitled.

III. Presentation of fraudulently obtained benefits **G.S. 108A-53(b)**

. . . unlawfully and willfully did (*choose one or both*: present; cause to be presented) to (*name person to whom benefits presented*) an electronic food and nutrition benefit in the amount of (*state amount*) for (*choose one or both*: payment; redemption), knowing the benefit to have been (*write* "received" *or* "transferred" *or state other way in which the benefits were used contrary to the statute or regulations*) in violation of the provisions of Part 5 of Article 2 of Chapter 108A of the General Statutes.

IV. Receiving fraudulently obtained benefits **G.S. 108A-53(c)**

. . . unlawfully and willfully did receive from (*name person from whom benefits received*) an electronic food and nutrition benefit in the amount of (*state amount*) for consumable items, (*state generally the nature of the consumable items for which the benefits were received, giving value if that aids the description*), knowing that the food and nutrition benefits were procured fraudulently in violation of [*choose one or both*: G.S. 108A-53(a); G.S. 108A-53(b)].

V. Receiving benefits in exchange for prohibited items **G.S. 108A-53(d)**

. . . unlawfully and willfully did receive from (*name person from whom benefits received*) an electronic food and nutrition benefit in the amount of (*state amount*), in exchange for (*name prohibited item for which the benefits were received*), a consumable item whose exchange for electronic food and nutrition benefits is prohibited by the United States Department of Agriculture (USDA).

Notes about Charging Language:

- Offenses I and II are misdemeanors if the value of the benefit is $400 or less. In that case, allege "unlawfully and willfully," not "unlawfully, willfully, and feloniously."
- Offense I may also be committed by aiding and abetting. In such a case, make appropriate changes to the charging language.
- For Offense V, although not legally required, you may wish to consider citing the USDA regulation that prohibits the exchange.

Sample Charge:

I. Obtaining benefit by fraud **G.S. 108A-53(a)**

. . . unlawfully, willfully, and feloniously did knowingly obtain from the Food and Nutrition Services program of the Durham County Department of Social Services an electronic food and nutrition benefit in the amount of $500, to which the defendant was not entitled, by making the following willfully false statement: a statement in his application for food coupons, dated July 16, 2017, that he had no income other than a $75-per-week disability check when in fact he had income in excess of $200 per week.

AOC Forms for This Offense:

None.

Punishment:

Offenses I and II are Class I felonies if the value of the electronic food and nutrition benefit is more than $400. Otherwise, they are Class 1 misdemeanors. Offenses III, IV, and V are Class 1 misdemeanors.

G.S. 108A-53.1
Illegal Possession or Use of Food and Nutrition Benefit
April 2024
Page 1 of 2

Introductory Comment:
None.

Charging Language:

I. Buying, selling, or possessing with intent to sell and distribute **G.S. 108A-53.1(a)**

. . . unlawfully, willfully, and feloniously did knowingly (*choose one or more*: buy; sell; distribute; possess with intent to sell and distribute) (*choose one or both*: electronic food and nutrition benefits; electronic food and nutrition benefit access devices) in a manner contrary to that authorized by Part 5 of Article 2 of Chapter 108A of the General Statutes and regulations issued pursuant thereto. The defendant (*describe illegal act*).

II. Using, acquiring, or possessing **G.S. 108A-53.1(b)**

. . . unlawfully, willfully, and feloniously did knowingly (*choose one or more*: use; transfer; acquire; alter; possess) (*choose one or both*: electronic food and nutrition benefits; electronic food and nutrition benefit access devices) in a manner contrary to that authorized by Part 5 of Article 2 of Chapter 108A of the General Statutes and regulations issued pursuant thereto. The defendant (*describe illegal act*). The value of the (*choose one or both*: electronic food and nutrition benefits; electronic food and nutrition benefit access devices) was (*give value*).

Notes about Charging Language:

- Much of the conduct prohibited by Offense II will also be prohibited by Offense I. In such a case, because Offense I does not require the State to prove the specific value of the electronic food and nutrition benefits or access devices at issue, and because Offense I is often a crime of higher grade than Offense II, it may be preferable to charge Offense I.
- Offense II is a misdemeanor if the value of the electronic food and nutrition benefits or access devices is less than $500. In such a case, allege "unlawfully and willfully," not "unlawfully, willfully, and feloniously."

Sample Charge:

I. Buying, selling, or possessing with intent to sell and distribute **G.S. 108A-53.1(a)**

. . . unlawfully, willfully, and feloniously did knowingly sell electronic food and nutrition benefits in a manner contrary to that authorized by Part 5 of Article 2 of Chapter 108A of the General Statutes and regulations issued pursuant thereto. The defendant sold $200 worth of benefits to Peter Smith for $50 and used the proceeds to buy a video game console.

AOC Forms for This Offense:
None.

Punishment:
Offense I is a Class H felony. Offense II is a Class 1 misdemeanor if the value of the electronic food and nutrition benefits or access devices is less than $100; a Class A1 misdemeanor if the value is at least $100 but less than $500; a Class I felony if the value is at least $500 but less than $1,000; and a Class H felony if the value is $1,000 or more.

G.S. 108A-63
Medicaid Fraud by Provider
April 2024
Page 1 of 2

Introductory Comment:
None.

Charging Language:

I. Misrepresentation or concealment of fact **G.S. 108A-63(a), (b)**

. . . unlawfully, willfully, and feloniously did knowingly, as a provider of medical assistance under Part 6 of Article 2 of Chapter 108A of the General Statutes, (*choose one or more*)

(1) make and cause to be made a false statement and false representation of a material fact in an application for payment for medical assistance under Part 6,

(2) make and cause to be made a false statement and false representation of a material fact for use in determining entitlement to a payment for medical assistance under Part 6,

(3) make and cause to be made a false statement and false representation of a material fact with respect to the conditions and operations of the defendant's facility in order to qualify and remain qualified to provide medical assistance under Part 6,

(4) conceal and fail to disclose a fact affecting the defendant's (*choose one or both*: initial; continued) entitlement to payment under Part 6,

(5) conceal and fail to disclose a fact affecting the amount of payment to which the defendant was entitled under Part 6,

in that the defendant did (*describe the false statement or failure to disclose and state how it affected the payment for medical assistance*).

II. Scheme to defraud **G.S. 108A-63(e)**

. . . unlawfully, willfully, and feloniously did knowingly, as a provider of medical assistance under Part 6 of Article 2 of Chapter 108A of the General Statutes, in connection with the (*choose one or both*: delivery of; payment for) (*choose one or more*: benefits; items; services) under Part 6, (*choose one or both*: execute; attempt to execute) a scheme and artifice to (*choose one or more*)

(1) defraud the Medical Assistance Program,

(2) obtain (*choose one or both*: money; property) (*choose one or both*: owned by; under the custody and control of) the Medical Assistance Program by means of false and fraudulent (*choose one or more*: pretenses; representations of material fact; promises of material fact),

in that the defendant did (*describe the fraudulent conduct*).

III. Obstruction of investigation **G.S. 108A-63(f)**

. . . unlawfully, willfully, and feloniously did knowingly, as a provider of medical assistance under Part 6 of Article 2 of Chapter 108A of the General Statutes, with the intent to (*choose one or more*: obstruct; delay; mislead) an investigation of a violation of G.S. 108A-63 by the Attorney General's office, (*choose one or more*: make a false entry in; cause a false entry to be made in; alter; destroy; conceal; make a false statement about) a record related to the provision of a (*choose one or more*: benefit; item; service) under Part 6, in that the defendant did (*describe the obstructive conduct*).

Notes about Charging Language:

- The term "provider" is defined in G.S. 108A-63(d).
- For Offense I, options (1) through (3), the statute makes it illegal to "make" or "cause to be made." If one of those terms is inappropriate, it may be omitted. The statute likewise applies to a "false statement" or to a "false representation." If one of those terms is inappropriate, it may be omitted.
- For Offense I, option (3), the statute makes it illegal to make a false statement to "qualify" or "remain qualified." If one of those terms is inappropriate, it may be omitted.
- For Offense I, options (4) and (5), the statute makes it illegal to "conceal" or "fail to disclose." If one of those terms is inappropriate, it may be omitted.
- For Offense II, the statute makes it illegal to execute a "scheme" or an "artifice." If one of those terms is inappropriate, it may be omitted.

Sample Charges:

I. Misrepresentation or concealment of fact **G.S. 108A-63(a), (b)**

. . . unlawfully, willfully, and feloniously did knowingly, as a provider of medical assistance under Part 6 of Article 2 of Chapter 108A of the General Statutes, make and cause to be made a false statement and false representation of a material fact in an application for payment for medical assistance under Part 6, in that the defendant stated that he had examined and x-rayed Louisa C. Childers on November 16, 2019, when in fact he had not done so.

III. Obstruction of investigation **G.S. 108A-63(f)**

. . . unlawfully, willfully, and feloniously did knowingly, as a provider of medical assistance under Part 6 of Article 2 of Chapter 108A of the General Statutes, with the intent to obstruct and mislead an investigation of a violation of G.S. 108A-63 by the Attorney General's office, alter a record related to the provision of a service under Part 6, in that the defendant altered his office copy of an application for payment for medical assistance under Part 6 to omit any reference to conducting a biopsy on Steven Higgins, even though the copy of the application that the defendant had previously submitted for payment included a statement that the defendant had conducted the biopsy.

AOC Forms for This Offense:

None.

Punishment:

Offenses I and III are Class I felonies. Offense II is a Class H felony. Conspiracy to commit Offense II is a Class I felony.

G.S. 108A-64
Medicaid Fraud by Recipient
April 2024
Page 1 of 2

Introductory Comment:
Although this manual does not provide charging language for G.S. 108A-64(b1), that subsection applies to individuals who "deliberately misuse a Medicaid identification card," for example, by borrowing a card and impersonating the beneficiary.

Charging Language:

I. False statement **G.S. 108A-64(a)**

. . . unlawfully, willfully, and feloniously did knowingly and with intent to defraud (*choose one or more*)

(1) make and cause to be made a false (*choose one or both*: statement; representation) of a material fact in an application for payment for medical assistance under Part 6 of Article 2 of Chapter 108A of the General Statutes,

(2) make and cause to be made a false (*choose one or both*: statement; representation) of a material fact intended for use in determining entitlement to medical assistance under Part 6 of Article 2 of Chapter 108A of the General Statutes,

in that the defendant did (*describe the false statement or false representation and state how it affected assistance*). The value of the assistance wrongfully obtained was (*state amount*).

II. Failure to disclose **G.S. 108A-64(b)**

. . . unlawfully, willfully, and feloniously did knowingly and with intent to defraud, as a(n) (*choose one*: applicant; recipient; person acting on behalf of an applicant; person acting on behalf of a recipient), conceal and fail to disclose a (*choose one or more*: fact; condition; event) affecting the (*choose one*: applicant's; recipient's) entitlement to assistance under Part 6 of Article 2 of Chapter 108A of the General Statutes, in that the defendant did (*describe the false statement or failure to disclose and state how it affected the payment for medical assistance*). The value of the assistance wrongfully obtained was (*state amount*).

Notes about Charging Language:
- If the amount of assistance received was not more than $400, these offenses are misdemeanors. In such a case, allege "unlawfully and willfully" rather than "unlawfully, willfully, and feloniously."
- For Offense I, the statute makes it unlawful to "make" *or* "cause to be made" a false statement, etc. If one of those terms is inapplicable, delete it.
- For Offense II, the statute makes it unlawful to "conceal" *or* "fail to disclose" a fact affecting payment. If one of those phrases is inapplicable, delete it.
- G.S. 108A-64 provides that "[p]roof of intent to defraud does not require proof of intent to defraud any particular person."

Sample Charge:

I. False statement **G.S. 108A-64(a)**

. . . unlawfully, willfully, and feloniously did, knowingly and with intent to defraud, make a false statement of a material fact in an application for medical assistance under Part 6 of Article 2 of Chapter 108A of the General Statutes in that the defendant did falsely state that he made $2,000 annually when in fact he made $20,000 annually. As a result of the false statement, he received medical assistance to which he was not entitled. The value of the assistance wrongfully obtained was $650.

AOC Forms for This Offense:
None.

Punishment:
If the value of the assistance wrongfully obtained was more than $400, the offense is a Class I felony. If the value was not more than $400, the offense is a Class 1 misdemeanor.

G.S. 115C-378(a)
Violation of School Compulsory Attendance Law
April 2024
Page 1 of 2

Introductory Comments:
The charging language below concerns subsection (a) of G.S. 115C-378. Note, however, that any person who "encourage[s], entice[s] or counsel[s] any child of compulsory attendance age to be unlawfully absent from school" violates subsection (b) of the statute. Charging language for that subsection is not provided in this manual. It appears that an offense under that subsection could be charged immediately, without the preliminary measures described in subsections (e) and (f) and incorporated into the charging language below.

Charging Language:
. . . unlawfully and willfully did, as a (*choose one*: parent; guardian; custodian) having charge and control of (*name child*), a child between 7 and 16 years old, fail to cause that child to attend school continuously for a period equal to the time which the public school to which the child was assigned, (*name public school to which assigned*), must be in session. After (*name child*) had accumulated three unexcused absences during the (*specify year*) school year, (*name person*), the (*choose one*: principal of; designee of the principal of) (*name school*) notified the defendant of the child's excessive absences. After (*name child*) had accumulated six unexcused absences during the (*specify year*) school year, (*name person*), the (*choose one*: principal of; designee of the principal of) (*name school*) notified the defendant by mail that the defendant may be in violation of the North Carolina compulsory school attendance law. After (*name child*) had accumulated ten unexcused absences during the (*specify year*) school year, (*name person*), the (*choose one*: principal of; designee of the principal of) (*name school*) conferred with the defendant and the child to determine whether the defendant had received the above-referenced notifications and whether the defendant had made a good-faith effort to comply with the law. The defendant did not make a good-faith effort to comply with the law.

Notes about Charging Language:
- For cases regarding the sufficiency of a criminal pleading that charges this offense, see *State v. Lewis*, 194 N.C. 620 (1927), and *State v. Johnson*, 188 N.C. 591 (1924). *See also* State v. Frady, 195 N.C. App. 766 (2009) (listing elements).
- Sending a child to a nonpublic school satisfies the statute if the school meets the standards set forth in G.S. 115C-378(d)—generally, the school must meet the curriculum and schedule standards that apply to the public schools.
- A parent, guardian, or custodian of a child under age 7 "who is enrolled in a public school in grades kindergarten through two" also violates the statute by failing to ensure attendance, "unless the child has withdrawn from school." In such a case, make appropriate changes to the charging language.
- The statute states that the ten-missed-days conference must take place "if possible." If it was not possible for the conference to take place, modify the sentence of the charging language concerning the conference appropriately.

Sample Charge:

. . . unlawfully and willfully did, as a parent having charge and control of Sally Smith, a child between 7 and 16 years old, fail to cause that child to attend school continuously for a period equal to the time which the public school to which the child was assigned, Grant Elementary School, Grantville, N.C., must be in session. After Sally Smith had accumulated three unexcused absences during the 2018–19 school year, Delia Castor, the principal of Grant Elementary School, notified the defendant of the child's excessive absences. After Sally Smith had accumulated six unexcused absences during the 2018–19 school year, Delia Castor, the principal of Grant Elementary School, notified the defendant by mail that the defendant may be in violation of the North Carolina compulsory school attendance law. After Sally Smith had accumulated ten unexcused absences during the 2018–19 school year, Delia Castor, the principal of Grant Elementary School, conferred with the defendant and the child to determine whether the defendant had received the above-referenced notifications and whether the defendant had made a good-faith effort to comply with the law. The defendant did not make a good-faith effort to comply with the law.

AOC Forms for This Offense:

None.

Punishment:

Class 1 misdemeanor. G.S. 115C-380.

G.S. 148-45
Escape from State Prison System
April 2024
Page 1 of 2

Introductory Comment:
This statute applies only to escapes from the state prison system. Escapes from local confinement facilities are governed by G.S. 14-256.

An escape otherwise punished as a misdemeanor instead is punished as a felony if it is committed by a defendant who previously has been convicted of escaping or attempting to escape from the state prison system. G.S. 148-45(b)(5). An indictment or an information for the recidivist offense must comply with G.S. 15A-928, which requires that the defendant's prior convictions be alleged either (1) in a separate count of the indictment or information than the substantive offense or (2) in a separate indictment or information. In such a case, the separate count or separate indictment should set forth the date and court in which the prior conviction occurred. This requirement does not apply to arrest warrants or magistrates' orders, which still must allege the defendant's prior convictions but need not do so in a separate count or separate charging instrument. G.S. 15A-928 also requires that the name or title of an offense elevated by prior convictions must not make reference to such prior convictions.

Charging Language:

I. Escape from the confines of a prison unit **G.S. 148-45(a), (b)**

. . . unlawfully, willfully, and feloniously did escape from (*name the prison unit from which the prisoner escaped*), a unit of the state prison system, while the defendant was there in the lawful custody of the Department of Correction serving a sentence for a conviction of a (*choose one*: felony; misdemeanor), that sentence having been imposed at the (*give date*) session of the (*choose one*: Superior; District) Court of (*name county*).

II. Escape by failing to return after authorized absence **G.S. 148-45(g)(1)**

. . . unlawfully, willfully, and feloniously did escape from (*name the prison unit from which the prisoner escaped*), a unit of the state prison system, while the defendant was there in the lawful custody of the Department of Correction serving a sentence for a conviction of a (*choose one*: felony; misdemeanor), that sentence having been imposed at the (*give date*) session of the (*choose one*: Superior; District) Court of (*name county*). The defendant escaped while on (*state authorized reason for defendant leaving unit, such as* work release, community volunteer leave, *etc.*) by willfully failing to return to the prison unit at the designated time.

Notes about Charging Language:

- An escape that is a violation of G.S. 148-45(a)—generally, escape by a misdemeanant—is a Class 1 misdemeanor. If that is the case, allege "unlawfully and willfully" rather than "unlawfully, willfully, and feloniously."
- The North Carolina Supreme Court ruled in *State v. Stallings*, 267 N.C. 405 (1966), that it is not necessary to describe the crime for which the defendant is in prison, as long as the pleading alleges that the defendant is imprisoned for a felony or misdemeanor conviction.

- This offense is also committed when a person (1) has been charged with a misdemeanor or felony and has been committed to the custody of the Department of Correction under G.S. 162-39 (transfer from local confinement facility for various reasons) or (2) has been convicted of a misdemeanor or felony and committed to the custody of the Department of Correction for a presentence diagnostic study under G.S. 15A-1332(c). If one of these conditions existed, make appropriate changes in the charging language.

Sample Charge:

I. Escape from the confines of a prison unit **G.S. 148-45(a), (b)**

. . . unlawfully, willfully, and feloniously did escape from Central Prison, Raleigh, N.C., a unit of the state prison system, while the defendant was there in the lawful custody of the Department of Correction serving a sentence for a conviction of a felony, that sentence having been imposed at the March 16, 2018, session of the Superior Court of Mecklenburg County.

AOC Forms for This Offense:

AOC-CR-132 (Indictment, for Offense I)
AOC-CR-131 (Indictment, for Offense II)

Punishment:

The punishment for an escape that is a violation of G.S. 148-45(a)—generally, escape by a misdemeanant—is a Class 1 misdemeanor. The punishment for an escape that is a violation of G.S. 148-45(b)—generally, escape by a felon—is a Class H felony. A person who commits Offense II is subject to the same punishment provisions applicable to Offense I.

Case Index

North Carolina Courts

North Carolina Supreme Court

North Carolina Court of Appeals

Federal Courts

United States Supreme Court

Circuit Courts of Appeals

District Courts

Subject Index

A

B

C

D

F

G

H

M

N

O

P

R

S

T